Preventing Suicide

Preventing Suicide

An Evidence-Based Approach

Edited by

Rob Poole
Bangor University

Murad M. Khan
Aga Khan University

Catherine A. Robinson
University of Manchester

CAMBRIDGE
UNIVERSITY PRESS

CAMBRIDGE
UNIVERSITY PRESS

Shaftesbury Road, Cambridge CB2 8EA, United Kingdom

One Liberty Plaza, 20th Floor, New York, NY 10006, USA

477 Williamstown Road, Port Melbourne, VIC 3207, Australia

314–321, 3rd Floor, Plot 3, Splendor Forum, Jasola District Centre,
New Delhi – 110025, India

103 Penang Road, #05–06/07, Visioncrest Commercial, Singapore 238467

Cambridge University Press is part of Cambridge University Press & Assessment,
a department of the University of Cambridge.

We share the University's mission to contribute to society through the pursuit of
education, learning and research at the highest international levels of excellence.

www.cambridge.org
Information on this title: www.cambridge.org/9781108965620

DOI: 10.1017/9781108963763

When citing this work, please include a reference to the DOI 10.1017/9781108963763

Artist: Catherine A Robinson
Medium: acrylic on stretched canvas
From a piece titled "There is only today"
Photographer: Steve Hammond

First published 2026

A catalogue record for this publication is available from the British Library

A Cataloging-in-Publication data record for this book is available from the Library of Congress

ISBN 978-1-108-96562-0 Paperback

Contents

Contributors

Rob Poole
Professor of Social Psychiatry, Centre for Mental Health and Society, Bangor University, Bangor, UK

Murad M. Khan
Emeritus Professor of Psychiatry and Consultant, Brain and Mind Institute (BMI), Aga Khan University, Karachi, Pakistan

Catherine A. Robinson
Professor of Social Care Research and Director, Social Care and Society, School of Health Sciences, University of Manchester, Manchester, UK

Mohammed T. Abou-Saleh
Professor of Psychiatry, St George's, University of London, London, UK

Johnny Andoh-Arthur
Senior Lecturer, Department of Psychology, University of Ghana, Accra, Ghana

Oyedeji Ayonrinde
Associate Professor and Division Chair, Community Psychiatry, Queen's University, Kingston, Ontario, Canada

Emily Bebbington
Welsh Clinical Academic Training Fellow in Public Health, School of Medical and Health Sciences, Bangor University, Bangor, UK

Silvia Sara Canetto
Professor of Applied Social and Health Psychology, Department of Psychology, Colorado State University, Fort Collins, Colorado, US

Erminia Colucci
Professor of Visual Psychology and Cultural and Global Mental Health, Department of Psychology, Middlesex University, London, UK

Ananta Dave
Chief Medical Officer and Consultant Psychiatrist, NHS Black Country Integrated Care Board, Wolverhampton, West Midlands, UK

Linda Gask
Emerita Professor of Primary Care, School of Health Sciences, University of Manchester, Manchester, UK

Keith Hawton
Professor of Psychiatry, Oxford Centre for Suicide Research, Department of Psychiatry, University of Oxford, Oxford, UK; Oxford Health NHS Foundation Trust, Oxford, UK

Sarah Hetrick
Associate Professor, Department of Psychological Medicine, University of Auckland, Auckland, New Zealand

Sirar Jaroudy
Mental Health and Psychosocial Support Consultant, Independent Global Mental Health Researcher, United Arab Emirates

Nomusa Mngoma
Research Scientist, Centre for Studies in Primary Care, Department of Family Medicine, Queen's University, Kingston, Ontario, Canada

Angela Nicholas
Senior Research Fellow in Mental Health, Centre for Mental Health, Melbourne

School of Population and Global Health, University of Melbourne, Melbourne, Victoria, Australia

Thomas Niederkrotenthaler
Professor of Public Health, Suicide Research and Mental Health Promotion Unit, Department of Social and Preventive Medicine, Center for Public Health, Medical University of Vienna, Vienna, Austria

Joseph Osafo
Professor of Clinical and Health Psychology, Department of Psychology, School of Social Science, University of Ghana, Accra, Ghana

Melissa Pearson
Research Fellow, Centre for Pesticide Suicide Prevention, University of Edinburgh, Edinburgh, Scotland and South Asian Clinical Toxicology Research Collaboration, University of Peradeniya, Kandy, Central Province, Sri Lanka

Jane Pirkis
Professor and Director, Centre for Mental Health, Melbourne School of Population and Global Health, University of Melbourne, Melbourne, Victoria, Australia

Alexandra Pitman
Professor of Psychiatry and Consultant Psychiatrist, Division of Psychiatry, University College London, London, UK; Camden and Islington NHS Foundation Trust, London, UK

Thilini Rajapakse
Professor of Psychiatry, Department of Psychiatry and South Asian Clinical Toxicology Research Collaboration, Faculty of Medicine, University of Peradeniya, Kandy, Central Province, Sri Lanka

Mohsen Rezaeian
Professor of Epidemiology, Epidemiology and Biostatistics Department, Occupational Environment Research Center, School of Health, Rafsanjan University of Medical Sciences, Rafsanjan, Kerman Province, Iran

Jo Robinson
Associate Professor, Orygen Youth Health Research Centre, Victoria, Australia; Centre for Youth Mental Health, University of Melbourne, Melbourne, Victoria, Australia

Mark Sinyor
Associate Professor, Department of Psychiatry, Sunnybrook Health Sciences Centre, University of Toronto, Toronto, Canada

Alex Thomson
Consultant Liaison Psychiatrist, Northwick Park Hospital, London North-West Healthcare NHS Trust and Central and North-West London NHS Foundation Trust, London, UK

Ellen Wilkinson
Consultant Psychiatrist, Cornwall Partnership NHS Foundation Trust, Truro, Cornwall, UK

Katrina Witt
Senior Research Fellow, Centre for Youth Mental Health, University of Melbourne, Melbourne, Victoria, Australia

Introduction

Rob Poole, Catherine A. Robinson and Murad M. Khan

The aim of this book is to provide evidence to inform the development and implementation of suicide prevention globally. It covers a range of topics that are relevant from local to national levels. It has an unapologetic emphasis on social determinants of suicide and a global perspective, with utility across the world as a primary resource by practitioners and policymakers. It aims at accessibility, with an emphasis on what can be achieved given the current knowledge base.

A central message of this book is the importance of using rigorous evidence to guide suicide prevention, whilst recognising that the best evidence is always partial. Key research is cited in the text and readers are, in places, directed to public-domain digital resources. The book aims to have relevance in low- and middle-income countries, as well as in high-income countries. It is not a country-by-country international overview. Instead, it addresses issues of common interest thematically and sometimes offers thought-provoking opinions. Consequently, there are some contradictions between chapters. The emphasis is on what can be practically done to reduce deaths due to suicide, from the organisation of clinical teams to national and international public health policy.

There are a considerable number of excellent scholarly books about suicide and self-harm, some which have been edited or co-authored by contributors to this book. Existing titles differ from this book because they are long and directed at an academic or research readership. In contrast, this book is directed at a professional/clinical readership that understands scientific evidence but is seeking authoritative guidance of practical usefulness in developing clinical services and suicide prevention strategies.

In keeping with our global aspirations, we have not confined ourselves to UK authors, with significant contributions from researchers in low- and middle-income countries. Through our international roles in self-harm and suicide research, we have been fortunate to have attracted a large number of high-quality contributors. They provide an answer to 'What would I need to know in practice to do this effectively and without delay if I was not an expert?', whether in policy formation or clinical practice. There is reference to key evidence, and where there is no reliable evidence, the basis of opinions is clear.

The content moves through three sections in a logical progression: Section 1 is concerned with public health measures at the population level that can affect suicide rates. Section 2 tackles the challenges and controversies in suicide prevention and seeks to guide the non-specialist to a path that remains within the bounds of evidence and good practice. It examines both factors of universal applicability (e.g., access to means) as well as those that are more specific in some regions of the world (such as the high female proportion of suicide in South Asia and the phenomenon of self-immolation across much of Asia). Section 3 addresses specific practical problems (e.g., establishing surveillance mechanisms and responding after a suicide has taken place).

In all of this there is a need to balance devoting one's efforts to public health measures, which can save a lot of lives but take a long time to implement, as opposed to clinical intervention, which is more immediate in its effects but only reaches those who can access services. In addressing the former, population-level needs, it is important to recognise that 'policymaker' means people with a professional interest in suicide prevention who wish to influence policy and politicians. Senior clinicians often influence both practice and policy. 'Policy-making' is not solely the work of inaccessible civil servants and politicians. It is a process that is not necessarily rational but can be influenced by clinicians and researchers, as well as those with vested interests. Finally, implementation involves more than good intentions. This is the key challenge in the field.

This book was started during the COVID-19 pandemic and has been slowed in its completion by episodes of life-threatening illness, natural disasters, displacement and civil unrest. Such is the nature of the world we live in. For better or worse, this is not an epoch of certainties. We wish to thank our co-authors, both those who produced their contributions promptly (only to find that the delays were so long they had to bring them up to date) and those who had to work more slowly, in the face of difficult circumstances. We also wish to thank Sioned Davies, who attempted to keep track of the various versions and correspondence.

Chapter 1

Suicide Is a Global Problem

Rob Poole, Catherine A. Robinson and Murad M. Khan

This book is informed by some key propositions: that suicide is a major public health issue, that effective suicide prevention requires both clinical and public health measures, that culture and the ways in which societies are organised have a direct and measurable impact on suicide, that suicide has a significant human rights dimension. These concepts are not controversial to most of us involved in suicide and self-harm research, but they can be difficult for policymakers to take on board. They have implications and consequences. Understanding suicide as a global and interconnected phenomenon introduces an important perspective that is equally as important for high-income countries (HICs) as it is for low- and middle-income countries (LMICs).

1.1 Suicide Can Be Prevented

Taking one's own life is an act that evokes powerful emotional reactions, and it has an extraordinary social impact. Each instance has ramifications that ripple out through social networks, often extending far beyond those who had a direct relationship with the deceased [1]. For the bereaved, reactions to and the consequences of suicide can continue to resonate for decades and over several generations [2].

Suicide is not inevitable, and each case is a potentially avoidable death. For the bereaved, these life-changing events have multiple meanings, commonly including regret, grief, stigma, shame and loss of social/economic security. Suicide stands as one of the most difficult forms of loss in all cultures across the world. Loss of life in this way is untimely by definition. It is not surprising that suicide has raised special concern throughout modern history. Durkheim's choice of suicide as one of the first subjects for systematic study at the birth of sociology in the late nineteenth century was neither coincidental nor arbitrary [3].

We can only take action to reduce the number of people who take their own life when it is accepted that preventing suicide is possible and desirable. Despite high levels of professional and public concern across the world, there is a surprising degree of resistance to the idea that prevention can be effective in mental health in general and particularly with regard to suicide. This skepticism falls broadly into two categories, which are not mutually exclusive.

One is a fatalistic belief that can be summarised as 'if they're going to do it, no one can stop them'. This attitude is not uncommon amongst mental health professionals, where it may have roots in a difficulty in coping with the heavy emotional burden of their work and a particular difficulty in instilling hope in people who find life unbearable. The fear of failure is sometimes rationalised through a belief that human intervention cannot alter a suicidal trajectory. Fatalism is a form of denial, in this case denial of the human capacity to help other people or to improve their world. It is hard to think of another cause of avoidable death that regularly evokes a reaction of 'what will be will be'. There is ample evidence that this is simply not true.

As a matter of public policy, it is universally accepted that mental health services should make strenuous efforts to avoid loss of life amongst patients, although there are genuine controversies over how best to achieve this; the use of incarceration is particularly contentious. Professional and public fatalism are not harmless opinions. They have a negative impact on the effort taken to prevent death by suicide.

There is often a conflation of assessment of suicide risk (in other words, *prediction* at the individual level) and prevention of suicide. Assessment of suicide risk has been repeatedly shown to be very difficult or impossible to operationalise [4,5]. No risk assessment instrument has been shown to have the optimal combination of sufficient sensitivity and specificity to be useful in clinical practice, other than as an adjunct to clinical assessment. Fortunately, successful suicide prevention does not necessarily depend on identifying those individuals at particularly high risk. Measures that affect groups of people known epidemiologically to be at elevated risk are important and effective (e.g., eliminating ligature points in psychiatric inpatient facilities) [6], as are some measures that affect the population at large (such as restriction of access to particular lethal poisons and drugs) [7]. For mental health services, the most important suicide prevention measure is to ensure that care is accessible in a timely way for everyone who needs it, irrespective of the degree to which the individual is ostensibly at risk of suicide. It is particularly important that this includes those with the least resources. Within services, consistent adherence to standards of good practice is critical, including for patients who are consistently hard to help or challenging to professionals (such as people with substance misuse problems or who have been diagnosed as having a personality disorder).

Prevention is demonstrably possible and has been achieved in many parts of the world at different times. It may not be possible to be certain exactly whose lives have been saved, but the fact that lives have been saved can be established by examination of rigorously collected surveillance data. Evaluation of intervention is one of the reasons that surveillance is a key element in any suicide prevention strategy [8].

Therapeutic intervention by health services at the individual level has limitations in all forms of prevention and health promotion. For example, typhoid is a disease that can be treated with antibiotics, but prevention depends on good sanitation and vaccinations. Individual lives can be saved through the treatment of typhoid infection, but this is insufficient to have a major impact on death rates in the population at large. The same principles apply equally to suicide. It would be unconscionable to make no effort to prevent suicide of individuals in crisis, but major reductions in suicide rates involve measures that affect whole populations.

It has been known since the nineteenth century that suicide rates are affected by social conditions and by fluctuations in the economy [3]. The second category of skepticism is a response to the suggestion that suicide might be prevented through macro-socio-economic action, for example by avoiding high rates of unemployment, which are known to be associated with increased rates of suicide in the general population. The skeptic will generally acknowledge the abstract possibility that this might work, but the real-life task is construed as too big, over-ambitious or so disruptive to the economy as to be wildly unrealistic. Consequently, the proposition that public health and social measures can have sufficient impact to reduce suicide rates is often met with an eye-rolling cynicism and the implication that these are the utopian dreams of the hopelessly over-optimistic naïf. Similar reactions are seen in response to efforts to address the social determinants of health. The latter are closely related to, or the same as, the factors that affect suicide and self-harm, namely 'the social and environmental conditions in which people are born, grow, live, work, and age' [9].

This negativity is not congruent with the evidence, particularly when the problem is examined from a global perspective. There is no need to create a perfect world to achieve reductions in avoidable deaths, including by suicide. Each individual measure often has a relatively small effect, but when combined with other measures as a coherent strategy, it is possible to achieve significant change over time. Sometimes, surprisingly large reductions can occur relatively quickly, although not always as a consequence of a planned suicide prevention strategy. A key example is the reduction in suicide rates in China in recent years [10]. Between 1999 and 2017, the per capita suicide rate in China dropped by 63% overall and by considerably more for some sections of the population. This appears to have been due to exceptionally rapid socio-economic change, with an intense urbanisation of the population combined with large increases in per capita income for the new city dwellers. Most countries cannot expect socio-economic change on this scale, but it does clearly show that change can occur, accompanied by improvements in public mental health.

In the face of systemic resistances to suicide prevention measures, it is important to demonstrate that the potential to save lives and improve population well-being are not items of faith. Empirical evidence clearly indicates that suicide can be prevented within the world as it exists, with all of its imperfections and in the absence of utopian socio-political transformations. Measures affecting the whole population can result in reductions in suicide mortality rates. As suicide is a problem that affects a large number of people, suicide prevention is firmly in the arena of public health.

1.2 The Scale of the Problem

According to the World Health Organization (WHO), approximately 700,000 people across the world die by suicide each year. There are marked differences in rates per 100,000 population between nations, with equally marked differences in the distribution of deaths across age groups and according to gender. Seventy-seven per cent of those who take their own lives each year reside in low- and middle-income countries (LMICs). In 2016 suicide was the second-commonest global cause of death in 15- to 19-year-olds. In some LMICs, such as India, population rates of suicide are far higher than in most high-income countries (HICs) [11].

Rates of death alone do not reflect the full extent of the health burden related to suicide. The number of people who harm themselves but survive is believed to far exceed the number who die. A significant proportion of survivors suffer enduring physical, social and psychological sequelae. There is a similarly large number of people who are bereaved by suicide [12]. The impacts on survivors and on the bereaved are major and constitute significant public health problems in their own right. The WHO has made suicide a public health priority, which is reflected in the title of its 2014 document 'Preventing Suicide: A Global Imperative' [13]. The extent of avoidable loss of life is such that prevention merits a major commitment of effort and resources, because even partially successful measures can prevent a large number of deaths and much suffering. In any local, regional or national health strategy, prevention of a major public health problem has to be considered one of the highest priorities. It is achievable.

There are major differences between nations in the ways in which deaths are registered and recorded, in the definitions used to classify cause of death and in methods of collation to generate national statistics. Some countries do not collate data or claim very low rates of suicide. As a result, the WHO figures are based on best estimates for some countries. It is arguable that the failure to attempt to accurately report these deaths represents a collusion with human rights infringements (as discussed later in this chapter). Nonetheless, many international comparisons are based on reliable figures with a known level of accuracy. Descriptions of trends across the world are not based on speculation. As a general pattern, the highest rates of suicide arise in societies with large agrarian populations, with poorly developed health infrastructure and high levels of inequality. Many of these LMICs have experienced disruption to social infrastructure as a result of socio-economic change, conflict or natural disaster. In fact, whether by coincidence or not, they are societies with similar problems to those prevalent in Europe when Durkheim did his early research on suicide.

In 1971 a Welsh family doctor, Julian Tudor Hart, set out his Inverse Care Law [14]. This states that the availability of good medical care varies inversely to the need for it in the population served. Tudor Hart attributed this to the effects of health care being distributed wholly or partly as a market commodity. The Inverse Care Law has proven to capture a profound truth. The inverse relationship between the availability of health care and the need for it inexorably follows as a result of the effects of the social determinants of health, whereby the healthiest part of the population is also the wealthiest. It applies within nations and between nations. The same pattern is seen with regard to suicide; within and between nations, the lowest per capita health resource is expended on those populations that suffer the highest rates of suicide.

1.3 Low- and Middle-Income Countries / High-Income Countries

Although the majority of people who take their own lives reside in LMICs, what we know about suicide, self-harm and their prevention is dominated by evidence from HICs. Research in (and therefore evidence from) LMICs is gradually increasing and this tells us that whilst there are some similarities with HICs, there are also major differences. Neither LMICs nor HICs are homogenous, and there are differences between nations in each category. Age and gender distributions differ markedly, as does the proportion of people with diagnosable mental disorders amongst those who harm themselves and those who take their own lives. These differences are not surprising, as many cultural, social and economic factors influence patterns of suicide.

A recent systematic review, based mainly on HIC findings, suggests that people with a diagnosable mental disorder have an eightfold increase in the risk of suicide compared with the general population [15]. There is a correspondingly high rate of psychiatric disorders amongst patients presenting to hospital with self-harm [16]. Taken from a narrow secondary health care perspective, the implication would seem to be that suicide is commonly a consequence of mental illness and that prevention should focus on its treatment. The ability to access care and treatment for mental illness is certainly important for a range of humanitarian and human rights reasons. However, mental illness and social stress are intimately connected. For example, high levels of structural income inequality make a significant proportion of the population vulnerable to financial stress. Financial stress is associated with both depression and suicide. Provision of secondary mental health care is not necessarily highly effective as a suicide prevention measure for the population at large. This is not to suggest that mental health services are useless or that they could be safely eliminated. Where mental health services exist, closing them would almost certainly lead to a noticeable increase in rates of suicide, together with other untoward consequences. It does mean that establishing such services, or improving those that already exist, is only likely to be effective in achieving major reductions in suicide where services are one part of a broader suicide prevention strategy.

The limited data from LMICs appears to show a key difference in that a lower proportion of people who harm themselves have diagnosable mental illness in some (though not all) LMICs [17]. HIC findings are not completely irrelevant to suicide prevention in LMICs, but there is a need for caution to avoid supposing that findings from well-conducted research in HICs are not culture-bound. Data from HICs must be placed in a global context where there appears to be considerable variation in the extent to which suicide, self-harm and mental disorders have an intimate association. The evidence as it stands shows that the stressors leading to suicide play out differently in different parts of the world. A key exemplar is the much higher proportion of death by suicide in women in some parts of South Asia. Women are disadvantaged compared to men everywhere, but there is clearly something different about life as a woman in countries where female suicide is as common as male.

In HICs, the evidence suggests that the most obvious linear causal chain (whereby social stress leads to mental illness, which then causes hopelessness and eventually suicide) is only one of a range of complex relationships between social factors, mental illness and suicide. Although studies using psychological autopsy suggest that the majority of people in HICs who take their own life are mentally ill at the time, there is a substantial minority who are not.

Amongst those people who are mentally ill, the relationship between their mental health problem and their social environment is complex. Social factors can be divided into structural background factors (affecting segments of the population collectively) and social stressors (which tend to be current and individual). Social determinants of mental health in childhood (predominantly poverty and marginalisation) are also associated with suicide later in life, but it should be noted that psychosis is associated with urbanicity, whilst suicide is associated with rurality. There is an element of common causation, as well as causal bidirectionality. Episodes of acute mental illness are associated with current social stress but also worsen it – or at least make it more difficult to resolve. Under some common circumstances, the relationship is still more complicated; there are consistent findings showing that the period immediate after discharge from psychiatric inpatient facilities is a high-risk period, at a time when it might be supposed that symptoms of mental illness are likely to be improving, if not resolved [18]. In suicide prevention, treatment of mental illness, structural change to reduce vulnerability and enhanced support in the face of immediate social stressors are all of importance.

Similar complex relationships between social factors, mental illness and suicide are likely to exist in LMICs. An example is the role of financial stress in LMICs. Financial stress is believed to be a significant factor in suicide everywhere, but it can differ in nature and quality between LMICs and HICs. The pace at which financial ruination develops is probably faster in LMICs because the gap between an adequate income and destitution is smaller. A seasonal drought can completely destabilise whole families where they have no financial reserves, lack social capital or cannot access affordable credit. Despair may rapidly appear with or without the development of a full range of depressive symptoms. Help is needed for symptoms and finances. Identifying and treating mental illness is relevant in LMICs, but suicide prevention in HICs and LMICs involves both social and clinical domains.

Comparison of trends in suicide underlines the need to develop good quality longitudinal surveillance data in every country, across all types of society, in order to develop effective strategies that are socially, economically and culturally appropriate to local conditions. There are lessons from LMICs for HICs; the dramatic reduction in suicide rates in China cited above being a case in point. Evidence of this sort casts a light upon international data, pointing to those factors that might be most usefully addressed in HICs as well as LMICs. It underlines that clinical intervention for mental illness cannot be the sole strategy to bring down suicide rates.

1.4 Targeting the Cause of the Causes

Professor Sir Michael Marmot is the world authority on the social determinants of health. He draws an important distinction between health inequalities, which are the differences in morbidity and mortality between various populations, and health inequity, which is a lack of fairness in the ill-health burden experienced by different demographic groups [9]. Generally speaking, the most powerless, marginalised and economically vulnerable people suffer the worst health outcomes everywhere. Their socio-economic disadvantage is principally determined by factors beyond their control, such as where they were born, their ethnicity, their gender and their family circumstances.

Although ill health is often mediated by modifiable behaviours such as smoking, alcohol consumption, obesity and lack of exercise, the degree to which people are free to make healthy choices is severely constrained by marginalisation and disadvantage. For example, the wealthy can exercise safely in a gym, but it is hard to exercise in crowded inner-city areas where unaccompanied women are not safe. It is a public health truism that the single most important choice anyone could make to avoid ill health would be to choose not to be born poor. A steep gradient of diminishing agency and control over one's own life across the socio-economic spectrum accounts for the concentration of poor lifestyle 'choices' in the least wealthy part of the population.

These effects are obvious as they apply to the poorest of the poor, but the gradient of health disadvantage affects people all the way up the social hierarchy, except for those at the very top [19]. Each group has less control and worse health than the groups above them. Health inequity affects the vast majority of the population, and health inequalities are most marked in the most unequal societies, a category that includes the United States as well as many LMICs. Fairness and social justice have a direct and measurable impact on public health. Health improvement and suicide prevention involve targeting a range of social inequities, particularly income inequality. After 40 years of neoliberal domination of economic policy, the doctrine that the unconstrained pursuit of wealth at the top of society 'trickles down' to those lower in the hierarchy has no credibility. The most enthusiastically neoliberal HIC countries, such as the US and the UK, have seen marked increases in inequality. It is not the case that good public health can only be achieved if everyone has the same income, but it is incontrovertible that countries with the largest difference between the income of the top 10% and the bottom 10% experience the worst health inequalities [19]. Whilst suicide is also modified by specific factors that vary between countries and sub-populations, in general it follows the same patterns as every other public health problem.

The relationship between inequality and the risk of ill health is only one type of health inequity. As mentioned earlier, the Inverse Care Law dictates that access to treatment is worst for those with the greatest health needs. Tudor Hart's Inverse Care Law is not a natural law like thermodynamics and entropy, immutably woven into the fabric of the universe. It is a reflection of the ways in which societies choose to distribute health care. The part of Tudor Hart's paper that states that the Inverse Care Law applies where health care was distributed as a market commodity, wholly or in part, is important. The market model is not inevitable or the only way of paying for health care. It is certainly not the most cost-efficient way of distributing health care, as public sector health care systems have lower overheads than for-profit ones. There are equitable models, including the UK's National Health Service (NHS; despite slowly progressive privatisation) and Cuba's high-quality health care system, which was developed in a poor country subject to economic sanctions by the US [20]. Neither country could be regarded as a utopia, although each of them has aspired to be a socio-political exemplar, of the free market in the case of the UK and of socialism in the case of Cuba. What they illustrate is that inequitable distribution of health resources can be addressed (albeit without being fully resolved) within imperfect societies. Failure to distribute health care by need rather than by wealth is a choice, not an inevitability.

Suicide prevention must also address what Marmot has labelled 'the cause of the causes' [9], those structural obstructions to well-being that lie behind the circumstances that lead people to become ill or take their own lives.

1.5 Suicide and Human Rights

Suicide is most often thought of as a personal choice, albeit a misguided one with awful consequences. It is understood as a decision that is made by the individual. In the European intellectual frame of reference established during the Enlightenment, a person weighs up the advantages and disadvantages of the proposed course of action, including considerations of legalities and other consequences; makes a free choice; and acts. This is how the relationship between circumstances and actions are understood in the law, in theology, in fiction and in clinical psychiatry. It is captured in Hamlet's soliloquy, as he poetically ponders the pros and cons of continuing to live. The English coronial system, which is a strong influence in many jurisdictions across the world, expends as much effort in deciding the precise intentions of a person who appears to have taken their own life as it does in finding out what actually happened. Unfortunately, this abstracted decision-making process does not correspond to the psychological, psychiatric or social evidence on how behaviour is motivated or how self-harm incidents unfold, still less the factors that are known to influence them.

Standing back from individual circumstances to survey global patterns, variations in suicide rates between different parts of the population and between different nations clearly have some relationship with the extent to which human rights are respected. It seems highly likely that the relationship is causal, at least in part. There are plausible ways in which systematic and individual human rights violations can lead to suicide. For example, a lack of choice in who to marry and where to live, together with a lack of redress regarding domestic violence, can easily be seen to have implications for female suicide rates. The Universal Charter of Human Rights was proclaimed at the United Nations General Assembly in Paris on 10 December 1948 [21]. It is a remarkable document. Few of any political persuasion have felt able to contradict or reject it, either as a whole or in part. Seventy-five years after it was drafted, even a cursory reading shows that very few countries in the world (if any at all) are fully compliant with its articles. Most of the structural societal factors that are known to have a direct impact on suicide rates occur in contradiction of one or more its provisions.

We have no hesitation in unequivocally stating that structural health inequities are human rights violations. These violations and inequities create the context against which individuals decide to take their own life or, rather, come to feel that they have no other choice open to them. Supporting human rights does not entail acceptance of any particular political doctrine, but it does rest upon acceptance of values to the effect that everyone is of equal worth, irrespective of any personal characteristic that they have no control over. There is a profound relationship between public mental and physical health and human rights.

1.6 Interconnectedness

In mental health practice, understanding context is essential. Karl Jaspers' approach to phenomenological psychopathology [22] was based on the recognition that individual subjective experience could only be understood in relation to a general emotional and psychological state of mind. Difficult behaviours and relationship disruptions occur in the context of reciprocal relationships and social environment, including culture. These have a causal as well as a pathoplastic role when people develop mental ill health.

In public mental health, 'the cause of the causes' has a global dimension. International trade has existed for thousands of years, and it creates an interconnectedness in human affairs that has a tangible impact on health. For example, trade and travel are vectors that create the potential for global pandemics from the Black Death to COVID-19 [23]. In matters of economic policy, local decisions in Paris, Beijing or Washington have an impact on people in rural South Asia and Sub-Saharan Africa. When a container ship blocks the Suez Canal, as occurred in 2021, the effects are felt around the world.

Throughout history, powerful HICs have exported inequities and social injustice, most recently through globalisation. The ability of private companies to source cheap labour in LMICs has allowed them to bypass health and safety and other regulation in HICs. Products are made to a standard by third-party businesses, creating a distance between HIC company ownership and a LMIC labour force. European countries, including the UK, tolerate employment practices in Asia involving a form of modern slavery in order to manufacture cheap clothes for sale in markets where these employment practices are illegal [24]. These Asian workforces, predominately female, have high rates of suicide [25]. There is reluctance amongst HIC governments to create adequate penalties for companies benefiting from modern slavery abroad. The strength of these international networks of causation is tangible when the causes of the causes are examined closely.

The impact of interconnectedness flows back to HICs. Many LMICs correctly see themselves as having been treated unfairly from the days of slavery through the age of empire and, more recently, as a consequence of the modern form of economic imperialism that is generally described as 'globalisation'. There have also been adverse consequences of international social injustice for HICs at home. Prior to Brexit and the COVID-19 pandemic, the UK had the sixth-largest economy in the world, but the outsourcing of inequity to LMICs resulted in many towns and cities in the north of England sinking into a state of post-industrial decay. It would be difficult to persuade residents in British former mill towns that outsourcing fabric and garment manufacture to South Asia greatly benefitted their communities. Similar processes have created the so-called Rust Belt in the US. Attended high unemployment has an impact on domestic suicide rates, as can be seen starkly in Northern Ireland [26]. Neither HIC nor LMIC general populations benefit as a result of inequality and injustice.

The world's population has become highly mobile during the twenty-first century. A large proportion of people in HIC urban areas are either migrants or live amongst migrants. In the UK 2011 census, 37% of Londoners stated that they were born outside of the UK [27]. As a general rule, when people migrate, they slowly take on the characteristics of the population and culture that they join. Sometimes these changes take several generations, and patterns of ill health from their heritage culture disappear only slowly. These patterns include self-harm and suicide. Understanding what happens in migrant countries of origin, and those factors that relate to migration itself, are highly relevant to the development of comprehensive suicide prevention strategies in host HICs.

If social justice is a solution to 'the cause of the causes', we are bound to recognise that social justice cannot be achieved in one part of the world alone. The pursuit of social justice has to be a public health objective shared by a substantial proportion of the international health community. In the context of the COVID-19 pandemic, the WHO has repeatedly stated that 'no-one is protected unless everyone is protected' [28]. HIC governments acknowledge this but find it hard to act upon. At the simplest level, allowing COVID-19 to rage in LMICs whilst vaccinating whole populations in HICs simply creates a crucible for viral mutation and vaccine escape, which has the potential to prolong or repeat the pandemic. At a more complex level, the overall world economy cannot recover if some countries experience continued waves of infection and economic recession.

The need to address suicide globally is just as pressing. Worldwide, people engaged in agriculture are at particularly high risk of suicide, and this is the sector of the economy most affected by climate change. Agricultural infrastructure takes time to develop. Because farming is part of the rural ecosystem, changes to crops to accommodate changes in seasonal weather patterns are not easy and can have unforeseen consequences. Environmental degradation disproportionally affects the poorest people in the poorest nations. Drought and flooding cause crop failures, which in turn lead to high suicide rates amongst small farmers in LMICs. The solution involves action in both HICs and LMICs, which in turn must involve reductions in inequality within them and between them. The very richest do not have to be impoverished, but they will have to survive on a smaller multiple of average income than at present. We need a global scientific consensus to support a universal human rights approach to public health.

1.7 Evidence Saves Lives

If the previously noted points were simply matters of conviction or dogma, they would be political opinions. Instead, they rest on a well-established evidence base. They are facts that politicians and other policymakers need to accommodate. There is overwhelming evidence against contrary views to the effect that public health improves as wealth trickles down and that health inequalities are due to genetics and freely made personal choices. As applied scientists we can tell policymakers that whilst it is for them to form whatever strategies they consider appropriate, if they choose not to take action on 'the cause of the causes', then they will limit their own effectiveness. This is not the same as having no effect, but we can do much better than partial effects.

In emphasising the importance of issues of socio-economic structure, there is a danger of seeming to imply that all other efforts are futile. This is far from the case. The evidence shows that a good deal can be done, including building a locally relevant evidence base. Suicide and self-harm surveillance are essential components to an effective suicide prevention strategy. It is impossible to track what is happening with respect to suicide and self-harm in a population without reliable national and local data collection and analysis. Tracking changes and trends gives invaluable information as to where effort should be targeted and whether suicide prevention measures are having any discernible effect. Surveillance gives information about commonly used suicide methods.

One of the most robust findings in the suicide literature is that restriction of access to common means of suicide can produce a significant reduction in rates of suicide. For example, campaigns to reduce access to ligature points in UK psychiatric inpatient facilities have resulted in a significant and persistent decrease in suicide amongst inpatients [29]. Globally the most common means of suicide are hanging, firearms and ingestion of pesticides. Suicide rates are substantially higher where access to firearms and/or pesticides is unrestricted. Neither are easily obtained in the United Kingdom, which has relatively low rates of suicide by international standards, whereas India (where pesticides are freely available) has a much higher rate, as does the United States, where 50% of the population live in a household where there is a gun.

1.8 Conclusion: 'No One Is Protected Unless We Are All Protected'

It is a truism to say that the COVID-19 pandemic and the climate emergency have profoundly increased the urgency of global cooperation on health to tackle the challenges that lie ahead. Suicide is one of these. Suicide prevention is achievable. It requires a multifaceted approach that goes beyond the provision of mental health services. Local, national and global factors are important. A key strategy to tackle suicide worldwide is the coordinated development of local solutions to this global problem. This involves building on existing international networks of cooperation among researchers, clinicians and policymakers to facilitate the reduction of suicide rates everywhere.

References

1. Niederkrotenthaler T, Voracek M, Herberth A, Till B, Strauss M, Etzersdorfer E, et al. Role of media reports in completed and prevented suicide: *Werther v. Papageno* effects. *British Journal of Psychiatry*. 2010; **197**(3): 234–43.
2. Ranning A, Madsen T, Hawton K, Nordentoft M, Erlangsen A. Transgenerational concordance in parent-to-child transmission of suicidal behaviour: A retrospective, nationwide, register-based cohort study of 4,419,642 individuals in Denmark. *Lancet Psychiatry*. 2022; **9**(5): 363–74.
3. Durkheim É. *Suicide: A Study in Sociology*. Abingdon: Routledge, 2002.
4. Harriss L, Hawton K. Suicidal intent in deliberate self-harm and the risk of suicide: The predictive power of the Suicide Intent Scale. *Journal of Affective Disorders*. 2005; **86** (2–3): 225–33.
5. Saunders K, Brand F, Lascelles K, Hawton K. The sad truth about the SADPERSONS Scale: An evaluation of its clinical utility in self-harm patients. *Emergency Medicine Journal*. 2014; **31**: 796–8.
6. Hunt IM, Windfuhr K, Shaw J, Appleby L, Kapur N, National Confidential Inquiry into Suicide and Homicide. Ligature points and

ligature types used by psychiatric inpatients who die by hanging: A national study. *Crisis: The Journal of Crisis Intervention and Suicide Prevention*. 2012; **33**(2): 87–94.

7. Hawton K, Townsend E, Deeks J, Appleby L, Gunnell D, Bennewith O, et al. Effects of legislation restricting pack sizes of paracetamol and salicylate on self poisoning in the United Kingdom: Before and after study. *BMJ*. 2001; **322**: 1203.
8. Cwik MF, Tingey L, Maschino A, Goklish N, Larzelere-Hinton F, Walkup J, et al. Decreases in suicide deaths and attempts linked to the White Mountain Apache Suicide Surveillance and Prevention System, 2001–2012. *American Journal of Public Health*. 2016; **106**: 2183–9.
9. Marmot M. *The Health Gap: The Challenge of an Unequal World*. London: Bloomsbury; 2015.
10. Zhang J. Suicide reduction in China. *American Journal of Public Health*. 2019; **109**(11): 1533–4.
11. World Health Organization. *Suicide Worldwide in 2019: Global Health Estimates*. Geneva: World Health Organization; 2021.
12. Pitman A, Osborn D, King M, Erlangsen A. Effects of suicide bereavement on mental health and suicide risk. *Lancet Psychiatry*. 2014; **1**(1): 86–94.
13. World Health Organization. *Preventing Suicide: A Global Imperative*. Geneva: World Health Organization; 2014.
14. Tudor Hart, J. The Inverse Care Law. *Lancet*. 1971; **297**(7696): 405–12.
15. Too LS, Spittal MJ, Bugeja L, Reifels L, Butterworth P, Pirkis J. The association between mental disorders and suicide: A systematic review and meta-analysis of record linkage studies. *Journal of Affective Disorders*. 2019; **259**: 302–13.
16. Hawton K, Saunders K, Topiwala A, Haw C. Psychiatric disorders in patients presenting to hospital following self-harm: A systematic review. *Journal of Affective Disorders*. 2013; **151**(3): 821–30.
17. Knipe D, Williams AJ, Hannam-Swain S, Upton S, Brown K, Bandara P, et al. Psychiatric morbidity and suicidal behaviour in low- and middle-income countries: A systematic review and meta-analysis. *PLOS Medicine*. 2019; **16**(10): e1002905.
18. Chung DT, Ryan CJ, Hadzi-Pavlovic D, Singh SP, Stanton C, Large MM. Suicide rates after discharge from psychiatric facilities: A systematic review and meta-analysis. *JAMA Psychiatry*. 2017; **74**(7): 694–702.
19. Wilkinson R, Pickett K. *The Spirit Level: Why More Equal Societies Almost Always Do Better*. London: Allen Lane; 2009.
20. Cooper RS, Kennelly JF, Orduñez-Garcia P. Health in Cuba. *International Journal of Epidemiology*. 2006; **35**(4): 817–24.
21. United Nations. *Universal Declaration of Human Rights*. New York: United Nations; 1948. www.un.org/en/universal-declaration-human-rights.
22. Jasper K. The phenomenological approach in psychopathology. *British Journal of Psychiatry*. 1968; **114**: 1313–23.
23. Burns J, Movsisyan A, Stratil JM, Biallas RL, Coenen M, Emmert-Fees KMF, et al. Travel-related control measures to contain the COVID-19 pandemic: A rapid review. *The Cochrane Database of Systematic Reviews*. 2020; **10**: CD013717.
24. Richards, H. Risk, reporting and responsibility: Modern slavery, colonial power and fashion's transparency industry. *International Journal for Crime, Justice and Social Democracy*. 2022; **11**(2): 47–60.
25. Do HN, Nguyen AT, Nguyen HQT, Bui TP, Nguyen QV, Tran NTT, et al. Depressive symptoms, suicidal ideation, and mental health service use of industrial workers: Evidence from Vietnam. *International Journal of Environmental Research and Public Health*. 2020; **17**(8): 2929.
26. O'Neill S, O'Connor RC. Suicide in Northern Ireland: Epidemiology, risk factors, and prevention. *Lancet Psychiatry*. 2020; **7**(6): 538–46.

27. UK Office of National Statistics (ONS). *Census 2011*. 2011. www.ons.gov.uk/census/2011census.

28. World Health Organization. *No One Is Safe from COVID-19 until Everyone Is Safe*. Geneva: World Health Organization; 2021. www.who.int/news-room/photo-story/photo-story-detail/No-one-is-safe-from-COVID19-until-everyone-is-safe.

29. Hunt IM, Windfuhr K, Shaw J, Appleby L, Kapur N. National confidential inquiry into suicide and homicide: Ligature points and ligature types used by psychiatric inpatients who die by hanging – a national study. *Crisis: The Journal of Crisis Intervention and Suicide Prevention*. 2012; **33**(2): 87–94.

Chapter 2

Mental Health Gap and Suicide

Oyedeji Ayonrinde and Nomusa Mngoma

Although mental disorders impose an enormous toll on society, with the global burden of these disorders estimated at 418 million disability-adjusted life years (DALYs) in 2019 and $5 trillion (USD) in economic costs, by some calculations [1] most of the people affected (e.g., 75% in many low-income countries) do not have access to the treatment they need [2,3]. The chronic underfunding of mental health services, with governments spending on average 2% of their national health budget on mental health services, perpetuates the lack of access [3]. Furthermore, where mental health services exist, the uneven distribution of resources contributes to disparities in access. Because mental disorders affect not only individuals but families, communities and economies [4,5] – and are often associated with physical health concerns [6], poverty and poor quality of life [1] – it is imperative to find innovative strategies to improve access to care and mitigate the negative consequences of mental disorders, such as those linked to suicide.

One of the targets of the United Nations' Sustainable Development Goals (SDCs) is to achieve a 30% reduction in premature mortality from non-communicable diseases by 2030, of which suicide is an indicator [7]. Goal 3 of the SDGs is to 'ensure healthy lives and promote well-being for all at all ages'. Target 3.4 is to 'by 2030, reduce by one third premature mortality from non-communicable diseases through prevention and treatment and promote mental health and well-being', of which target 3.4 (suicide rate) is an indicator (see specifically target 3.4.2) [7]. There is a considerable gap between the ability of different countries to meet this goal [8].

2.1 The Mental Health Gap

In many parts of the world, mental health services are insufficient, inadequate, inaccessible or not equitably accessible for the people who need them in a timely manner, thus creating a mental health gap [2]. One of the grave consequences of this gap between need and the availability of mental health services is the risk of suicide. Limited access to mental health services, stigma and lack of awareness contribute to this gap, creating barriers to timely assessment and treatment [1].

In addition, affordability remains an important barrier to accessing mental health services in countries where there is no universal health coverage or where a two-tier health system creates inequitable access. Other barriers include location (e.g., rural and remote location), wait times and language [9,10]. A lack of culturally sensitive or relevant mental health services presents a barrier, as individuals may avoid seeking care or follow-up if they don't feel safe, seen or heard [3,11]. Even when initial contact has been made, these barriers can significantly limit a person's ability to adhere to treatment.

In many parts of the world, the provision of formal and informal mental health care and support is an amalgamation of Indigenous, traditional, Western and non-Western resources and systems [12]. Expanding the definition of mental health care to include interventions by non-specialists and away from institutionalised care would refocus the size of the problem. In many instances, 'treatment' seems to refer to a medical model of Western-type treatments provided by specialised health care providers such as psychiatrists. In some health systems, the barriers to care may be addressed by the presence of universal health coverage, decentralisation of mental health services, shortened wait times, anti-stigma measures, training of health workers and subsidised costs of medication.

In light of these factors, the World Health Organization (WHO) developed a Mental Health Gap Action Programme (mhGAP) [13] which aims at addressing gaps in national health care systems by scaling up prevention and management services for priority mental, neurological and substance use disorders, particularly in lower- and middle-income countries (LMICs). The intent of the mhGAP programme is to increase access to prevention and management mental health services through a multilevel approach, including psychosocial assistance and medication for depression, schizophrenia and other psychotic disorders, suicide, epilepsy, dementia and substance use disorders. This chapter focusses on recognition of the mental health gap, along with the development and implementation of measures to narrow the gap, particularly related to the assessment and management of suicidal individuals.

2.2 The Mental Health Workforce

One significant barrier to access to mental health care in many regions of the world is the shortage of mental health practitioners. The number of mental health practitioners per 100,000 population varies significantly across different countries within the same continent (e.g., Zimbabwe has 28.4 mental health practitioners per 100,000 people, while Ghana only has 7.3 mental health practitioners per 100,000 people) [8]. This shortage of specialists, including psychiatrists, psychologists, psychiatric nurses and social workers, further limits the ability of mental health services to support severely ill individuals with the greatest mental health needs [8].

Another important consideration is the availability of health care facilities, such as clinics and hospitals, to support mental health services. The number of mental/psychiatric hospitals, general hospital psychiatric units, residential care facilities and community health / non-hospital mental care health centres varies across countries. For instance, Argentina has 162 mental hospitals, while Ukraine has 69 inpatient psychiatric facilities [8]. These variations impact the accessibility of mental health care and the mental health gap.

The demand on mental health resources can be impacted by conflict, mass migration and global events, such as the COVID-19 pandemic, which significantly disrupted health systems with a direct impact on health care workers, who have faced increased stress, burnout and mental health problems of their own [14]. Globally the loss of health care workers due to the pandemic has further strained mental health services and the care of patients.

2.3 COVID-19 and Suicide Rates

The disruptions caused by the pandemic have led to a rise in serious mental health disorders. Limited access to early mental health interventions has contributed to an increase in cases of major depressive disorder and suicidal ideation. The prevalence of suicidal ideation has increased during and after the pandemic [15].

The impact of the COVID-19 pandemic on mental distress has been significant globally. Fear, social isolation, grief, unemployment and the constant stream of distressing news have contributed to increased mental health problems, such as depression and anxiety [15]. Certain populations, including those with pre-existing mental health conditions, racialised groups, children and youths and individuals experiencing homelessness or financial difficulties, have been disproportionately affected [16].

Workforce fluctuations with economic or other forms of migration further contribute to the mhGAP in many LMICs. Given the dearth of mental health workers, it is also important to develop foundational resources and capability within individual communities alongside traditional health and providers, alongside practitioners trained under Western models of care [16].

2.4 Displaced Populations, Global Conflicts and Natural Disasters

Armed conflict and natural or human-made disasters, with or without displacement, are associated with loss of protective factors and take a toll on mental health, causing fear, anxiety, depression, post-traumatic stress disorder, injuries and a range of other mental distress symptoms associated with hopelessness [17,18]. Loss of life and disruption of family and support structures, and loss of communities, often lead to feelings of grief. These consequences lead to an increased mental health burden and an increased need for services, often at a time when there may be a destruction or disruption of health resources. Conflict situations and other disasters, therefore, further worsen the gap between those requiring mental health services and the capacity to meet the increased demands. Limited availability of humanitarian health supports means that, of necessity, physical injuries are prioritised over mental health care and support.

2.5 Suicide and Mental Health Disorders

Mental health disorders play a significant role in the risk of suicide, particularly when untreated. While depression, anxiety disorders, substance misuse, bipolar disorder and schizophrenia are among the most common mental health conditions associated with suicide, evidence-based interventions can reduce the burden of illness and improve outcomes in illness trajectories. The WHO reports that approximately 90% of individuals who die by suicide have a diagnosable mental disorder at the time of their death [19]. Identifying and treating these conditions is crucial for suicide prevention.

2.6 Suicide Risk Factors

Various risk factors contribute to an individual's vulnerability to suicide. These include a history of previous suicide attempts, family history of suicide, social isolation, access to means of self-harm, exposure to suicidal behaviours and lack of mental health resources [19]. Additionally, socio-economic factors such as poverty, unemployment and inequality can further increase suicide risk. Chronic pain, chronic difficulties or physical health conditions may also contribute to the risk of suicide. Contextual understanding of these risk factors is essential for developing targeted interventions to reduce the mental health gap [19].

2.7 Impact of the Mental Health Gap on Suicide Rates

The mental health gap has a direct impact on suicide rates. When individuals are unable to access timely and appropriate mental health care, their risk of suicidal thoughts and behaviours increases [19]. Quoting the WHO, studies have shown that improved mental health services and support can significantly reduce suicide rates. Conversely, countries with limited mental health resources may experience higher suicide rates. Bridging the mental health gap is therefore vital for preventing suicide and promoting the overall well-being of individuals and their communities.

2.8 Narrowing the Mental Health Gap

The global gap between the need, demand and available provision of health services to prevent, screen, identify and treat mental, neurological and substance use (MNS) disorders has been widely documented. Recognising the dearth of secondary, tertiary-of-specialist services, the WHO's World Mental Health Report [19] recommended the assessment and management of MNS disorders in primary health care (PHC) and community settings, as outlined in the Mental Health Action Plan [20] to efficiently advance evidence-based care. The delivery of locally adapted primary care and community mental health care requires health staff to receive standardised training in the assessment, diagnosis and management of mental disorders with appropriate supervision and support. At the core of this global agenda is the WHO Mental Health Gap Action Programme (mhGAP) supported by an intervention guide (IG) – the mhGAP-IG [21].

The mhGAP-IG is an evidence-based tool for the assessment, treatment or management of priority MNS disorders, with structured and operationalised guidelines for clinical decision-making. Targeted at non-specialist community and primary care workers in LMICs, the mhGAP-IG is used by policymakers, governments and non-governmental organisations (NGOs) in the delivery and evaluation of interventions. Given the variable health terrain in countries or regions experiencing natural disaster or conflict, the mhGAP Humanitarian Intervention Guide (HIG) [22] was developed for interventions in resource sparse high trauma settings. In addition, an mhGAP-IG mobile device application [23] was developed to allow immediate and portable access to implementation and knowledge resources.

Addressing the mental health gap requires a comprehensive and multifaceted approach to supporting or developing health systems to meet their needs. Quoting the WHO, several evidence-based interventions have proven effective in reducing suicide rates, including the following [13]:

1. Enhancing mental health literacy and awareness. Education campaigns can help reduce stigma and increase public knowledge about mental health issues and available resources.
2. Expanding access to mental health services. Governments and health care systems should invest in improving mental health infrastructure, including increasing the number of mental health professionals, establishing community-based services and integrating mental health care into primary health care settings.
3. Strengthening suicide prevention strategies. Implementing national suicide prevention strategies that involve collaboration among government agencies, health care providers and community organisations can help identify at-risk individuals and provide appropriate support and intervention.

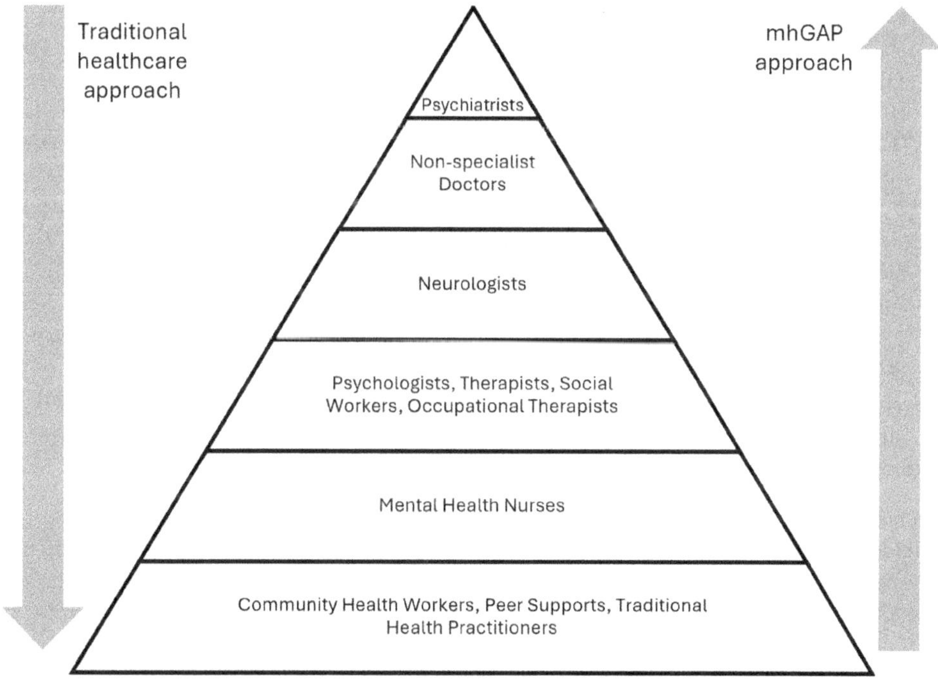

Figure 2.1 Illustration of the number of mental health workers per 100,000 population. Adapted from the Organisation for Economic Development and Co-operation and the World Health Organization, 2022 [24].

4. Promoting early identification and intervention. Training health care professionals, educators and community members to recognise early warning signs of mental distress and suicidal behaviour can facilitate timely intervention and support.
5. Providing psychosocial support. Creating supportive environments, such as help lines, crisis centres and peer support groups, can offer individuals in distress a safe space to seek help and support.

With the mhGAP, the reduced availability of mental health human resources underscores the need for decentralised care from the traditional health care approach to the mhGAP approach, particularly in remote and rural areas. Non-traditional forms of the mental health workforce can be helpful and include (1) Indigenous healers, (2) faith healers, (3) herbalists and (4) community elders (such as the 'grandmother's bench' practice popularised in Zimbabwe, which provides a communal space for mentoring and advice).

While national data on mental health workforces per 100,000 population give an insight into resource availability, the disaggregation of these numbers within a country are important, as there may be significant disparity between rural and urban areas or remote geographies. Furthermore, access to technologies (e.g., internet access) may have specific geographical distribution. Another consideration for disaggregation is the different demographic and vocational risk factors associated with suicide, such as farmers in agrarian communities with access to pesticides and firearms or remote areas with adverse climatic conditions. (see Figure 2.1)

In understanding the mhGAP in different communities, it is important to take the following into consideration [25]:

1. Traditional cultural beliefs regarding suicide.
2. Spiritual or faith beliefs. Many faiths discourage suicide based on a primary belief that life is a gift of a higher being who has authority over birth and death. The process of taking one's life is therefore considered against the observations of the faith. In some cultures, suicide is also felt to banish the individual from a happy reincarnation in an afterlife.
3. Gender roles. Cultural attributions of masculinity, courage and strength may impair or delay help-seeking during periods of distress, particularly when acknowledging difficulty coping is perceived to be a sign of weakness.
4. Taboos. While some cultures consider suicide abhorrent or a taboo conversation or acts, these beliefs may also be at odds with the intended mhGAP programme.
5. Stigma and shame. Stigma regarding mental health and specific mental disorders is universal to different degrees. As noted previously, this may have a direct or indirect impact on help-seeking or the support provided within communities.

Each of the considerations listed here are important illustrations of why the mhGAP for suicide educators and trainers requires a good knowledge of the attitudes to mental disorders and suicide in the target society. The buy-in of critical stakeholders and influencers, such as respected community leaders through direct or facilitated engagement, can reduce resistance to the interventions. In addition, careful consideration should be given to the perception of threats (knowledge, financial, status, cultural) to existing care models or frameworks in the community from an intervention that may be perceived to be foreign and esoteric to existing ways of knowing [13].

Mental health resource issues contributing to the mhGAP include (1) funding, (2) manpower, (3) logistics, (4) technology, (5) medication, (6) infrastructure, (7) training, (8) policy and (9) legislation, particularly mental health legislation [13].

2.9 mhGAP Implementation: How to Plan Pre-service Delivery Awareness and Education Using the mhGAP

As mentioned previously, the delivery of a universal and evidence-based suicide intervention programme requires extensive standardised training. In some cases, this is targeted at enhancing a pre-existing curriculum, while in other cases, there may not be any curriculum whatsoever. The mhGAP Implementation Guide (mhGAP-IG) serves to ensure core consistency with local adaptation in the development and delivery process to strengthen or enhance a curriculum. It can be divided into seven main phases, as illustrated in Figure 2.2; however, not all phases need to be followed in the order given and not all of them need to be included in the model development. The WHO encourages each teaching institution to have its own process, tailored to its resources and specific needs [21].

2.10 Phase 1: Create Awareness and Understanding

Although the mhGAP-IG has been used widely in more than 100 countries, its application in pre-service education is quite limited. It is important to involve key decision makers and clinical professionals about the potential benefits and impacts on their services and communities. On the surface this may appear straightforward. However, cultural beliefs, health

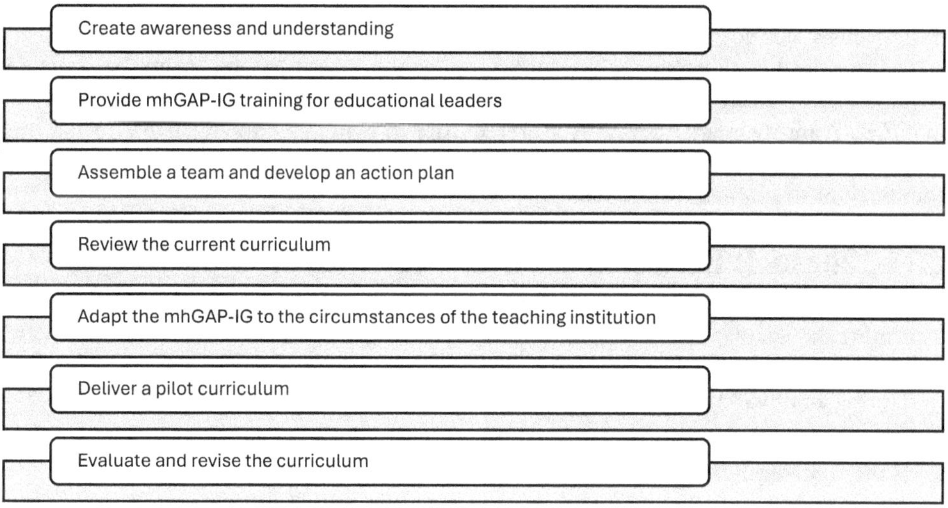

Figure 2.2 The seven phases of mhGAP-IG training. From the World Health Organization, 2020 [21].

system structures and competing priorities may require tailored approaches to raising awareness. Invariably, a baseline understanding of and direct consultations with key stakeholders enhances the creation of awareness.

2.11 Phase 2: Provide mhGAP-IG Training for Educational Leaders

The mhGAP-IG training manuals are based on the 'cascade' model, with two tiers of educators: (1) 'master trainers' responsible for training the teaching faculty staff and (2) teaching faculty staff who then instruct learners and students. The benefits of this model are not only through engaging educational stakeholders in the development, adaptation and delivery of curricula, but also in scaling up the teaching, for instance across regional health programmes. Through workshops, seminars and adapted pedagogies, the objective is to develop competent trainees to become trainers.

Alongside both clinical and teaching experience, the personal communication, collaborative approaches, self-reflection and innovative adaptation of teaching methods should be carefully considered with programmed development.

2.12 Phase 3: Assemble a Team and Develop an Action/Work Plan

As expected with the development of a project or team, the selection of a leader with prerequisite educational and leadership skills is key. In partnership with a committed group of individuals and educational networks, the assembly of a team is important. Where possible, team diversity and range of skills can be optimised to enhance the reach. Where possible, the involvement of both mental health specialists and non-specialists can create a knowledge balance to ensure that resource limitations for mental health professionals do not restrict the capacity for programme development. Alongside an educational lead responsible for the curriculum enhancement process, team members are responsible for needs assessments, development, strengthening and integration of the mhGAP. Team member training is a prerequisite to being able to effectively review and adapt the curriculum with mhGAP-IG materials. Where possible, the involvement of students can strengthen engagement.

2.13 Phase 4: Review the Current Curriculum

The mhGAP-IG suicide pre-service delivery team can review the pre-existing curriculum to determine the adaptability or relevance of materials against the local situation and WHO standardised materials.

During an mhGAP curricula review, the following questions should be considered [21]:

1. What is the current state of suicide awareness and education on interventions?
2. Is there currently a suicide prevention curriculum?
3. What are the strengths and weaknesses of the current curriculum?
4. Is there a need to enhance and strengthen the current teaching process and curriculum?
5. What is the objective of the new or modified curriculum?
6. What would the 'ideal' curriculum look like?
7. How can mhGAP-IG materials designed for suicide prevention help achieve goals and objectives?
8. In what way can mhGAP-IG materials designed for suicide prevention be adapted without losing the fidelity of the models?

Overall, this process involves ensuring the existing suicide awareness curriculum contains relevant and updated mental health information related to suicide risk and associated health conditions in different demographic populations across the lifespan.

Through a systematic review of pre-existing material, the suicide intervention guide reviews the following implementation strategies:

1. Promotion. This involves the dissemination of awareness and knowledge through the most appropriate range of media available (e.g., radio, town crier, faith groups, digital and social media).
2. Prevention. The identification of high risk or common suicide methods in the community (e.g., pesticides, hanging, jumping from heights at specific locations).
3. Management. The most appropriate interventions for suicidality, suicide attempts and the consequences of completed suicides.
4. Referral options and pathways. This is dependent on the primary, secondary and tertiary care resources available in the health system and engagement with these resources.
5. Practical practice application of teaching and learning materials. This includes opportunities to simulate interventions and realistic practice case material for the community based on recognised trends.

2.14 Phase 5: Adapt mhGAP-IG Suicide Content to the Circumstances of the Teaching Institution

Given the diverse range of cultures, educational, health systems and inequity in the mhGAP, it is pertinent that each centre tailor adaptation to the best model or fit. There are a number of important considerations involved, including the following questions:

1. How extensive an adaptation is needed?
2. Which specific modules are needed?
3. How should the mhGAP-IG suicide prevention content be introduced into the current curriculum?

The practical application of mhGAP materials involves a distinctions-based tailoring of the content to the local health system, while aligning and adapting materials with appropriate national treatment guidance, guidelines and policies within legislative frameworks. To be acceptable to the population served and health providers, the cultural practice and epistemological context of health and disease need to be considered.

At a very basic level, adaptation may only require replacing names in case studies with the incorporation of recognisable locations, while in other situations, complex changes may be required to ensure the material is sufficiently realistic and contextual with local explanatory models and beliefs. Though early versions of the mhGAP-IG were initially in English, French, Spanish, Italian, Marathi and Russian, translations into other languages are actively in progress. Where possible, it is advisable that translation through translation and back translation should be implemented at the earliest convenience to ensure all curriculum team members have equitable access to the available mhGAP content.

2.15 Phase 6: Deliver a Pilot Curriculum

As soon as mhGAP-IG content is incorporated into a curriculum and the identified teaching staff have received training, a pilot of the enhanced curriculum can then be carried out. Where possible, all the educational materials should be available at the time of launch to ensure seamless transition. It is understandable that not all providers have the print and technological resources to develop and deliver high-end outputs. Ultimately the key content should include a printed version of the mhGAP-IG: training package presentations, videos, role-plays and customised teaching tools created by faculty staff such as leaflets and presentations. Allowing flexibility of application, mhGAP-IG content can be presented during didactic teaching or small group teaching reinforced with knowledge and skills testing.

2.16 Phase 7: Evaluate and Revise the Curriculum

The evaluation process can be simultaneous with the delivery of the pilot curriculum with a view to identifying barriers, challenges and facilitators, as well as successes with the enhanced curriculum.

Ideally, both quantitative and qualitative methods should be applied in evaluation, adapted to and factoring in the local requirements and resources. Importantly,

1. Acceptability and applicability with the enhanced curriculum against the stated objectives.
2. Institutional or organisational support for the enhanced curriculum as well as from educational staff.

3. Educational processes involving the mhGAP-IG, such as the number of learners, resource use and teaching time.
4. Teaching outcomes and student assessment results. These evaluation results are incorporated into the quality improvement process and shared with key partners, including the WHO.

2.17 The Self-Harm/Suicide mhGAP Training Manual

The following section provides excerpts from the self-harm/suicide module of the mhGAP training manual for health care providers [21]. Each centre is encouraged to adapt the content to the specific cultural, social, demographic and suicide risks of their community.

Over nearly four hours, participants are involved in five sessions and five training activities with clear learning objectives. At the end of the training, a short review of the knowledge and evaluation quiz reinforces the lesson. Each of these learning objectives is further enhanced by the collaborative efforts of mental health specialists and local/community expertise. Table 2.1 includes details of relevant sessions, objectives and training activities.

Visual aids are an integral component of the training material for ease of learning, recognising different learning styles. For instance, the interplay between suicide risk factors and protective factors in Figures 2.3 and 2.4 highlights the equilibrium and escalation of risk under different conditions.

In the absence of digital resources and mobile telephone applications, Figure 2.5 provides workers with an easily rehearsed and memorable 'one-handed' guide to the key steps in the mhGAP training manual for the management and support of suicidal individuals.

Overall, participants in the mhGAP suicide curriculum and evolving communities of practice will develop universal core knowledge and share the following key messages (simplified with the 'hand' depiction in Figure 2.5):

1. Common presentations of self-harm/suicide:
   a. Extreme hopelessness and despair.
   b. Current thoughts/plan/acts of self-harm/suicide or history thereof.
   c. Act of self-harm with signs of poisoning/intoxication, bleeding from self-inflicted wounds, loss of consciousness and/or extreme lethargy.
2. Anyone with other priority MNS conditions must be assessed for self-harm/suicide.
3. Anyone with self-harm/suicide must be assessed for other priority MNS conditions, chronic pain and emotional distress.
4. You can use effective communication skills to provide psychosocial interventions to the person and to the whole family.
5. Refer a person with self-harm/suicide to a mental health specialist, if available.
6. It is essential to offer regular follow-up care to a person with self-harm/suicide.

2.18 Barriers to the Implementation and Sustainability of mhGAP

A thematic review of the cultural context of the mhGAP [24] identified six major sets of challenges associated with the implementation of mhGAP in different communities, namely

Table 2.1 Details of sessions, objectives and training activities based on the mhGAP

Session	Learning objectives	Duration	Training activities
1. Introduction to self-harm/ suicide	Know the common presentations of self-harm/ suicide. Promote respect and dignity for people with self-harm/suicide.	40 minutes	**Activity 1: Person stories followed by group discussion.** Use the person stories to introduce self-harm/suicide. **Presentation to supplement first-person accounts discussion.** Use the first-person stories as a basis for discussions on: • Common presentations of self-harm/suicide • Risk factors • Why it is important to learn how to manage self-harm/ suicide in non-specialised health settings
2. Assessment of self-harm/ suicide	Know the principles of assessment of self-harm/suicide. Perform assessments for self-harm/suicide. Assess and manage comorbid physical health in self-harm/suicide. Assess and manage emergency presentations of self-harm/suicide. Refer to specialists and links to outside agencies for self-harm/suicide, as appropriate.	40 minutes 30 minutes	**Activity 2: Video demonstration: Assessment** Use videos/demonstration role-play to show an assessment of self-harm/suicide and allow participants to follow the process according to the mhGAP-IG assessment algorithm **Activity 3: Role-play: Assessment** How to assess someone for self-harm/suicide
3. Management of self-harm/ suicide	Know the management principles of self-harm/suicide. Provide psychosocial interventions to a person with self-harm/suicide.	30 minutes 30 minutes	Presentation on psychosocial interventions and brief group discussion **Activity 4: Role-play: Management interventions**
4. Follow-up	Offer follow-up for self-harm/suicide, as appropriate.	40 minutes	**Activity 5: Role-play: Follow-up**
5. Review	Review knowledge and skills from the session.	15 minutes	Multiple-choice questions and discussion

Total duration (without breaks) = 3 hours, 45 minutes.
Source: World Health Organization, 2017 [13].

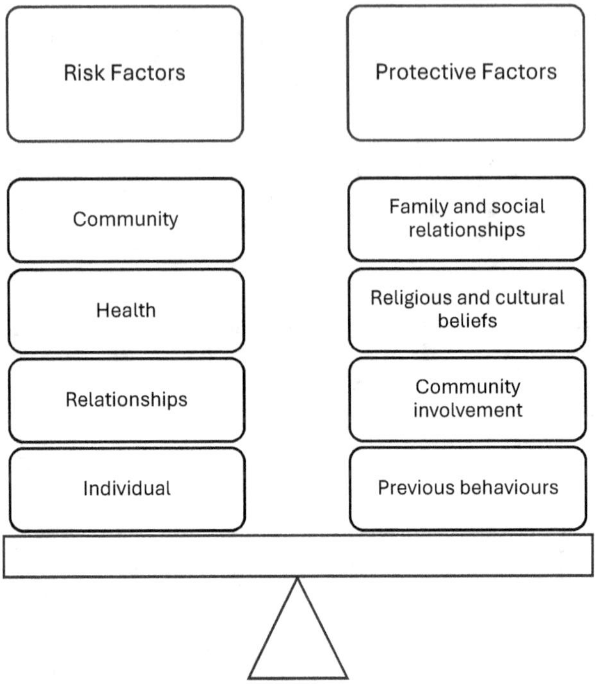

Figure 2.3 Illustration of the interplay between risk and protective factors in equilibrium. Adapted from the World Health Organization, 2017 [13]. Licence: CC BY-NC-SA 3.0 IGO.

(1) cultural differences in explanations of and attitudes towards mental disorder; (2) the structure of the local health care system; (3) the level of supervision and support available post-training; (4) the level of previous education, knowledge and skills of trainees; (5) the process of recruitment of trainees; and (6) the larger socio-political context. The researchers proposed several approaches to addressing these challenges, such as (1) cultural and contextual adaptation of training, (2) meaningful stakeholder and community engagement and (3) supervisory and support systems for trainees (e.g., communities of practice).

Contextual and cultural factors can present major barriers to mhGAP implementation and the sustainability of services. The interaction between local trainees and their educators can have great advantage in the knowledge process, whereby trainees are able to effectively apply their local cultural knowledge and mhGAP training needs to (1) address assumptions, biases and stigma associated with mental health symptoms and problems; (2) provide an explicit framework to guide the integration of cultural knowledge into assessment, treatment negotiation and delivery; and (3) address the specific kinds of problems, modes of clinical presentations and social predicaments seen in the local population. Table 2.2 documents some facilitators and barriers to the implementation of the mhGAP-IG.

In recent years, there has been international growth in mhGAP training, implementation, evaluation and diverse global practice supported by research and literature. There remain research gaps from some geographical regions and among individuals with severe mental illness25. As mhGAP gets embedded in health service delivery, it is anticipated that the local, linguistic and community contextual adaptation of brief psychological

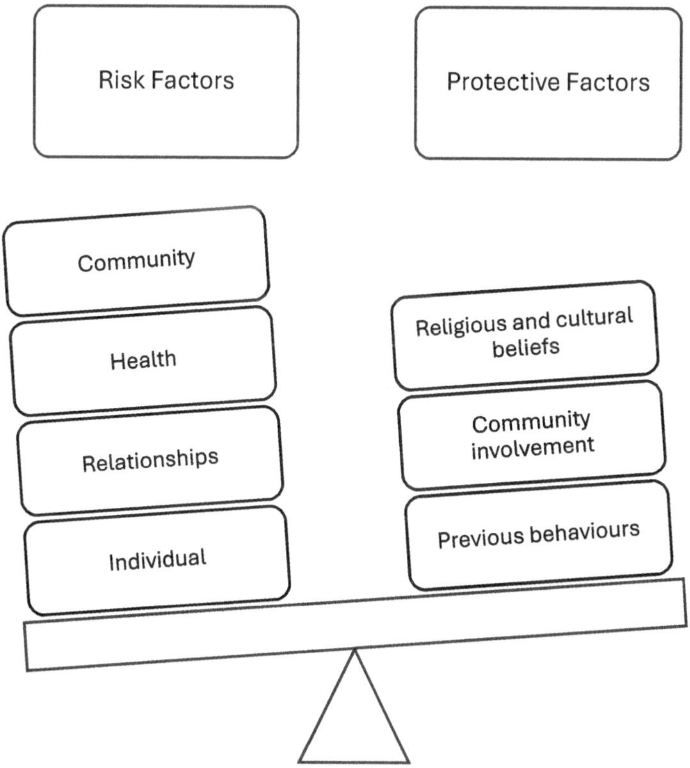

Figure 2.4 Illustration of the interplay between risk and protective factors out of equilibrium. Adapted from the World Health Organization, 2017 [13]. Licence: CC BY-NC-SA 3.0 IGO.

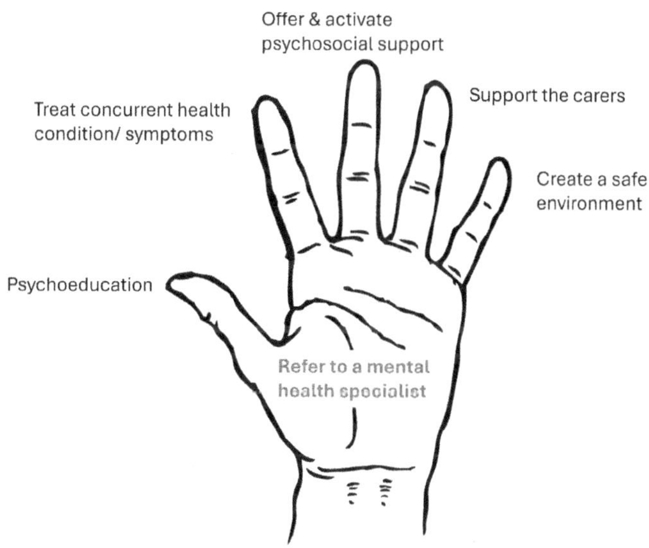

Figure 2.5 A 'one-handed' depiction of key steps for the management and support of suicidal individuals. Adapted from the World Health Organization, 2016 [21].

Table 2.2 Facilitators and barriers to mhGAP-IG implementation success

System level	Facilitators	Barriers
Service user	Co-delivery of traditional and biomedical care Increased community awareness	Cultural differences between biomedical models Different treatment perspectives Rural location and distance from health resources Non-interventional expectation of resolution Cost of treatment Resistance to treatment
Staff	Health worker motivation Sharing research findings collaboratively	Resistance from faculty members Time constraints and workload Stigma Mistrust of informal health providers, cultural misunderstandings
Service	Supervision Onward referral Reliable psychotropic medication procurement Trained female community health volunteers	Few specialist staff to deliver supervision Lack of financial resources Limited referral systems Staff turnover/retention Inadequate privacy/confidential consultation space
Leadership	Strong political and organisational support	Lack of institutional support

Adapted from Keynejad et al., 2021 [26]. Creative Commons CC BY 4.0.

interventions, stigma reduction and awareness will serve to reduce the burden of suicide across societies.

The implementation of an mhGAP suicide reduction initiative requires an awareness of the current mental health resources available in each country and the unique communities therein. With an appreciation of communities, pathways to help-seeking and the potential synergy or divergence between the models of care, the mhGAP can be implemented to reduce suicide rates in diverse settings.

References

1. Arias D, Saxena S, Verguet S. Quantifying the global burden of mental disorders and their economic value. *EClinical Medicine.* 2022 Sep 28; **54**: 101675.
2. Roberts T, Esponda GM, Krupchanka D, et al. Factors associated with health service utilisation for common mental disorders: A systematic review. *BMC Psychiatry.* 2018; **18**: 262.
3. World Health Organization. *World Mental Health Report: Transforming Mental Health for All.* Geneva: World Health Organization, 2022.
4. Patel V, Chisholm D, Parikh R, et al. Global priorities for addressing the burden of

mental, neurological, and substance use disorders. In *Mental, Neurological, and Substance Use Disorders: Disease Control Priorities*, vol. 4, 3rd ed. Washington, DC: International Bank for Reconstruction and Development / The World Bank; 2016.

5. Trautmann S, Rehm J, Wittchen HU. The economic costs of mental disorders: Do our societies react appropriately to the burden of mental disorders? *EMBO Reports*. 2016 Sep; **17**(9): 1245–9.
6. Ohrnberger J, Fichera E, Sutton M. The relationship between physical and mental health: A mediation analysis. *Social Science and Medicine*. 2017 Dec; **195**: 42–9.
7. UN Department of Economic and Social Affairs (UN DESA). *The Sustainable Development Goals Report 2016*. New York: UN DESA; 2016.
8. World Health Statistics. *Monitoring Health for the SDGs, Sustainable Development Goals*. Geneva: World Health Organization; 2021.
9. Elliott KP, Hunsley J. Evaluating the measurement of mental health service accessibility, acceptability, and availability in the Canadian Community Health Survey. *American Journal of Orthopsychiatry*. 2015; **85**(3): 238–42.
10. Wang PS, Aguilar-Gaxiola S, Alonso J, et al. (2007). Use of mental health services for anxiety, mood, and substance disorders in 17 countries in the WHO world mental health surveys. *Lancet*. 2007 Sep 8; **370**(9590): 841–50.
11. Watungwa Y. *Equitable Access to Mental Health Care for Black and Indigenous Peoples in Canada: A Scoping Review*. Unpublished honours thesis, Dalhousie University, Halifax, Nova Scotia, 2022.
12. Wu J, Smye V, Hill B, Antone J, MacDougall A. Exploration of existing integrated mental health and addictions care services for Indigenous Peoples in Canada. *International Journal of Environmental Research and Public Health*. 2023; **20**(11): 5946.
13. World Health Organization. *mhGAP Training Manuals for the mhGAP Intervention Guide for Mental, Neurological and Substance Use Disorders in Non-specialized Health Settings, Version 2.0 (for field testing; WHO/MSD/MER/17.6)*. Geneva: World Health Organization; 2017. https://iris.who.int/handle/10665/259161.
14. Pragholapati A. *Mental Health in Pandemic COVID-19*. SSRN; 2020.
15. World Health Organization. *World Mental Health Report: Transforming Mental Health for All*. Geneva: World Health Organization; 2022.
16. Kola L, Kohrt BA, Hanlon C, et al. COVID 19 mental health impact and responses in low-income and middle-income countries: Reimagining global mental health. *Lancet Psychiatry*. 2021; **8**(6): 535–50.
17. Munro A, Kovats RS, Rubin GJ, et al. Effect of evacuation and displacement on the association between flooding and mental health outcomes: A cross-sectional analysis of UK survey data. *Lancet Planet Health* 2017; **1**: e134–41.
18. Keya TA, Leela A, Habib N, Rashid M, Bakthavatchalam P. Mental health disorders due to disaster exposure: A systematic review and meta-analysis. *Cureus*. 2023; **15**(4): e37031.
19. Pirkis J, John A, Shin S, DelPozo-Banos M, Arensman E. Preventing suicide: A public health approach to a global problem. *Lancet Public Health*. 2024; **9**(10): e787–95.
20. World Health Organization. *Mental Health Action Plan, 2013–2020*. Geneva: World Health Organization; 2013. www.who.int/publications/i/item/9789241506021.
21. World Health Organization. *Enhancing Mental Health Pre-service Training with the mhGAP Intervention Guide: Experiences and Lessons Learned*. Geneva: World Health Organization; 2020. www.who.int/publications/i/item/9789240007666.
22. World Health Organization. *mhGAP Humanitarian Intervention Guide (mhGAP-HIG)*. Geneva: World Health Organization; 2015. www.who.int/mental_health/publications/mhgap_hig/en.
23. Luitel NP, Neupane V, Lamichhane B, et al. (2023). Experience of primary healthcare workers in using the mobile app-based

WHO mhGAP intervention guide in detection and treatment of people with mental disorders: A qualitative study in Nepal. *SSM Ment Health*. 2023 Dec 15; **4**: 100278.

24. Organisation for Economic Development and Co-operation and the World Health Organization. Psychiatrists, per 100,000 population, 2020 or latest year available. In *Health at a Glance: Asia/Pacific 2022: Measuring Progress towards Universal Health Coverage*. Paris: OECD Publishing; 2022.

25. Faregh N, Lencucha R, Ventevogel P, et al. Considering culture, context and community in mhGAP implementation and training: Challenges and recommendations from the field. *Journal of Mental Health Systems*. 2019 Aug 24; **13**: 58.

26. Keynejad R, Spagnolo J, Thornicroft G. WHO mental health gap action programme (mhGAP) intervention guide: updated systematic review on evidence and impact. *BMJ Ment Health*. 2021 Apr 26; **24**(3): 124–30.

Chapter 3

Preventing Male Suicide

Silvia Sara Canetto

3.1 Introduction

Men comprise the majority of those who die of suicide [1]. This pattern is often taken as an indication that suicide is a male behaviour and a male problem, and that men are naturally and perhaps inevitably more prone to suicide than women (see Canetto's studies in 1992–3 and 2021 [2,3] and Kushner's 1993 study [4] for critical analyses of this idea).

Suicide, however, is not always more common in men than in women when the data is examined over time, by country and within country by age groups. For example, as recently as 2012, men were less likely to die of suicide than women in China, Indonesia, Iraq and Pakistan [5]. These countries compose a major proportion of the global population, so their suicide patterns cannot be dismissed as minor exceptions. Also, currently, in some countries, men are less likely to die of suicide than women in certain age groups. For example, in Bangladesh, India, Nepal and Pakistan, adolescent and adult men are less likely to die of suicide than adolescent and adult women [6]. This variability in male suicide rates, relative to female rates, by country and over time, and within country by age, suggests cultural influences [7,8].

It is also worth noting that generally men have lower rates of non-fatal suicidal behaviour but a higher mortality by suicide than women. This gender paradox of suicide is another indication of cultural influences on suicidality [9].

3.2 Dominant Theories of Male Suicide Focus on Men's Public-Life Behaviours, Particularly on Employment

Many theories have been proposed to explain high male suicide mortality. Most theories link men's suicide to their public-life roles and specifically their economic roles. These theories assume that male suicide rates would be higher when men experience threats to employment or the end of employment (as is the case, for example, in times of economic crisis or following retirement). Some theories postulate that male suicide rates would also be higher in societies and/or at times when female employment is also higher, presumably related to how female employment challenges male entitlement to economic dominance in the family and society [10–13].

Parts of this chapter have been previously published in Ms Magazine (By Assuming More Family Caregiving Responsibilities, Men May Reduce Their Suicide Vulnerability https://msmagazine.com/2022/01/26/men-suicide-rates-caregiving-kids-education-family-build-back-better/)

3.3 Research Challenges to the Role of Employment in Men's Suicide

Economic adversities, including unemployment and retirement, do not necessarily explain high rates of suicide mortality in men. To start with, research shows that men's suicide rates are not consistently higher in times of economic recession. For example, a multinational study of suicide and unemployment found marked country variations in suicide rates during the 2008–10 economic recession. In Austria, men's suicide rates did not increase when unemployment rose, while in the United States, unemployment produced only a small proportion of variance in men's suicide rates [14].

It is unclear what accounts for the substantial cross-country variations in suicide rates during times of economic recession. One theory is that the association between unemployment and suicide is weaker in countries that have work-protection programmes (e.g., programmes providing expenditures to compensate for unemployment) or active-labour programmes (e.g., programmes that assist with finding employment). Studies, however, indicate that the impact of work-protection programmes varies widely, by country and region of a country, by type of programme and by demographic group (e.g., age group) [15,16,17]. For example, an Italian study found that between 1990 and 2014, active-labour programmes were effective in moderating the association between unemployment and suicide only among men ages 45–54 and only in central Italy [16].

A Hong Kong study of suicide rates in relation to both regional unemployment rates and individual employment status during the economic recession of 2000–3 and the economic recovery period of 2003–6 found a strong correlation between unemployment rates and suicide rates for the full study period (2000–6). Contrary to prediction, however, it was the suicide rates of the employed that raised during the economic recession. The suicide rates of the unemployed *decreased* in the period of economic recession, and they increased in the period of recovery [18].

Retirement does not explain men's high suicide rates, either. In the United States, men's suicide rates (post–typical retirement age) are highest among men of European descent. If retirement was a universal suicide risk factor for men, it would impact the suicide rates of older adult men across ethnicities, not just those of older adult men of European descent [19].

Another challenge to employment theories of male suicide are the patterns of female suicide, over time. If employment challenges were suicidogenic per se, women's suicide rates should have skyrocketed in recent decades in countries where women's participation in the paid labour force grew. This is what dominant suicide theories have predicted – and also what women were warned about [12]. But women's suicide rates did not raise concomitant with women's increased participation in the paid labour force, including in the United States, where men's suicide mortality is still significantly higher than women's suicide mortality [19].

3.4 New Theory on Men and Suicide

Since the 1990s, I have been theorizing that men's suicide mortality is not just a response to the adversities that men may encounter in their public lives, including loss of employment [2,19–22]. My perspective is that men's vulnerability to suicide is related to men's private-life behaviours – specifically men's low engagement in family care work. Men tend to generally overinvest in economic-provider work and underinvest in family care work. This pattern leaves men vulnerable to all sorts of psychological and social problems, especially when their economic-provider role is threatened or when employment is lost or ends.

I have predicted that men's suicide vulnerability would be lower if men invested in family care work – that is, if men actually did family care work [19,21,22]. My hypothesis is based on a diversity of evidence, including the fact that in several countries, including Italy and the United States, older adult women have lower suicide mortality than older adult men [19,23,24], despite the fact that women experience more systemic adversities than men. Across the lifespan, and especially in late life, women have higher rates of chronic illnesses, poverty and widowhood than men [25]. The fact that in the United States White men have the highest suicide rates of all older adults, across sex and ethnicity, is thus an adversity paradox [19,20].

A suicide-relevant difference between US women's and men's life experiences, in recent decades, is that most women do family care work as well as financial-provider work, while most men primarily do financial-provider work [26,27].

My prediction has been that male suicide vulnerability will not be reduced via employment-focussed social protection programmes, because these programmes reinforce men's already strong investment and identification with work/economic-provider roles. It is by adding family responsibilities to the economic-provider work responsibilities that men can likely boost their suicide protection. When men assume care work responsibilities, they diversify their social investments and psychological identifications; as a result they increase their social networks and capital and have the potential to develop more psychological resilience [19–22,28].

3.5 New Research on Men and Suicide

My theory that family care work could have a suicide-protective effect for men (considering that men already have substantial paid-work commitments) [19–22] was tested in a study by an international and multidisciplinary team [28]. In this study, Chen and colleagues examined suicide, male family care work and unemployment in 20 countries, including Austria, Belgium, Canada, Italy, Japan and the United States. Family care giving was defined as, for example, providing personal care or education for a child and/or providing care for a dependent adult.

Chen and colleagues found that suicide rates were lower in countries where men reported more family care work [28]. The study also found that higher unemployment rates were not associated with higher suicide rates in men in countries where men reported more such care work. By contrast, in countries where men reported less family care work, higher unemployment rates were associated with elevated male suicide rates.

Chen and colleague's findings suggest that doing family care work may boost men's suicide resilience, particularly during difficult economic periods, such as when unemployment rates are high [28]. These findings are consistent with my theories that men's vulnerability to suicide is related to their private-life behaviours, not only their public-life situation, and specifically that men's vulnerability to suicide is amplified by an over-investment in economic-provider work and an underinvestment in family care work.

A diversity of evidence, including Chen and colleagues' study [28], challenges the long-standing theory that men's suicide is predicated upon their public-life roles and situation (specifically their employment status). Growing evidence also challenges the idea that men's private-life roles and behaviours (specifically men's engagement in family care work) are not important for determining men's likelihood of suicide [10,11,12].

This new evidence points to new directions for theory, research and the prevention of men's suicide.

3.6 New Directions for Theory on Men and Suicide, and on Men and Health Broadly

Chen and colleagues' findings on men, suicide, unemployment and family care work [28] challenge the dominant theory that public-life problems, specifically unemployment, are the main drivers of male suicide mortality [10,11,12]. They are consistent with a diversity of empirical evidence indicating that for men as for women, having both family care work and family economic responsibilities is more conducive to well-being, health and longevity than a gendered division of labour (see Barnett and Hyde's 2001 review [27]; see also Heymann et al.'s 2019 study of programmatic, legal and policy approaches to improving female and male health via reducing female–male inequalities [29]).

This has been known about women for a long time [30]. Women's well-being, health and longevity have increased concomitant with increases in their participation in the paid labour force. One reason employed women tend to do better than unemployed women is that they have independent financial resources, which contributes to their greater power outside as well as within the home. Another reason employed women tend to do better is that they enjoy broader social networks as well as greater self-esteem and confidence than unemployed women. Women's paid employment also enhances the well-being of their children. For example, a study of 29 countries found that adult daughters of employed mothers were more likely to be employed and, if employed, were more likely to hold supervisory responsibility and earn higher incomes than adult daughters of mothers who were not employed. Adult sons of employed mothers spent more time caring for family members [31].

The benefits for men of participating in family care work have been less well-documented. This is in part because men have yet to assume family care work responsibilities to the same degree that women have taken on family financial responsibilities [26]. Men still do about 2 to 10 times *less* family care work than women [32].

Until recently, family care work was considered a cost and a burden to be assumed by social subordinates – that is, women. *Not doing* family care work can be considered a status symbol and a way for men to retain their higher status and power in the family and the community (see Barnett and Hyde's 2001 review [27]).

Indeed, men's low family care work participation contributes to men's labour market advantages: for example, their greater and more time-sustained labour force participation, their higher wages and the higher quality of their jobs [32]. Men's limited family care work participation also comes with costs, including possibly greater suicide vulnerability [28].

Chen and colleagues' findings are most closely related to those of Reeves and Stuckler using data for 20 European Union countries for the years 1991–2011 [33]. Reeves and Stuckler found that countries with more female/male egalitarian systems and practices (e.g., greater female representation in parliament) had lower suicide mortality (especially male suicide mortality) during periods of higher unemployment [33]. Together, the findings of Chen and colleagues [28] and those of Reeves and Stuckler [33] challenge a trope that male suicide is a symptom of a crisis of masculinity triggered by the growing (however slow-growing) social and economic equality of women and men [34]. Chen and colleagues' findings are consistent with evidence [26,29,35–9] that in societies where women and men are afforded more equality, they both enjoy better physical and mental health.

The study conducted by Chen's and colleagues on suicide, unemployment and family care work identified population-level social and economic factors that may be driving suicide patterns [28]. They point to an association between men's suicide rates and their participation in family care work, including under conditions of high unemployment.

It is not known what accounts for the association between lesser engagement in family care work and suicide – that is, how family care work may reduce suicide mortality. One possibility is that family care work is protective because it diversifies people's sources of meaning and purpose, as well as their social capital and networks. Understanding the pathways linking men's family care work and men's suicide, over time, is a direction for future research.

Chen and colleagues' study is limited, including mostly European and Christian-majority countries. It is important to test the questions raised by the study across greater geographical and cultural diversity of countries. Another limitation is that the study focussed on suicide mortality. In future studies, other forms of suicidality (e.g., non-fatal suicidal behaviour) and other indicators of distress should be included as outcomes in order to capture the different ways men may express and experience pain and suffering [2–3,23,40–1]. It is also important to track a diversity of social and economic adversities, in addition to unemployment.

Chen and colleagues' findings on unemployment and family care work [28], together with a wide range of evidence on men, women and health [36–39], point to new directions for the prevention of men's suicide, for suicide prevention in general and for promoting men's health and well-being broadly. To start with, Chen and colleagues' findings support going beyond the idea of suicide as a mental health problem to be solved with mental health 'treatments'. The idea that a medical model of suicide is at a minimum insufficient, and in fact problematic, is gaining momentum [22,42–44].

The findings of Chen and colleagues also support expanding men's suicide prevention beyond the traditional emphasis on employment. Dominant approaches to the prevention of men's suicide have focussed on providing men with employment safeguards, for example, via employment-protection programmes. A limitation of these approaches is that they reinforce men's already strong identification with work and men's perhaps excessive investment in the economic-provider role, instead of diversifying men's social identifications and investment [21,22,28].

Chen and colleagues' findings [28], together with a diversity of evidence on men, women and health [26,38], point to the potential value of incorporating universal education and support for boys and men's engagement in family care work in programmes aimed at reducing men's suicide rates [36,39]. The findings, together with other evidence on men, women and health, indicate that by adding family care work to their economic-provider responsibilities, men can not only boost their suicide protection but also improve their health and general well-being.

References

1. World Health Organization. *Suicide Worldwide in 2019: Global Health Estimates.* Geneva: World Health Organization; 2021. www.who.int/publications/i/item/9789240026643.

2. Canetto, SS. She died for love and he for glory: Gender myths of suicidal behavior. *Omega – Journal of Death and Dying*. 1992–3; **26**: 1–17.

3. Canetto, SS. Language, culture, gender, and intersectionalities in suicide theory, research, and prevention: Challenges and changes. *Suicide and Life-Threatening Behavior*. 2021; **51**: 1045–54.

4. Kushner HI. Gender and the irrelevance of medical innovation: The social construction

of suicide as a male behavior in nineteenth century psychiatry. In Lowy I, ed., *L'innovation en Medicine: Etudes Historiques et Sociologiques*. Paris: Les Editions INSERM/Libby Eurotext; 1993. 421.

5. World Health Organization. *Preventing Suicide: A Global Imperative*. Geneva: World Health Organization; 2014. https://apps.who.int/iris/bitstream/handle/10665/131056/9789241564779_eng.pdf?sequence=1.
6. Vijayakumar L, Balaji M. Suicide in South Asia. In Pompili M, ed., *Suicide Risk Assessment and Prevention*. Cham: Springer; 2022. 719–37.
7. Canetto SS, Lester D. Gender and the primary prevention of suicidemortality. *Suicide and Life-Threatening Behaviour*. 1995; **25**: 58–69.
8. Canetto SS, Cleary A. Men, masculinities and suicidal behaviour. *Social Science and Medicine*. 2012; **74**: 461–5.
9. Canetto SS, Sakinofsky I. The gender paradox in suicide. *Suicide and Life-Threatening Behaviour*. 1998; **28**: 1–23.
10. Durkheim É. *Suicide: A Study in Sociology*. New York: The Free Press; 1897/1951.
11. Dublin LI. *Suicide: A Sociological and Statistical Study*. New York: Ronald; 1963.
12. Platt S, Hawton K. Suicidal behaviour and the labour market. In Hawton K, van Heeringen K, eds., *The International Handbook of Suicide and Attempted Suicide*. London: Wiley; 2000. 309–85.
13. Stack S. The relationship of female labour force participation to suicide: A comparative analysis. *Archives of Suicide Research*. 1998; **4**: 249–61.
14. Reeves A, McKee M, Stuckler, D. Economic suicides in the Great Recession in Europe and North America. *British Journal of Psychiatry*. 2014; **205**(3): 246–7.
15. Kaufman JA, Livingston MD, Komro, KA. Unemployment insurance program accessibility and suicide rates in the United States. *Preventive Medicine*. 2020; **141**: 106318.
16. Mattei G, Pistoresi B, De Vogli R. Impact of the economic crises on suicide in Italy: The moderating role of active labor market programs. *Social Psychiatry and Psychiatric Epidemiology*. 2019; **54**(2): 201–8.
17. Stuckler D, Basu S, Suhrcke M, Coutts A, McKee,M. The public health effect of economic crises and alternative policy responses in Europe: An empirical analysis. *Lancet*. 2009; **374** (9686): 315–23.
18. Yip PS, Caine ED. Employment status and suicide: The complex relationships between changing unemployment rates and death rates. *Journal of Epidemiology and Community Health*. 2011; **65**(8), 733–6.
19. Canetto SS. Suicide: Why are older men so vulnerable? *Men and Masculinities*. 2017; **20**: 49–70.
20. Canetto SS. Gender and suicide in the elderly. *Suicide and Life-Threatening Behaviour*. 1992; **22**(1): 80–97.
21. Canetto SS. Gender issues in the treatment of suicidal individuals. *Death Studies*. 1994; **18**: 513–27.
22. Canetto SS. Gender and suicidal behavior: Theories and evidence. In Maris RW, Silverman MM, Canetto SS, eds., *Review of Suicidology*. New York: Guilford; 1997. 138–67.
23. Canetto SS. Genere nella psicoterapia degli anziani. In Scocco P, De Leo D, Pavan L, eds., *Manuale di psicoterapia dell'anziano*. Turin: Bollati Boringhieri; 2001. 32–48.
24. Ghirini, S, Vichi, M. Caratteristiche e andamento temporale della mortalità per suicidio in Italia: uno studio descrittivo sugli ultimi 30 anni. *Bollettino Epidemiologico Nazionale*. 2020; **1**(2): 1–8.
25. Homan P. Structural sexism and health in the United States. *American Sociological Review*. 2019; **84**(3): 486–516.
26. Barker G. A radical agenda for men's caregiving. *Institute of Development Studies Bulletin*. 2014; **45**: 85–90.
27. Barnett RC, Hyde JS. Women, men, work, and family: An expansionist theory. *American Psychologist*. 2001; **56**(10): 781–96.
28. Chen YY, Cai ZY, Chang Q, Canetto SS, Yip PSF. Caregiving as suicide

prevention: An ecological 20-country study of men's family carework, unemployment, and suicide. *Social Psychiatry and Psychiatric Epidemiology*. 2021; **56**: 2185–98.

29. Heymann J, Levy JK, Bose B, Rios-Salas V, Mekonen Y, Swaminathan H, Omidakhsh N, Gadoth A, Huh K, Greene ME, Darmstadt GL, Gender Equality and Health Steering Committee. Improving health with programmatic, legal, and policy approaches to reduce gender inequality and change restrictive gender norms. *Lancet*. 2019; **393** (10190): 2522–34.
30. United Nations (UN) Women. *Transforming Economies, Realizing Rights: Progress of the World's Women 2015–2016 Summary*. New York: United Nations (UN) Women; 2015. www.unwomen.org/en/digital-library/progress-of-the-worlds-women.
31. McGinn KL, Castro MR, Lingo EL. Learning from mum: Cross-national evidence linking maternal employment and adult children's outcomes. *Work, Employment and Society*. 2019; **33**(3): 374–400.
32. Ferrant G, Pesando LM, Nowacka K. *Unpaid Care Work: The Missing Link in the Analysis of Gender Gaps in Labour Outcomes*. Ethiopia: OECD Development Centre. 2014. www.oecd.org/dev/development-gender/Unpaid_care_work.pdf.
33. Reeves A, Stuckler D. Suicidality, economic shocks, and egalitarian gender norms. *European Sociological Review*. 2016; **32**(1): 39–53.
34. Jordan A, Chandler A. Crisis, what crisis? A feminist analysis of discourse on masculinities and suicide. *Journal of Gender Studies*. 2019; **28**(4): 462–74.
35. Stanistreet D, Bambra C, Scott-Samuel A. Is patriarchy the source of men's higher mortality? *Journal of Epidemiology and Community Health*. 2005; **59**(10): 873–6.
36. Kavanagh SA, Shelley JM, Stevenson C. Does gender inequity increase men's mortality risk in the United States? A multilevel analysis of data from the National Longitudinal Mortality Study. *Social Science and Medicine Population Health*. 2017; **3**: 358–65.
37. Van de Velde S, Huijts T, Bracke P, Bambra C. Macro-level gender equality and depression in men and women in Europe. *Sociology of Health and Illness*. 2013; **35**(5): 682–98.
38. Kavanagh SA, Shelley JM, Stevenson C. Is gender inequity a risk factor for men reporting poorer self-rated health in the United States? *PloS One*. 2018; **13**(7): e0200332.
39. Holter ØG. 'What's in It for Men?': Old Question, New Data. *Men and Masculinities*. 2014; **17**(5): 515–48.
40. Canetto SS. Men who survive a suicidal act: Successful coping or failed masculinity? In Sabo D, Gordon D, eds., *Men's Health and Illness: Gender, Power, and the Body*. Oxford: Sage; 1995. 292–304.
41. Canetto SS, Lester D. Gender, culture and suicidal behaviour. *Transcultural Psychiatry*. 1998; **35**: 163–91.
42. Canetto S. Suicidal behaviour among Muslim women: Patterns, pathways, meanings, and prevention. *Crisis: The Journal of Crisis Intervention and Suicide Prevention*. 2015; **6**: 447–58.
43. Hjelmeland H, Knizek BL. Suicide and mental disorders: A discourse of politics, power and vested interests. *Death Studies*. 2017. https://doi.org/10.1080/07481187.2017.1332905.
44. Canetto, SS, Rezaeian M. Protest suicide among Muslim women: A human rights perspective. In Button ME, Marsh I, eds., *Suicide and Social Justice: New Perspectives on the Politics of Suicide and Suicide Prevention*. London: Routledge; 2020. 102–21.
45. Canetto SS. Gender roles, suicide attempts, and substance abuse. *Journal of Psychology*. 1991; **125**: 605–20.

Chapter 4

National Suicide Prevention Policies

Murad M. Khan

4.1 Introduction

This chapter addresses national suicide prevention policies and strategies/programmes. Policies set out desired goals together with a set of objectives to help to meet them. Strategies/programmes are action oriented. They are coordinated patterns of activities intended to achieve objectives and thus help meet policy goals. Policies include values and concepts, as well as an overall course of action. Strategies are concerned with specific steps to be taken. Although the terms clearly have quite different meanings, *policy* and *strategy* are used interchangeably (as are *strategy* and *programme*) in the literature and elsewhere.

In many countries, suicide prevention is part of a national mental health policy. In others, a suicide prevention strategy is entirely separate. Indeed, sometimes a national suicide prevention strategy exists in the absence of a corresponding explicit policy of any sort. In the interest of clarity, this chapter follows the convention of treating *policy* and *strategy* as if they are synonyms, despite the fact that this is, strictly speaking, incorrect.

4.2 Background

Suicide is a major public health problem. Globally, more than 700,000 people die by suicide every year (with a rate of 10.5 in 100,000), according to the most recent figures [1]. No region or nation, and no ethnic or religious group, is free from suicide. However, there are significant differences in patterns of suicide between countries and between different parts of the same country. There are variations in rates of suicide and self-harm, in the methods used, and in the distribution of suicide risk according to age group, gender, occupation and other demographic characteristics.

On a total worldwide basis, men take their own lives more frequently than women. The global age-standardised rate of suicide amongst men is 13.7/100,000, which is almost twice the rate amongst women, which is 7.5/100,000 [1]. Suicide is a major cause of death amongst young people. It is the second leading cause of death amongst young people aged between 15 and 29 years, and notwithstanding generally high rates for men, it is the second leading cause of death for females aged between 15 and 19 years [2].

As is the case for many other major public health problems, countries across the world show wide variation in the extent to which they are systematically addressing suicide prevention at a national level. At the time of writing, only 40 countries around the world have adopted a national suicide prevention strategy [2]. About one-third of upper-middle- and high-income countries have a stand-alone government-adopted national suicide prevention strategy. In low- and lower-middle-income countries, where the 79% of global suicides occur, around 10% of countries have a national strategy [2].

For many countries, including the majority of low- and middle-income countries (LMICs), neither suicide prevention nor mental health has a high priority, despite the high death toll in these settings. In some LMICs, national suicide statistics are collated but there is little else in terms of a suicide prevention strategy or specific policy. Some countries do not collate information on deaths by suicide at all, and there are no national suicide statistics. These nations rely on World Health Organization (WHO) estimates.

4.3 National Suicide Prevention Strategies

The concept of a national suicide prevention strategy first came to prominence with the publication of the United Nations report *Prevention of Suicide: Guidelines for the Formulation and Implementation of National Strategies* [3]. These guidelines, which were developed in consultation with the WHO, called for a multidisciplinary and intersectoral approach to suicide prevention. At that time, Finland was the only country known to have developed and implemented a government-sponsored, systematic, national response to suicide. Finland's early development of a strategy reflected Finnish public concern over an unusually high rate of suicide at the time.

In 2012 the UN document was superseded by the WHO's *Public Health Action for the Prevention of Suicide: A Framework*, which identified necessary individual components and set out clear steps for developing a national suicide prevention strategy [4].

In 2013 the World Health Assembly declared suicide a serious global public health problem and called on all countries to develop national suicide prevention plans [5]. The assembly adopted *the WHO Mental Health Action Plan 2013–2020*, with suicide prevention considered an 'important priority'. It set the global target of reducing national suicide rates by 10% by 2020 [5]. The plan was adopted by health ministers of all 194 UN member states.

In 2014 WHO published its first-ever world suicide prevention report, *Preventing Suicide: A Global Imperative* [6]. The publication of this report was timely, and it was a major strategic step intended to increase the commitment of health ministers and national governments to move from policy and strategy development to implementation of tangible suicide prevention measures [7]. In the report, the WHO Director-General made a call to action for countries to employ a multisectoral approach to address suicide in a comprehensive manner, bringing together different stakeholders based on their resources and contexts.

In 2015 the United Nations General Assembly (UNGA) adopted Sustainable Development Goals (SDGs) [9]. Target 3.4 of the SDGs was to reduce premature mortality due to non-communicable diseases (NCDs) by one-third by 2030 through prevention and treatment and the promotion of mental health and well-being. Suicide rates are a named indicator for target 3.4. The 'prevention of premature mortality due to suicide' was not only considered achievable; it was understood to be something that would have far-reaching benefits for individuals and families, as well as society at large [8].

The financial toll of suicide on society is also costly. In the US in 2020, suicide and non-fatal self-harm cost the nation more than $500 billion in medical, work-loss, value-of-statistical-life and quality-of-life costs [9].

4.4 Why National Suicide Prevention Strategies Are Important

Suicidal behaviour is a highly complex, and tackling it requires a coordinated and multifaceted approach. It is recognised and accepted to be a significant public health issue by governments across the world, whether or not they have an explicit suicide prevention policy. A national suicide prevention strategy is a method of systematically developing a comprehensive and integrated national response to suicidal behaviour, together with a structural framework to support effective suicide prevention action and evaluation [7].

National suicide prevention policies are important for many reasons. At the most fundamental level, they indicates a government's seriousness and commitment to address a major preventable cause of premature death [10]. Adopting a national strategy signals that the government is concerned about the safety and welfare of its people and, in the case of suicide, especially its young people.

A national suicide prevention strategy creates a framework that brings together the disparate elements of suicide prevention, which include surveillance, early detection and treatment of mental disorders, restriction of access to the means of suicide and policy changes that may range from access to mental health care to limitations on the retail of potentially lethal medications, as well as population-wide advocacy and educational measures [7,10,11]. It identifies the various stakeholders and brings them together under one umbrella. This includes sectors that are not primarily concerned with health issues, such as educational and welfare organisations, or associations representing high-risk occupational groups. A policy creates strategic direction for suicide prevention, taking an overview of the implementation of evidence-based interventions [4,10]. In the process, it should identify gaps and obstructions and include provision for developing ways to address them. A strategy creates an imperative for governments to make human and fiscal resources available. This imperative is much stronger once a policy and strategy have been developed, and a way forward can be understood and properly costed [4,10].

Attempted suicide and self-harm are still criminal offences in some major countries, and this is a major obstruction in suicide prevention. Far from having a deterrent effect, criminalisation makes suicide prevention more difficult. One function of a national suicide prevention strategy is that it can act as an impetus towards legislation to decriminalise distressed people. Such legislation is controversial in those cultures, where there is a high level of religious observance, and placing it within a framework to reduce suicide can be politically helpful.

High-quality leadership is needed to ensure sustained implementation of suicide prevention strategies [10]. There is a need for constant coordination between various stakeholders and the promotion of evidence-based activities. Critically, national policies and associated strategies must include provision and funding for monitoring and evaluation of effectiveness, as well as documentation of unforeseen consequences [7,10]. Evaluation is not straightforward and has to be robust to accommodate secular social changes that effect suicide rates (such as fluctuations in national economies), as well as the inevitable modifications to the strategy that are likely to be necessary over time. In short, although many factors can influence national suicide rates, a national policy and/or strategy is critical in order to realise any aspiration to achieve a permanent reduction in the incidence of self-harm and suicide.

4.5 Main Elements of a National Suicide Prevention Strategy

Suicidal behaviour can rarely be attributed to simple causal pathways. Instead, it is the result of a nexus of factors interacting with each other in complex ways. These factors come together at a certain point in time to put the individual on the suicidal 'pathway'. These include social, psychological/psychiatric, biological, political, cultural and economic aspects of the person's life. Their effects can be distal or proximal, macro or micro, and they usually act synergistically. Hence strategies to prevent suicidal behaviours necessarily comprise a range of approaches and actions [7]. In addition to the WHO global report [6], Platt, Arensman and Rezaeian [7]; Arensman [11]; and Platt and Niederkrotenthaler [12] have elucidated essential elements of national suicide prevention strategies. These include the following:

- Surveillance of suicide and self-harm acts
- Restriction of access to commonly used methods of suicide
- Improving access to mental health and social care services
- Access to crisis intervention services
- Promotion of responsible media reporting of suicide and self-harm
- Addressing stigma around suicide
- Gatekeeper training to help non-professionals recognise and respond appropriately to situations with a high risk of suicide or self-harm
- Improvements in the care of those with a history of repeated suicidal behaviour
- Awareness raising and encouragement of help-seeking
- Postvention
- Monitoring and evaluation of each initiative
- Leadership of the strategy to drive implementation through oversight and coordination

In addition to a plan for awareness raising, tackling stigma, media communication and advocacy, it is important to outline a strategic research agenda that addresses suicidal behaviour in the local context [10]. The problem of suicide may be global, but the solutions always have to be relevant to local conditions. Without good local evidence, suicide prevention cannot be effective.

4.6 Are National Suicide Prevention Programmes Effective?

In keeping with a commitment to evidence-based suicide prevention, whole suicide prevention programmes should be evaluated. However, this is a major challenge. As Kerkhof and Clark [13] state in an editorial in *Crisis: The Journal of Crisis Intervention and Suicide Prevention*, there are major limitations in studying the effectiveness of large-scale programmes that are obvious to anyone with a knowledge of research design. There is no possibility of a control condition, whereby one part of the population is not exposed to the suicide prevention strategy, so evaluation is bound to be, at very best, quasi-experimental in nature. Consequently, very few research findings have been published that investigate the effect of national suicide prevention programmes. In contrast, there is significant literature on local interventions and programmes to prevent suicide and suicide attempts, where the methodological challenges are smaller [14]. Nonetheless, there is a small literature that is worthy of examination.

In 1985 Finland became the first country to develop a national suicide prevention programme [15]. The National Suicide Prevention Project in Finland consisted of a research phase (1986–91), an implementation phase (1992–6) and an evaluation phase (1997–8). The primary aim of the project was to lower the national suicide rate by 20% over a 10-year period. The first two phases of the project developed prevention strategies and implemented these at national and local levels.

The project was evaluated internally, but there was also an external evaluation by an international expert peer group. The internal evaluation was conducted by the implementation team, focusing on the objectives, strategies, contents and results of the strategy. The main goals of the external evaluation were to assess the purposefulness, appropriateness and results of the project. There was also assessment of the usefulness of the project strategy within Finland and the international implications of the findings. The research phase was evaluated only with regard to the usefulness of its findings during the intervention phase.

The frequency of suicide in Finland increased during the first years of the project to peak in 1990, followed by a reduction of 20% between 1991 and 1996, which coincided with the implementation phase. It eventually dropped to 9% below the initial level. Although the project was found to have many shortcomings, the final report concluded that the achievements of the strategy greatly outweighed its limitations [15].

The success of the Finnish suicide prevention project stimulated international interest in the effectiveness of prevention activities. As a consequence, in the years that followed, many countries around the world developed their own national suicide prevention programmes.

Matsubayashi and Ueda [16] evaluated suicide prevention in 21 nations belonging to the Organisation for Economic Co-operation and Development (OECD) nations to assess whether it had an effect in reducing suicide rates. Eleven of the countries (Australia, Denmark, Finland, France, Germany, Ireland, New Zealand, Norway, Sweden, United Kingdom and United States) had established national suicide prevention programmes, while 10 (Austria, Belgium, Canada, Greece, Italy, Japan, Netherlands, Portugal, Spain and Switzerland) did not have a national government-endorsed strategy. There was analysis of data between 1980 and 2004 with a fixed-effect estimator, and testing of whether there was a statistically significant difference in the suicide rates before and after the implementation of national suicide prevention programmes in those countries that had them.

The panel data analysis showed that, overall, suicide rates decreased after nationwide suicide prevention programmes were introduced. These government-led suicide prevention programmes were most effective in preventing suicides amongst the elderly and the young. In contrast, suicide rates of working-age groups, irrespective of gender, did not seem to improve following the introduction of national prevention programmes. The authors concluded that their findings suggested that the existence of a national governmentally endorsed strategy can be effective in reducing suicide rates [16].

Lewitzka, Sauer, Bauer and Felber analysed the effectiveness of national suicide prevention programmes using a statistical approach involving segmented regression analysis of interrupted time series data. Four locations (Finland, Norway, Sweden and Australia) were chosen as countries with comprehensive suicide prevention programmes that were well-established and had been operational for at least five years. All these countries had published comprehensive data on national suicide before and during the implementation of their programmes. Data from these countries were compared with data from control countries (including Canada, Austria, Switzerland and Denmark). The criteria for the choice of control countries were culture and religion, historical and political factors, socio-demographic structure, population size and quality of published statistics (for details on the criteria, see Lewitzka, Sauer, Bauer and Felber [17]).

The study demonstrated that national suicide prevention programmes are effective, but this effect seemed to be more marked amongst men and in younger age groups. The data showed a statistically significant decline in suicide rates in countries with established suicide prevention programmes, with the strongest effects in men in the 25-to-44-years and 45-to-64-years age groups. There were reductions in suicides amongst older people, but these were not shown to be statistically significant in comparison with countries without a programme [17].

Despite the difficulties of assessing complex interventions across entire national populations, there appears to be a reasonable level of evidence that national suicide prevention strategies make an important contribution to the reduction of national suicide rates.

4.7 Country Examples of National Suicide Prevention Programmes/Strategies

In the following section we consider the suicide prevention strategy of a high-income country (England) and the corresponding strategy of a low- and middle-income country (Iran).

4.7.1 A High-Income Country: England

The National Suicide Prevention Strategy for England was developed in 2002 [18]. The strategy used evidence-based criteria for its priorities and emphasised goals that included specific, preventive measures that were practical and had visible preventive potential. It had six key goals:

1. Reduce risk in key high-risk groups.
2. Promote mental well-being in the wider population.
3. Reduce the availability and lethality of suicide methods.
4. Improve reporting of suicidal behaviour in the media.
5. Promote research on suicide and suicide prevention.
6. Improve monitoring of progress towards the *Saving Lives / Our Healthier Nation* target for reducing suicide (discussed later in this chapter).

Other guiding principles were that suicide preventive measures and initiatives would be open to monitoring and evaluation, and that revisions and updates of the strategy would be made regularly. Thus it was an evolving strategy [19].

Annual reviews in the following years highlighted the progress of the prevention strategy and underscored the importance of continuous monitoring of suicide rates to demonstrate the effectiveness of the strategy. Research and continued clinical audit were seen as essential, and the National Institute for Mental Health in England (NIMHE) produced a *Suicide Prevention Toolkit* which audited the acute care with respect to suicide and suicide risk [20].

It is relevant to point out that the *National Suicide Prevention Strategy* develop in 2002 was preceded by the *Health of the Nation* white paper [21], a strategic health initiative for England that included targets to reduce the overall suicide rate by at least 15% and, for those with severe mental illness, by at least 33% by the year 2000. In 1999 two further policy documents were published, *Our Healthier Nation* [22] and *Saving Lives* [23], in which a new target was set to reduce the death rate from suicide and undetermined injury by at least a further sixth (17%) by 2010.

Other developments in the UK included the national suicide prevention strategy *Preventing Suicide in England: A Cross-government Outcome Strategy to Save Lives* [24], published in 2012, with the key aims of reducing overall suicide rates and establishing support services for those bereaved by suicide.

In 2016 the *NHS Five Year Forward View for Mental Health* [25] was published, with a target to reduce suicide rates in England by 10% by 2020 (compared to 2015). All Clinical Commissioning Groups (CCGs) were asked to deliver local multi-agency suicide prevention plans.

In 2019 the *Cross-government Suicide Prevention Workplan* [26] committed every area of government to taking action on suicide. It set out clear deliverables and timescales against which key commitments in the suicide prevention strategy were monitored. Crucially, £57 million in funding was allocated for suicide prevention work up to 2023–4.

The fifth progress report on the implementation of the national strategy (March 2021) [27] set out additional government support and funding for suicide prevention to address pressures caused by the COVID-19 pandemic. This included £5 million to support suicide prevention work by voluntary and community sector organisations in 2021–2. The report noted that although full data was not yet available, early indications did not suggest a rise in the number of suicides when comparing pre- and post-lockdown figures for January to August 2020.

England's suicide prevention strategy is noteworthy for a number of reasons. First, there is comprehensive involvement of many social sectors in the strategy, such as education, employment, social security, transport, prisons and media, amongst others. Even if the mental health services are specially purposed for preventing suicide, the problem cannot be solved by measures in this sector alone. Research indicates that up to three quarters of those who die by suicide in England are not in contact with mental health services [28]. Second, the strategy is evidence-based, grounded in published research. Third, suicide prevention measures have been specific, practical and open to monitoring. Fourth, the strategy has been continuously evaluated and changed, when necessary. Finally, the government's commitment has been underlined by its making adequate funding available.

4.7.2 A Low- and Middle-Income Country: Iran

Although a number of LMICs (e.g., Guyana, Bhutan and India) have developed a national suicide prevention plan, Iran is one of the few LMICs that has taken it beyond the initial stages of development [10].

Iran is an Islamic country of more than 81 million inhabitants in the WHO's Eastern Mediterranean Region (EMR). During the last three decades, a primary health care (PHC) network has been established throughout the country in an attempt to narrow the health inequalities gap between rural and urban areas [29]. PHC services in rural areas are now delivered in 'Health Houses' (HHs). The HHs serve between 1,000 and 1,500 residences in two or three villages. These are staffed by two community health workers (known as *Behvarzes* locally). Behvarzes come from the villages they serve and receive two years of basic training in preventive health care. A rural 'Health Centre' (HC) supports 10 to 15 HHs. An HC is staffed by one or two primary care physicians, two health technicians and, on occasion, a nurse. The service area for each rural HC consists of 10,000 to 15,000 residents. Health Houses serve as the first point of contact with the community in rural areas. As needed, patients are referred to rural HCs or to a district hospital.

In urban areas, this network is not well developed and for the most part functions through urban health posts and health centres, which recruit health volunteers to work with Behvarzes. The health volunteers have some level of high school education, are recruited from their own districts and serve as the intermediaries between 50 to 80 households in their neighbourhood and the health centre in their district. They receive basic health care training for two months, during which they learn how to fill out health information cards for the households they visit and deliver them to the health technicians [29].

Since 2009 a comprehensive national registry of suicide and non-fatal suicidal behaviour has been developed by the Iranian Ministry of Health [30].

In 2010 a new national suicide prevention programme (NSPP) was introduced into the public health care system in Iran [31]. The programme covers nine specific objectives and related strategic actions. The specific objectives include the following:

1. Enhancing the knowledge of health care personnel about the management, care and follow-up of patients presenting with suicidal behaviour
2. Enhancing the capacity of health care workers to assist patients presenting with suicidal ideation
3. Increasing awareness amongst school principals, teachers and counsellors on how to respond to and manage suicidal behaviour
4. Enhancing public understanding of mental health and removing the stigma attached to suicide
5. Improving the national self-harm data registry system (including demographic and familial data, risk factors, protective factors and so forth)
6. Offering suicide prevention services at health care centres and crisis intervention phone lines
7. Improving the media reporting of suicide (inter-sector cooperation with the Iranian Broadcasting Organization and the press)
8. Establishing a supervision system between the Ministry of Health and Health Houses
9. Reducing access to the means of suicide (toxins, oil, drugs and so forth)

A cross-sectoral approach was adopted, with the Ministry of Health being the lead stakeholder but working in collaboration with other relevant government departments and stakeholders, such as the Ministry of Agriculture contributing to the development and implementation of strategies to reduce access to pesticides [31].

Rezaeian, Platt and Arensman [32] have highlighted the strengths and challenges of Iran's suicide prevention programme. First amongst the strengths was a national commitment to reducing the incidence of suicide by promoting good mental health and by addressing some of the social and political determinants of poor mental health: tackling poverty and inequalities, prohibiting the use of alcohol and drugs, and promoting social justice and human rights. The second was that both suicide and self-harm are decriminalized in Iran, making it relatively easier to address the underlying causes of both as well as better quality data, which is critical to inform evidence-based prevention initiatives. Third, and crucially, Iran has a well-established and functioning public funded health system, especially a primary health care system, particularly within rural areas, making it accessible for those who would otherwise struggle to receive health and mental health interventions.

In 2015 Iran implemented a comprehensive national health information system, including screening of mental health status. Some of the challenges to this system include the absence of official oversight or a national governing body. This makes it difficult to engage other (non-health) sectors in implementing an NSPP and delivering cross-sectoral actions [32]. Funding continues to remain a major challenge for suicide prevention initiatives for

Iran, given the current economic situation, made worse by US-led international sanctions over the past four decades

While both England's and Iran's national suicide prevention plans/strategies have much in common, the strategy in England was developed much earlier, is well-established, is continuously monitored and has undergone several evaluations and changes made accordingly. Crucially, funding has been made available and the strategy is overseen by the National Suicide Prevention Strategy Advisory Group.

Iran's suicide prevention programme is more recent. There are many challenges, but the programme is integrated into the primary health care system and there is a well-established surveillance system for suicide and self-harm, both of which are decriminalised. However, the absence of oversight or a national governing body poses significant challenges for the delivery of cross-sectoral actions. Making adequate resources available, including funding, remains a major challenge for suicide prevention initiatives for Iran. Despite this, Iran's suicide prevention programme provides an excellent example for other LMICs as they develop their own suicide prevention programmes.

4.8 Conclusions

Suicide is a major public health problem that is highly complex, with multifaceted causes. It is one of the preventable causes of premature deaths, and the rising rates of suicides in young people around the world is cause for major concern. Suicide prevention requires a systematic approach to developing a framework that brings together different elements of a prevention strategy. By developing suicide prevention programmes/strategies, governments around the world show their commitment for the welfare of their population. It is imperative that these programmes/strategies are evidence-based, informed by local research, continuously monitored and regularly evaluated for effectiveness. There are many examples of such programmes/strategies, from both high-income as well as middle- and low-income countries, which can guide governments that consider developing their own suicide prevention programmes.

References

1. World Health Organization. *Suicide Worldwide in 2019: Global Health Estimates.* Geneva: World Health Organization; 2021. www.who.int/publications/i/item/9789240026643.
2. World Health Organization. *Global Health Estimates.* Geneva: World Health Organization; 2018. www.who.int/healthinfo/global_burden_disease/en.
3. United Nations. *Suicide Prevention: Guidelines for the Formulation and Implementation of National Strategies.* New York: United Nations; 1996.
4. World Health Organization. *Public Health Action for the Prevention of Suicide: A Framework.* Geneva: World Health Organization; 2012.
5. World Health Organization. *Global Mental Health Action Plan, 2013–2020.* Geneva: World Health Organization; 2013. www.who.int/mental_health/publications/action_plan/en/.
6. World Health Organization. *Preventing Suicide: A Global Imperative.* Geneva: World Health Organization; 2014.
7. Platt S, Arensman E, Rezaeian M. National suicide prevention strategies: Progress and challenges. *Crisis.* 2019 Mar; 40(2): 75–82.
8. World Health Organization. *Health in 2015: From MDGs (Millennium Development Goals) to SDGs (Sustainable Development Goals).* Geneva: World Health Organization; 2015.

9. Centers for Disease Control and Prevention. *Suicide Prevention*. Atlanta: Centers for Disease Control and Prevention; 2023. www.cdc.gov/suicide/facts/index.html.
10. World Health Organization. *National Suicide Prevention Strategies: Progress, Examples and Indicators*. Geneva: World Health Organization; 2018. www.who.int/publications/i/item/national-suicide-prevention-strategies-progress-examples-and-indicators.
11. Arensman E. Suicide prevention in an international context: Progress and challenges (editorial). *Crisis*. 2017; 38(1): 1–6.
12. Platt S, Niederkrotenthaler T. Suicide prevention programs: Evidence base and best practice. In Arensman E, De Leo D, Pirkis J, ed., *Suicide Prevention in the Global Context: Progress and Challenges*. Boston: Hogrefe; 2019.
13. Kerhof JF, Clark DC. How to evaluate national suicide programs? *Crisis*. 1998; 19: 2–3.
14. Ono Y, Sakai A, Otsuka K, Uda H, Oyama H, Ishizuka N, Awata S, Ishida Y, Iwasa H, Kamei Y, Motohashi Y. Effectiveness of a multimodal community intervention program to prevent suicide and suicide attempts: A quasi-experimental study. *PLoS One*. 2013 Oct 9; 8(10): e74902.
15. Beskow J, Kerkhof A, Kokkola A, Uutela A. Suicide Prevention in Finland 1986–1996: External Evaluation by an International Peer Group. 1999. www.julkari.fi/bitstream/handle/10024/145672/Jan%20Beskow%20et%20al%201999%20Suicide%20prevention%20in%20Finland%201986%961996.pdf?sequence=1.
16. Matsubayashi T, Ueda M. The effect of national suicide prevention programs on suicide rates in 21 OECD nations. *Social Science & Medicine*. 2011 Nov 1; 73(9): 1395–400.
17. Lewitzka U, Sauer C, Bauer M, Felber W. Are national suicide prevention programs effective? A comparison of 4 verum and 4 control countries over 30 years. *BMC Psychiatry*. 2019 Dec; 19: 1–10.
18. UK Department of Health. *National Suicide Prevention Strategy for England*. London: Department of Health; 2002.
19. Mehlum L. A suicide prevention strategy for England. *Crisis*. 2002; 25(2): 69.
20. National Institute for Mental Health in England (NIMHE). *Preventing Suicide: A Toolkit for Mental Health Services*. London: Department of Health; 2003.
21. UK Department of Health. *The Health of the Nation*. London: HMSO; 1992.
22. UK Department of Health. *Our Healthier Nation*. London: HMSO; 1999.
23. UK Department of Health. *Saving Lives*. London: HMSO; 1999.
24. UK Department of Health. *Preventing Suicide in England: A Cross-government Outcomes Strategy to Save*. London: HMSO; 2012.
25. The Mental Health Taskforce. *NHS Five Year Forward View for Mental Health*. London: NHS Mental Health Taskforce; 2016.
26. HM Government. *Cross-government Suicide Prevention Workplan*. 2 London: HMSO; c019.
27. HM Government. *Preventing Suicide in England: Fifth Progress Report of the Cross Government Outcomes Strategy to Save Lives*. London: HMSO; 2021.
28. Appleby L, Shaw J, Amos T, McDonnell R, Harris C, McCann K, Kiernan K, Davies S, Bickley H, Parsons R. Suicide within 12 months of contact with mental health services: National clinical survey. *BMJ*. 1999; 318(7193): 1235–9.
29. Tabrizi JS, Pourasghar F, Nikjoo RG. Status of Iran's primary health care system in terms of health systems control knobs: a review article. *Iranian Journal of Public Health*. 2017 Sep; 46(9): 1156.
30. Hajebi A, Ahmadzad-Asl M, Ershadi M, Nikfarjam A, Davoudi F. National registration system of suicide behaviors in Iran: Barriers and challenges. *Archives of Suicide Research*. 2013 Oct 1; 17(4): 416–25.

31. Malakouti SK, Nojomi M, Ahmadkhaniha HR, Hosseini M, Fallah MY, Khoshalani MM. Integration of suicide prevention program into primary health care network: A field clinical trial in Iran. *Medical Journal of the Islamic Republic of Iran*. 2015; 29: 208.

32. Rezaeian M, Platt S, Arensman E. Iran's national suicide prevention program. *Crisis*. 2021 May; 43(4): 344–7.

Chapter 5

Using Evidence in Suicide Prevention

Rob Poole

Evidence is the essential underpinning of suicide prevention. Scientific evidence is, by nature, complicated and ambiguous. Existing knowledge is always partial and it constantly evolves. The application of evidence in the real world involves compromise, because it has to be applied to situations where there are practical, political and economic obstacles. A judgement has to be made as to whether adjustments to accommodate what *can* be done mean that interventions have strayed too far from the evidence on what *should* be done.

It can be difficult to predict the extent to which evidence about suicidal behaviour gathered from one population will apply to a different population, which calls into question the validity of recommending the general use of interventions that have not been shown to be effective in a wide range of socio-cultural settings. There is a separate problem with the appropriation of the label 'evidence-based' by individuals, organisations and governments who pursue their own agenda whilst citing research in ways that are misleading. This chapter explores what 'evidence-based suicide prevention' means in practice for clinicians and policymakers.

5.1 The Nature of Scientific Evidence in Suicide Prevention

A high proportion of all scientific papers published in peer-reviewed journals end with a statement to the effect that 'more research is needed'. This is a safe conclusion for authors because it is always true. Decisions about action to prevent suicide cannot be delayed until an imagined future date when the evidence on suicide prevention will be complete and when the advice given to policymakers will therefore be perfect. The suggestion that there could ever be an evidence end-point like this is risible and intrinsically unscientific. All decisions about interventions and policies have to be made in the face of uncertainty, and the degree of this uncertainty must be understood. One uncomfortable possibility is that interventions that have been developed on the basis of the best evidence at a particular point in time may not have the hoped-for effects when implemented on a wider scale. There is always a risk that even the most carefully thought through and tested interventions may turn out to cause more harm than good under real-life conditions.

The evaluation of what happens, for good or ill, during implementation of preventative measures is critical. It is part of an iterative scientific process that should support all interventions aimed at individuals, as well as population-wide public health measures. The world learned hard lessons about the importance of post-implementation evaluation from the thalidomide disaster of the 1960s [1]. Assumptions that the drug's apparently innocuous safety profile in clinical trials on animals meant that it would be safe in humans proved to be wildly wrong. Thousands of children exposed to thalidomide in utero were born with severe limb malformations. This led to major changes in drug safety procedures across the world, but it took a long time for those lessons to be applied to non-pharmacological interventions. Where research has been carried out, there have been examples of well-intended psychosocial interventions that have been shown to have marked adverse effects under some circumstances [2]. Unfortunately, post-implementation evaluation is frequently neglected due to political pressures to produce positive results and good news.

It is possible to describe an idealised cycle of implementation of suicide prevention. Generally speaking, both individual-level and public health interventions start with concepts that are derived from clinical observation or are extrapolated from scientific or statistical information. Occasionally they arise from application of untestable 'first principles', in which case the utility of the idea is highly dependent on whether these a priori principles are sound. This first phase can be labelled 'observation-innovation'. It should be followed by an experimental phase, where the intervention is piloted in a formal study to see whether there is prima facie evidence that it 'works' when applied to a small number of people under ideal conditions. If so, this should be followed by a phase of larger studies, to show that the intervention produces better results than doing nothing at all or 'works' better in comparison to an alternative intervention.

During these two experimental phases, modifications to the intervention can be made according to experience and the emerging evidence. The next phase is implementation and evaluation to test what happens when the intervention is deployed in the real world. Critically, this includes measurement of the extent of both foreseeable and unexpected adverse consequences. If results are favourable, post-implementation evaluation should be maintained in the long term, as initial positive effects are not always maintained. It takes time for low-frequency adverse consequences to emerge. The effectiveness of psychosocial or public health measures is not independent of socio-economic context, and circumstances change overtime. This can affect their impact. Needless to say, this idealised cycle of evidence rarely happens, but it is possible to achieve key elements of it, even where resources are limited.

5.2 National Evidence-Based Suicide Prevention

By global standards, the UK has excellent suicide surveillance infrastructure, although there are some notable flaws. There is a reasonably rigorous and consistent system of death certification. In England, Wales and Northern Ireland, where a death is deemed 'unnatural' (including deaths that may be due to accident, misadventure, suicide or neglect), the coronial [3] system provides judicial oversight of the attribution of cause of death. (Different processes exist in Scotland.) These nationwide data sources generate national statistics which provide information about trends in suicide rates. However, the scope of centrally collated information from coroners' courts is relatively limited. There is very little information about individual circumstances that is analysable. There are difficulties in capturing and collating the full range of information available to coroners during their deliberations. Research has consistently found that a proportion of deaths categorised by coroners as 'accidental', 'misadventure' or 'open' are likely to be due to suicide [4], which is further complicated by the modern development of non-categorical narrative verdicts, which can be difficult to aggregate [5].

In high-income countries (HICs), there is a close relationship between self-harm and suicide. A significant proportion of people who harm themselves go on to take their own lives [6]. Presentation to the hospital for treatment of self-harm therefore represents an important opportunity to intervene in order to prevent subsequent suicide. Furthermore, understanding more about the circumstances leading to self-harm provides proxy information about the antecedents to suicide. In the 1970s this led to the development of self-harm registers based in secondary care, including the world's longest standing register, which is held in Oxford. Self-harm registers can generate important, rigorous and relatively detailed information about people who harm themselves. The data can be used to capture changes in self-harming and suicidal behaviour that arise over time.

Since the mid-1990s the UK has had a unique national system to monitor and investigate deaths by suicide amongst people under the care of mental health services, the National Confidential Inquiry into Suicide and Safety in Mental Health (NCISH), based at the University of Manchester. When a mental health patient's death is found by a coroner to be due to suicide, the doctor in charge of their care is asked to complete a detailed proforma about the person and the circumstances of their death [7]. Open (or undetermined) verdicts are treated in the same way, due to the evidence that an especially high proportion of these are deaths are due to suicide. The rate of data return is high. This rich information has allowed NCISH to make recommendations for services to improve patient safety. Crucially, NCISH is able to evaluate the extent to which recommendations are implemented and relate this to associated changes in suicide rates. More recently, the UK government has developed an additional system of near to real-time surveillance of suspected suicides using different data sources [8], which allowed them to report rapidly on suicide during the COVID-19 pandemic [9].

NCISH has published data on changes in suicide rates amongst patients over time. They have explored whether there are differences between those services that have implemented their recommendations and those that have not. As a consequence, they have found that a high proportion of people who take their own life whilst inpatients in mental health units do so by hanging. NCISH have made recommendations that strenuous efforts should be made to eliminate ligature points from the fabric of inpatient units, amongst other recommendations to improve patient safety during inpatient admissions. In the years that have followed, they have reported an overall reduction in suicides in inpatient units. This has been more marked in those services that have followed a high proportion of their recommendations. There has been a particularly sharp reduction in deaths by hanging [10].

NCISH has been cautious in interpreting these findings, as implementation of their recommendations is by no means the only change to services that has occurred [11]. Other changes included a substantial reduction in the number of available inpatient beds. A causal relationship between their recommendations and improvements in inpatient safety cannot be demonstrated with certainty. Furthermore, NCISH has found that alongside a reduction in suicides in mental health inpatient units, there have been some unwelcome changes. For example, there has been an increase in the number of suicides amongst acutely unwell patients being cared for by mental health services in their own home.

The elimination of ligature points in inpatient areas is sometimes regarded as a task-and-finish project, which is not repeated after an initial effort. As structural and organisational changes mean that new potential ligature points continue to be unwittingly generated on inpatient units, it is evident that ligature points can only be minimised through a continuous process to detect and eliminate them.

Near to real-time surveillance of suspected suicides is an important innovation, but it is important to understand its nature. The system in England is separate from and uses a somewhat different method to the Welsh system, for example [8]. There are several problems with coronial data, the most serious of which is the delay between the incident and the recording of a coronial verdict. The delay is caused by the need to gather evidence and various legal processes. The duration of these vary from case to case. This means that suicide data based on coroners' verdicts is always somewhat out of date. It also creates problems in ensuring that incidents occurring on a particular year are analysed by date of death rather than date of inquest, which is important in understanding trends and the effects of specific events like the financial crash of 2008.

Real-time data on suspected suicide, on the other hand, has the advantage of being available almost immediately as the events occur. The English system collates information on notification of suspected suicides from coroners' offices and from police forces on attendance at the scene of suspicious deaths. The Welsh system relies solely upon police data. On the one hand, this allowed NCISH to report promptly on the impact of the COVID-19 pandemic on suicide rates. On the other hand, the figures are bound to include false positives (deaths that eventually turn out to be due to non-suicidal causes) and to omit false negatives (suicides that only become evident on further investigation). It is important not to conflate real-time data with more reliable but slower surveillance information. Like all scientific evidence, no single data source produces an unambiguous result. Evidence builds from multiple sources, each of which is important, but none of which is sufficient on its own.

Surveillance is dealt with more fully in a later chapter, but the point of describing the UK systems here is to draw out the way that evidence interacts with suicide prevention under the favourable circumstances of high-quality national systems and a near-monopoly provider of emergency services (the UK National Health Service). Even under good conditions, findings are not certain or clear-cut, and recommendations have to be made on the basis of a balance of probabilities. Even when an intervention appears to have been successful, it is important to be cautious over claims of success. Attention to associated adverse changes is equally important, and active steps are needed to sustain improvements. Despite the caveats, it is evident that linking evidence to intervention makes an important contribution when it is done properly and that it is a much better option than using no evidence to guide policy or practice.

5.3 Good Intentions and a Priori Reasoning

In order to evaluate a preventative measure, it is necessary to demonstrate a double negative – that is, to convincingly show that something undesirable has not happened. This requires a degree of certainty over what is likely to happen if no intervention is made, which can be difficult. Where a positive change is seen, there is a further challenge in demonstrating a causal link, to show that the effect was most likely a consequence of the intervention. This is possible, but it requires good quality data, time and a commitment to rigour in interpreting data. Despite the hurdles, we have good evidence that some types of prevention work and other types do not.

Sometimes, putative preventative interventions are shown to actually make things worse. Single-intervention psychological debriefing following mass psychological trauma is a key example. This was developed as a means to prevent post-traumatic stress disorder amongst combat troops and civilians caught in disasters or atrocities. A set of first principles was applied to develop the intervention, in particular the a priori belief that going over the traumatising events one-to-one with a therapist would help people make sense of what had happened to them, that it would provide an opportunity for early catharsis and that it would facilitate coming to terms with the trauma. It was widely deployed for some years before evidence started to emerge that it was ineffective. In some studies, far from having the desired effects, people exposed to the intervention appeared to be more likely to develop post-traumatic stress disorder than those who were not [12]. The approach is not recommended in any major international guidance. It appears that early one-to-one rehearsal of the events can sometimes reinforce the trauma and make it more difficult to get over; furthermore, the therapists who conduct the debriefing may be at risk of becoming vicariously traumatised themselves.

This does not mean that no psychological help should be offered to people exposed to awful events, nor does it not mean that all interventions are ineffective or harmful. It does mean that it is important to act on evidence and not just on what seems like a good idea at the time. There is a large group of people who make a good recovery from psychological trauma without any professional help. Timely help should be offered to those who are especially distressed or who do not get over the events in the early months. People who are persistently distressed following trauma can benefit from psychotherapy, but the belief that psychotherapeutic techniques are intrinsically benign and therefore can be applied indiscriminately is wrong.

The way that the application of first principles proved misleading in the case of psychological debriefing has implications for suicide prevention. The fact that it was based on good intentions did not prevent it from being harmful, which is a recurrent hard lesson in the history of medicine; the first principles it was based upon proved to be less well-founded than initially thought, which is another recurrent theme. The urge to *do something* without waiting for evidence can cause harm to a significant number of people.

A practical example of the dangers of good intentions is attempting to dissuade someone from suicide by suggesting that they weigh up the pros and cons of continuing to live. Although an analogous process does have a role in some specific interventions, it is a risky and dangerous approach when taken in isolation and applied indiscriminately. The reasons for this can be understood through brief consideration of the psychological process of decision-making. Throughout the English-speaking world, the dominant model of decision-making and personal responsibility derives from the British legal system. This holds that people decide that they want to do something; they weigh up the advantages and disadvantages of doing so, including any legal prohibition and penalty; and then make a choice whether to act or not. In criminal law, this is known as *mens rea*, or guilty mind. It is distinguished from the *actus rea*, or guilty act. For some but not all offences in English law, both should be present – intention and act. Unfortunately, there is ample evidence from psychology that this is not how human beings make decisions [13]. Indeed, many actions do not involve a cognitive decision-making process at all, and there are significant problems in applying the legal cognitive model (as set out in the England and Wales Mental Capacity Act) to real-life decisions [14].

The assumptions inherent to this decision-making model are so ubiquitous that it can appear to be 'common sense' to try to argue people out of bad decisions, including whether to take their own life. In mental health services, this is a novices' error and psychiatric trainees have long been warned not to ask patients to weigh up in the balance the reasons to live or die [15]. It is not that this inevitably leads to disaster, but it is certainly very risky when the person concerned is suffering from severe depression. Under these circumstances, the cognitive bias that affects people with a profound mood disturbance is likely to make the person give little weight to optimistic thoughts and far greater weight to pessimistic and hopeless ones. The process of weighing things up, far from discouraging them, can help to confirm in their mind that suicide is the only option open to them. Despite the good intentions behind it, such a procedure is so unhelpful that it should be completely avoided outside of a specific, properly evaluated, therapy. There have been unevaluated suicide prevention interventions promoted by individuals and companies in the past that have drawn loosely on cognitive behaviour therapy and recommended indiscriminate use of the pros and cons process, and they were wrong to do this; good intentions are simply not enough.

5.4 Right Intervention, Wrongly Applied

When a new intervention is implemented, the evidence supporting its use usually comes from experimental application amongst people who have specific demographic or clinical characteristics. The population at large is bound to display more disparate characteristics. Consequently, a high proportion of evidence-based complex interventions are initially shown to work within a specific population but are implemented in populations that are rather different. This is unavoidable. It can be very difficult to predict the extent to which these differences matter, which is one of the reasons why post-implementation evaluation is important. A degree of judgement is needed to assess whether the real-life population is so different from the experimental population that a completely new evaluation of effectiveness is necessary. Continuing evaluation allows action to be taken should evidence of ineffectiveness or unforeseen adverse effects become apparent.

To take a practical example, dialectical behaviour therapy (DBT) has been shown to be effective in reducing recurrent self-harm in people diagnosed with emotionally unstable personality disorder in the US and UK [16]. One of its strengths is that it is an intrinsically cooperative approach, which avoids the situation where a therapist tries to control the patient in order to secure their safety. Attempts to control people who recurrently harm themselves are notoriously unproductive, and this can make their problems worse, increasing risk rather than reducing it. Accordingly, DBT therapists often acknowledge to their patients that they cannot prevent them from taking their own lives. Instead, a different way forward is offered. If such an approach is uncritically applied to people who are suicidal outside of the context of recurrent self-harm and emotional dysregulation, the consequences can be catastrophic. DBT is not a panacea. Although it is being evaluated for a range of other psychiatric conditions, routine use with people with those diagnoses requires clear evidence. For people who are suicidal in the context of a transient mental illness, such as an episode of severe depression, a statement of helplessness by a mental health professional is open to misinterpretation as shared hopelessness. The key role of a mental health professional working with someone who is suicidal is to keep the flame of hope alive within the therapeutic relationship. In clinical practice, suicides are prevented mainly through that relationship.

Suicide prevention measures that have been shown to be helpful in HICs cannot be assumed to work everywhere. DBT, like most therapies, is culture-laden. It involves elements of both cognitive behaviour therapy and mindfulness. These cannot be assumed to be culturally-acceptable or appropriate in low- and middle-income countries (LMICs), as they rely upon culture-bound assumptions. It is relevant that DBT is highly labour intensive, which makes it expensive, so that it may have very limited application in LMICs with large populations and low levels of health provision.

There is a dearth of replication studies to show that suicide interventions that work in HICs are also effective in the range of LMIC settings, but a lack of evidence does not imply that all of the measures that have been successfully applied elsewhere are of no relevance. In particular, public health measures of proven value are likely to have wide application (as discussed later in this chapter). Restriction of access to means of self-harm is one of the most effective suicide prevention approaches, and it is reasonable to work on the assumption that this is likely to be true everywhere unless evidence to the contrary emerges. An evidence-based approach does not imply inaction until locally relevant evidence is available, but it does demand steps to ensure that, should an intervention be adopted in a different environment, data is collected to ensure that it is having the effects that were intended.

5.5 Intervention-Lite

A related pitfall in applying evidence is to succumb to the temptation to develop your own, more easily implemented version of an intervention, a kind of *intervention-lite*. The driver for this is usually the imperative to reduce cost. However, for complex interventions applied to individuals, fidelity to the model is always a critical issue [17]. In trials of psychological interventions, it is essential to know that the participants have all been exposed to the same intervention. In the experimental setting, great care is taken over fidelity to the model. It is more of a problem in clinical practice, where a variety of contextual factors can drag treatment approaches off-piste. Deliberately slimming down the treatment approach as a matter of policy is a high-risk strategy which is likely to undermine effectiveness. This can mean that far from saving money, it results in money being wasted on an approach that does not work. Intervention-lite has to be approached with great caution and, on balance, is usually best avoided.

5.6 Predicting Behaviour Using Clinical Suicide Risk Assessment Instruments

'Risk assessment' is a commonly used term which is open to much misinterpretation. On the face of it, risk assessment is self-evidently a good thing, and under many circumstances this is true. Furthermore, the use of manualised procedures is known to improve both risk assessment and safety in a wide variety of settings, although these are often unpopular with and resisted by those who are expected to use them. Although often resisted, the WHO Surgical Safety Checklist is a very simple measure that has been shown to reduce complications and mortality related to surgical procedures across the world, with particularly improvements in LMIC settings [18]. It is therefore disappointing to report that the use of clinical suicide risk assessment instruments to prevent patients from taking their own life has been unsuccessful [19] and that it is most unlikely that an effective instrument will be developed in the future. Furthermore, the continuing use of such instruments in clinical practice may well be counterproductive.

The most common scenario that requires a clinician to assess the risk that an individual patient will attempt to take their own life is in the aftermath of an act of self-harm. This is a common occurrence, and such individuals are known to be at high risk of taking their own life. In the UK, the risk of suicide in the first year after an act of self-harm leading to assessment in hospital is 49 times higher than the general population risk [20]. This means that 0.5% of people presenting to an emergency department will go on to kill themselves in the year that follows; 99.5% will not die by their own hand within a year. It is important for services to find appropriate responses to the needs of these individuals, because presentation with self-harm is a key opportunity to intervene and prevent subsequent suicide. Consider that 0.5% of a large group is a small proportion, but it is still a significant number of people.

The problem with risk assessment under these circumstances is reliably identifying who is at lower risk amongst a group of people who are generally at elevated risk. The risk factors for suicide are well understood in HIC populations, but they are factors that are very widespread in the population. These are mainly fixed characteristics such as male gender, age and previous attempts. Those dynamic risk factors that change over short periods of time, such as mental state or suicidal intentions, are hard to measure reliably using instruments that can be administered in clinical settings. In addition to this, amongst people under psychiatric treatment (known to be generally at higher risk than the general population), there are more suicides amongst people who are regarded as at low risk than those considered at high risk. This has been a consistent finding of NCISH over many years.

In 2018 NCISH published findings from a survey of all NHS mental health providers in the UK about their use of clinical risk instruments [21]. There had been clear evidence in the scientific literature for some time that suicide risk assessment instruments lacked sufficient specificity and sensitivity to be clinically useful, but nonetheless, NCISH found that every single NHS mental health provider in the UK used such instruments. Organisations often used more than one, and many of the instruments had been developed locally, either from scratch or by adapting a validated instrument. The report firmly recommended that these instruments were not reliable. The most worrying aspect of the use of such instruments as a key aid to clinical decision-making is that they can create a false sense of security that an individual patient is not likely to take their own life. Tick box procedures that generate categorical findings with regard to risk (high, medium and low) are attractive to organisations, especially in overstretched clinical services where professional time is at a premium. However, the evidence is clear; this is not an appropriate way of managing risk.

This is not counsel of despair. Whilst predicting suicide is difficult, careful systematic assessment of is patients is important. Plans that recognise the ambiguities with regard to risk are better plans than those that depend on an illusory degree of certainty.

5.7 Making Inferences from Evidence

The application of evidence often involves making inferences on the basis of what is known, in order to work out what might be helpful for a particular population out there in the real world. This is entirely respectable, but it depends on either having an excellent grasp of the literature or making a proper search of all the evidence that might be relevant to the situation. Problems arise when the people guiding the process have an overattachment to a particular approach based on either beliefs that are untestable (e.g., a strong attachment to a specific theoretical stance or a religious faith) or a conflict of interest (e.g., a financial interest in the intervention or personal prestige related to developing the intervention). No one is free of opinions and biases, which emphasises the need for awareness of these factors in the promotion of preventative strategies.

5.8 The Role of Charities and Businesses in Suicide Prevention

Suicide and suicide prevention have never been the exclusive preserve of public services. Religious groups have taken an interest, with varying results. One of the oldest suicide prevention charities in the UK is the Samaritans, which was founded by an Anglican clergyman, Chad Varah [22]. It is an important organisation that has developed far beyond its origins. Volunteers provide a nationwide call-line service that is well-known amongst the general public and heavily used as a first-line support by people in distress, as well as those who are suicidal. Amongst its other activities, it supports the development of suicide prevention evidence and policy. Its charitable nature and its religious origins do not represent a weakness.

STORM, on the other hand, is a social enterprise (a regulated private company that reinvests financial surpluses to achieve specific social objectives) based in Manchester. It provides suicide prevention training courses, some of which attract a fee. It was established in the 1990s on the basis of work with an academic department of psychiatry. The STORM website states, 'We are the first fully evaluated suicide prevention skills training package for the frontline; supported by over 20 years of peer-reviewed academic research' [23]. The latter statement contains a web link to the original research publications.

The Samaritans and STORM are organisations making different but important contributions to suicide prevention in the UK. They illustrate that there are real advantages in doing this outside of the public sector, where politics and bureaucracy can cause indefinite delay in taking action. They both have a firm attachment of evidence and evaluation, and demonstrate that this is just as important and achievable in the charitable and independent sectors as it is in the public sector, if not more so.

Set against this, within the suicide prevention field there is an array of less useful, and in some cases highly questionable, organisations offering services which are provided for a fee that includes a significant margin of surplus value. One of the things that they have in common is that they do not conduct proper evaluation of their products. Confusingly, some claim that their courses or training programmes are 'evidence-based' or 'peer-reviewed'. This implies that findings are available in the public domain and have been subject to a fully independent peer review, for example, through publication in an indexed scientific journal. These organisations sometimes apply a different, idiosyncratic, meaning to these terms. The claim is seriously misleading where there are no references to public domain journals or none can be found using standard research search engines. The use of the words 'evidence-based' and 'peer-reviewed' is a red flag rather than a mark of quality when there is little or nothing available in the public domain.

Under all circumstances, evidence is only valuable if it is properly understood. Many organisations and public bodies with responsibility for the development or implementation of suicide prevention lack the expertise to interpret research findings. Fortunately, more or less everywhere in the world there are universities and other academic or research bodies with relevant expertise that can be consulted. Seeking independent advice is particularly important where interventions are to be provided by an external body, no matter how respectable it may appear. This is an essential protection for the population. No legitimate organisation could object to scrutiny of the evidence for their product's effectiveness prior to purchase.

5.9 The Men's Mental Health Movement

Over the past decade or so, there has been a remarkable growth of a men's mental health movement in HICs. It has led to the proliferation of countless informal self-help groups and charities, both small and large. The primary focus is on the much higher rate of suicide amongst men than women in those countries. Many groups have been formed as a reaction to the death by suicide of a particular individual. Some groups are named after the person whose death inspired their formation.

The men's mental health movement generally takes the view that men lack a safe place to talk about difficult feelings and that men are inhibited about seeking support from each other. The result has been a plethora of men's mental health projects being established, including across the UK (e.g., programs by Mental Health UK) [24]. These organisations are almost certainly important to individuals. They probably save lives. They have the distinct advantage of existing outside of the public sector, being self-organising, based on mutual respect and creating space for men to talk about their problems, which is a rare opportunity in UK society. They make no money and probably influence general population attitudes in a positive way. There is no opportunity loss – which is to say, they are not funded at the expense of another program.

These are major advantages that are seen in other non-cost suicide prevention initiatives. However, they are bound to reach only a proportion of men at-risk. They cannot effect population level risk, as this would involve reaching all men in a given population. At the level of the general public, this is impossible to achieve. The other major problem is the downside of their self-organising nature. They are very difficult to regulate. Overall, we are supportive of the men's movement, which is a judgement based on the balance of a number of factors. We include a list of online resources at the end of this chapter.

5.10 Implementing Public Health Evidence

There are a few consistent findings in the literature that have proven robust over time. The effectiveness of reducing access to common means of suicide is one; increases in suicide during times of widespread economic hardship is another. Consequently, there are excellent grounds to believe that significant numbers of deaths by suicide can be prevented across the whole population by implementing two public health targets: first, restriction of access to common means of suicide and, second, minimisation of unemployment and economic hardship. There are several examples of the former being successful [25]. Unemployment and economic hardship, on the other hand, tend to be regarded as acts of God which cannot be influenced. In my opinion, an objective consideration of facts shows that both are achievable but are usually overlooked, because policymakers are either unaware of the evidence or, rather more likely, regard the economic cost as too high a price to pay for the achievable benefit, namely the avoidance of loss of life and human suffering.

Pesticide poisoning is the one of the commonest means of suicide in South Asia. When countries have banned the agricultural use of the most toxic pesticides, suicide rates have fallen [26]. Some Indian states have restricted some pesticides, usually temporarily, and have sometimes seen a fall in suicide rates, but the range of highly toxic pesticides available there has meant that overall rates of death by self-poisoning remain exceptionally high. Bans of highly toxic pesticides are resisted on the grounds that they are essential to tropical agriculture; the counter-argument is that there are less toxic options that are no more expensive, which, if used as part of a pest management strategy, are also less environmentally damaging. Irrespective of the strength of these arguments, the continuation of free access to highly toxic chemical that are common means of suicide is a policy choice which could be changed, given the political will.

If deaths involving firearms are excluded, the US and UK have broadly similar suicide rates. The UK has very few firearm-related suicides, because firearm ownership is uncommon and highly regulated. In the US, there are as many suicides by firearm as suicidal deaths by other means, so that the US suicide rate is twice that of the UK. Indeed, two-thirds of all US firearm deaths relate to suicide [27]. A reduction of firearm ownership in the US to UK levels would be likely to prevent thousands of deaths by suicide each year. There is no need to rehearse the controversies over gun control in the US, other than to say that most HICs seem to have safer societies than the US in absence of firearms. Although high school killings are understandably the main focus in the US gun control debate, the lack of discussion of suicide by firearm is puzzling in the light of the large number of deaths involved, not to mention US-specific phenomena such as suicide by police officer [28].

The link between unemployment and suicide in the UK is well understood. On 16 May 1991, the Chancellor of the Exchequer at the time, Norman Lamont, told the UK's House of Commons that 'rising unemployment and the recession have been the price that we have had to pay to get inflation down. That price is well worth paying' [29]. The remark became famous, or notorious, as a very clear statement that rises of unemployment, which had been regarded as anathema under the Keynesian economic policies of UK governments following the Second World War, were now seen as acceptable means of achieving neoliberal economic objectives. I do not suggest that Lamont's use of the phrase 'That price is well worth paying' indicates that he was indifferent to the human cost in terms of increased suicides. I do suggest that he was clearly indicating that there was a choice to be made. Using the epidemiological evidence might have allowed a more comprehensive weighing of the costs and benefits. This might well have led to the conclusion that the price was, in fact, not worth paying and that it might be better to make some compromises between population health and profitability.

It is sometimes suggested that recommending significant socio-economic change to achieve health benefits is unrealistic. However, the advantage of population-wide changes to prevent suicide, like any other health problem, is that they save many more lives than is possible through individual-level intervention. Furthermore, there are real costs savings when such measures are successful, not just to health services but across the whole socio-economic infrastructure. Objections are frequently made through *reductio ad absurdum* arguments that a perfect world is unattainable. However, the impact of economic hardship exists on a gradient, not as an all-or-nothing effect. Partial reductions in unemployment and easing of economic hardship have an effect of health, so that lives can be saved without achieving unrealistic political change.

It is hard to prevent politicians from making bad public health choices, but we can make sure that decisions are made with full knowledge of the relevant evidence. It is important to avoid being defeatist because of a low expectation that politicians will make difficult decisions to achieve health improvements. Change does sometimes happen, and when it does, it can come unexpectedly. Work to improve the knowledge of policymakers is rarely wasted, even when the measurable impact comes only slowly. Finland has shown that a successful suicide prevention strategy can be followed for decades, with substantial benefits – not an elimination of suicide but, nonetheless, many lives saved [30].

5.11 Influencing Policymakers

To prevent suicides, it is necessary to influence policymakers, whether organisational, local, regional, national or international. Policy is much more than an unending stream of governmentally endorsed documents, which generally do not have identifiable authors and are rarely fully implemented. Policy emerges from a climate of opinion. It is formed in an array of locations, committees and forums, but also in private conversations between individuals. Policymakers include people who are influential in professional and political communities. People further down the hierarchy who are responsible for policy implementation are also de facto policy makers. They often make choices about which national policies to implement, the sequencing of implementation and the priority given to different parts of policy.

Evidence is only one factor that impresses policymakers. Persuasive argument, charisma, financial implications, *realpolitik*, preconceptions and a range of other influences all have an impact. Evidence is often very dry for readers beyond the research community. There is a strong temptation to overstate the strength of evidence and to promise more than can be delivered. The problem with trying to achieve one's ends through the use of exaggeration, charm or Machiavellian manipulations is that the results are short-term and prone to unravel when outcomes prove disappointing or worse. It is inevitable that evidence must be rendered understandable to policymakers and presented in ways that are palatable to them. Nonetheless, allowing what you tell them to part company with evidence is a mistake. Science and evidence retain their credibility through a track record in solving problems, and the mental health community will only influence the world in a positive way if it stays true to its empirical roots. We must continue to evaluate, to rigorously collect data and research. The resulting information becomes incrementally better but also harder to interpret. We must stay true to our empirical mission, to present policy makers with information that is truthful, always partial and, although beset by caveats, also can help save some of the countless lives that are lost through suicide.

5.12 Conclusions: Multiple Interventions of Small Effect

Suicide prevention occurs in at least three different levels. First, individual intervention. People who are suicidal are sometimes deflected from this course through the intervention of a mental health professional, one of their family/friends or a concerned stranger. Second, through a social change of large effect. Sometimes social, economic or cultural condition shift accidentally improves the situation and leads to a relatively large and rapid change in suicide rates, like the one that has been seen in China over the last 20 years, which is not yet fully understood [31]. Finally, strategically. Multiple interventions, each of relatively small effect, can collectively have a large impact. Most suicide prevention belongs to the first and the last categories. Measures and interventions should not be dismissed because their impact is limited when taken alone. There is a constant need for rigorous surveillance, which may seem dull but underpins everything else. The need to continuously monitor the suicide rates will never disappear, especially if suicide prevention is to remain evidence based. This is crucial to ensure that the impact of suicide prevention is real, and that there is evaluation before and after implementation of all interventions that are made with the general population.

5.13 Online Resources

See the following websites for more information on groups devoted to men's mental health (last accessed 18 September 2024):

https://andysmanclub.co.uk/who-we-are/

www.jamesplace.org.uk/news-research/research/

www.supportline.org.uk/problems/mens-support/

www.manhealth.org.uk/

https://uk.movember.com/mens-health/mental-health

References

1. Ward SP. Thalidomide and congenital abnormalities. *BMJ*. 1962; **2**(5305): 646–7.
2. Rose S, Bisson J, Wessely S. A systematic review of single-session psychological interventions ('debriefing') following trauma. *Psychother Psychosom* 2003; **72**(4): 176–84.
3. UK Ministry of Justice. *A Guide to Coronial Services*. 2020. www.gov.uk/government/publications/guide-to-coroner-services-and-coroner-investigations-a-short-guide.
4. Gunnell D, Bennewith O, Simkin S, Cooper J, Klineberg E, Rodway C, Sutton L, Steeg S, Wells C, Hawton K, Kapur, N. Time trends in coroners' use of different verdicts for possible suicides and their impact on officially reported incidence of suicide in England: 1990–2005. *Psychological Medicine*. 2013; **43**(7): 1415–22.
5. Gunnell D, Hawton K, Kapur N. Coroners' verdicts and suicide statistics in England and Wales. *BMJ*. 2011; **343**: d6030.
6. Hawton K, Bergen H, Cooper J, Turnbull P, Waters K, Ness J, Kapur N. Suicide following self-harm: Findings from the multicentre study of self-harm in England, 2000–2012. *Journal of Affective Disorders*. 2015; **175**: 147–51.
7. National Confidential Inquiry into Suicide and Safety in Mental Health. *Annual Report: England, Northern Ireland, Scotland and Wales*. University of Manchester. 2021. https://sites.manchester.ac.uk/ncish/reports/annual-report-2021-england-northern-ireland-scotland-and-wales/.
8. Office for Health and Disparities Near to Real Time Suspected Suicide Surveillance (NRTSSS) for England. *Statistical Report: NRTSSS for England for a 15-Month Period to August 2023*. 2024. www.gov.uk/government/statistics/near-to-real-time-suspected-suicide-surveillance-nrtsss-for-england/statistical-report-near-to-real-time-suspected-suicide-surveillance-nrtsss-for-england-for-the-15-months-to-august-2023.
9. Appleby L, Richards N, Ibrahim S, Turnbull P, Rodway C, Kapur N. Suicide in England in the COVID-19 pandemic: Early observational data from real time surveillance. *Lancet Regional Health – Europe*. 2021; **4**: 100110.
10. Hunt IM, Windfuhr K, Shaw J, Appleby L, Kapur N. Ligature points and ligature types used by psychiatric inpatients who die by hanging: a national study. *Crisis*. 2012; **33**(2): 87–94.
11. Kapur N, Hunt IM, Windfuhr K, Rodway C, Webb R, Rahman MS, Shaw J, Appleby L. Psychiatric in-patient care and suicide in England, 1997 to 2008: A longitudinal study. *Psychological Medicine*. 2013; **43**(1): 61–71.
12. Rose SC, Bisson J, Churchill R, Wessely S. Psychological debriefing for preventing post traumatic stress disorder (PTSD). *Cochrane Database of Systematic Reviews*. 2002; 2: CD000560.
13. Dror IE. Cognitive and human factors in expert decision making: Six fallacies and the eight sources of bias. *Analytical Chemistry*. 2020; **92**(12): 7998–8004.

14. Price A, McCormack R, Wiseman T, Hotopf M. Concepts of mental capacity for patients requesting assisted suicide: A qualitative analysis of expert evidence presented to the Commission on Assisted Dying. *BMC Med Ethics*. 2014; **15**: 32.

15. Poole R, Higgo R. *Clinical Skills in Psychiatric Treatment*. Cambridge: Cambridge University Press; 2008.

16. Priebe S, Bhatti N, Barnicot K, Bremner S, Gaglia A, Katsakou C, Molosankwe I, McCrone P, Zinkler M. Effectiveness and cost-effectiveness of dialectical behaviour therapy for self-harming patients with personality disorder: A pragmatic randomised controlled trial. *Psychother Psychosom*. 2012; **81**(6): 356–65.

17. McHugo GJ, Drake RE, Whitley R, Bond, GR, Campbell K, Rapp CA, Goldman HH, Lutz WJ, Finnerty MT. Fidelity outcomes in the national implementing evidence-based practices project. *Psychiatric Services*. 2007; **58**: 1279–84.

18. Jain D, Sharma R, Reddy S. Surgery checklist: Barriers to universal acceptance. *J Anaesthesiol Clin Pharmacol*. 2018. **34**(1); 7–10.

19. Andreotti ET, Ipuchima JR, Cazella SC, Beria P, Bortoncello CF, Silveira RC, Ferrão YA. Instruments to assess suicide risk: A systematic review. *Trends Psychiatry Psychother*. 2020 Jul–Sep; **42**(3): 276–81.

20. Hawton K, Bergen H, Cooper J, Turnbull P, Waters K, Ness J, Kapur N. Suicide following self-harm: Findings from the Multicentre Study of Self-Harm in England, 2000–2012. *Journal of Affective Disorder*. 2015; **175**: 147–51.

21. National Confidential Inquiry into Suicide and Safety in Mental Health. *The Assessment of Clinical Risk in Mental Health Services*. Manchester: University of Manchester; 2018. https://sites.manchester.ac.uk/ncish/reports/the-assessment-of-clinical-risk-in-mental-health-services/.

22. The Samaritans. *Our History*. www.samaritans.org/about-samaritans/our-history/.

23. STORM website. https://stormskillstraining.com/.

24. Men's Mental Health UK website. https://mentalhealth-uk.org/mens-mental-health/.

25. Hawton K, Bergen H, Simkin S, Dodd S, Pocock P, Bernal W, Gunnell D, Kapur N. Long term effect of reduced pack sizes of paracetamol on poisoning deaths and liver transplant activity in England and Wales: Interrupted time series analyses. *BMJ*. 2013; **346**: f403.

26. Lee YY, Chisholm D, Eddleston M, Gunnell D, Fleischmann A, Konradsen F, Bertram MY, Mihalopoulos C, Brown R, Santomauro DF, Schess J, van Ommeren M. The cost-effectiveness of banning highly hazardous pesticides to prevent suicides due to pesticide self-ingestion across 14 countries: An economic modelling study. *Lancet Glob Health*. 2021; **9**: e291–300.

27. Rhee P, Prabhakaran K, Joseph B, Simely A, Okumura K, Klein J, Policastro A, Lombardo G, Latifi R. Firearm deaths are increasing and endemic in the USA: It is a problem of suicides and not homicides. *World J Surg*. 2021; **45**: 1323–9.

28. Homant RJ, Kennedy DB. Suicide by police: A proposed typology of law enforcement officer-assisted suicide. *Policing: An International Journal*. 2024; **23**(3): 339–55.

29. Hansard. Interest Rates. Thursday, 16 May 1993. https://hansard.parliament.uk/Commons/1991-05-16/debates/bc7daf42-76d1-4c4b-b5d9-881c3d48a1f4/InterestRates?highlight=price%20worth%20paying.

30. Wilson, JF. Finland pioneers international suicide prevention. *Ann Intern Med*. 2004; **140**: 853–6.

31. Jiang H, Niu L, Hahne J, Hu M, Fang J, Shen M, Xiao S. Changing of suicide rates in China, 2002–2015. *Journal of Affective Disorders*. 2018; **240**: 165–70. www.sciencedirect.com/science/article/pii/S0165032718303768.

Chapter 6

Suicide and the Media

Angela Nicholas, Thomas Niederkrotenthaler, Jo Robinson, Mark Sinyor and Jane Pirkis

6.1 Introduction

Interventions for minimising harm and promoting protective effects through media portrayals of suicide have emerged as a key avenue for population-based suicide prevention. Research on the effects of media reporting of suicide has shown clear evidence that certain types of reporting can produce substantial negative effects [1,2], most notably increases in the number of subsequent suicides but also other potential negative impacts such as increased stigma regarding suicide, distress and reductions in help-seeking. For example, providing details on locations and methods of suicide, along with sensationalist reporting, particularly with celebrity suicides, can lead to large increases in subsequent suicide rates [1,3]. Conversely, emerging evidence shows that suicide reporting focussed on positive narratives of recovery from suicidal thoughts may confer protective benefits and lower subsequent suicides rates [3].

As suicide prevention research and practice have evolved over time, so too have the types of media being studied. In recent years, the media ecosystem has shifted dramatically from heavy reliance on traditional media such as print, radio and television to online content and social media [4]. The interactivity and rapidly changing content of social media contrasts with the didactic nature and slower cycling of traditional media. The creation of content for traditional media is largely undertaken by journalists and therefore easier to monitor and modify, to some degree, compared with social media, where all users can create their own content. Social networks and social media have swiftly evolved to include substantial discourse about suicide, including sharing one's own experiences with suicidal feelings, reaching out for help and memorialising those who have died by suicide [5]. The interactive nature of the internet and social networks, and their capacity to reach users quickly and across geographical boundaries, presents both unprecedented opportunities for suicide prevention and a continuously changing range of challenges, depending on the type of content being shared [5].

In addition to these various media types, there are also numerous ways that suicide is portrayed and discussed in the media. For example, there are both factual and fictional portrayals of suicide, and some cases where the distinction is blurred. Portrayals may involve depictions of death or survival or stories without an individual focus, such as those that report suicide statistics or research. While the research discussed in this chapter emphasises individual stories, the principles that guide safe and positive media portrayals may have broader applicability.

This chapter provides a brief discussion of a possible theoretical mechanism for the impact of media portrayals of suicide on subsequent suicides; the history of research into the effects of media portrayals of suicide, focussing on novel research findings in the area; interventions that attempt to optimise the safety of media portrayals of suicide; and interventions that utilise media for suicide prevention purposes.

6.2 A Mechanism by Which the Media May Have an Influence on Suicide

The precise mechanisms behind the effects of media portrayals of suicide are not fully understood. The current dominant model is Bandura's (1977) [6] social learning theory. In summary, the theory posits that humans, in part, learn behaviour by imitating others. These learning effects are especially strong when the learner observes a person with whom they identify (a 'model'), such as someone they see as similar to themselves or whom they admire.

This notion is consistent with the observed negative media effects on suicide mentioned previously and discussed in more detail throughout this chapter. For example, increases in suicidal behaviour occur more frequently in population groups that are similar to those who are depicted in the media as having died by suicide [7]. Researchers term this phenomenon the 'Werther Effect' in reference to the titular character from Goethe's 1774 novella *The Sorrows of Young Werther*. Werther's experience of unrequited love is presented as the cause of his suicide. The publication of the novella was linked to increased suicides, and particularly imitative suicides, in which young men died under similar circumstances to those described in the novella.

Furthermore, the reporting of celebrity suicides is known to have a particularly strong effect on subsequent suicide rates [8,9]. Identification with the circumstances or characteristics of a person who has died by suicide can enhance the magnitude of such effects [10]. When these influences are paired with broad recognition, as with celebrities, the likelihood of negative effects across populations may be amplified.

Since any behaviour can be imitated, social learning could explain negative or positive effects of different media exposures. For example, Bandura noted that people trying to overcome phobias learned more from observing others overcoming their own phobias than from observing those without phobias succeeding in the feared environment. He concluded that observing 'effortful coping behaviour' can demonstrate to a person in distress that they too can 'succeed through perseverance' ([6], p. 197). This is in line with the findings of Niederkrotenthaler and Till [11], which indicated that people with suicidal thoughts who read about a person who overcame suicidal thinking experience a decrease in suicide risk. However, no such effect was observed when the same ideas were presented by an expert. Niederkrotenthaler et al. [3] coined the term 'Papageno effect' to describe this phenomenon, in which media reporting has a positive effect on suicide. The Papageno effect refers to the central character in Mozart's opera *The Magic Flute*. In the opera, Papageno, devastated by his fear of losing his beloved Papagena, sings about his intention to die by suicide and takes steps to end his life. However, he is supported through his suicidal crisis by three boys, and Papageno ultimately masters the crisis and lives on. Researchers are actively seeking to better understand the mechanisms of the Papageno effect and how it may be leveraged as a suicide prevention tool, rather than focussing media efforts towards simply trying to minimise harm.

6.3 Negative Impacts of Media Portrayals of Suicide

Most research examining media portrayals of suicide has focussed on news reporting in traditional forms of media. Numerous studies illustrate that news reporting of suicides can be followed by an increase in suicides, especially when the reporting is high volume, prominent, details suicide methods and/or refers to celebrity suicides [3,7,12]. This effect has been observed in adults [1] and young people [7].

Media reporting of celebrity suicides has become a strong focus of research in recent years. A recent meta-analysis [13] of data from 20 international studies concluded that there was an overall 13% increase in suicides in the period after media reporting of a celebrity's suicide. Where the method of the suicide was reported, there was a 30% increase in suicides by that method.

The suicide of popular actor and comedian Robin Williams in 2014 provided an unfortunate opportunity for suicide prevention researchers to study the effects of reporting of celebrity suicide. Fink and colleagues [8] reported a 10% increase in suicide in the US [14] in the five months following Williams' suicide and a 32% increase in suicides by hanging, the same method as Williams used [8]. In Australia, there was an 11% increase, largely among men aged 30 to 64 [9], and in Canada, there was a 16% increase, also mostly among men over 30 and mostly by hanging [15]. These findings highlight the magnitude of the negative effects of media reporting of celebrity suicides and the necessity for more responsible reporting. Pitman and colleagues [16], however, found no excess suicides in England and Wales following Williams' suicide. It is unclear why England and Wales differed from other countries.

Researchers have sought to understand whether similar increases in suicide occur following social media discussions of suicide. Sinyor and colleagues [17] identified 787 suicide-related tweets over a one-year period geolocated to Toronto, Canada, from sources with a high level of social media influence, such as journalists and news organisations, celebrities and social media influencers [17]. They examined the relationship between various characteristics of these tweets and suicides in Toronto in the seven days following each tweet. Tweets reporting suicides were associated with increased suicides. Consistent with previous studies of traditional media reporting, they found that the largely sensationalist reporting of the suicide of a local news reporter was associated with the strongest increase in suicides.

Compared with studies of the effects of news media reporting of suicide, studies on the effects of fictional depictions of suicide remain relatively limited [18]. A recent meta-analysis suggested that the number of studies on fictional media of adequate quality was still very limited but that more recent studies, which were more methodologically rigorous, generally found evidence of increases in suicides after fictional portrayals of suicide [18].

Regarding possible mechanisms, Till and colleagues [10] conducted a laboratory experiment with 95 adults with varying levels of suicidality who watched one of three films in which the protagonist died by suicide, recovered from their suicidal crisis or died by natural causes, respectively. Participants who had stronger suicidal thinking and who watched the film depicting a suicide death experienced an increase in suicidality. The degree to which their suicidality increased depended on how much the participant identified with the protagonist who had died, consistent with Bandura's Social Learning Theory [6].

An opportunity for the observation of the effects of fictional portrayal of suicide under real-world circumstances came with the March 2017 worldwide release of the popular Netflix teen series *13 Reasons Why*. The release of this series afforded an unprecedented yet unfortunate opportunity for observation of the effects of a fictional depiction of suicide that violated numerous recommendations for safe presentation of suicide. In the initial 13-part season of *13 Reasons Why*, the series' central character, 17-year-old Hannah Baker, records and posthumously releases the reasons for her suicide on audiotapes. The tapes are aimed at specific people in her life who, she explains, each had a role in causing her suicide. The show was widely viewed in the 30 days following its release [19] and sparked more than 3.5 million tweets in its first week [20]. The series triggered immediate criticism from mental health and suicide prevention organisations for contravening guidelines on media depiction of suicide. Central to this criticism was the vivid and detailed depiction of Hannah's method of suicide and a clear message from Hannah's character that seeking help from others for suicidal thoughts is futile [21]. These individuals and groups expressed their concern that this portrayal could result in imitative suicides, particularly among vulnerable young people, who were most likely to identify with the protagonist [18,21,22].

Several studies have shown that an increase in the number of suicides among young people following the release of the *13 Reasons Why* is likely to have occurred [18]. These effects have been shown both in the US among 10- to 19-year-olds [22] and in Canada among those aged 29 and under [21]. Other studies of the effects of exposure to the series showed an increase in emergency department presentations and hospitalisations for self-harm and self-reported feelings of distress and suicidal thoughts after viewing the show [22,23].

6.4 Positive Impacts of Media Portrayals of Suicide

As research into suicide and the media has progressed, increasing evidence has also emerged that while the negative effects of certain types of media portrayals of suicide are incontrovertible, some suicide reporting appears to induce a reduction in suicides [3,11,24–6].

Niederkrotenthaler and colleagues [3] examined the association between the content of 497 Austrian print media articles on subsequent suicide rates. They found that reports of mastery of suicidal crises were associated with a reduction in suicide rates [3]. In these reports, individuals talked about their suicidal thoughts but did not act on them (there was no accompanying suicide attempt or death), instead finding other ways of coping. This replicates findings of others who have shown that a discussion of suicidal thoughts without behaviour may confer protection [12,17].

To test whether content could be created specifically for the purpose of eliciting these protective effects, Niederkrotenthaler and Till [11] conducted a study in which they exposed people who reported recent suicidal thinking or a recent suicide attempt to one of three new articles written for the study. In two experimental conditions, participants read a story talking about how to cope with suicidal thoughts. In one, a person who had their own experience of suicidal thoughts talked about how they had coped with their crisis, and in the other, an expert discussed the same topic. In the third control condition, participants read an article in which someone talked about an initiative to build a railway. Niederkrotenthaler and Till found that only those participants who read the article about a person with lived experience mastering their crisis experienced a decrease in suicide risk. A subsequent study included only articles with educational content from suicide prevention experts and found no effects on a range of suicide-related outcomes. This study suggests that stories of 'personal perspective of hope, recovery, and healing' ([27], p. 6) may be necessary to create a Papageno effect. A meta-analysis that has combined the evidence from across published trials found that across six published trials evaluating effects of stories of hope and recovery, there was evidence for a small-sized reduction in suicidal thoughts in participants exposed to such content as compared to control groups. With regard to help-seeking attitudes and intentions, no significant effect was found across studies [26].

Counterintuitively, Sinor and colleagues [17] found that tweets including the specific suicide method of jumping or falling from a height were associated with protective effects. They noted that discussions of these methods were embedded within tweets with narratives that portrayed suicide as 'undesirable, tragic and/or preventable', which may have led to the observed effects ([17], p. 6). These positive findings led the authors to speculate about the potential importance of the overarching narrative of media presentations in comparison to specific elements of content. Importantly, in this study, Twitter messages of hope and tweets about suicidal ideation in the absence of a suicide or suicide attempt were also associated with decreases in suicides, consistent with a Papageno effect. In a different study, Sinyor and colleagues [24] observed that news media articles describing railways suicides and suicide by cutting or stabbing were followed by fewer suicides and proposed that the 'gruesome' nature of such methods might act as a deterrent [24].

Niederkrotenthaler and colleagues [28] similarly found some surprising positive effects of participating in 'suicide' message boards (online discussion forums where participants hold conversations via posted messages) run by non-professionals, even when the given message board was characterised as 'pro-suicide' [28]. The researchers sought to understand whether certain communication styles used on boards have positive psychological effects on those who post. They observed positive psychological effects on the primary posters of message threads when the online community responded to posts with encouragement of 'constructive needs' (e.g., getting help) and discouragement of 'destructive needs' (e.g., self-destruction). They isolated helpful strategies for achieving positive outcomes as 'constructive advice, active listening and collaborative problem solving, as well as expression of sympathy, debunking of suicide myths, and provisions of alternatives to suicidal behaviour and positive stories of lived experience'. Unexpectedly, these positive effects were observed even on pro-suicide message boards. That is, if responding posters showed empathy, adopted active listening and described how they coped during a suicidal crisis, positive psychological effects were observed among primary posters, even on these 'pro-suicide' message boards. Notably, however, such responses were much rarer in pro-suicide message boards, and thus there were fewer instances of improved psychological well-being arising on those boards compared with 'anti-suicide' boards.

The finding that protective effects are observed in relation to reporting or discussions of suicide that, on the face of it, might be expected to be harmful illustrates that understanding the effects of discussions of suicide is complex and likely depends on the interaction of a range of factors, including narrative, audience and medium. Niederkrotenthaler's study of message boards also shows the importance of the interaction between exposure to a primary message about suicide and public responses to that message on social media, producing either protective or harmful effects. This interaction is not yet well understood, though some insight is beginning to emerge. Researchers are increasingly attempting to test the speculation that positive effects could arise because the discussion of suicide is embedded within a positive narrative.

Potential positive effects of fictional portrayals of survival are also scant. However, Niederkrotenthaler and colleagues conducted a notable study of Logic's hip hop song '1-800-273-8255'. The song tells the story of a character surviving a suicide crisis and calling a help-line. During the month of maximum interest in the song, there were nearly 10,000 more calls to the US national help-line and 245 fewer suicides than expected across the US [29].

Lastly, media presentations of suicide in 'villains', such as criminals and others with whom people generally do not identify, have also been associated with some reductions in suicides [30]. This is an intuitive finding with respect to social learning theory. However, since stigmatising those who die by suicide or creating a cultural expectation that suicide is an accepted behaviour for such 'villains' is unethical, this finding has little practical implication for suicide prevention.

6.5 Media Interventions

In line with evolving knowledge regarding both the possible negative and positive effects of media discussions of suicide, media-based suicide prevention interventions are increasingly being developed not only to minimise harm relating to suicide portrayals in the media but also to increase the positive effects of such portrayals and to encourage helpful discussions of suicide in the media.

6.6 Media Guidelines

There are multiple examples of media guidelines for journalists aimed at improving reporting on suicides. Examples of these include the World Health Organization and International Association for Suicide Prevention's Guidelines, *Preventing Suicide: A Resource for Media Professionals-Update 2017* [31], Everymind's (Australian) *Reporting Suicide and Mental Ill-Health: A Mindframe Resource for Media Professionals* [32], Canada's *Media Guidelines for Reporting on Suicide: 2017 Update of the Canadian Psychiatric Association Policy Paper* [33] and Austria's *Leitfaden zur Berichterstattung über Suizid (Reporting Guide about Suicide)* [34]. Generally, these guidelines discourage reporting on suicide methods and locations, prominent reporting such as publication of suicides as 'front page news' and sensational language like 'suicide epidemic'; oversimplification of the cause of a suicide as attributable to one particular incident; and romanticising or idealising suicide, including through use of images of funerals or memorials. These guidelines also aim to promote the publication of information to encourage help-seeking, such as statements that suicide is preventable, stories of survival, information on how to access help-lines and mental health services, and other general information on suicide prevention [31,32,35].

These guidelines, however, are indeed just guidelines, and are voluntarily implemented by some journalists familiar with their existence. Research assessing the adoption of media guidelines has shown that knowledge of guidelines and subsequent implementation in reporting of suicide varies worldwide. For example, in Australia, awareness of the *Mindframe* guidelines [32] is widespread and, generally speaking, uptake is strong [36–38]. However, recent studies of the quality of media reporting in the United Kingdom [39,40], Bangladesh [41], China [42] and India [43] have shown that adherence to media guidelines is poor. Greater exposure to, and training for, media professionals in relation to guidelines on suicide reporting appears worthwhile. A review by Bohanna and Wang of the effectiveness of the guidelines, when implemented, showed they can mitigate negative effects on suicide [44]. The authors highlighted the importance of a collaborative approach with media personnel in achieving such positive outcomes, and evidence from Australia [45] and Austria [46] provides support for this suggestion.

6.7 Social Media Guidelines

In 2015 Robinson and colleagues [47] surveyed suicide prevention researchers and organisations, and social media users about their current and potential use of social media for suicide prevention. The study identified a lack of, and urgent need for, 'clear protocols and ethical standards for suicide prevention activities using social media' (p. 32). Subsequently, Robinson and colleagues [5] conducted a systematic review of 30 studies to inform understanding of how social media was being used by young people for suicide prevention purposes. They concluded that social media designed to be used as a tool for suicide prevention had significant potential to reach hard-to-engage people and to foster a sense of connection. They also concluded that social media provided opportunities for intervention when people at risk posted their suicidal intent online and for users to give and receive anonymous peer support for people at risk of suicide and bereaved by suicide [5]. However, they highlighted the absence of intervention studies and that greater understanding of the safety and efficacy of social media approaches to suicide prevention are needed.

Until recently, there had been no guidelines regarding the discussion of suicide on social media where many users are young people, all users are creators of their own content and the environments are by nature hard to regulate. Existing media guidelines largely target journalists and are oriented towards professionals. Given the great potential for social media in suicide prevention, particularly among young people [48], but also the lack of guidance on how online discussions of suicide might occur safely, Robinson and colleagues developed the #chatsafe guidelines [49]. The aim of the guidelines is to equip young people to have suicide-related conversations safely.

The guidelines were developed using a Delphi expert consensus method [48] and are structured around the ways in which young people reported using social media to communicate about suicide – namely, (1) things to consider before posting online about suicide (e.g., 'Be aware that what goes online may be there forever'); (2) sharing your own thoughts, feelings or experience with suicidal behaviour online (e.g., 'Consider that other people in your life . . . might find this out as a result of your post'); (3) communicating about someone you know who is affected by suicidal thoughts, feelings or behaviour (e.g., 'Where possible, ask permission before posting or sharing content about another person'); (4) responding to someone who may be suicidal (e.g., 'Always take content that suggests a person may be thinking about suicide seriously'); and (5) creating memorial websites, pages and closed groups to honour the deceased (e.g., 'Include a "Terms of Use" that outlines the rules for participating in the online memorial page or group'). In 2020 the guidelines were adapted for an additional 11 regions around the world [50], and accompanying resources were developed for educators and communities affected by a youth suicide. The guidelines are currently being updated. The new version will expand to include guidance on how to communicate safely online about self-harm, as well as how to respond to livestreams, suicide games and hoaxes. They will also include specific guidance for influencers [51].

However, because guidelines alone are unlikely to have much traction with young people, they were enhanced via a social media campaign co-designed with young people from across Australia [52]. The campaign predominantly adopted a harm minimisation approach with content focussed on safe ways to communicate about suicide. However, more active content was also developed (e.g., tips on how to respond to expressions of suicide risk, which provided young people with practical skills to use across platforms). The impact of the #chatsafe guidelines and social media campaign has been tested in two pilot studies, one with a general population sample of 189 young Australians and one with a sample of 199 young people recently been bereaved by suicide. Participants in both studies reported improvements in their willingness to intervene against suicide and in their self-efficacy, confidence and safety when communicating on social media about suicide. The authors conclude that this presents a promising picture for the potential impact of a suicide prevention campaign delivered through social media, including among young people bereaved by suicide [53]. The #chatsafe bereavement, or postvention campaign content, is now being used as part of a postvention response following the suicide of a young person in several jurisdictions in Australia and has been shown to reach large numbers of individuals quickly [54]. There is also the potential for guidelines to target the social media industry itself. The industry, which is frequently blamed for the increased rates of youth suicide [55], would almost certainly benefit from evidence-based guidance regarding how to manage suicide-related content on various platforms.

6.8 Suicide Prevention Media Campaigns

Suicide prevention campaigns that use a range of media are an increasingly common element of national suicide prevention strategies. Generally speaking, these are campaigns that are promoted via various media such as television, radio, billboards, posters and social media, and tend to focus on warning signs for suicide risk, decreasing the stigma of sharing suicidal thoughts, promoting help-seeking among those at risk and in some cases educating the public about how to be helpful in responding to people in suicidal crises [56].

The evidence for the effectiveness of these campaigns is mixed [57]. Typically, they are successful in improving knowledge and awareness related to suicide, and most are effective in creating improvements in attitudes to suicide [57]. The evidence for whether the campaigns boosts help-seeking is more varied [57]. Given the low incidence of suicide, statistically speaking, there are relatively few studies that have shown that these campaigns can reduce suicides, though there is limited evidence that they may [57].

The #chatsafe campaign provides an example of how a social media campaign can be used to educate young people about safe ways to communicate about suicide and how to respond to online expressions of risk. It also provides an example of how a social media campaign can be used as part of a real-time postvention response following a suicide death. Another example of a social media campaign for suicide prevention is the Australian #YouCanTalk campaign, which aimed to educate Australian adults on how to identify when a family member or friend is at risk of suicide and how best to respond. The campaign was led by the major Australian not-for-profit mental health organisation Beyond Blue, with nine other major partners. The campaign messages are based on a series of studies carried out by Australian researchers [58–62], who used a range of methods, including an expert consensus study [62] and nationally representative telephone survey [58,59,61] to develop the content based on the education needs of the population. The campaign had significant reach, with an audience of 5.65 million people across all social media platforms, and an analysis of web traffic indicated that the campaign audience was accessing web pages hosting specific information on how to help a loved one at risk of suicide [63].

Australian researchers King and colleagues [64] have also taken a novel approach to the use of media for suicide prevention by creating a suicide prevention documentary aimed at Australian men [64]. These researchers contracted a film company to create a three-part documentary series. The documentary follows a host, Gus Worland (a popular Australian radio personality), as he tries to understand why males dominate suicide statistics and to create his own suicide prevention campaign aimed at Australian men. The documentary, called *Man Up*, is based on underlying theoretical assumptions that suicide among men may in part relate to their socialisation into typically masculine traits of stoicism and self-reliance. Though they may be adaptive in some circumstances, these traits may inhibit men from seeking help for mental health difficulties which may contribute to suicide [64].

King and colleagues tested the effectiveness of this documentary on the help-seeking intentions of those men who viewed it [64]. In a randomised controlled trial involving 354 men allocated to view either *Man Up* or a control documentary, they found that viewing the documentary was related to a significant increase in intentions to seek help if faced with mental health difficulties. King and colleagues stated that this trial shows the 'potential for men's health outcomes to be positively impacted by novel, media-based public health interventions that focus on traditional masculinity' ([64], p. 86). Moreover, this trial showed the potential for suicide prevention organisations and researchers to look beyond traditional media campaigns to create more novel suicide prevention approaches.

6.9 Conclusion

Over time, suicide prevention researchers have developed a better understanding of suicide-related media content and narratives that confer harm and those that may be beneficial, and the likely mechanisms underpinning these effects. Consistent with this knowledge, the field has evolved from purely attempting to understand and minimise the harms of suicide reporting to actively using discussions of suicide in the media for suicide prevention. The media landscape is ever-changing. Suicide prevention research and practice need to continue to be agile, given how rapidly media is evolving. There must be increased efforts to translate what has been learned about suicide portrayals in the media, and their effect on suicides, to encourage the creation of helpful media content and measure its impact.

References

1. Pirkis J, Blood RW. *Suicide and the News and Information Media: A Critical Review.* Canberra: Commonwealth of Australia; 2010.
2. Sisask M, Värnik A. Media roles in suicide prevention: A systematic review. *International Journal of Environmental Research and Public Health.* 2012; **9**(1): 123–38.
3. Niederkrotenthaler T, Voracek M, Herberth A, et al. Role of media reports in

completed and prevented suicide: *Werther v. Papageno* effects. *British Journal of Psychiatry*. 2010; **197**(3): 234–43.

4. Pew Research Center. More than eight-in-ten Americans get news from digital devices. 2021.
5. Robinson J, Cox G, Bailey E, et al. Social media and suicide prevention: A systematic review. *Early Intervention in Psychiatry*. 2016; **10**(2): 103–21.
6. Bandura A. Self-efficacy: Toward a unifying theory of behavioral change. *Psychological Review*. 1977; **84**: 191–215.
7. Gould MS, Kleinman MH, Lake AM, Forman J, Midle JB. Newspaper coverage of suicide and initiation of suicide clusters in teenagers in the USA, 1988–96: A retrospective, population-based, case-control study. *Lancet Psychiatry*. 2014; **1**(1): 34–43.
8. Fink DS, Santaella-Tenorio J, Keyes KM. Increase in suicides the months after the death of Robin Williams in the US. *PLoS One*. 2018; **13**(2): e0191405-e.
9. Pirkis J, Currier D, Too LS, et al. Suicides in Australia following media reports of the death of Robin Williams. *Australia and New Zealand Journal of Psychiatry*. 2020; **54**(1): 99–104.
10. Till B, Strauss M, Sonneck G, Niederkrotenthaler T. Determining the effects of films with suicidal content: A laboratory experiment. *British Journal of Psychiatry*. 2015; **207**(1): 72–8.
11. Niederkrotenthaler T, Till B. Effects of suicide awareness materials on individuals with recent suicidal ideation or attempt: Online randomised controlled trial. *British Journal of Psychiatry*. 2020; **217**(6): 693–700.
12. Pirkis JE, Burgess PM, Francis C, Blood RW, Jolley DJ. The relationship between media reporting of suicide and actual suicide in Australia. *Social Science and Medicine*. 2006; **62**(11): 2874–86.
13. Niederkrotenthaler T, Braun M, Pirkis J, et al. Association between suicide reporting in the media and suicide: Systematic review and meta-analysis. *BMJ*. 2020; **368**: m575.
14. National Centre for Injury Prevention and Control. *10 Leading Causes of Death by Age Group, United States 2014: Centre for Disease Control and Prevention*. 2014. www.cdc.gov/injury/wisqars/pdf/leading_causes_of_death_by_age_group_2014-a.pdf.
15. Whitley R, Fink DS, Santaella-Tenorio J, Keyes KM. Suicide mortality in Canada after the death of Robin Williams, in the context of high-fidelity to suicide reporting guidelines in the Canadian media. *Canadian Journal of Psychiatry*. 2019; **64**(11): 805–12.
16. Pitman A, Fink DS, Whitley R. Patterns of suicide mortality in England and Wales before and after the suicide of the actor Robin Williams. *Social Psychiatry and Psychiatric Epidemiology*. 2021; **56**(10): 1801–8.
17. Sinyor M, Williams M, Zaheer R, et al. The association between Twitter content and suicide. *Australia and New Zealand Journal of Psychiatry*. 2021; **55**(3): 268–76.
18. Niederkrotenthaler T, Kirchner S, Till B, et al. Systematic review and meta-analyses of suicidal outcomes following fictional portrayals of suicide and suicide attempt in entertainment media. *eClinicalMedicine*. 2021; **36**: 100922.
19. Spangler T. *Netflix's* Marvel's The Defenders *Poised for Binge-Viewing Pop, Data Indicates*. Variety. 2017. https://variety.com/2017/digital/news/netflix-marvel-thedefenders-binge-viewing-data-ratings-1202532453.
20. Seventeen. *'13 Reasons Why' Just Broke a Netflix Record*. 2017. www.seventeen.com/celebrity/movies-tv/news/a46406/13-reasons-why-netflixbroke-record/.
21. Sinyor M, Williams M, Tran US, et al. Suicides in young people in Ontario following the release of '13 Reasons Why'. *Canadian Journal of Psychiatry*. 2019; **64**(11): 798–804.
22. Niederkrotenthaler T, Stack S, Till B, et al. Association of increased youth suicides in the United States with the release of *13 Reasons Why*. *JAMA Psychiatry*. 2019; **76**(9): 933–40.

23. Sinyor M, Mallia E, de Oliveira C, et al. Emergency department visits for self-harm in adolescents after release of the Netflix series '13 Reasons Why'. *Australia and New Zealand Journal of Psychiatry*. 2022; **56**(11): 1434–42.

24. Sinyor M, Schaffer A, Nishikawa Y, et al. The association between suicide deaths and putatively harmful and protective factors in media reports. *Canadian Medical Association Journal*. 2018; **190**(30): E900–7.

25. Niederkrotenthaler T, Laido Z, Gould M, et al. Associations of suicide-related media reporting characteristics with help-seeking and suicide in Oregon and Washington. *Australia and New Zealand Journal of Psychiatry*. 2022: 48674221146474.

26. Niederkrotenthaler T, Till B, Kirchner S, et al. Effects of media stories of hope and recovery on suicidal ideation and help-seeking attitudes and intentions: Systematic review and meta-analysis. *Lancet Public Health*. 2022; **7**(2): e156–68.

27. Till B, Tran US, Niederkrotenthaler T. The impact of educative news articles about suicide prevention: A randomized controlled trial. *Health Communication*. 2020: 1–8.

28. Niederkrotenthaler T, Gould M, Sonneck G, Stack S, Till B. Predictors of psychological improvement on non-professional suicide message boards: Content analysis. *Psychological Medicine*. 2016; **46**(16): 3429–42.

29. Niederkrotenthaler T, Tran US, Gould M, et al. Association of Logic's hip hop song '1-800-273-8255' with Lifeline calls and suicides in the United States: Interrupted time series analysis. *BMJ*. 2021; **375**: e067726.

30. Stack S. Celebrities and suicide: A taxonomy and analysis, 1948–1983. *American Sociological Review*. 1987; **52**(3): 401–12.

31. World Health Organization and International Association for Suicide Prevention. *Preventing Suicide: A Resource for Media Professionals – Update 2017*. Geneva: World Health Organization; 2017.

32. Everymind. *Reporting Suicide and Mental Ill-Health: A Mindframe Resource for Media Professionals*. Newcastle, Australia: Everymind; 2020.

33. Sinyor M, Schaffer A, Heisel MJ, et al. *Media Guidelines for Reporting on Suicide: 2017 Update of the Canadian Psychiatric Association Policy Paper*. Canadian Psychiatric Association; 2017.

34. Tomandl G, Sonneck G, Stein C, Niederkrotenthaler T. *Leitfaden zur Berichterstattung über Suizid*. Vienna: Krisen interventionszenterum; 2019.

35. Samaritans. *Media Guidelines for Reporting Suicide Surrey*. London: Samaritans; 2020.

36. Machlin A, Skehan J, Sweet M, et al. Reporting suicide: Interpreting media guidelines. *Australian Journalism Review*. 2012; **34**: 45–56.

37. Skehan J, Greenhalgh S, Hazell T, Pirkis J. Reach, awareness and uptake of media guidelines for reporting suicide and mental illness: An Australian perspective. *International Journal of Mental Health Promotion*. 2006; **8**(4): 29–35.

38. Skehan J, Paton E, Tynan R. The uptake of evidence-informed guidelines for reporting suicide into media codes of practice and policies in Australia. *Health Promotion Journal of Australia*. 2020; **31**(3): 482–90.

39. Duncan S, Luce A. Using the responsible suicide reporting model to increase adherence to global media reporting guidelines. *Journalism*. 2020: 1464884920952685.

40. Utterson M, Daoud J, Dutta R. Online media reporting of suicides: Analysis of adherence to existing guidelines. *BJPsych Bull*. 2017; **41**(2): 83–6.

41. Arafat SMY, Khan MM, Niederkrotenthaler T, Ueda M, Armstrong G. Assessing the quality of media reporting of suicide deaths in Bangladesh against World Health organization guidelines. *Crisis*. 2020; **41**(1): 47–53.

42. Fu K-W, Chan Y-Y, Yip PSF. Newspaper reporting of suicides in Hong Kong, Taiwan and Guangzhou: Compliance with

WHO media guidelines and epidemiological comparisons. *Journal of Epidemiology and Community Health.* 2011; **65**(10): 928–33.

43. Armstrong G, Vijayakumar L, Niederkrotenthaler T, et al. Assessing the quality of media reporting of suicide news in India against World Health Organization guidelines: A content analysis study of nine major newspapers in Tamil Nadu. *Australia and New Zealand Journal of Psychiatry.* 2018; **52**(9): 856–63.
44. Bohanna I, Wang X. Media guidelines for the responsible reporting of suicide. *Crisis.* 2012; **33**(4): 190–8.
45. Pirkis J, Dare A, Blood RW, et al. Changes in media reporting of suicide in Australia between 2000/01 and 2006/07. *Crisis.* 2009; **30**(1): 25–33.
46. Niederkrotenthaler T, Sonneck G. Assessing the impact of media guidelines for reporting on suicides in Austria: Interrupted time series analysis. *Australian and New Zealand Journal of Psychiatry.* 2007; **41**(5): 419–28.
47. Robinson J, Rodrigues M, Fisher S, Bailey E, Herrman H. Social media and suicide prevention: Findings from a stakeholder survey. *Shanghai Archives of Psychiatry.* 2015; **27**(1): 27–35.
48. Robinson J, Hill NTM, Thorn P, Battersby R, Teh Z, Reavley NJ, Pirkis J, Lamblin M, Rice S, Skehan J. The #chatsafe project. Developing guidelines to help young people communicate safely about suicide on social media: A Delphi study. *PLoS One.* 2018; **13**(11): e0206584.
49. Orygen. *Chatsafe: Tools and Tips to Help Young People Communicate Safely Online about Suicide.* Melbourne, Australia: Orygen. www.orygen.org.au/chatsafe.
50. Robinson J, Teh Z, Lamblin M, Hill NTM, La Sala L, Thorn P. Globalization of the #chatsafe guidelines: Using social media for youth suicide prevention. *Early Intervention in Psychiatry.* 2021; **15**: 1409–13.
51. Robinson J, Thorn P, McKay S, et al. #chatsafe 2.0: Updated guidelines to support young people to communicate safely online about self-harm and suicide – A Delphi study. *PLoS One.* 2023 Aug; **18**(8): e0289494.
52. Thorn P, Hill NTM, Lamblin M, et al. Developing a suicide prevention social media campaign with young people (The #chatsafe Project): Co-design approach. *JMIR Mental Health.* 2020; **7**(5): e17520.
53. La Sala L, Teh Z, Lamblin M, et al. Can a social media intervention improve online communication about suicide? A feasibility study examining the acceptability and potential impact of the #chatsafe campaign. *PLoS One.* 2021; **16**(6): e0253278.
54. La Sala L, Pirkis J, Cooper C, Hill NT, Lamblin M, Rajaram G, Rice S, Teh Z, Thorn P, Zahan R, Robinson J. Acceptability and potential impact of the #chatsafe suicide postvention response among young people who have been exposed to suicide: Pilot study. *JMIR Human Factors.* 2023 May; **10**: e44535.
55. Luxton DD, June JD, Fairall JM. Social media and suicide: A public health perspective. *American Journal of Public Health.* 2012; **102**(Suppl 2): S195–200.
56. Ftanou M, Cox G, Nicholas A, et al. Suicide prevention public service announcements (PSAs): Examples from around the world. *Health Commun.* 2017; **32**(4): 493–501.
57. Pirkis J, Rossetto A, Nicholas A, Ftanou M, Robinson J, Reavley N. Suicide prevention media campaigns: A systematic literature review. *Health Communication.* 2019; **34**(4): 402–14.
58. Nicholas A, Niederkrotenthaler T, Reavley N, Pirkis J, Jorm A, Spittal M. Belief in suicide prevention myths and its effect on helping: A nationally representative survey of Australian adults. *BMC Psychiatry.* 2020; **20**(303).
59. Nicholas A, Pirkis J, Jorm A, Spittal MJ, Reavley N. Helping actions given and received in response to suicide risk: Findings from an Australian national survey. *SSM-Population Health.* 2019; **9**: 100483.
60. Nicholas A, Pirkis J, Reavley N. Helpful and unhelpful responses to

communications of suicide risk: An online questionnaire study. *Journal of Mental Health.* 2022; **1**(4): 496–505.

61. Nicholas A, Pirkis J, Rosetto A, Jorm A, Spittal M, Reavley N. Confidence and intentions to help a person at risk of suicide: A nationally representative telephone survey. *Suicide and Life-Threatening Behavior.* 2020; **50**(1): 138–50.
62. Nicholas A, Rossetto A, Jorm A, Pirkis J, Reavley N. Importance of messages for a suicide prevention media campaign: An expert consensus study. *Crisis.* 2018; **39**(6): 438–50.
63. Beyond Blue. *The Research behind Suicide Prevention Campaign #YouCanTalk.* https://australianrotaryhealth.org.au/research/the-research-behind-suicide-prevention-campaign-youcantalk/.
64. King KE, Schlichthorst M, Spittal MJ, Phelps A, Pirkis J. Can a documentary increase help-seeking intentions in men? A randomised controlled trial. *Journal of Epidemiology and Community Health.* 2018; **72**(1): 92–8.

Chapter 7

Suicide and Violence

Emily Bebbington and Mohsen Rezaeian

7.1 Introduction

Suicide is not simply a typology of violence. All forms of violence are interrelated, and preventative action should tackle the common antecedents to all. Understanding what these are, and how they differ between regions and cultures, is key to developing effective violence prevention strategies that extend beyond suicide. In this chapter we will discuss the relationship between suicide and other forms of violence, then factors influencing volume and direction of violence, before finally moving on to preventative action that considers all forms of violence under the same framework. Throughout the chapter real-world examples will be given for important concepts, with particular reference to self-immolation, as it is the authors' area of research expertise.

7.2 The Relationship between Suicide and Other Forms of Violence

The World Health Organization (WHO) defines violence as 'the intentional use of physical force or power, threatened or actual, against oneself, another person, or against a group or community, that either results in or has a high likelihood of resulting in injury, death, psychological harm, maldevelopment or deprivation' [1]. Considering each of the components of this definition of violence in turn highlights the complexity of violence as a major public health problem. The nature of violence can be physical, emotional, neglectful or sexual; the type of violence can be directed towards oneself (e.g., suicide), against another (e.g., homicide) or collective (e.g., war); the outcome of violence can be acute or latent and affects the individual, their community and wider society. There is particular merit to clinicians, researchers and policymakers remembering this broad definition because many forms of violence go hand in hand. If a patient or population is recognised to be experiencing one form of violence, they are likely to be at risk of others as well.

When considering deaths from physical violence only, it is the leading cause of deaths for people aged 15–44 [1]. The crude ratio of deaths globally from self-harm to interpersonal violence to collective violence and legal intervention is 4.3 to 2.6 to 1 (Table 7.1) [2]. The vast majority of deaths due to violence occur in low- and middle-income countries. High-income countries have a disproportionate amount of suicides compared to other forms of violent death. The highest age-specific death rates for self-harm are in high-income countries and lower-middle income countries. The highest age-specific death rates for interpersonal violence and deaths from collective violence and legal interventions are in low-income countries. It is important to understand that low- and middle-income countries have less complete and reliable mortality data. The WHO estimates mortality by cause using a variety

Table 7.1 Estimated global violence deaths in 2016 by World Bank income group

	Global		LIC			LMIC			UMIC			HIC		
Type of violence	**Deaths**	**ASDR**	**Deaths**	**ASDR**	**%**	**Deaths**	**ASDR**	**%**	**Deaths**	**ASDR**	**%**	**Deaths**	**ASDR**	**%**
Self-harm	793,307	10.5	44,873	10.8	6%	319,672	11.4	40%	260,582	9.0	33%	168,179	11.5	21%
Interpersonal violence	476,898	6.4	57,501	9.3	12%	178,215	6.1	37%	207,336	7.8	43%	33,847	3.0	7%
Collective violence and legal intervention	183,691	2.5	40,398	6.6	22%	94,982	3.1	52%	47,325	1.9	26%	986	0.1	1%

LIC, low-income country; LMIC, lower-middle-income country; UMIC, upper-middle-income country; HIC, high-income country; ASDR, age-specific death rate per 100,000 population; %, percentage of total global deaths.

Data aggregated from *Global Health Estimates 2016: Deaths by Cause, Age, Sex, by Country and by Region, 2000–2016*. Geneva: World Health Organization; 2018 [2].

of statistical models. This allows comparisons between member states, but figures should not be regarded as exact so only general trends can be inferred [3,4].

Typologies of violence are rarely considered at a national level using a unified approach. Suicide is treated as a medical problem, homicide as a crime, and armed conflict as political action. England has a National Suicide Prevention Strategy prepared by the Department of Health [5] and a Serious Violence Strategy focussing on homicide and other forms of interpersonal violence, prepared by the Home Office [6]. These strategies are not aligned despite both acknowledging that interpersonal violence increases risk of suicide and self-harm, and vice versa, and that there are common drivers such as drug and alcohol misuse, poverty and adverse childhood experiences [5,7]. A key report that bucked this trend was the *National Confidential Inquiry into Suicide and Homicide by People with Mental Illness*, which has been a cornerstone of UK suicide prevention evidence since 1996. It reports both suicide and homicide statistics for the general population and those who are confirmed to have had contact with mental health services 12 months prior to the incident. It uses rigorous methods and sets a precedent to work with both police and clinicians to compile high-quality data. In 2018 *homicide* was omitted from the title, changing the name to *The National Confidential Inquiry into Suicide and Safety in Mental Health*, and in 2019 general population statistics for homicide were removed from the report [8–10]. The changes to this important work no doubt reflect reduced interest at a national level in the UK in homicide as a health problem, and likely reflects a growing unease towards interpersonal violence in mental health as a whole [11].

Distancing research and prevention strategies on suicide and self-harm from homicide and other forms of interpersonal violence simplifies the compilation of statistics, accountability and separation into different specialties. The knock-on effect of this is lack of recognition of how intertwined the concepts are, leading to wide variation in approaches to prevention. The danger of this is that in some circumstances classification of violence may be arbitrary and misleading (Box 7.1).

Decriminalisation of suicide has been hugely beneficial in changing the narrative of suicide from that of personal culpability to recognition and prevention of the broader social pressures that lead to suicide. There is not the same narrative for interpersonal violence, which is usually treated as a law-and-order matter. The rapid rise in knife crime in the UK has necessitated new initiatives to reduce violence. Scotland's Violence Reduction Unit reframed interpersonal violence as a 'disease affecting communities', recognising it as a symptom of poverty, inequality and despair. New initiatives that engage communities, those with lived experience and school education programmes have resulted in large reductions in crimes of handling an offensive weapon and hospital admissions for assault [24].

Historically, suicide and homicide have been considered under the same theoretical framework. Stream Analogy suggests that common social and cultural factors lead to the conditions that favour suicidal and homicidal behaviour (known as forces of production) and that social and structural factors dictate whom that behaviour is directed towards (known as forces of direction). Blame attributed externally results in homicide, whereas blame attributed internally leads to suicide when applying this model [26].

Wu used county-level data from the *Multiple Cause of Death Study in the United States* to investigate forces of production and direction for suicide and homicide [25]. The volume of both suicide and homicide violence were associated with infant mortality, percentage of non-white residents in a county, rate of unemployment and rate of teen pregnancy (forces of

Box 7.1 Difficulty in Differentiating between Accidental, Suicidal and Homicidal Burns in India

There are between 1 and 7 million moderate to severe burns in India annually, with 160,000 burn deaths [12 14]; 40% of deaths are in women aged 15–34. Women are three times more likely to die of fire-related injuries than men [14]. Age patterns for fire-related death in women match the age structure of fertility, suggesting that conditions that favour child-bearing also exacerbate the risk of fire-related death [14]. Statistics from small-scale epidemiological studies report accidents as the most common cause of burns, followed by self-harm and assault. This pattern is reported for both sexes [15–17]. Intentional burns are more commonly reported by women. Research about female burn deaths in India have revealed that clinicians may have a suspicion of intentionality based upon inconsistencies in the story and pattern of burns, even where the patient continues to report the burn as accidental [18].

Suicide by burning is often referred to as 'self-immolation'. India, Iran and neighbouring countries have the highest rates of self-immolation in the world – known as the 'geographical belt of self-immolation' [19]. Self-immolation disproportionately affects young women of low socio-economic status. Suicide is illegal or only recently decriminalised in many countries with high rates of self-immolation. Reporting of deaths is open to manipulation in many low- and middle-income countries, such that suicide may be recorded as an accident for the benefit of family or the community.

Homicides may be misclassified in records as accidents or suicide. There are methods reported in the popular press and literature that are commonly attributed to certain regions, though their true contribution to overall deaths is difficult to quantify.

'Dowry death' is a class of homicide in India which applies if the victim is a woman, has been married for less than seven years and there is found to be evidence of dowry-related harassment. A 'dowry' is the payment of money from the bride's family to the bridegroom's family when getting married. If the sum is deemed to be too little, it can lead to harassment of the bride by the groom and his family [20]. It is not difficult to imagine how harassment of this nature may be as likely to lead a woman to self-immolation or other forms of self-harm out of coercion or desperation as it is to lead to homicide.

Sati is the practice of a widow dying by burning either at the funeral pyre of her husband or shortly afterwards. It was particularly emphasised as a means of death in India in reporting by British Victorian newspapers. This was used as a justification for colonialisation, to ensure enforcement of the 1829 law against sati. Two popular narratives existed – that of the woman as a willing participant wishing to honour her husband or that of the woman as a victim of her cruel family [21]. *Sati* means 'virtuous woman', and it was the highest praise that could be bestowed upon a woman. A woman left alone was by default 'asati', where the only means of regaining sati is through purification, ideally immolation. The idea that the most a woman can hope to achieve with her life is to honour her husband with her own death is the epitome of misogyny. It has been theorised that women left alone emotionally by abusive or absent husbands may be driven to self-immolation to prove their innocence [22]. The last widely publicised case of sati was by Roop Kanwar in 1987. She died 158 years after the practice became illegal, but she is still worshipped in her hometown [23]. This highlights that although sati may be illegal, the pervasive social construct of the inferiority of women is still widely accepted.

Understanding the interface between accidental, suicidal and homicidal burns is currently an area of missing, and misleading, data. Focussing too heavily on the reported cause of a burn in countries with incomplete data, at risk of misclassification, can mean that prevention strategies are misdirected. Recognising the potential for misclassification, and the social inequalities leading to this misclassification, are essential for appropriately targeted prevention strategies.

production). Wu gives an example of what this means in real-world terms: 'Counties with a higher infant mortality rate are more likely to have a higher level of lethal violence. In other words, a community's susceptibility to murder and suicide is strongly linked to its inability to prevent infant mortality, which is a result of poverty' [25].

Wu also found that a county was more likely to express lethal violence as homicide where there was a higher percentage of non-white residents, higher rates of unemployment, greater income inequality and more racial inequality (forces of direction). This is a crucial finding – structural, not cultural, factors affect forces of direction. Considering suicide and homicide under the same theoretical framework of Stream Analogy highlights that suicide and homicide should be considered as related health outcomes, where both are determined by social, cultural and structural inequalities.

Calculating the suicide–homicide ratio (SHR) is a simple way to express force of direction. SHR is calculated using the following formula:

Suicide–homicide ratio (SHR) = suicide rate / (suicide rate + homicide rate)

A ratio of greater than 0.5 means fatal violence is expressed more as suicide. A ratio of less than 0.5 means fatal violence is expressed more as homicide. A study conducted using data from the WHO Global Burden of Disease project in 2000 found three distinct patterns when calculating the SHR for six regions of the WHO [27]. Europe, South-East Asia and Western Pacific regions express fatal violence more as suicide. Africa expresses fatal violence more as homicide. Eastern Mediterranean and the Americas have a mixed picture.

SHR varies with age, sex and income group of the country. Men in the Eastern Mediterranean region express violence more frequently as homicide, except in the age group of men over 60 from high-income countries, where it is expressed more as suicide. Women in the Eastern Mediterranean region express violence more frequently as suicide, except in the 5–14 age group in low- and middle-income countries and over-60 age group in high-income countries, where homicide is more common [28]. The rates of suicide and homicide in the Eastern Mediterranean region are higher in low- and middle-income countries than high-income countries for all age groups and both sexes. Men from low- and middle-income countries have the highest rates of suicide and homicide across all age groups (except the 5–14 age group, where women have higher rates of homicide and suicide, and the 15–29 age group, where women have higher rates of suicide; Box 7.2). Again, this study used WHO *Global Burden of Disease* data from the year 2000. New studies are required, using up-to-date estimates of SHR across age, sex and income group of countries.

The cause-of-death data for 74 of 133 (56%) low- and middle-income countries was rated as unavailable or unusable by the WHO in 2019 (analysis of data 2000–2016) due to quality issues, compared to only 2 of 48 (4%) high-income countries [34]. Experts consider the most reliable estimates of suicide death data in Eastern Mediterranean region are from international organisations (e.g., WHO) that integrate the best available national data with statistical modelling [35]. Although these data fill a void, they should not alleviate a state's responsibility to collect nationally representative statistics. In a world progressively dominated by big data, statistical modelling risks overlooking systematically missing data that may represent minority groups, further perpetuating health inequalities.

These data highlight important regional, sex, age and income variations in the volume and direction of violence. The next part of the chapter will explore the social, cultural and structural factors that may explain these variations.

Box 7.2 Young Female Suicides in the Eastern Mediterranean Region

The Eastern Mediterranean region comprises 22 countries extending from Morocco to Pakistan. There are large socio-economic differences across the region; there are five low-income countries (Afghanistan, Somalia, Sudan, Syrian Arab Republic, Yemen), six lower-middle-income countries (Djibouti, Egypt, Morocco, Pakistan, Tunisia, Palestine), five upper-middle-income countries (Islamic Republic of Iran, Iraq, Jordan, Lebanon, Libya) and six high-income countries (Bahrain, Kuwait, Oman, Qatar, Saudi Arabia, United Arab Emirates) [29,30].

The region has been exposed to considerable political upheaval and conflict, with more than 85% of the population exposed to emergency situations in the past 25 years. The median age of the regional population is only 23 years, meaning that many have grown up exposed to extreme stressors known to increase the risk of mental ill health [31].

Young females in the Eastern Mediterranean region have higher rates of suicide and homicide than men of the same age. Suicides in young women in this region more often use highly lethal means such as self-immolation, hanging and firearms than their European counterparts. Self-immolation is a particularly prevalent method of suicide in young married women from low socio-economic backgrounds with poor levels of literacy. There is some evidence that the women do not recognise the lethality of these means, and they are 'chosen' out of availability and not necessarily a desire to die [32]. Rates of depression have been found to be higher in women than men in this region [31], but it is unlikely this completely accounts for the difference in suicide rates. It has been suggested that social factors including gender-based violence perpetuated by forced child marriage and a patriarchal society lead to higher rates of suicide [32,33]. The same social factors preserve regional practices of 'Honour' killing that may be misclassified as suicide or accidental death. 'Honour killing' refers to the homicide of a woman who is deemed to have brought shame on her family. 'Honour' killing are typically associated with Islamic countries, but the practice existed in the Eastern Mediterranean region before Islam [20].

The primary religion of the Eastern Mediterranean region is Islam. The Koran condemns suicide, which is likely to lead to under-recognition and under-reporting of suicide deaths. It is important to note that the Koran states men and women are equal in the eyes of God – the maltreatment of women in this region is due to social values, not beliefs that are intrinsic to Islam [32].

7.3 Health Inequities Influencing Suicide and Other Forms of Violence

Michael Marmot eloquently describes the difference between health inequalities and health inequities in his 2020 report *Health Equity in England: The Marmot Review 10 Years On*:

> We refer to health inequities as those systematic inequalities between social groups that are judged to be avoidable by reasonable means and are not avoided – hence they are unfair. The evidence we rely on suggests that many of the health inequalities we see can be avoided. Putting them right is a matter of social justice. [36]

The United Nations' Sustainable Development Goals (SDGs) lay out the required standards to improve global environmental, social and health equity [11]. There are five targets of particular relevance to this chapter:

- Target 5.2: Eliminate all forms of violence against all women and girls in the public and private spheres, including trafficking and sexual and other types of exploitation.

- Target 5.3: Eliminate all harmful practices, such as child, early and forced marriage and female genital mutilation.
- Target 16.1: Significantly reduce all forms of violence and related death rates everywhere.
- Target 16.2: End abuse, exploitation, trafficking and all forms of violence against and torture of children.

It is important to note is that target 16.1 does not include suicide as a form of violence. Suicide is included in target 3.4 with non-communicable diseases:

➢ Target 3.4: By 2030, reduce by one-third premature mortality from non-communicable diseases through prevention and treatment and promote mental health and well-being.

The suicide mortality rate is one of the indicators for target 3.4, along with the mortality rate attributed to cardiovascular disease, cancer, diabetes or chronic respiratory disease.

➢ High-income countries have much higher rates of suicide than homicide and deaths from war and legal interventions. Whereas, low- and middle-income countries have high rates of suicide, and homicide and deaths from war and legal intervention.

This raises the question of whether separating suicide from other forms of fatal violence is in itself a manifestation of global health inequity.

Health inequities play a role at all phases of a violent event and apply to multiple risk factors. Haddon's matrix is a commonly used framework for planning primary, secondary and tertiary injury prevention measures (Figure 7.1) [37]. It was initially applied to traffic accidents but has subsequently been used for a variety of injuries, including self-poisoning from pesticides in Sri Lanka and filicide by parents with substance misuse problems [38,39].

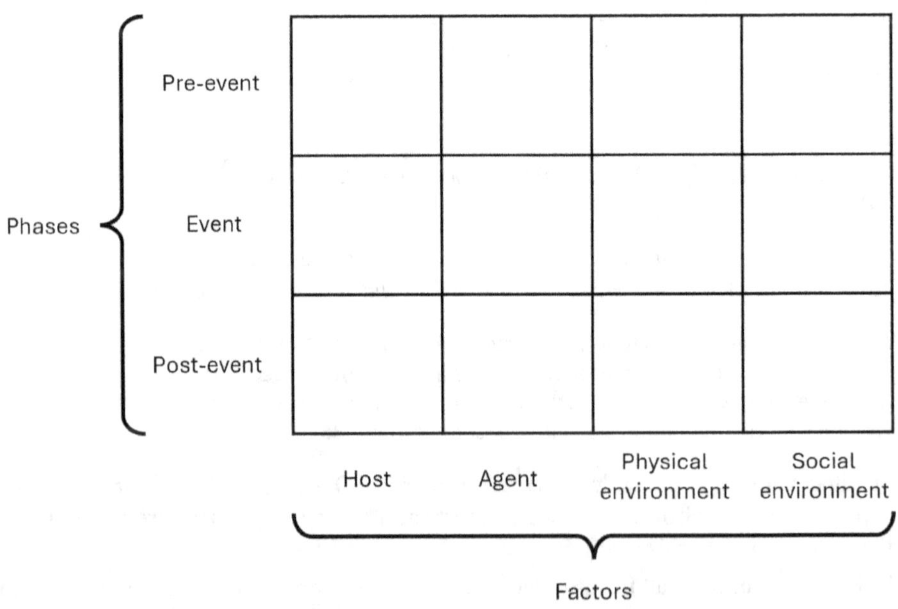

Figure 7.1 Haddon's matrix: A framework used to understand injuries and develop prevention measures.

Success of the model undoubtedly hinges on its accessibility, breaking the injury down into phases of the event (before, during, after) and factors causing the injury. Factors causing the injury require some modification from the original when applied to violent events – the host is the victim of violence and the agent is the perpetrator of the violence (which would be the same as the host for suicide). In this chapter we will not discuss every risk factor common to suicide and other forms of violence. Instead, we will discuss some key issues that have important prevention implications.

7.4 Violence against Women and Girls

Globally the ratio for male to female deaths due to self-harm is 1.8 to 1, whereas the risk of death from interpersonal violence is 4 to 1, and collective violence and legal intervention is 2.5 to 1 (Table 7.2) [2]. Interpersonal violence contributes 0.21 years to the reduced life expectancy between males and females globally; this pattern is most marked in low-income countries [11]. Lower-middle-income countries have the most similar number of suicides across both sexes (crude ratio 1.4 to 1). There are striking sex differences in the number of homicides across all World Bank income groups. Risk factors for homicide in a society include the proportion of men in the 15–29 age group, availability of guns, alcohol misuse and poverty.

Violence against men is more likely to be public. Violence against women occurs in private. This can take many forms, including intimate partner violence, femicide, forced marriage, female genital mutilation, trafficking and sexual violence. A total of 6% of homicides in men are caused by an intimate partner, whereas 38% of homicides are caused by an intimate partner in women. Female death rate by these causes is inversely proportional to income [11].

It is widely recognised that women and girls who have experienced violence are at increased risk of suicide and self-harm. This should not be viewed as individual vulnerability but instead as a manifestation of human rights violation. In 1979 the United Nations General Assembly adopted the Convention of the Elimination of All Forms of Discrimination against Women, and in 1993 it adopted *Resolution 48/104: Declaration on the Elimination of Violence against Women* [40]. The reframing of violence against women and girls as a human rights issue emphasises that this violence occurs because of structural inequalities that are the responsibility of the state to address, not the individual – it is a matter of social justice.

The *Declaration on the Elimination of Violence against Women* defines violence against women as 'any act of gender-based violence that results in, or is likely to result in, physical, sexual or psychological harm or suffering to women, including threats of such acts, coercion or arbitrary deprivation of liberty, whether occurring in public or in private life' [41]. It incorporates violence against women and girls occurring at all levels of society:

- Family (e.g., domestic violence, degrading practices such as child marriage)
- Community (e.g., rape, sexual assault, forced prostitution, stalking, femicide such as honour killings and dowry deaths)
- State (e.g., conflict, imprisonment)
- Transnational (e.g., refugees, migrant workers, sexual slavery during armed conflict, peacekeeper exploitation)

In 1994 the UN appointed a Special Rapporteur on 'violence against women, its causes and consequences' [42]. This role still continues today. The Special Rapporteur completes this

Table 7.2 Estimated global violence deaths in 2016 by sex and World Bank income group

		Global		LIC		LMIC		UMIC		HIC	
Type of violence	**Sex**	**Deaths**	**M:F**	**Deaths**	**M:F**	**Deaths**	**M:F**	**Deaths**	**M:F**	**Deaths**	**M:F**
Self-harm	Male	507,730	1.8	30,820	2.2	189,098	1.4	164,775	1.7	123,037	2.7
	Female	285,577	–	14,053	–	130,574	–	95,807	–	45,143	–
Interpersonal violence	Male	381,829	4.0	44,466	3.4	136,225	3.2	175,465	5.5	25,673	3.1
	Female	95,069	–	13,035	–	41,990	–	31,871	–	8,173	–
Collective violence and legal intervention	Male	131,326	2.5	28,539	2.4	67,527	2.5	34,344	2.6	917	13.3
	Female	52,365	–	11,859	–	27,455	–	12,981	–	69	–

LIC, low-income country; LMIC, lower-middle-income country; UMIC, upper-middle-income-country; HIC, high-income country; M:F, crude ratio of numbers of male deaths divided by female deaths.
Data aggregated from *Global Health Estimates 2016: Deaths by Cause, Age, Sex, by Country and by Region, 2000–2016*. Geneva: World Health Organization; 2018 [2].

mandate through thematic reports, country missions, consultations, expert meetings and government communications [43].

Family violence is the most pervasive and entrenched form of violence against women. A total of 30% of women have experienced intimate partner violence worldwide [44]. Women who are also part of other marginalised groups (e.g., racial, sexual, income, literacy, etc.) are at greater risk of violence. The increased social disadvantage and risk of adverse outcomes of occupying more than one marginalised identity category is known as 'intersectionality' – a term coined by Kimberley Crenshaw in her landmark 1991 paper *Mapping the Margins* [45]. Identity politics became a groundbreaking concept because the depth of acceptance of these harmful practices is often not realised at an individual, community and state level. For example, women in Kyrgyzstan aged 15–49 believed their husband had the right to beat them under various circumstances, including leaving the home without permission, disagreeing with the husband, refusing to have sex, burning food or taking inadequate care of their children [46]. Victims are unlikely to report family violence due to fear of further violence from the perpetrator or community, fear that their complaints will not be responded to by the police, inadequate support services and economic entrapment in their current circumstances (Box 7.3) [43]. Rates of prosecution for family violence are low in many parts of the world, and police may promote informal resolutions as opposed to arrests. Prosecution is further complicated in 'honour' killings, which are often perpetrated by multiple family members and condoned by the community (Box 7.2). Regarding the policing of 'honour' killings in Sweden, the Special Rapporteur noted, 'This collective element makes it extremely difficult to separate the victim from actual or potential perpetrators, unless she is willing to break off all relations with her family and begin a new life outside her social frame of reference' [47].

Box 7.3 Interviews with Female Burn Patients in India and Iran: The Firestarter Nexus and Narrative Precedent

Daruwalla and colleagues completed qualitative interviews with female patients and professionals at tertiary burn units in Delhi and Mumbai [18]. Common themes emerged from the interviews which were used to construct a model of risk factors for burn injuries in women in India. The model applies to all burns in women, as the authors found that the features, particularly of suicidal and homicidal burns, cluster so closely that it is difficult to differentiate between them.

The model consists of the *firestarter nexus* and the *narrative precedent*. The *firestarter nexus* are the physical environmental risk factors (as per Haddon's matrix) that increase the chance of a burn injury. These include black market kerosene that is decanted from larger government-issued cylinders to smaller non-safety-tested cylinders, readily available kerosene in the home, poorly manufactured and maintained stoves that are kept on the floor in a small living space and flammable synthetic clothing that is at risk of catching alight while cooking and going unnoticed. The *narrative precedent* are the socio-cultural factors that increase the risk of a woman sustaining a burn injury. These include mythological and traditional depictions of burns in women (e.g., dowry death, sati), poor understanding of the effects of burns reinforced by media depictions that show no scarring and a condoned culture of violence against women.

These women described a common scene in which firstly the *narrative precedent* dominates; their husband would be unemployed, drink to excess, then regularly beat them or inflict other types of abuse. The burn incident would occur either as a challenge from the husband to set herself alight or as a threat by the woman to try to provoke a sense of responsibility in her husband. This was preceded by a history of violence that had been condoned by the woman's natal and affinal family. Second, the *firestarter nexus* dominates, as there is access to means for the burn and a reasonable alternative explanation that the injury was sustained during cooking. Prosecution is unlikely to succeed in such cases due to a general reluctance of women to disclose intentional injuries, difficulty in getting the police to register and investigate the case, conflicting narratives between parties, long delays going to court and associated fees and lack of forensic evidence.

Similar discourse was found in interviews conducted with female patients in Iran who disclosed the cause of their burn as self-immolation [33]. Additional risk factors that could be added to the *narrative precedent* include self-immolation as an unplanned act completed in response to severe family stress, exposure to self-immolation by other family members legitimising it as a method to cope with life stress, and the subjugation of women through child marriage and unacceptability of divorce. These studies demonstrate systematic gender-based inequality at all levels of society. In some cases these inequalities lead to suicide or homicide, but the root causes remain the same.

The Special Rapporteur, Rashida Manjoo, perfectly summarises the need to understand all forms of violence under the same framework and tackle their common causes:

> States must acknowledge that violence against women is not the root problem, but that violence occurs because other forms of discrimination are allowed to flourish. By situating violence along a continuum, States may appropriately contextualise violence and recognise that the deprivation of water, food, and other human rights can be just as egregious and debilitating as family violence. Although these forms of violence are by no means the same, they can be viewed as parallel and similar when considering their interrelationship. [43]

7.5 Adverse Childhood Experiences, Alcohol and Drugs

Adverse childhood experiences (ACEs) are stressors experienced before the age of 18 that are known to increase the risk of adverse physical and mental health outcomes later in life [48]. ACEs include any type of abuse or neglect; living in a household where there is family dysfunction such as parental separation, mental illness, domestic violence, substance misuse and criminality; and exposure to peer, community or collective violence [36,49].

Experience of ACEs is proportional to level of deprivation [6,36]. Half of the world's children – approximately 1 billion – are exposed to violence each year [50]. For many children exposure to violence occurs in several spheres of their life, leading to poly-victimisation. In his book *Poverty Safari*, Darren McGarvey explains the effect of the threat of violence from multiple sources, including his mother who was an alcoholic, while growing up in Glasgow:

> In a community like this, the threat of violence is so pervasive that even when there is no reason to be afraid, the state of hypervigilance keeps you on the alert regardless, making daily life considerably stressful.... The only reason I ever overcame my fear of bullies was because it was dwarfed by my fear of my mother. [51]

Those who experience four or more ACEs are more likely have adverse physical and mental health outcomes later in life compared to those who experience none. The association is strongest for developing problematic alcohol and drug use, interpersonal violence (perpetrator and victim) and suicide [48]. This research applies to low-, middle-, and high-income countries.

ACEs confer eight times the risk of perpetrating a violent crime [48]. Young people with experience of ACEs and a history of poor mental health are particularly vulnerable to becoming involved in violent crime [52]. The UK is seeing increasing rates of knife crime and drug-related gang crime among young people. Rates of knife crime are highest in young males from deprived backgrounds, many of whom go on to be excluded from school, further perpetuating entry into a life of organised crime. Areas with the largest cuts to spending on young people have seen the greatest increases in knife crime rates [36]. Young people from deprived backgrounds, school-excluded children and homeless people are targeted by organised drug gangs to seek new markets outside of cities – known as *County Lines* [7]. The operationalisation of drug distribution in recent years has led to increased violence compared to more informal dealer-buyer relationships of previous decades. Illicit drugs are a major driver of homicide trends. The greatest impact is from system effects of the illegal drug trade leading to organised crime and violence as a means of resolving disputes. Gang presence in a community has a greater effect on homicide rates than poverty or any other structural factors [7]. Drug use can also increase the risk of violence at a personal level through psycho-pharmacological effects and necessity to pay for illicit drugs.

ACEs confer almost six times the risk of problematic alcohol use [48]. Hazardous drinking culture is associated with increased risk of alcohol associated homicide. Alcohol is particularly implicated in domestic violence–related homicides. There are two possible theories for why alcohol misuse is associated with homicides. First, alcohol reduces self-control and can increase aggression. Second, alcohol may increase the number of people in a space, increasing the risk of homicide [7]. Schizophrenia and other psychoses are associated with violence and homicide. This increased risk can be explained by higher rates of alcohol and drug misuse. When comparing those with psychoses and a history of substance misuse to people with a history of substance misuse without psychoses, the rates of violence are the same [53,54]. McGarvey later goes on to eloquently expresses the pervasive synergism of ACEs, alcohol and drug misuse in *Poverty Safari* [51]:

> I toured mental health services for years, genuinely believing I was either severely depressed or insane, when really, I was an exhausted, malnourished alcoholic, oscillating wildly between the high of inebriation and the crushing low of withdrawal and financial ruin.. . . Because I wasn't ready to honestly examine my problems which were, in the end, as much about my own attitudes and behaviour as they were about poverty or child abuse, I stubbornly continued on a path of delusional self-obliteration.

ACEs, deprivation and substance misuse are a deadly triad of interrelated factors known to increase risk of interpersonal and self-directed violence. Separating suicide from other forms of violence is arbitrary for many people, given the common antecedents. That is not to say that crimes should be excused but rather that prevention strategies must move away from a model exclusively focussed on personal culpability and problem behaviours to one that recognises broader social pressures and drivers that lead to violence.

7.6 Extreme Stressors

Natural disasters, war and pandemics are extreme stressors with the potential to have adverse health outcomes, no matter when in a person's life course they are experienced. If support is not given at a personal and state level to mitigate these stressors, the risk of suicide and homicide is amplified [55].

There is no consistent evidence that the COVID-19 pandemic led to a change in suicidal and self-harm behaviour globally, although data availability and methodological quality limit these conclusions [56–8]. There was, however, an increase in domestic violence during the COVID-19 pandemic, most likely mediated by increased household stress and confinement to a single shared living space [59,60]. Increase in domestic violence has been reported in other epidemics, including Ebola in west Africa [61]. The long-term effects on suicide and other forms of violence are more difficult to calculate, even in retrospect, because events may occur a long time after the initial 'extreme stressor' event [55,62]. It is likely that the long-term social consequences (e.g., unemployment, austerity, increased deprivation) of the COVID-19 pandemic are more likely to affect rates of suicide and other forms of violence than direct psychological stress from the event itself, as was seen in the aftermath of the 2008 financial crisis [36,59,63].

War is possibly the most extreme stressor. It acts as a facilitator to the displacement of people, collapse of social harmony and failure of policy and law enforcement [64]. Vulnerable groups such as women, children, unemployed and minority ethnic groups become more vulnerable to exploitation and violence [64]. Human trafficking, the mediator of modern slavery, is a real threat for vulnerable groups. A total of 71% of people in modern slavery are women and girls [65]. Attempted suicide or seeking health care following assault may be the only opportunity for professionals to recognise modern slavery; thus training and access to referral services are essential in primary and secondary care [66]. The loss of human life from war disproportionately affects low- and lower-middle income countries, particularly in the African and Eastern Mediterranean regions [67]. Literature on the negative effects of war and the positive effects of peace are lacking, further reflecting inequity in the volume of epidemiological research conducted in low- and middle-income countries [67]. The primary prevention effects of reinforcing peace through high-quality peace epidemiology go beyond suicide prevention (and the scope of this book chapter), but undoubtedly the reader will note the same structural inequalities that must be tackled as many of the other risk factors discussed earlier, and that secondary and tertiary prevention is inadequate in isolation [67].

7.7 *Primevention*

Throughout this chapter we have argued that prevention strategies should consider suicide and other forms of violence under the same framework. We have emphasised that the same societal factors that influence risk of suicide also influence other forms of violence. Prevention strategies must therefore take a public health approach to rectify social inequities. These strategies can be implemented at all levels of society (international, national, community and individual).

Arguably the greatest responsibility for preventative action falls at the level of the state. The first step is to recognise and take responsibility for the structural factors leading to suicides and other forms of violence. The next is to develop a strategy to tackle these. Only a third of high-income countries and a tenth of low- and middle-income countries have a national suicide prevention strategy [68]. For low- and middle-income countries, the rates of suicide and other forms of violence are much more similar than in high-income countries, so having a national prevention strategy for all forms of violence may be appropriate.

Suicide prevention activities can be divided into universal (for everyone irrespective of risk), selective (for subgroups at an increased risk) and indicated (for people at very high risk) [63,69]. Postvention is the facilitation of grieving for close contacts of a person who has died by suicide to reduce suicide contagion [69]. These activities fall under indicated suicide prevention activities. We feel that none of the current subcategories of prevention activities go upstream enough to tackle social inequities that lead to all forms of violence. This might include tackling causes of poverty, unemployment, housing, illiteracy and the status of women. In contrast to postvention, we have coined this approach *primevention*. The WHO recognises that more upstream approaches are likely to simultaneously improve a wide range of outcomes such as suicide, other forms of violence and substance misuse [70]. However, it will require considerable bravery from governments to invest in *primevention* research and evaluation, as by its very nature the benefits may not be realised for many years.

References

1. Etienne G, Krug LLD, Mercy JA, Zwi JA, Lozano R. *World Report on Violence and Health*. Geneva; 2002. https://apps.who.int/iris/bitstream/handle/10665/42495/9241545615_eng.pdf?sequence=1.
2. World Health Organization. *Global Health Estimates 2016: Deaths by Cause, Age, Sex, by Country and by Region, 2000–2016*. Geneva; 2018. www.who.int/healthinfo/global_burden_disease/estimates/en/.
3. The Global Health Observatory. *nMx – Age-Specific Death Rate between Ages x and x+n: World Health Organization*.www.who.int/healthinfo/global_burden_disease/estimates/en.
4. Department of Information Evidence and Research. *WHO Methods and Data Sources for Country-Level Causes of Death 2000–2016*. World Health Organization; 2018. www.who.int/healthinfo/global_burden_disease/GlobalDALY_method_2000_2016.pdf.
5. UK Department of Health. *Preventing Suicide in England*. 2012. https://assets.publishing.service.gov.uk/government/uploads/system/uploads/attachment_data/file/430720/Preventing-Suicide-.pdf.
6. UK Government HM. *Serious Violence Strategy*. 2018. https://assets.publishing.service.gov.uk/government/uploads/system/uploads/attachment_data/file/698009/serious-violence-strategy.pdf.
7. Morgan N, Shaw O, Mailley J, Channing R, Sweiry A, Kruithof K, et al. *Trends and Drivers of Homicide*. 2020. https://assets.publishing.service.gov.uk/government/uploads/system/uploads/attachment_data/file/870188/trends-and-drivers-of-homicide-main-findings-horr113.pdf.
8. Appleby L, Kapur N, Shaw J, Hunt IM, Ibrahim S, Turnbull P, et al. The National Confidential Inquiry into Suicide and Safety in Mental Health. *Annual Report: England, Northern Ireland, Scotland and Wales*. Manchester University; 2019. http://documents.manchester.ac.uk/display.aspx?DocID=46558.
9. The National Confidential Inquiry into Suicide and Homicide by People with Mental Illness. *Annual Report: England, Northern Ireland, Scotland and Wales*. Manchester University; 2017. http://documents.manchester.ac.uk/display.aspx?DocID=37560 .
10. The National Confidential Inquiry into Suicide and Safety in Mental Health. *Annual Report: England, Northern Ireland, Scotland, Wales*. Manchester University; 2018. http://documents.manchester.ac.uk/display.aspx?DocID=38469.
11. World Health Organization. *World Health Statistics 2019: Monitoring Health for the SDGs, Sustainable Development Goals*. Geneva; 2019. https://apps.who.int/iris/handle/10665/324835.
12. Rastogi A. *Burns: National Health Portal of India*. 2020. www.nhp.gov.in/disease/skin/burns.
13. World Health Organization. *Burns: World Health Organisation*. 2023. www.who.int/en/news-room/fact-sheets/detail/burns.

14. Sanghavi P, Bhalla K, Das V. Fire-related deaths in India in 2001: A retrospective analysis of data. *Lancet*. 2009; **373**: 1282–8.

15. Ganesamoni S, Kate V, Sadasivan J. Epidemiology of hospitalized burn patients in a tertiary care hospital in South India. *Burns*. 2010; **36**: 422–9.

16. Kumar N, Kanchan T, Unnikrishnan B, Rekha T, Mithra P, Venugopal A, et al. Clinico-epidemiological profile of burn patients admitted in a tertiary care hospital in coastal South India. *J Burn Care Res*. 2012; **33**: 660–7.

17. Natarajan M. Differences between intentional and non-intentional burns in India: Implications for prevention. *Burns*. 2014; **40**: 1033–9.

18. Daruwalla N, Belur J, Kumar M, Tiwari V, Sarabahi S, Tilley N, et al. A qualitative study of the background and in-hospital medicolegal response to female burn injuries in India. *BMC Women's Health*. 2014; **14**: 142.

19. Rezaeian M. The geographical belt of self-immolation. *Burns*. 2017; **43**: 896–7.

20. Belur J, Tilley N, Daruwalla N, Kumar M, Tiwari V, Osrin D. The social construction of 'dowry deaths'. *Social Science and Medicine*. 2014; **119**: 1–9.

21. Gilmartin S. The sati, the bride, and the widow: Sacrificial women in the nineteenth century. *Victorian Literature and Culture*. 1997; **25**: 141–58.

22. Sutherland SJ. Suttee, sati, and sahagamana: An epic misunderstanding? *Economic and Political Weekly*. 1994; **29**: 1595–605.

23. Khan H. India's last known case of Sati: 'She ceased to be a woman . . . was a Goddess'. *The Indian Express*. 2019. https://indianexpress.com/article/india/she-ceased-to-be-a-woman-was-a-goddess-6016915/.

24. Evans L. *A Radical Approach to Tackling Knife Crime in Scotland*. Gov.uk; 2019. https://quarterly.blog.gov.uk/2019/07/04/a-radical-approach-to-tackling-knife-crime-in-scotland/.

25. Wu B. Testing the stream analogy for lethal violence: A macro study of suicide and homicide. *Western Criminology Review*. 2003; **4**: 15–25.

26. Bills CB, Li G. Correlating homicide and suicide. *Int J Epidemiol*. 2005; **34**: 837–45.

27. Rezaeian M. An analysis of WHO data on lethal violence: Relevance of the New Western Millennium. *Asia Pac J Public Health*. 2011; **23**: 163–70.

28. Rezaeian M. Suicide/homicide ratios in countries of the Eastern Mediterranean region. *Eastern Mediterranean Health Journal*. 2008; **14**: 1459–65.

29. The World Bank. *World Bank Country and Lending Groups*. https://datahelpdesk.worldbank.org/knowledgebase/articles/906519-world-bank-country-and-lending-groups.

30. World Health Organization. *WHO's Eastern Mediterranean Region*. www.emro.who.int/countries.html.

31. Charara R, El Bcheraoui CC, Khalil I, Moradi-Lakeh M, Afshin A, Kassebaum NJ, et al. The burden of mental disorders in the Eastern Mediterranean region, 1990–2015: Findings from the global burden of disease 2015 study. *International Journal of Public Health*. 2018; **63**: 25–37.

32. Rezaeian M. Suicide among young Middle Eastern Muslim females. *Crisis*. 2010; **31**: 36–42.

33. Rezaie L, Hosseini SA, Rassafiani M, Najafi F, Shakeri J, Khankeh HR. Why self-immolation? A qualitative exploration of the motives for attempting suicide by self-immolation. *Burns*. 2014; **40**: 319–27.

34. World Health Organization. *Suicide in the World: Global Health Estimates*. Geneva; 2019.www.who.int/publications/i/item/suicide-in-the-world.

35. Rezaeian M, Khan MM. Suicide prevention in the Eastern Mediterranean region. *Crisis*. 2020; **41**: S72–9.

36. Marmot M, Allen J, Boyce T, Goldblatt P, Morrison J. *Health Equity in England: The Marmot Review 10 Years On*. London: Institute of Health Equity; 2020. www.heal

th.org.uk/publications/reports/the-marmot-review-10-years-on.

37. Runyan CW. Using the Haddon matrix: Introducing the third dimension. *Injury Prevention.* 1998; **4**: 302.

38. Eddleston M, Buckley N, Gunnell D, Dawson A, Konradsen F. Identification of strategies to prevent death after pesticide self-poisoning using a Haddon matrix. *Injury Prevention : Journal of the International Society for Child and Adolescent Injury Prevention.* 2006; **12**: 333–7.

39. Hartney E, Barnard DK. A framework for the prevention and mitigation of injury from family violence in children of parents with mental illness and substance use problems. *Aggression and Violent Behavior.* 2015; **25**: 354–62.

40. United Nations General Assembly. *Background: Taking a Stand against Gender-Based Violence.* 2023. www.un.org/en/observances/ending-violence-against-women-day/background.

41. United Nations General Assembly. *Declaration on the Elimination of Violence against Women.* A/RES/48/104; 1993. http://undocs.org/A/RES/48/104.

42. United Nations Human Rights Office of the High Commissioner. *Violence against Women.* www.ohchr.org/EN/Issues/Women/WRGS/Pages/VAW.aspx.

43. United Nations General Assembly. *Report of the Special Rapporteur on Violence against Women, Its Causes and Consequences.* New York: United Nations; 2011.

44. World Health Organization. *Global and Regional Estimates of Violence against Women: Prevalence and Health Effects of Intimate Partner Violence and Non-partner Sexual Violence.* Geneva: World Health Organization; 2013.

45. Crenshaw K. Mapping the margins: Intersectionality, identity politics, and violence against women of color. *Stanford Law Review.* 1991; **43**: 1241–99.

46. Manjoo R. *Report of the Special Rapporteur on Violence against Women, Its Causes and Consequences. Addendum: Mission to Kyrgyzstan.* A/HRC/14/22/Add2; 2010. https://undocs.org/A/HRC/14/22/Add.2.

47. Ertürk Y. *Report of the Special Rapporteur on Violence against Women, Its Causes and Consequences. Addendum: Mission to Sweden.* A/HRC/4/34/Add3; 2007. www.undocs.org/A/HRC/4/34/Add.3.

48. Hughes K, Bellis MA, Hardcastle KA, Sethi D, Butchart A, Mikton C, et al. The effect of multiple adverse childhood experiences on health: A systematic review and meta-analysis. *Lancet Public Health.* 2017; **2**: e356–e66.

49. World Health Organization. *Adverse Childhood Experiences International Questionnaire (ACE-IQ) Geneva.* www.who.int/violence_injury_prevention/violence/activities/adverse_childhood_experiences/en/.

50. Human Rights Council. *Annual Report of the Special Representative of the Secretary-General on Violence against Children.* 2019. https://undocs.org/en/A/HRC/43/39.

51. McGarvey D. *Poverty Safari: Understanding the Anger of Britain's Underclass.* 2018.

52. Haylock S, Boshari T, Alexander EC, Kumar A, Manikam L, Pinder R. Risk factors associated with knife-crime in United Kingdom among young people aged 10–24 years: A systematic review. *BMC Public Health.* 2020; **20**: 1451.

53. Appleby L, Kapur N, Shaw J, Hunt I, Flynn S, Ibrahim S, et al. *The National Confidential Inquiry into Suicide and Homicide by People with Mental Illness. Making Mental Health Care Safer: Annual Report and 20-Year Review.* 2016. https://documents.manchester.ac.uk/display.aspx?DocID=37580.

54. Fazel S, Gulati G, Linsell L, Geddes JR, Grann M. Schizophrenia and violence: Systematic review and meta-analysis. *PLoS Med.* 2009; **6**: e1000120.

55. Rezaeian M. The association between natural disasters and violence: A systematic review of the literature and a call for more

epidemiological studies. *J Res Med Sci.* 2013; **18**: 1103–7.

56. John A, Pirkis J, Gunnell D, Appleby L, Morrissey J. Trends in suicide during the COVID-19 pandemic. *BMJ.* 2020; **371**: m4352.

57. John A, Eyles E, Webb R, Okolie C, Schmidt L, Arensman E, et al. The impact of the COVID-19 pandemic on self-harm and suicidal behaviour: Update of living systematic review [version 2; peer review: 1 approved, 2 approved with reservations]. *F1000Research.* 2021; **9**. doi: 10.12688/f1000research.25522.2

58. Knipe D, John A, Padmanathan P, Eyles E, Dekel D, Higgins JPT, et al. Suicide and self-harm in low- and middle- income countries during the COVID-19 pandemic: A systematic review. *PLoS Global Public Health.* 2022; **2**: e0000282.

59. Marmot M, Allen J, Goldblatt P, Herd E, Morrison J. *Build Back Fairer: The COVID-19 Marmot Review. The Pandemic, Socioeconomic and Health Inequalities in England.* London: Institute of Health Equity; 2020.

60. Kourti A, Stavridou A, Panagouli E, Psaltopoulou T, Spiliopoulou C, Tsolia M, et al. Domestic violence during the COVID-19 pandemic: A systematic review. *Trauma, Violence, & Abuse.* 2023; **24**: 719–45.

61. Chandan JS, Taylor J, Bradbury-Jones C, Nirantharakumar K, Kane E, Bandyopadhyay S. COVID-19: A public health approach to manage domestic violence is needed. *Lancet Public Health.* 2020; **5**: e309.

62. Rezaeian M. Epidemiology of suicide after natural disasters: A review on the literature and a methodological framework for future studies. *Am J Disaster Med.* 2008; **3**: 52–6.

63. Gunnell D, Appleby L, Arensman E, Hawton K, John A, Kapur N, et al. Suicide risk and prevention during the COVID-19 pandemic. *Lancet Psychiatry.* 2020; **7**: 468–71.

64. Rezaeian M. The emerging epidemiology of human trafficking and modern slavery. *Middle East Journal of Business.* 2016; **11**.

65. WF Foundation. Global Slavery Index. 2018. www.globalslaveryindex.org/resources/downloads/.

66. Rezaeian M. The frequency of burns among the victims of sex trafficking in some lower-middle-income countries. *Burns.* 2017; **43**: 245–6.

67. Rezaeian M. 'War epidemiology' versus 'peace epidemiology': A personal view. *Archives of Iranian Medicine.* 2020; **23**: S38–42.

68. World Health Organization. *National Suicide Prevention Strategies: Progress, Examples and Indicators.* Geneva; 2018. www.who.int/mental_health/suicide-prevention/national_strategies_2019/en/.

69. Platt S, Niederkrotenthaler T. Suicide prevention programs. *Crisis.* 2020; **41**: S99–124.

70. World Health Organization. *Preventing Suicide: A Global Imperative.* Geneva; 2014. www.who.int/mental_health/suicide-prevention/world_report_2014/en.

Chapter 8

Suicide Prevention in Young People

Katrina Witt, Sarah Hetrick and Jo Robinson

8.1 Introduction

Suicide in young people (variously defined as those aged up to 24–29 years) is a growing public health concern worldwide. Worldwide, suicide is the third leading death for children aged 10 to 14 years, and the second leading cause of death amongst adolescents (aged up to 19 years) and young adults (aged between 20 and 24 years). The mean suicide rate for this age group, based on the latest global data from 2016, is 5.8 per 100,000 persons [4]. Whilst, overall, age-standardised suicide rates have been decreasing over recent decades [5], rates have been increasing in young people across a number of countries [6]. Additionally, although data from 21 countries, including 16 high-income and five upper-middle-income countries, suggests there has been no evidence of a significant increase in suicide rates as a result of the Severe Acute Respiratory Coronavirus-2 (SARS-CoV-2/COVID-19) pandemic to date [7], there are concerns that suicide rates may rise in this age group in the post-COVID-19 recovery phase as young people [8], and particularly young women [9], have been disproportionally affected by job loss and associated financial stress as a consequence of the lockdowns implemented in many countries to prevent the spread of the pandemic.

Non-fatal self-harm is more common than suicide. For every young male who dies by suicide, there are an estimated 100 episodes of hospital-presenting self-harm, whilst for every young female who dies by suicide, there are approximately 1,000 episodes of hospital-presenting self-harm [10]. Many more young people engage in self-harm in the community without ever presenting to hospital or other clinical services [10]. An estimated one out of every five young people report having engaged in self-harm at least once in their lifetime [11]. Rates of non-fatal self-harm have also been increasing over recent decades, both in the community [12] and according to the number of episodes resulting in presentation to hospitals [13]. This increase may be attributable to a number of factors, including younger age of self-harm onset [13], changes in the potential lethality of methods used by children and adolescents [13], increased risk of repetition in children and adolescents relative to young adults (i.e., 20- to 24-year-olds) [14], and changes in clinical documentation and improved administrative coding of cases of self-harm in children and adolescents, resulting in a higher detection rate of self-harm in young people presenting to services [15].

Suicide and self-harm both show distinct age, gender/sex and geographic patterns.

8.2 Age Patterns

Suicide in children is rare, and rates are generally higher in older adolescents and young adults [6]. Globally there is an average of 1.3 suicide deaths per 100,000 per annum in children aged 10–14 years, compared with 7.0 per 100,000 for those aged 15–19 years and 10.3 per 100,000 for those aged 20–24 years [4]. There are notable differences in age patterns for suicide both over time and between countries, however [16]. For example, some work has demonstrated that, over recent decades, a pattern of gradual increase in suicide with increasing age has been replaced in several western countries by a bimodal pattern with peaks in young people and again in later life. In several Asian regions, in contrast, suicide rates tend to be characterised by a gradual increase reaching a peak in later life. These geographic and temporal differences likely reflect changing macro socio-economic conditions and other factors.

Self-harm also typically onsets in adolescence, which also represents the peak age of onset for a number of mental illnesses. In a meta-analysis of community-based studies of self-harm in adolescents aged 12–18 years, for example, the mean age of self-harm onset was 12.8 years (95% confidence interval, 11.8 to 13.8 years), peaking in those aged 16 years [17]. A younger age of self-harm onset has been associated with a number of adverse outcomes, including greater risk of self-harm repetition, self-harm severity and suicide death [13], highlighting the importance of early intervention to prevent both the onset and maintenance of self-harm in young people.

8.3 Gender/Sex Patterns

Suicide rates are generally higher in young males (global average: 8.4 per 100,000) as compared to young females (global average: 3.2 per 100,000), although there are some notable exceptions to this general pattern in Asia (e.g., Bangladesh, China, India, Pakistan, Myanmar) and Northern Africa (e.g., Morocco), where suicide rates are higher in females as compared to males [4]. However, suicide rates have been increasing amongst young women in some countries [18,19], resulting in a narrowing of the gender/sex ratio, particularly for younger age groups, in recent years.

In contrast to suicide, rates of non-fatal self-harm are typically higher in young females, although the gender/sex ratio does change throughout the lifespan, peaking at approximately five to six times in 12- to 14-year-olds before decreasing with age [13,20].

Young people who identify as lesbian, gay, bisexual, transgender, queer, intersex or other sexual minority identities (LGBTQI+) may be at greater risk as compared to their peers. It is also important to remember there may be intersectionality between these identities [21]. With regards to non-fatal self-harm, available data has shown that almost one out of every two gender diverse young people (47%) and one out of every three sexual minority young people (30%) report engaging in self-harm in their lifetime [22]. However, gender/sexual orientation is seldom recorded in official registers at death, leading to likely under-identification of the scale of the problem [23].

8.4 Geographic Patterns

There is evidence that suicide rates vary by country. Based on WHO data from 2010–16, for example, suicide rates have been found to be highest in several countries that were formerly part of the Soviet Union and New Zealand [6]. A number of theories have been advanced to explain these geographic patterns. For example, rapid political and socio-economic changes, coupled with increased per capita availability of alcohol, following the fall of the Soviet Union in 1991, have been used to explain the rapid increases in suicide rates noted across a number of former Soviet Union countries, whilst high rates of suicide amongst Indigenous young people in New Zealand have been used to explain the high rates of suicide observed in this country [6]. However, many of these theories remain relatively unsatisfying and have not been thoroughly investigated empirically.

Geographic variation in lifetime self-harm rates has also been observed in some studies, with higher lifetime rates found in some European countries [17]. Rates of self-harm repetition also vary by country, with lower rates of repetition generally being found in Asian countries as compared with western countries [24]. The use of different measures to enumerate repeat self-harm does not appear to explain this difference. Instead, differences in rates of self-harm repetition may be explained by differences in self-harm methods. Methods associated with greater case fatality ratios are generally used with greater frequency in certain Asian countries, so that fewer patients are at risk of repetition [24]. Between-country variation in patient characteristics, access to treatment following an episode of non-fatal self-harm and other factors may also contribute to this difference.

8.5 Factors Associated with Suicide in Young People

There is rarely one single cause of youth suicide or self-harm. Instead, both are often the result of a complex interplay between genetic, biological, psychological, psychiatric, social, cultural and other factors [25], including method choice.

8.6 Genetic and Biological Factors

Suicide rates are between four- and sevenfold higher in young people with a first-degree relative (i.e., parent, sibling) who has also died by suicide, even following adjustment for the presence of psychiatric disorders and other relevant factors [26]. This risk appears to remain elevated even into adulthood [27]. A genetic contribution to suicide risk is also indicated by a higher-than-expected concordance for suicide in monozygotic (i.e., identical) twins as compared to dizygotic (i.e., fraternal or non-identical) twins [28]. There is some evidence to suggest that suicide method preference may also cluster within families [29], although it is unclear to what extent this may represent the contribution of genetic influences as compared to environmental factors (e.g., availability and/or familiarity with a given method). Despite this, heritability estimates range between 30% and 55% [28].

The fact that the genetic contribution to suicide risk has been found to be so variable suggests that the genetic component of suicide may be polygenic (i.e., not related to the presence or absence of any one particular gene) [30]. The majority of those genes that have been linked with suicide and self-harm in Genome Wide Association Studies (GWAS) have also previously been associated with other mental health comorbidities, personality disorders or plausible biochemical pathways, such as disturbances to the serotonergic and stress response systems [31], which have also been associated with suicide and self-harm risk [32,33]. However, the strength of association for many of these biochemical factors is also relatively weak [34], again suggesting there is a significant role of psychological, psychiatric and social factors.

8.7 Psychological Factors

A history of self-harm, and particularly frequently repeated self-harm, is the strongest risk factor for suicide [35]. Whilst the use of higher lethality methods during an episode of self-harm is often considered to indicate greater suicidal risk, there is no clear and consistent pattern between self-harm method choice over time and subsequent suicide [36]. This is because method switching between self-harm episodes is relatively common and largely unpredictable [37].

Problems in interpersonal relationships have also been linked with both suicide and self-harm in young people. Up to half of those who die by suicide experienced relationship problems with parents and/or friends prior to their death, whilst up to one quarter experienced problems with intimate partners/spouses [38]. This may differ by age with relationship problems with family members more common in younger children, whilst in older adolescents and young adults, problems with peers and partners/spouses may become more pronounced [39]. Problems in peer relationships, including experiences of (cyber)bullying, have also been associated with increased suicide risk in young people.

8.8 Psychiatric Factors

Psychiatric disorders are strongly associated with both frequent repetition of self-harm [40] and suicide death [41] in young people. Between one-third [42] and 70.4% [43] of young people who died by suicide had either a psychiatric diagnosis and/or symptoms consistent with a probable psychiatric disorder at the time of their death. Of these, recurrent major depression is most strongly associated with suicide in young people, followed by schizophrenia and other psychoses, bipolar disorder and borderline personality disorder [44]. Alcohol use disorder has also been associated with a significant population attributable risk fraction for suicide in young people [44]. Comorbidity between these disorders is relatively common and may further increase risk. However, despite this strong association between psychiatric factors and suicide, studies have shown that as many as one-third of young people who died by suicide were not receiving mental health care at the time of their death [45].

8.9 Social Factors

Experiences of childhood adversity, which can include exposure to parental interpersonal violence as well as neglect, maltreatment, emotional, physical and/or sexual abuse, have been linked with self-harm [46] and suicide [47] in young people. In many studies, associations remain significant after adjustment for covariates (e.g., demographic, psychological and psychiatric factors) [48]. Various mechanisms for this association have been proposed. Experiences of childhood adversity, for example, have been prospectively associated with the development of anxiety and depressive symptomatology [49]. These symptoms, in turn, have been associated with both self-harming behaviour and suicide in young people [40].

Lower socio-economic status (SES) is associated with youth suicide [41]. Compared with young people in the highest tertile of the SES distribution, those in the lowest tertile have been found to be at increased risk of suicide after adjustment for the presence of psychiatric disorder and other relevant factors [41]. Frequent changes of address, which may represent a proxy variable for social and/or economic disadvantage and/or disruption, has been linked with suicide in young people [50]. Several indicators of educational disadvantage, including school non-attendance [51], experiencing academic difficulties at school [52] and non-completion of compulsory schooling, are linked to suicide risk, particularly in adolescents. In young adults, not being in education, employment or training (NEET) has been associated with increased suicide risk, particularly for young males [45]. However, it may be that these factors represent the consequences of deteriorating mental health status, rather than being a direct cause of suicide or self-harm [53].

Alcohol use (both acute intoxication and chronic use) is associated with suicide risk in young people. Studies consistently find that one-third of those who die by suicide had consumed alcohol, and one quarter were intoxicated by alcohol at the time of their death. Acute alcohol misuse is associated with fluctuations in impulsivity [54] and negative rumination [55] – both known risk factors for self-harm and suicide. Chronic alcohol dependence has been associated with executive dysfunction which, in turn, is associated with reductions in problem-solving and future orientation – further risk factors for both self-harm and suicide [56]. Lastly, both acute and chronic alcohol use have also been associated with greater tolerance of pain [57] and disinhibition of psychological barriers against death [58]. Through these mechanisms, alcohol use may be associated with greater risk of using methods associated with greater lethality [59].

Area-level indices of socio-economic disadvantage (e.g., poverty, educational disadvantage and the proportion of social welfare recipients per capita) and unemployment rates are associated with high suicide rates [60], particularly for older adolescents, as well for males [60]. Other area-level indicators of social disadvantage, such as alcohol outlet density, have been associated with suicide rates in young people, once again, particularly for young males.

8.10 Cultural Factors

Worldwide, suicide rates amongst persons of Indigenous origin have been found to be up to 20-fold higher than their non-Indigenous peers [61]. For young Indigenous persons specifically, studies have found rates are elevated between two- to 40-fold [62,63]. Whilst the reasons for this are complex, intergenerational trauma and ongoing disconnection from culture, family and language as a result of experiences of colonisation are likely to be important factors. Experience of continuing discrimination are common. Many of these factors interact with the social factors as highlighted previously, as Indigenous people experience high levels of economic, educational and/or employment disadvantage compared to non-Indigenous populations [64]. Indigenous people may find it more difficult to access services during a time of crisis. For those living in rural/remote communities, this may be due to a complete lack of available services. Absence of culturally appropriate services may also discourage Indigenous persons from seeking help [65].

8.11 Clustering

Suicidal behaviour can cluster. Knowing another person who has attempted or completed suicide has been found to be a risk factor for suicide [66]. Suicide clustering may be more common in young people compared to older age groups [67]. Whilst the mechanisms underlying suicide clustering are not yet fully understood, imitation, changes to descriptive norms, social transmission and assortative relating have all been implicated [68]. Young people may imitate the behaviour of others, particularly those they view as role models. Geographical, social and/or psychological identification with the deceased may further increase the risk of imitation. Repeated exposure to suicide within their community may cause changes to descriptive norms, resulting in some young people viewing suicide as an acceptable coping strategy. Finally, assortative relating may occur particularly where young people share close social ties with others who are at risk of suicide, for example in school [67].

8.12 Method Choice

Self-harm method choice influences suicide risk. Those who use methods associated with higher potential lethality are more likely to die by suicide on their first attempt as compared to those who use methods typically associated with lower potential lethality, owing to limited opportunity for preventive intervention. Males, particularly young males, often use methods associated with greater potential lethality compared to females [69]. However, there is accumulating evidence that method switching is common. Around one-third of those who engage in frequent self-harm switch methods between successive episodes [37], although encouragingly there is little evidence at present of a consistent pattern of method escalation across episodes [36]. Nevertheless, almost half of those who die by suicide use a different method from that used in previous episodes of non-fatal self-harm [37].

8.13 Interventions for the Prevention of Youth Suicide and Self-Harm

Given the range of factors that have been associated with suicide and self-harm risk in this age group, their prevention requires multi-sector approaches delivered across community-based, educational, clinical and digital settings that can address each source of risk [70], as well as interventions that can operate in tandem across the universal, selective and indicated levels of the prevention hierarchy [71].

8.14 Universal Interventions

Universal interventions operate at the population level and aim to reduce risk factors and/or strengthen protective factors for all young people, regardless of level of risk. These interventions typically aim to improve knowledge about risk factors for suicide, provide information on how to help a person who might be at risk of suicide, remove barriers to accessing care (e.g., stigma) and strengthen protective processes (e.g., social connection within an at-risk community) [72]. These interventions have typically been delivered in community-based settings, include suicide awareness campaigns, reduction of alcohol availability and reduction of access to certain highly lethal suicide methods.

8.15 Community-Based Settings: Suicide Awareness Campaigns

Public suicide awareness campaigns aim to promote open discussion of suicide, provide information about how suicide can be prevented and provide advice on how to support a person who is at risk of suicide [73]. Whilst these campaigns have been found to be effective in reducing levels of suicide-related stigma, in increasing individuals' knowledge of risk factors for suicide and in improving preparedness to talk about suicide [74, 75], their effects on help-seeking behaviour are less clear, particularly in young people [76]. Evaluations of these campaigns have lacked the necessary statistical power to detect effects on rates of non-fatal self-harm and suicide [75]. Nevertheless, suicide awareness campaigns are an important aspect of multicomponent suicide prevention strategies [74]. As young people may be more likely to use social media to communicate about suicide and self-harm, public awareness campaigns should seamlessly integrate both offline and online/digital content to ensure wide reach.

Consideration should be given to enhancing access and capacity within mental health and other services in parallel to public awareness campaigns, as their aim is to increase help-seeking. Any resulting increase in referrals must be responded to appropriately. Simulation studies suggest that improving access, capacity and coverage of mental health services, so that all young people receive timely and ongoing mental health care when needed, could avert as many as one in four suicide deaths [77].

8.16 Restricting Access to Suicide Methods

Across the age range, a number of initiatives to reduce access to suicide methods, including regulation of the sale of firearms [78]; safe storage of firearms [79]; installing physical barriers to prevent suicide by jumping [80, 81]; bans of the sale of certain poisons, particularly pesticides [82], and other measures to reduce their availability; and legislation to reduce the pack sizes of analgesic medications [81] have all been found to be effective in reducing suicide deaths. Reducing access to toxic gasses by switching domestic gas supply from town gas to natural gas and installing catalytic converters into motor vehicles [83,84] may also be effective in reducing suicide. The longer-term impact of some of these initiatives, however, remains unclear, as few studies have been designed to evaluate the impact of these initiatives at the time of their introduction and evaluating their effects are often difficult to assess retrospectively [85]. Few studies have specifically investigated the impact of restricting access to suicide methods in young people. There is some evidence that young people who die by suicide are more likely than adults to use methods which are hard to restrict, particularly hanging [86]. Further work is needed on restriction of access to suicide methods amongst young people.

8.17 Reducing Alcohol Availability

At the population level, alcohol consumption has been associated with high suicide rates, particularly in young males [87]. Policies to restrict the per capita consumption of alcohol, for example by reducing availability through increases in excise, taxation and/or reductions in alcohol retail outlet density, may be effective in contributing towards reductions in self-harm and suicidal behaviour [88], although the effects may be smaller amongst young females [89].

8.18 Educational Settings: Suicide Awareness Campaigns

A number of evaluations of suicide awareness campaigns have been delivered in educational settings, primarily schools. Curriculum-based suicide prevention programs have generally been shown to be beneficial, at least in terms of improved knowledge of suicide risk factors, attitudes to help-seeking and reduced suicidal ideation [90]. However, the long-term effects of these programs are unclear. As with suicide awareness campaigns delivered in the community, consideration should be given to a concomitant improvement in accessibility and capacity of school-based and other mental health services.

8.19 Selective Interventions

Selective interventions focus on at-risk subgroups of a population that may be at increased risk of suicide as a result of the presence of certain risk factors (e.g., people with a diagnosed mental illness or a previous episode of self-harm) and/or absence of certain protective factors (e.g., disengaged young people who are neither in education or employment). The aim of these interventions is therefore to prevent the onset of self-harm and suicide [72]. These interventions have been delivered in community-based and educational settings, and have included gatekeeper training and screening interventions.

8.20 Community-Based Settings: Gatekeeper Training for Community Leaders

Young people are more likely to initially disclose suicidal ideation, self-harm and/or suicidal behaviour to informal sources (e.g., family members, peers and others) than to health care professionals [91,92]. Providing suicide awareness training to so-called gatekeepers in the community may be effective in reducing suicide in young people. As a result of their regular contact with young people, these gatekeepers may be in a good position to notice changes in a young person that signal increasing suicidal risk [93]. This training might usefully be combined with peer support.

Whilst a range of programs have been developed, there are some common elements, including providing psycho-education on risk and protective factors for self-harm and suicide in young people, and information on how to refer an at-risk young person to health services. Gatekeeper training programs have been developed for clergy [94], cultural leaders [95], sports coaches and parents. However, to date, there have been no comprehensive and independent evaluations of community-based gatekeeper programs.

8.21 Educational Settings: Gatekeeper Training for Teachers and School Well-Being Professionals

Gatekeeper training programs have been implemented for teachers and school well-being staff. These programs are effective in improving the knowledge, skills and confidence of trainees in responding to students who are at risk of self-harm and/or suicide [96]. However, the effect of these program on behavioural change (e.g., increases in referral to or use of services) are less clear [97]. There is an absence of evidence on the effectiveness of these programs in preventing suicide deaths [90]. Few studies have considered the role that institutional policies and school culture play in influencing the effectiveness of these programmes. For example, policies that manage risk by referring all students to external services may paradoxically reduce levels of help-seeking behaviour amongst low-risk students who seek confidential advice and/or support [98]. In those programmes that include peer support, careful selection of peers is necessary to ensure that peers represent different subgroups within the student body.

8.22 Screening

Screening programs use questionnaire-style instruments to detect young people who may be at risk of self-harm and/or suicide. The key difference between screening and gatekeeper training is that screening is implemented using an instrument or tool, and therefore can be readily scaled up to reach larger numbers of people. These approaches may be particularly effective for young people in the light of work that has found young people are more likely to disclose suicidal ideation and/or behaviours on a questionnaire than to a person. Screening programs have been found to be effective in identifying young people who have not previously been in contact with services [99]. However, evidence of effects on suicide rates is lacking at present. Typically screening programs are integrated into multimodal suicide prevention programs, rather than implemented in isolation [100].

8.23 Digital and Online Settings

Given that young people spend a large part of their lives online, recent studies have investigated the impact of providing training to young people in how to respond to peers who may be expressing suicidal ideation and/or self-harm thoughts or content online. A six-week program to provide young people who have been exposed to suicide and/or who knew someone who had attempted suicide, for example, found that the provision of psycho-education via social media direct messages was associated with improvements in self-reported willingness to intervene against suicide online and perceived confidence and safety when communicating about suicide online [101,102]. The impact of these approaches on actual self-harm and/or suicidal behaviour, however, has not been established.

8.24 Indicated Interventions

Indicated interventions aim to reduce risk factors and/or enhance protective factors amongst those who have signs, symptoms and behaviours consistent with suicide risk – for example, those engaging in non-fatal self-harm and/or those reporting significant levels of suicidal ideation [72]. The majority of these interventions are therefore delivered in clinical settings (e.g., mental health services, hospitals), although indicated interventions have also been trialled in digital and online settings.

8.25 Clinical Settings

Indicated interventions delivered in clinical settings may involve pharmacological interventions, psychosocial interventions or a combination of the two.

8.26 Pharmacological Interventions

Mood disorders have been identified as key modifiable risk factors for suicide in young people, so pharmacological treatments may include antidepressants. However, there are concerns that certain classes of antidepressants, particularly serotonin reuptake inhibitors (SSRIs), may increase suicidal ideation in young people [103]. As a result, regulatory agencies in a number of countries have cautioned practitioners about the use of SSRIs in this age group. There is some evidence that these warnings have had unintended consequences, with some early evidence finding reduced rates of antidepressant prescribing following these warnings [104,105], although more recent evidence suggests ongoing increases in antidepressant prescribing [106,107]. Anti-psychotics, anxiolytics (including both benzodiazepines and non-benzodiazepine anxiolytics) and mood stabilisers (including anticonvulsants) may be used, depending on clinical indication.

There have been no randomised controlled trials of the effectiveness of pharmacological interventions for the prevention of repeat self-harm or suicide in young people [108]. In adults, the evidence for pharmacological interventions is poor, with most trials conducted to date being of poor methodological quality and including older medications that are no longer in routine clinical use [109]. Therefore, unless clinically indicated for the treatment of a psychiatric disorder, pharmacological interventions are generally not recommended solely for the prevention of self-harm or suicide. Where pharmacological agents are indicated due to the presence of mental illness, prescribers should be aware of the risk of intentional drug overdose in this population [110]. As a general rule, medications associated with lower potential toxicity profiles should be selected [109].

8.27 Psychosocial Interventions

Whilst there is no standard psychosocial treatment for self-harm and/or suicide in young people, these interventions typically involve manualised psychological therapy delivered in an individual, group-based or mixed format. Results from a recently updated Cochrane systematic review found that, for young people with symptoms consistent with emergent borderline personality disorder, there is some evidence of reduction of frequency of repeated self-harm and suicide from intensive prolonged forms of psychological therapy, such as dialectical behaviour therapy for adolescents (DBT-A) [108]. Given the evidence of favourable effects for cognitive behavioural therapy (CBT) in adults, there may also be benefits in terms of reduced repetition of non-fatal self-harm in adolescents for this form of therapy. [108].

Most of these interventions have been developed to treat depression and then extended to address suicidal ideation and non-fatal self-harm. Resolution in depressive symptomatology does not necessarily lead to improvements in suicidal ideation and/or self-harm in young people [111], so interventions with a specific focus on suicidal ideation and/or self-harm may be expected to achieve better results. Additionally, most therapeutic interventions trialled to date were originally developed in adults and only minimally adapted for young people [100]. They are of low-to-moderate methodological quality [108] and are typically underpowered to detect effects on suicide death rates [112]. These trials have rarely been co-designed, implemented and evaluated in partnership with young people. As a consequence, evidence on the effect of these interventions on outcomes of importance to young people is limited at present [113].

8.28 Digital and Online Settings

The effectiveness of delivering indicated suicide and self-harm interventions to young people in digital and online settings have been trialled. These interventions have taken a variety of different therapeutic approaches, ranging from internet-delivered forms of psychotherapy, such as internet-delivered CBT (iCBT) and DBT (iDBT), to mood monitoring, crisis planning and behavioural programs, for example, where participants are presented with a series of visual stimuli pairs, designed to condition aversive reactions to self-harming thoughts or behaviours [114].

Overall, there is some evidence of effectiveness for these interventions in reducing suicidal ideation, but there appears to be no effect on repetition of non-fatal self-harming behaviour [115]. Few studies have evaluated the effectiveness of these approaches on suicide death rates. Adherence to these interventions tends to be poor. In one review, up to half of those allocated to the intervention group did not complete all treatment modules [114]. This was not associated with large numbers of treatment modules. Long-term adherence may be even poorer. In one naturalistic trial, over half of the sample did not access the intervention at all over a one-month follow-up period [115]. Additional measures, such as moderated social therapy content and gamification, may be required to make these interventions engaging over the longer term [114].

8.29 Multimodal Interventions

A number of interventions have been developed that aim to address sources of risk across multiple levels of the prevention hierarchy. These interventions typically combine universal screening and gatekeeper training approaches to identify young people who are at high risk of suicide together with various selective and/or indicated interventions targeted specifically towards this high-risk group. These interventions have shown promising effects on rates of suicide and/or suicide-related behaviour across a number of studies, although the methodological quality of these studies has been variable [100].

8.30 Conclusions

Youth self-harm and suicide prevention remain a national priority in many countries, but evidence regarding the effectiveness of various interventions for at-risk youth is limited at present. There is a distinct lack of well-conducted, methodologically robust and adequately powered studies for us to draw any robust conclusions. Whilst some universal approaches, such as suicide awareness campaigns and gatekeeper training, do show promise in improving knowledge, skills and confidence in responding to young people who may be at risk of suicide, the effect of these approaches on behavioural change (e.g., referral to services by trained gatekeepers, use of services) are less clear. Additionally, whilst initiatives to reduce access to potentially lethal methods of suicide show promise in adults, their effect in young people has not been comprehensively evaluated to date. For young people at high risk of suicide, there is some evidence of benefit for certain forms of high-intensity clinical psychosocial therapies, such as dialectical behaviour therapy and possibly cognitive behavioural therapy. However, few studies have been co-designed, co-implemented and co-evaluated in partnership with young people. Fewer still investigate outcomes of importance to those at high risk of suicide.

References

1. Hawton K, Hariss L, Hall S, Simkin S, Bale E, Bond A. Deliberate self-harm in Oxford, 1990–2000: A time of change in patient characteristics. *Psychological Medicine*. 2003; **33**: 987–96.
2. Andover M, Morris B, Wren A, Bruzzese ME. The co-occurrence of non-suicidal self-injury and attempted suicide among adolescents: Distinguishing risk and psychosocial correlates. *Child and Adolescent Psychiatry and Mental Health*. 2016; **2012**: 11.
3. De Beurs D, Vancayseele N, van Borkulo C, Portzky G, van Heeringen K. The association between motives, perceived problems and current thoughts of self-harm following an episode of self-harm: A network analysis. *Journal of Affective Disorders*. 2018; **240**: 262–70.
4. World Health Organization. *Global Health Observatory Data Repository: Suicide Rate Estimates, Crude, 5-Year Age Groups up to 29 Years*. Geneva: World Health Organization; 2018. https://apps.who.int/gho/data/node.main.MHSUICIDE5YEARAGEGROUPS?lang=en.
5. Naghavi M. Global, regional, and national burden of suicide mortality 1990 to 2016: Systematic analysis for the Global Burden of Disease Study 2016. *British Medical Journal*. 2019; **364**: 194.
6. Glenn C, Kleiman E, Kellerman J, Pollak O, Cha C, Esposito E, et al. Annual research review: A meta-analytic review of worldwide suicide rates in adolescents. *Journal of Child Psychology and Psychiatry*. 2020; **61**: 294–308.
7. Pirkis J, John A, Shin S, DelPozo-Banos M, Arya V, Analuisa-Aguilar P, et al. Suicide

trends in the early months of the COVID-19 pandemic: An interrupted time-series analysis of preliminary data from 21 countries. *Lancet Psychiatry*. 2021; **8**: 579–88.

8. Montenovo L, Jiang X, Lozano Rojas F, Schmutte I, Simon K, Weinberg B, et al. *Determinants of Disparities in COVID-19 Job Losses*. Cambridge: National Bureau of Economic Research; 2020. www.nber.org/system/files/working_papers/w27132/w27132.pdf.
9. Churchill B. COVID-19 and the immediate impact on young people and employment in Australia: A gendered analysis. *Gender, Work and Organization*. 2020; **28**: 783–94.
10. Geulayov G, Casey D, McDonald K, Foster P, Pritchard K, Wells C, et al. Incidence of suicide, hospital-presenting non-fatal self-harm, and community-occurring non-fatal self-harm in adolescents in England (the iceberg model of self-harm): A retrospective study. *Lancet Psychiatry*. 2018; **5**: 167–74.
11. Lim K-S, Wong C, McIntyre R, Wang J, Zhang Z, Tran B, et al. Global lifetime and 12-month prevalence of suicidal behavior, deliberate self-harm and non-suicidal self-injury in children and adolescents between 1989 and 2018: A meta-analysis. *International Journal of Environmental Research and Public Health*. 2019; **16**: 4581.
12. Tørmoen A, Myhre M, Walby F, Grøholt B, Rossow I. Change in prevalence of self-harm from 2002 to 2018 among Norwegian adolescents. *European Journal of Public Health*. 2020; **30**: 688–92.
13. Griffin E, McMahon E, McNicholas F, Corcoran P, Perry I, Arensman E. Increasing rates of self-harm among children, adolescents and young adults: A 10-year national registry study 2007–2016. *Social Psychiatry and Psychiatric Epidemiology*. 2018; **53**: 663–71.
14. Bennardi M, McMahon E, Corcoran P, Griffin E, Arensman E. Risk of repeated self-harm and associated factors in children, adolescents, and young adults. *BMC Psychiatry*. 2016; **16**: 421.
15. McGill K, Hiles S, Handley T, Page A, Lewin T, Whyte I, et al. Is the reported increase in young female hospital-treated intentional self-harm real or artefactual? *Australian and New Zealand Journal of Psychiatry*. 2018; **53**: 663–72.
16. Snowdon J, Phillips J, Zhong B, Yamauchi T, Chiu HFK, Conwell Y. Changes in age patterns of suicide in Australia, the United States, Japan and Hong Kong. *Journal of Affective Disorders*. 2017; **211**: 12–9.
17. Gillies D, Christou MA, Dixon AC, Featherston OJ, Rapti I, Garcia-Anguita A, et al. Prevalence and characteristics of self-harm in adolescents: Meta-analyses of community-based studies 1990–2015. *Journal of the American Academy of Child and Adolescent Psychiatry*. 2018; **57**: 733–41.
18. Roh B, Jung E, Hong H. A comparative study of suicide rates among 10–19-year-olds in 29 OECD countries. *Psychiatry Investigations*. 2018; **15**: 376–83.
19. Kõlves K, De Leo D. Suicide rates in children aged 10–14 years worldwide: Changes in the past two decades. *British Journal of Psychiatry*. 2014; **205**: 283–5.
20. Diggins E, Kelley R, Cottrell D, House A, Owens D. Age-related differences in self-harm presentations and subsequent management of adolescents and young adults at the emergency department. *Journal of Adolescent Health*. 2017; **66**: 470–77.
21. Russon J, Washington R, Machado A, Smithee L, Dellinger J. Suicide among LGBTQIA+ youth: A review of the treatment literature. *Aggression and Violent Behavior*. 2020; **64**: 101578.
22. Liu RT, Sheehan AE, Walsh RFL, Sanzari CM, Cheek SM, Hernandez EM. Prevalence and correlates of non-suicidal self-injury among lesbian, gay, bisexual, and transgender individuals: A systematic review and meta-analysis. *Clinical Psychology Review*. 2019; **74**: 101783.
23. Skerrett DM, Kõlves K, De Leo D. Suicides among lesbian, gay, bisexual, and transgender populations in Australia: An

analysis of the Queensland Suicide Register. *Queensland Suicide Register* 2014; **6**: 440–6.

24. Carroll R, Metcalfe C, Gunnell D. Hospital presenting self-harm and risk of fatal and non-fatal repetition: Systematic review and meta-analysis. *PLoS One*. 2014; **9**: e89944.

25. Hawton K, Saunders K, O'Connor R. Self-harm and suicide in adolescents. *Lancet*. 2012; **379**: 2373–82.

26. Lee K, Li C, Chang K, Lu T, Chen Y. Age at exposure to parental suicide and the subsequent risk of suicide in young people. *Crisis*. 2017; **39**: 27–36.

27. Hua P, Bugeja L, Maple M. A systematic review on the relationship between childhood exposure to external cause parental death, including suicide, on subsequent suicidal behaviour. *Journal of Affective Disorders*. 2019; **257**: 723–34.

28. Voracek M, Loibl L. Genetics of suicide: A systematic review of twin studies. *Wiener klinische Wochenschrift*. 2007; **119**: 463–75.

29. Lu T, Chang W, Lin J, Li C. Suicide method runs in families: A birth certificate cohort study of adolescent suicide in Taiwan. *Suicide and Life-Threatening Behavior*. 2011; **41**: 685–90.

30. Docherty A, Shabalin A, Di Blasi E, Monson E, Mullins N, Adkins D, et al. Genome-wide association study of suicide death and polygenic prediction of clinical antecedents. *American Journal of Psychiatry*. 2020; **177**: 917–27.

31. Campos A, Verweij K, Statham D, Madden P, Maciejewski D, Davis K, et al. Genetic aetiology of self-harm ideation and behaviour. *Scientific Reports*. 2020; **10**: 9713.

32. Mann J. Neurobiology of suicidal behavior. *Nature Reviews Neuroscience*. 2003; **4**: 819–28.

33. van Heeringen K, Mann J. The neurobiology of suicide. *Lancet Psychiatry*. 2014; **1**: 63–72.

34. Chang B, Franklin J, Ribeiro J, Fox K, Bentley K, Kleiman E, et al. Biological risk factors for suicidal behaviors: A meta-analysis. *Translational Psychiatry*. 2016; **6**: e887.

35. Zahl D, Hawton K. Repetition of deliberate self-harm and subsequent suicide risk: Long-term follow-up study of 11, 583 patients. *British Journal of Psychiatry*. 2004; **185**: 70–5.

36. Witt K, Pirkis J, Scott D, Smith K, Lubman D. Trajectories in suicide attempt method lethality over a five-year period: Associations with suicide attempt repetition, all-cause mortality, and suicide mortality. *PLoS One*. 2021; **16**: e0245780.

37. Witt K, Daly C, Arensman E, Pirkis J, Lubman D. Patterns of self-harm methods over time and the association with methods used at repeat episodes of non-fatal self-harm and suicide: A systematic review. *Journal of Affective Disorders*. 2019; **245**: 250–64.

38. Karch D, Logan J, McDaniel D, Floyd C, Vagi K. Precipitating circumstances of suicide among youth aged 10–17 years by sex: Data from the national violent death reporting system, 16 States, 2005–2008. *Journal of Adolescent Health*. 2013; **53**: S51–3.

39. Sheftall A, Asti L, Horowitz L, Felts A, Fontanella C, Campo J, et al. Suicide in elementary school-aged children and early adolescents. *Pediatrics*. 2016; **138**: e20160436.

40. Witt K, Milner A, Spittal M, Hetrick S, Robinson J, Pirkis J, et al. Population attributable risk of factors associated with the repetition of self-harm behaviour in young people presenting to clinical services: A systematic review and meta-analysis. *European Child & Adolescent Psychiatry*. 2019; **28**: 5–18.

41. Page A, Morrell S, Hobbs C, Carter G, Dudley M, Duflou J, et al. Suicide in young adults: Psychiatric and socio-economic factors from a case–control study. *BMC Psychiatry*. 2014; **14**: 68.

42. Annor F, Zwald M, Wilkinson A, Friedrichs M, Fondario A, Dunn A, et al. Characteristics of and precipitating circumstances surrounding suicide among persons aged 10–17 years – Utah,

2011–2015. *Morbidity and Mortality Weekly Report*. 2018; **67**: 329–32.

43. Houston K, Hawton K, Shepperd R. Suicide in young people aged 15–24: A psychological autopsy study. *Journal of Affective Disorders*. 2001; **63**: 159–70.

44. Qin P. The impact of psychiatric illness on suicide: Differences by diagnosis of disorders and by sex and age of subjects. *Journal of Psychiatric Research*. 2011; **45**: 1445–52.

45. Hill N, Witt K, Rajaram G, McGorry P, Robinson J. Suicide by young Australians, 2006–2015: A cross-sectional analysis of national coronial data. *Medical Journal of Australia*. 2020; **214**: 133–9.

46. Serafini G, Canepa G, Adavastro G, Nebbia J, Belvederi Murri M, Erbuto D, et al. The relationship between childhood maltreatment and non-suicidal self-injury: A systematic review. *Frontiers in Psychiatry*. 2017; **24**: 149.

47. Castellví P, Miranda-Mendizábal A, Parés-Badell O, Almenara J, Alonso I, Blasco M, et al. Exposure to violence, a risk for suicide in youths and young adults: A meta-analysis of longitudinal studies. *Acta Psychiatrica Scandinavica*. 2017; **135**: 195–211.

48. Miller A, Esposito-Smythers C, Weismoore J, Renshaw K. The relation between child maltreatment and adolescent suicidal behavior: A systematic review and critical examination of the literature. *Clinical Child and Family Psychology Review*. 2013; **16**: 146–72.

49. Li M, D'Arcy C, Meng X. Maltreatment in childhood substantially increases the risk of adult depression and anxiety in prospective cohort studies: Systematic review, meta-analysis, and proportional attributable fractions. *Psychological Medicine*. 2016; **46**: 717–30.

50. Qin P, Mortensen P, Pedersen C. Frequent change of residence and risk of attempted and completed suicide among children and adolescents. *Archives of General Psychiatry*. 2009; **66**: 628–32.

51. Jung S, Lee D, Park S, Lee K, Kweon Y-S, Lee E-J, et al. Gender differences in Korean adolescents who died by suicide based on teacher reports. *Child and Adolescent Psychiatry and Mental Health*. 2019; **13**: 12.

52. Lee D, Jung S, Park K, Lee K, Kweon Y-S, Lee E-J, et al. Youth suicide in Korea across the educational stages: A postmortem comparison of psychosocial characteristics of elementary, middle, and high school students. *Crisis*. 2020; **41**: 187–95.

53. Milner A, Page A, LaMontagne A. Cause and effect in studies on unemployment, mental health and suicide: A meta-analytic and conceptual review. *Psychological Medicine*. 2013; **44**: 909–17.

54. Stamates A. *The Bidirectionality of Impulsivity and Alcohol Use: An Ecological Momentary Examination among Emerging Adults*. Norfolk, VA: Old Dominion University; 2019.

55. Simons J, Emery N, Simons R, Wills T, Webb M. Effects of alcohol, rumination, and gender on the time course of negative affect. *Cognition and Emotion*. 2017; **31**: 1405–18.

56. Witt K, Lubman D. Effective suicide prevention: Where is the discussion on alcohol? *Australian and New Zealand Journal of Psychiatry*. 2018; **52**: 507–8.

57. Amadi S, Berman M, Timmins M, Guillot C, Fanning J, Nadorff M, et al. Analgesic effect of alcohol mediates the association between alcohol intoxication and deliberate self-harm. *Archives of Suicide Research*. 2022; **26**: 1060–71.

58. Norström T, Rossow I. Alcohol consumption as a risk factor for suicidal behavior: A systematic review of associations at the individual and at the population level. *Archives of Suicide Research*. 2016; **20**: 489–506.

59. Lee J, Chang SJ, Kim H, Kim MH, Ahn JS, Park KC, et al. Prolonged risk of suicide reattempts in patients with alcohol use disorder and acute alcohol use: A register-based follow-up study (2010–2015). *Psychiatry Investigation*. 2019; **16**: 145–53.

60. Song J, Park S, Lee K, Hong H. Influence of area-level characteristics on the suicide rate in Korean adolescents. *Psychiatry Investigation*. 2019; **16**: 800–7.

61. Pollock N, Naicker K, Loro A, Mulay S, Colman I. Global incidence of suicide among Indigenous peoples: A systematic review. *BMC Medicine*. 2018; **16**: 145.

62. Child and adolescent health suicide in indigenous youth: An unmitigated crisis. *Lancet Child & Adolescent Health*. 2019; **3**: 129.

63. Harder H, Rash J, Holyk T, Jovel E, Harder K. Indigenous youth suicide: A systematic review of the literature. *Pimatisiwin: A Journal of Aboriginal and Indigenous Community Health*. 2012; **10**: 125–42.

64. Mitrou F, Cooke M, Lawrence D, Povah D, Mobilia E, Guimond E, et al. Gaps in Indigenous disadvantage not closing: A census cohort study of social determinants of health in Australia, Canada, and New Zealand from 1981–2006. *BMC Public Health*. 2014; **14**: 201.

65. Kilian A, Williamson A. What is known about pathways to mental health care for Australian Aboriginal young people? A narrative review. *International Journal for Equity in Health*. 2018; **17**: 12.

66. Hill N, Robinson J, Pirkis J, Andriessen K, Krysinska K, Payne A, et al. Association of suicidal behavior with exposure to suicide and suicide attempt: A systematic review and multilevel meta-analysis. *PLoS Medicine*. 2020; **17**: e1003074.

67. Hawton K, Hill N, Gould M, John A, Lascelles K, Robinson J. Clustering of suicides in children and adolescents. *Lancet Child and Adolescent Health*. 2019; **4**: 58–67.

68. Haw C, Hawton K, Niedzwiedz C, Platt S. Suicide clusters: A review of risk factors and mechanisms. *Suicide and Life-Threatening Behavior*. 2013; **43**: 97–108.

69. Jordan J, McNeil D. Characteristics of persons who die on their first suicide attempt: Results from the National Violent Death Reporting System. *Psychological Medicine*. 2020; **50**: 1390–97.

70. Rodway C, Tham S-G, Ibrahim S, Turnbull P, Kapur N, Appleby L. Children and young people who die by suicide: Childhood-related antecedents, gender differences and service contact. *British Journal of Psychiatry Open*. 2020; **6**: e49.

71. Mrazek P, Haggerty R. *Reducing Risk for Mental Disorders: Frontiers for Preventive Intervention Research*. Washington, DC: National Academy Press; 1994.

72. Nordentoft M. Crucial elements in suicide prevention strategies. *Progress in Neuro-Psychopharmacology and Biological Psychiatry*. 2011; **35**: 848–53.

73. Ftanou M, Cox G, Nicholas A, Spittal M, Machlin A, Robinson J, et al. Suicide prevention Public Service Announcements (PSAs): Examples from around the world. *Health Communication*. 2017; **32**: 493–501.

74. Torok M, Calear A, Shand F, Christensen H. A systematic review of mass media campaigns for suicide prevention: Understanding their efficacy and the mechanisms needed for successful behavioral and literacy change. *Suicide and Life-Threatening Behavior*. 2017; **47**: 672–87.

75. Pirkis J, Rossetto A, Nicholas A, Ftanou M, Robinson J, Reavley N. Suicide prevention media campaigns: A systematic literature review. *Health Communication*. 2019; **34**: 402–14.

76. Klimes-Dougan B, Klingbeil D, Meller S. The impact of universal suicide-prevention programs on the help-seeking attitudes and behaviors of youths. *Crisis*. 2013; **34**: 82–97.

77. Atkinson J, Page A, Heffernan M, McDonnell G, Prodan A, Campos B, et al. The impact of strengthening mental health services to prevent suicidal behaviour. *Australian and New Zealand Journal of Psychiatry*. 2018; **53**: 642–50.

78. Mann J, Michel C. Prevention of firearm suicide in the United States: What works and what is possible? *American Journal of Psychiatry*. 2016; **173**: 969–79.

79. Violano P, Bonne S, Duncan T, Pappas P, Christmas A, Dennis A, et al. Prevention of firearm injuries with gun safety devices and safe storage: An Eastern Association for the Surgery of Trauma systematic review. *Journal of Trauma and Acute Care Surgery*. 2018; **84**: 1003–11.

80. Okolie C, Wood S, Hawton K, Kandalama U, Glendenning A, Dennis M, et al. Means restriction for the prevention of suicide by jumping. *Cochrane Database of Systematic Reviews*. 2020; **2**: CD013543.

81. Zalsman G, Hawton K, Wasserman D, Van Heeringen K, Arensman E, Sarchiapone M, et al. Suicide prevention strategies revisited: 10-year systematic review. *Lancet Psychiatry*. 2016; **3**: 646–59.

82. Gunnell D, Knipe D, Chang S-S, Pearson M, Konradsen F, Lee W, et al. Prevention of suicide with regulations aimed at restricting access to highly hazardous pesticides: A systematic review of the international evidence. *Lancet Global Health*. 2017; **5**: e1026–37.

83. Routley V. Motor vehicle exhaust gas suicide: Review of countermeasures. *Crisis*. 2007; **28**: 28–35.

84. Sarchiapone M, Mandelli L, Iosue M, Andrisano C, Roy A. Controlling access to suicide means. *International Journal of Environmental Research and Public Health*. 2011; **8**: 4550–62.

85. Bateman D. Limiting paracetamol pack size: Has it worked in the UK? *Clinical Toxicology*. 2009; **47**: 536–41.

86. Arensman E, Bennardi M, Larkin C, Wall A, McAuliffe C, McCarthy J, et al. Suicide among young people and adults in Ireland: Method characteristics, toxicological analysis and substance abuse histories compared. *PLoS One*. 2016; **11**: e0166881.

87. Kim A. Alcohol consumption and suicide rate: A cross-sectional analysis in 183 countries. *Psychiatry Research*. 2020; **295**: 113553.

88. Kõlves K, Chitty K, Wardhani R, Värnik A, de Leo D, Witt K. Impact of alcohol policies on suicidal behavior: A systematic literature review. *International Journal of Environmental Research and Public Health*. 2020; **17**: 7030.

89. Markowitz S, Chatterji P, Kaestner R. Estimating the impact of alcohol policies on youth suicides. *Journal of Mental Health Policy and Economics*. 2003; **6**: 37–46.

90. Cusimano M, Sameem M. The effectiveness of middle and high school-based suicide prevention programmes for adolescents: A systematic review. *Injury Prevention*. 2011; **17**: 43–9.

91. Rowe S, French R, Henderson C, Ougrin D, Slade M, Moran P. Help-seeking behaviour and adolescent self-harm: A systematic review. *Australian and New Zealand Journal of Psychiatry*. 2014; **48**: 1083–95.

92. Michelmore L, Hindley P. Help-seeking for suicidal thoughts and self-harm in young people: A systematic review. *Suicide and Life-Threatening Behavior*. 2012; **42**: 507–24.

93. Menon V, Subramanian K, Selvakumar N, Kattimani S. Suicide prevention strategies: An overview of current evidence and best practice elements. *International Journal of Advanced Medical and Health Research*. 2018; **5**: 43–51.

94. Bazley R, Pakenham K. Feasibility evaluation of the HOLLY program: An ACT-based suicide prevention program for Christian faith-based organisations. *Advances in Mental Health*. 2020; **18**: 115–30.

95. Nasir B, Hides L, Kisely S, Ranmuthugala G, Nicholson G, Black E, et al. The need for a culturally tailored gatekeeper training intervention program in preventing suicide among Indigenous peoples: A systematic review. *BMC Psychiatry*. 2016; **16**: 357.

96. Pierret A, Anderson J, Ford T, Burn A. Education and training interventions, and support tools for school staff to adequately respond to young people who disclose self-harm – a systematic literature review of effectiveness, feasibility and acceptability. *Child and Adolescent Mental Health*. 2022; **27**: 161–72.

97. Torok M, Calear A, Smart A, Nicolopoulos A, Wong Q. Preventing adolescent suicide: A systematic review of the effectiveness and change mechanisms of suicide prevention gatekeeping training programs for teachers and parents. *Journal of Adolescence*. 2019; **73**: 100–12.

98. Evans R, Hurrell C. The role of schools in children and young people's self-harm and suicide: Systematic review and meta-ethnography of qualitative research. *BMC Public Health*. 2016; **16**: 401.

99. Peña J, Caine E. Screening as an approach for adolescent suicide prevention. *Suicide and Life-Threatening Behavior*. 2006; **36**: 614–37.

100. Robinson J, Bailey E, Witt K, Stefanac N, Milner A, Currier D, et al. What works in youth suicide prevention? A systematic review and meta-analysis. *eClinicalMedicine*. 2018; **4–5**: 52–91.

101. La Sala L, Teh Z, Lamblin M, Rajaram G, Rice S, Hill NTM, et al. Can a social media intervention improve online communication about suicide? A feasibility study examining the acceptability and potential impact of the #chatsafe campaign. *PLoS One*. 2021; **16**(6): e0253278.

102. La Sala L, Pirkis J, Cooper C, Hill NTM, Lamblin M, Rajaram G, et al. Acceptability and potential impact of the #chatsafe suicide postvention response among young people who have been exposed to suicide: pilot study. *Journal of Medical Internet Research: Human Factors*. 2023; **10**: e44535.

103. Healy D. Lines of evidence on the risks of suicide with selective serotonin reuptake inhibitors. *Psychotherapy and Psychosomatics*. 2003; **72**: 71–9.

104. Gibbons R, Brown C, Hur K, Marcus S, Bhaumik D, Erkens J, et al. Early evidence on the effects of regulators' suicidality warnings on SSRI prescriptions and suicide in children and adolescents. *American Journal of Psychiatry*. 2007; **164**: 1356–63.

105. Lu C, Zhang F, Lakoma M, Madden J, Rusinak D, Penfold R, et al. Changes in antidepressant use by young people and suicidal behavior after FDA warnings and media coverage: Quasi-experimental study. *British Medical Journal*. 2014; **348**: j3596.

106. Plöderl M, Hengartner M. Antidepressant prescription rates and suicide attempt rates from 2004 to 2016 in a nationally representative sample of adolescents in the USA. *Epidemiology and Psychiatric Sciences*. 2019; **28**: 589–91.

107. Whitely M, Raven M, Jureidini J. Antidepressant prescribing and suicide/self-harm by young Australians: Regulatory warnings, contradictory advice, and long-term trends. *Frontiers in Psychiatry*. 2020; **11**: 478.

108. Witt KG, Hetrick SE, Rajaram G, Hazell P, Taylor Salisbury TL, Townsend E, et al. Interventions for self-harm in children and adolescents. *Cochrane Database of Systematic Reviews*. 2021; **3**: CD013667.

109. Witt K, Hetrick S, Rajaram G, Hazell P, Taylor Salisbury T, Townsend E, et al. Pharmacological interventions for self-harm in adults. *Cochrane Database of Systematic Reviews*. 2021; **12**: CD013669.

110. Gjelsvik B, Heyerdahl F, Lunn D, Hawton K. Change in access to prescribed medication following an episode of deliberate self-poisoning: A multilevel approach. *PLoS One*. 2014; **9**: e98086.

111. Witt K, Madsen T, Berk M, Dean O, Chanen A, McGorry PD, et al. Trajectories of change in depression symptoms and suicidal ideation over the course of evidence-based treatment for depression: Secondary analysis of a randomised controlled trial of cognitive behavioural therapy plus fluoxetine in young people. *Australian and New Zealand Journal of Psychiatry*. 2021; **55**: 506–16.

112. Witt K, Townsend E, Arensman E, Gunnell D, Hazell P, Taylor Salisbury T, et al. Psychosocial interventions for people who self-harm: Methodological issues involved in trials to evaluate effectiveness. *Archives of Suicide Research*. 2020; **24**: S32–93.

113. Owens C, Fox F, Redwood S, Davies R, Foote L, Salisbury N, et al. Measuring outcomes in trials of interventions for people who self-harm: Qualitative study of service users' views. *British Journal of Psychiatry Open*. 2020; **6**: e22.

114. Witt K, Spittal M, Carter G, Pirkis J, Hetrick S, Currier D, et al. Effectiveness of online and mobile telephone applications ('apps') for the self-management of suicidal ideation and self-harm: A systematic review and meta-analysis. *BMC Psychiatry*. 2017; **17**: 297.

115. Franklin J, Fox K, Franklin C, Kleiman E, Ribeiro J, Jaroszewski A, et al. A brief mobile app reduces nonsuicidal and suicidal self-injury: Evidence from three randomized controlled trials. *Journal of Consulting and Clinical Psychology*. 2016; **84**: 544–57.

Chapter 9

Suicide and Minority Groups

Sirar Jaroudy and Erminia Colucci

9.1 Introduction: Overview

In 2019 more than 700,000 people died by suicide, equating to one in every 100 deaths, prompting the World Health Organization (WHO) to produce new guidance to help countries improve suicide prevention and care [1]. The impact of suicide extends far beyond the tragic loss of life. According to WHO, more lives are claimed by suicide each year than by HIV, malaria, breast cancer, war and homicide [1]. Children and adolescents are particularly vulnerable, with suicide ranking as the leading cause of death among individuals aged 15 to 29 [2]. The ripple effects of suicide are profound, placing an immense burden on families, communities and health care systems.

The aim of this chapter is to present and synthesise available literature on suicidal behaviour and prevention strategies among migrants, refugees, asylum seekers or internally displaced persons (IDPs), particularly in humanitarian settings in low-and-middle-income countries (LMICs). By exploring the current knowledge and identifying research needs, we aim to contribute to a better understanding of suicidal behaviours in these contexts and provide some suggestions for preventive efforts.

To clarify the terminology used in this chapter, 'suicidal behaviours' refers to self-harm, suicidal attempts, fatal and non-fatal suicide, suicidal ideation and planning for suicide, all of which are dimensions closely associated with suicidal death [3]. The term 'minority groups' refers to refugees, asylum seekers, IDPs and migrants or immigrants. 'Migrants' and 'immigrants' are broad, overarching terms that are used interchangeably across this chapter.

9.2 Suicide in Humanitarian Settings: Challenges and Research Gaps

Humanitarian settings refer to emergencies that threaten the basic needs and well-being of large communities, putting them at high risk of death or suffering. As of 2023 the United Nations (UN) [8] estimates that a very large number of people in many countries need humanitarian assistance and protection, with more than 110 million forcibly displaced individuals. Among the displaced population, more than 40% are children under 18 years old, fleeing war, armed conflict and persecution. IDPs make up approximately 62.5 million of the displaced population. The Syrian Arab Republic, Ukraine and Afghanistan are the most affected countries.

The majority of suicides occur in low-and-middle-income countries (LMICs), accounting for approximately 79% of all suicide deaths worldwide [9]. Overall the reported, suicide rates in LMICs are slightly lower than in high-income countries (HICs), with 11.2 suicides per 100,000 individuals in LMICs compared to 12.7 per 100,000 individuals in HICs,

Box 9.1 Definitions

Refugees: A refugee is defined as 'a person who, owing to a fear of being persecuted for reasons of race, religion, nationality, membership of a particular social group or political opinion, is outside the country of his nationality' [4].

Asylum seekers: An asylum seeker is defined as 'an individual who is seeking international protection. In countries with individualized procedures, an asylum seeker is someone whose claim has not yet been finally decided on by the country in which he or she has submitted it. Not every asylum seeker will ultimately be recognized as a refugee, but every recognized refugee is initially an asylum seeker' [5].

Internally displaced persons (IDPs): An IDP is defined as 'persons or groups of persons who have been forced or obliged to flee or to leave their homes or places of habitual residence, in particular as a result of, or in order to avoid the effects of, armed conflict, situations of generalised violence, violations of human rights or natural or human-made disasters, and who have not crossed an internationally recognised border' [6].

Migrants or immigrants: 'An umbrella term, not defined under international law, reflecting the common lay understanding of a person who moves away from his or her place of usual residence, whether within a country or across an international border, temporarily or permanently, and for a variety of reasons. The term includes a number of well-defined legal categories of people, such as migrant workers; persons whose particular types of movements are legally defined, such as smuggled migrants; as well as those whose status or means of movement are not specifically defined under international law, such as international students' [7].

although suicide mortality data are likely to be underestimated in LMIC contexts [9]. Nonetheless, suicide remains a significant cause of mortality, accounting for 1.4% of all deaths in LMICs and 1.7% in HICs [9]. In terms of public health concerns, suicide ranks seventeenth in LMICs and eleventh in HICs, underscoring the need for attention and resources [10]. However, limited resources hinder suicide prevention efforts in LMICs, despite the significant impact of suicidal behaviour.

While some studies have examined suicidal behaviours in LMICs, existing research often displays methodological constraints, including small sample sizes and a focus on clinical populations. These limitations affect the generalisability of findings, particularly among displaced populations like IDPs in humanitarian settings. Furthermore, the absence of data on non-fatal suicidal behaviour reported in primary care settings poses a significant challenge. In LMICs, there is a scarcity of mental health specialists, including psychiatrists and clinical psychologists, which means that most patients are unlikely to receive evaluations from these experts, further hindering the understanding of non-fatal suicidal behaviours. This highlights the need for more robust evidence in LMICs, including in-depth qualitative studies.

Addressing suicide prevention in crisis-affected populations, especially those displaced by disasters or conflicts, has gained recognition as a specific area of focus. This is evident in the establishment of a special thematic group in 2019 by the Inter-Agency Standing Committee (IASC), the highest global forum for humanitarian coordination, which aims to address suicide and self-harm in humanitarian settings. Refugee contexts often involve multiple stressors such as forced displacement, exposure to trauma, loss of support and opportunities and various forms of discrimination and abuse. These factors can contribute to mental health conditions, including traumatic stress, depression and anxiety, which are associated with an increased risk of suicide. However, there is limited consistent data available on the prevalence of suicidal behaviour among refugees.

9.3 Prevalence of Suicide among Minority Groups in High-Income Countries (HICs)

The prevalence of suicide among minority groups in high-income countries (HICs) is a significant public health concern. These groups, particularly refugees and immigrants, often face unique challenges that can exacerbate mental health problems and increase the risk of suicidal behaviour [11]. This section aims to delve into the prevalence of suicide among these minority groups in HICs, examining the contributing factors, the impact of the resettlement process and the role of underlying mental disorders.

Studies consistently show that minority groups in HICs have a higher risk of suicidal behaviours compared to the general population [3]. Among these minority groups, refugees exhibit a varied prevalence of suicidal behaviours, with suicidal ideation being the most common form and a significant predictor of death by suicide [12]. A recent systematic review found that suicidal ideation was more prevalent among refugees and immigrants than other types of suicidal behaviours, such as mortality, attempts and suicide planning [13].

Several factors contribute to increased risk of suicidal ideation among refugees. These include migration-related factors (e.g., forced migration, length of stay in the host country and lack of social support), mental health issues (e.g., depression, anxiety and post-traumatic stress disorder), socio-demographic factors (e.g., younger age, female gender and unmarried status) and cultural factors, such as stigma and religious beliefs [12,14,15]. Furthermore, the relationship between suicide and non-fatal suicidal ideation can vary across countries and cultures.

The process of resettlement in HICs can be stressful and challenging for refugees, contributing to a high prevalence of suicidal behaviours. These behaviours are often exacerbated by socio-economic difficulties, traumatic experiences and limited access to appropriate care. However, a recent Swedish study found that refugees, despite a high prevalence of mental disorders, may not have a higher risk of suicide compared to non-migrant populations due to strong reasons to live, survive and cope [16]. Nevertheless, evidence from other countries continues to show an association between refugee status and suicidal behaviours. For example, a study in Greece found high rates of suicide attempts among refugees who experienced psycho-social distress, mainly attributed to a scarcity in specialised mental health professionals and limited psychological care [17]. In the United States, Bhutanese refugees exhibited suicide rates twice as high as the general population [18]. Similar findings are observed in Europe, where a systematic review revealed a high prevalence of self-harm among detained asylum seekers [19]. Similarly, asylum seekers in Denmark showed a 340% higher rate of suicide attempts compared with the Danish general population, with risk factors including length of waiting for leave to stay, mental illness and a high number of rejected asylum applications [20]. Interestingly, in Canada, the rates of self-harm among youth from immigrant backgrounds are declining, which may be attributable to efforts to reduce mental health stigma, provide accessible mental health services and raise awareness [21].

In LMICs, a significant proportion of individuals who engage in suicidal behaviours have underlying mental disorders such as depression and substance abuse [22]. This highlights the importance of addressing substance abuse as a potentially modifiable risk factor in suicide prevention strategies in LMICs. However, further investigation is necessary to gain a comprehensive understanding of how substance abuse in humanitarian settings contributes to the risk of suicidal behaviours, taking into account variables such as socio-economic status, educational level, feelings of sadness or loneliness, experiences of parental neglect or abuse and co-occurring mental illnesses [23,24,25].

In studies of immigrants and refugees in different regions, suicide rates vary. In a systematic review and meta-analysis, Europe and America were found to have the lowest prevalence of suicide among immigrants, while Asia appeared to have the highest rate [13]. The likelihood of suicide was found to be lower in immigrants and refugees compared to the native population, although immigrants were more likely to attempt suicide and have a suicide plan [13]. This aligns with the World Health Organization's suicide fact sheet which outlines risk factors that increase susceptibility of immigrants and refugees to suicide.

Geographic differences in suicide rates are likely to be due to a range of factors, including social and economic disparities, such as limited employment opportunities and low income, and social and political factors, such as racism and discrimination.

9.4 Prevalence of Suicide among Minority Groups in Low-and-Middle-Income Countries (LMICs)

The majority of displaced populations reside in LMICs, yet the issue of suicide and associated behaviours remains insufficiently addressed, despite mental health and psychosocial support services gaining increased attention in humanitarian settings [26]. This gap is particularly evident in the limited research conducted on IDPs, with most studies focusing on refugees, migrants and asylum seekers who have resettled in HICs.

Research in LMICs, although limited, aligns with findings from HICs insofar as there is an association between psychiatric disorders and an increased likelihood of suicidal behaviours [22]. Studies conducted among Congolese refugees in Rwanda, Afghan mothers in Pakistan and former child soldiers in Northern Uganda highlight the impact of mental illnesses, such as depression and PTSD, on suicidal ideation [25,27,28]. Variations in prevalence rates of suicidal ideation were observed among Rohingya refugee women with children residing in Bangladesh, underscoring the influence of sample characteristics and identification methods used [29].

However, the association between psychiatric disorders and suicidal behaviours in LMICs is not as strong as in HICs, and interactions between various socio-economic factors that influence suicidal behaviours are likely to differ across cultures and locations. It cannot be assumed that suicidal behaviour is 'caused by' a mental disorder.

There is a scarcity of studies among IDP populations, but reports by international non-governmental organisations provide some insights. For example, a 2017 International Organisation for Migration report in Thailand highlighted a significant increase in suicide rates among refugees between 2015 and 2017, reaching 36.6 deaths per 100,000 people [30]. Save the Children has published multiple reports about the mental health and psychosocial needs of IDP children in Syria, emphasising the detrimental impact of prolonged war and uncertain futures on their mental well-being [31,32,33]. These reports indicate that children reported suicidal behaviours, drug use and feelings of grief or extreme sadness. A study of IDP adults in Central Sudan indicated a higher prevalence of suicide in urban areas compared to rural ones, with employment opportunities playing a significant role. There were high rates of post-traumatic stress disorder (PTSD), alcohol and substance abuse [34]. Overall, IDPs often exhibit worse mental health outcomes due to ongoing exposure to violence and instability, increasing their risk of suicide.

While the scientific literature about suicidal behaviours in LMICs is growing, specific knowledge about displaced populations is limited. This hinders the application of existing evidence to humanitarian settings in LMICs, where cultural differences, health care systems and exposure to adversity play an essential role in understanding suicidal behaviours. The lack of rigorous surveillance of suicide and self-harm in LMICs is discussed in later chapters.

There is an urgent need for robust evidence investigating suicidal behaviours among refugees, IDPs, asylum seekers and migrants in humanitarian settings within LMICs.

9.5 Culture and Gender

The interplay of cultural and gender is pivotal in understanding the multifaceted nature of suicide. These elements of diversity not only shape the intricate dynamics of suicide but also highlight their critical role in addressing this global public health issue [35,36,37]. The influence of cultural and gender-related factors is particularly significant among refugees, IDPs and other minority groups, who face unique challenges that can exacerbate the risk of suicide.

While the existing literature often associates mental illness with suicidal behaviours, it is essential to acknowledge that suicide is influenced by a wide range of other factors [38]. Suicide cannot be understood in isolation from the socio-cultural environment [39]. Suicide rates differ between cultures, and culture is crucial to the understanding of risk and protective factors, along with the expressions and experiences of suicide, which vary across countries and cultural populations.

Culture is a complex concept that includes elements of language, gender, class, religion and nationality which construct a group's shared values and norms [40]. Cultural ideologies and institutional practices influence our understanding of help-seeking behaviour, mental health and mental illness, access to services, treatment approaches and the quality of interactions between service providers and patients. They profoundly impact on perceptions of health, illness and well-being [40,41,42].

A recent study by Akhtar and colleagues [43] underscores the importance of adapting evidence-based psychological interventions to specific cultural contexts. Cultural adaptation involves systematically modifying treatment protocols to align with the clients' cultural patterns, meanings and values, ensuring the intervention's effectiveness and relevance. The literature strongly suggests that culturally adapted interventions are more effective than non-adapted interventions, likely due to increased acceptability and comprehension of the intervention material [44]. A systematic review found that more extensive cultural adaptations of minimally guided or self-help interventions were linked to higher effectiveness in reducing depression and anxiety symptoms [45]. These findings highlight the ethical necessity of adapting interventions to suit cultural contexts in humanitarian settings.

Studies have revealed that suicide rates among refugees and minority groups often mirror those of their countries of origin, indicating the influence of cultural contexts [46]. Second-generation immigrants exhibit suicide rates resembling those of their countries of origin, influenced by cultural-specific determinants transmitted across generations. Gender differences also play a significant role in suicide rates, with men globally experiencing higher rates of suicides, while women exhibit higher rates of non-fatal suicidal behaviours [27,47]. However, this pattern is not ubiquitous. Both China and India, the two most populous nations in the world, have rates of suicide among women that are comparable to the rates among men [48].

In many LMICs, a strong association has been observed between domestic violence and gender-based violence (GBV) and suicidal ideation among women [48]. Among refugee populations, these patterns persist [27,49]. Various risk factors contribute to the vulnerability of female refugees to suicidal behaviours. These include poor mental health, a sense of disconnectedness, conflicts within interpersonal relationships and the challenges of cultural adjustment after resettlement. These findings underscore the importance of considering domestic violence and GBV in the development of suicidal prevention efforts.

Findings from the Middle East and North Africa (MENA) region also demonstrate the particular vulnerability of women. For example, in Iraq, female patients admitted to the emergency department were more than three times more likely to present with self-harm or attempted suicide compared to males [50]. Among Iraqi and Syrian refugees in Turkey, 78% of those presenting with suicidal attempts were females [51]. In a study based in Jordan, the majority of 62 patients admitted for self-harm were single females and 85% were housewives. In Lebanon, females aged 22 to 49 years presenting symptoms of depression constituted the majority of patients admitted for suicidal attempts, and in Tunisia, a retrospective cohort study found the majority of patients admitted to hospital after suicide attempt were female [52]. Evidence indicates similar patterns in adolescent populations in the MENA region. For example, between 2012 and 2015, female adolescents made up 93.75% of those aged 11 to 16 presenting to a hospital in Morocco after attempting suicide [53]. Across the MENA region, interpersonal family issues and GBV were commonly identified as risk factors contributing to suicidal attempts, with the ingestion of pharmaceutical drugs being the commonest method among women.

Understanding these gender differences and cultural influences is essential for developing effective suicide prevention strategies and tailored interventions for diverse populations. It requires a comprehensive approach that considers the interplay of socio-cultural factors, mental health services and social support systems to effectively support those at risk and reduce the overall burden of suicide in both HICs and LMICs.

9.6 Suicide Prevention Strategies in Humanitarian Settings

Suicide prevention is a major public health concern in both HICs and LMICs. Effective strategies can significantly reduce suicide rates, prompting these nations to adopt comprehensive, multidimensional interventions. These interventions often employ a multilayered approach, addressing the issue through a range of different measures. Humanitarian settings pose unique challenges to suicide prevention efforts due to structural disruption, shifts in priorities and resource constraints [54]. The evidence for specific measures under these circumstances is, so far, not strong [26]. It is important to focus on immediate and feasible priorities for suicide prevention in these contexts.

The IASC has offered valuable advice in their 2022 Guidance Note, outlining key strategies for suicide prevention in humanitarian settings [55]. These strategies include promoting mental health and psychosocial support, enhancing community engagement and strengthening health systems. They align with broader suicide prevention efforts outlined in the WHO 2021 suicide prevention guide [54], which emphasises the importance of early identification and intervention, promotion of mental well-being and resilience and addressing risk factors associated with suicide. The guide also highlights the role of governments in considering the impact of emergencies on suicide risk factors and implementation of mitigation measures through multisectoral collaboration. Governments, in collaboration with various sectors, including health, protection, education, nutrition and refugee camp management, play a crucial role in supporting individuals facing financial distress, restricting access to means of suicide and providing access to mental health and crisis support services. Moreover, governments hosting individuals affected by emergencies, including refugees and migrants, should consider their specific risk factors and needs in suicide prevention efforts.

To ensure effective suicide prevention in humanitarian settings, special attention should be given to vulnerable groups such as young people and older persons who may have experienced loss of family support or separation from loved ones. Engaging the media is important to minimise sensationalised reporting of suicides within the affected community. Building the capacity of existing health and community workforces in early identification, assessment, management and follow-up of suicide risk is essential. This includes equipping community gatekeepers and non-specialist health workers with the necessary skills to confidently identify, support and refer individuals at risk of suicide. Priority should be given to integrating suicide prevention into primary health care services and programs focused on protection concerns, such as child protection and gender-based violence.

Moreover, while the WHO mental health gap humanitarian intervention guide [56] was developed to address the limited mental health resources and overall mental health and psychosocial support (MHPSS) services available, it is important to acknowledge its inherent limitations. Although the guide provides valuable guidelines for non-specialised health care providers, focusing on screening for suicidal behaviours, offering basic care principles and providing guidance to individuals affected by suicide and their families, its primary focus on clinical settings creates a gap in addressing community-level issues. This includes tackling misinformation, stigma and misconceptions surrounding suicide, which act as significant barriers to help-seeking. Recognising the importance of community engagement, both the IASC Guidance Note 2022 and the WHO 2021 suicide prevention guide emphasise the roles of promoting mental health and raising awareness about suicide. By integrating community-level strategies, this gap can be bridged, ensuring comprehensive support and prevention efforts in humanitarian settings.

Affirming the importance of community-level engagement, expert opinion strongly supports the implementation of awareness-raising and gatekeeper training as effective strategies in suicide prevention efforts, with some research support [26,34,57,58]. Gatekeeper training aims to equip individuals with the knowledge, attitudes and skills needed to identify individuals at risk of suicide, understand associated risk factors and warning signs, and refer them for further treatment. Save the Children funded a training in Syria based on an adaptation of Suicide prevention guidelines for people from migrant and refugee backgrounds Piloted by the authors, this training showcased the positive impact of suicide-specific community-based interventions and highlighted the importance of clear referral protocols [57]. The WHO further emphasise that establishing systems for remote support, protecting key personnel and providing information on mental health self-care and available services are vital components of suicide prevention in humanitarian settings [54].

Research has identified several effective interventions for suicide prevention among minority groups. These interventions include brief follow-up measures for individuals at risk of suicide, utilising Brief Intervention and Contact (BIC) and Safety Planning delivered by trained volunteers, and training health care workers in evaluating suicidal behaviours and conducting depression screenings, although the latter is based on the assumption that depression commonly mediates suicide in this population [26].

The Save the Children piloted study findings suggest that cultural adaptation of suicide interventions is a key aspect of suicide prevention in humanitarian settings. A study of the adaptation of the WHO's Problem Management Plus (PM+) intervention for displaced Venezuelans and Colombians in Colombia highlighted the importance of understanding local population characteristics, formulating adaptation hypotheses, local consultation and external evaluations [59]. The authors concluded that even in resource-scarce settings, cultural adaptation of suicide interventions is both possible and necessary, and it can significantly enhance the effectiveness of these interventions.

Incorporation of these strategies and interventions into suicide prevention efforts in humanitarian settings make it possible to address the specific challenges and needs of crisis-affected populations, promote mental health and psychosocial support and ultimately reduce suicide rates within these vulnerable contexts.

9.7 Conclusion

In conclusion, addressing suicide in minority groups within humanitarian settings calls for a comprehensive, culturally sensitive and tailored approach. It is evident that a one-size-fits-all approach is inadequate in effective suicide prevention in these populations. The unique challenges faced by these populations, coupled with the influence of their socio-cultural and political contexts (including traditional beliefs and spirituality/religion), necessitate tailored interventions that address the specific needs of these groups.

Cultural adaptation of psychological interventions has shown promise in aligning strategies with the values, meanings and patterns of the target population. Comprehensive strategies with integrated interventions, community engagement and gatekeeper training appear to be effective and should be adapted to LMICs and humanitarian settings.

The scarcity of mental health specialists and limited resources in LMICs and humanitarian settings pose significant challenges to suicide prevention efforts. Investment in mental health infrastructure and training is important, but there is an urgent need for robust research to inform more effective strategies and policies.

The influence of gender-related issues on suicide rates highlights the need for a gender-sensitive approach and consideration of cultural nuances in suicide prevention strategies. Addressing GBV and gender inequality, as well as understanding and respecting cultural influences, are crucial in reducing the burden of suicidal behaviours [60].

Addressing suicide in minority groups in humanitarian settings requires a comprehensive, multifaceted and culturally sensitive approach. By focusing on these areas, we can hope to make significant strides in reducing the global burden of suicide and improving the mental health and well-being of these populations.

References

1. World Health Organization. *One in 100 Deaths Is by Suicide*. Geneva: World Health Organization; 2021. www.who.int/news/item/17-06-2021-one-in-100-deaths-is-by-suicide.
2. Iemmi V, Bantjes J, Coast E, Channer K, Leone T, McDaid D, Palfreyman A,

Stephens B, Lund C. Suicide and poverty in low-income and middle-income countries: A systematic review. *Lancet Psychiatry*. 2016; **3**(8): 774–83.

3. Forte A, Trobia F, Gualtieri F, Lamis DA, Cardamone G, Giallonardo V, Fiorillo A, Girardi P, Pompili M. Suicide risk among immigrants and ethnic minorities: A literature overview. *International Journal of Environmental Research and Public Health*. 2018; **15**(7): 1438.
4. Tribe RH, Sendt KV, Tracy DK. A systematic review of psychosocial interventions for adult refugees and asylum seekers. *Journal of Mental Health*. 2019; **28**(6): 662–76.
5. International Organization for Migration. *Key Migration Terms*. Geneva: International Organization for Migration; 2016. www.iom.int/key-migration-terms.
6. UNHCR. *IDP Definition*. Geneva: UNHCR; 2020. https://emergency.unhcr.org/protection/legal-framework/idp-definition.
7. International Organization for Migration. *Key Migration Terms*. Geneva: International Organization for Migration; 2016. www.iom.int/key-migration-terms.
8. UNHCR. *Refugee Statistics*. Geneva: UNHCR; 2022. www.unhcr.org/refugee-statistics/.
9. Arensman E, Scott V, De Leo D, Pirkis J. Suicide and suicide prevention from a global perspective. *Crisis*. 2020; **41**: S3–7.
10. Vijayakumar L, Phillips MR, Silverman, MM, Gunnell D, Carli V. Suicide. In Patel V, Chisholm D, Dua T, Laxminarayan R, Medina-Mora ME, eds., *Mental, Neurological, and Substance Use Disorders: Disease Control Priorities*, vol. 7, 3rd ed. Washington, DC: World Bank; 2016.
11. Troya MI, Spittal MJ, Pendrous R, Crowley G, Gorton HC, Russell K, Byrne S, Musgrove R, Hannam-Swain S, Kapur N, Knipe D. Suicide rates amongst individuals from ethnic minority backgrounds: A systematic review and meta-analysis. *eClinicalMedicine*. 2022; **47**: e1002905.
12. Leiler A, Hollifield M, Wasteson E, Bjärtå A. Suicidal ideation and severity of distress among refugees residing in asylum accommodations in Sweden. *International Journal of Environmental Research and Public Health*. 2019; **16**(15): 2751.
13. Amiri S. Prevalence of suicide in immigrants/refugees: A systematic review and meta-analysis. *Archives of Suicide Research*. 2022; **26**(2): 370–405.
14. McKenzie K, Bhui K, Nanchahal K, Blizard B. Suicide rates in people of South Asian origin in England and Wales: 1993–2003. *British Journal of Psychiatry*. 2008; **193**(5): 406–9.
15. Panagioti M, Gooding P, Tarrier N. Post-traumatic stress disorder and suicidal behavior: A narrative review. *Clinical Psychology Review*. 2009; **29**(6): 471–82.
16. Hollander AC, Pitman A, Sjöqvist H, Lewis G, Magnusson C, Kirkbride JB, Dalman C. Suicide risk among refugees compared with non-refugee migrants and the Swedish-born majority population. *British Journal of Psychiatry*. 2020; **217**(6): 686–92.
17. Hermans MP, Kooistra J, Cannegieter SC, Rosendaal FR, Mook-Kanamori DO, Nemeth B. Healthcare and disease burden among refugees in long-stay refugee camps at Lesbos, Greece. *European Journal of Epidemiology*. 2017; **32**: 851–4.
18. Cochran J, Geltman PL. Suicide and suicidal ideation among Bhutanese refugees – United States, 2009–2012. *CDC: Morbidity and Mortality Weekly Report*. 2013; **62**: 533–6.
19. Gargiulo A, Tessitore F, Le Grottaglie F, Margherita G. Self-harming behaviours of asylum seekers and refugees in Europe: A systematic review. *International Journal of Psychology*. 2021; **56**(2): 189–98.
20. Staehr MA, Munk-Andersen E. Suicide and suicidal behavior among asylum seekers in Denmark during the period 2001–2003: A retrospective study. *Ugeskrift for Laeger*. 2006; **168**(17): 1650–3.
21. Saunders NR, Lebenbaum M, Stukel TA, Lu H, Urquia ML, Kurdyak P, Guttmann A. Suicide and self-harm trends in recent immigrant youth in Ontario, 1996–2012: A population-based

longitudinal cohort study. *BMJ Open*. 2017; **7**(9): e014863.

22. Knipe D, Williams AJ, Hannam-Swain S, Upton S, Brown K, Bandara P, Chang SS, Kapur N. Psychiatric morbidity and suicidal behaviour in low-and middle-income countries: a systematic review and meta-analysis. *PLoS Medicine*. 2019; **16**(10): e1002905.
23. Salama E, Castaneda AE, Suvisaari J, Rask S, Laatikainen T, Niemelä S. Substance use, affective symptoms, and suicidal ideation among Russian, Somali, and Kurdish migrants in Finland. *Transcultural Psychiatry*. 2022; **59**(1): 37–51.
24. Breet E, Goldstone D, Bantjes J. Substance use and suicidal ideation and behaviour in low-and middle-income countries: a systematic review. *BMC Public Health*. 2018; **18**: 1–8.
25. Rahman A, Hafeez A. Suicidal feelings run high among mothers in refugee camps: A cross-sectional survey. *Acta Psychiatrica Scandinavica*. 2003; **108**(5): 392–3.
26. Haroz EE, Decker E, Lee C, Bolton P, Spiegel P, Ventevogel P. Evidence for suicide prevention strategies with populations in displacement: A systematic review. *Intervention Journal of Mental Health and Psychosocial Support in Conflict Affected Areas*. 2020; **18**(1): 37–44.
27. Ingabire CM, Richters A. Suicidal ideation and behavior among Congolese refugees in Rwanda: Contributing factors, consequences, and support mechanisms in the context of culture. *Frontiers in Psychiatry*. 2020; **11**: 473847.
28. Ertl V, Pfeiffer A, Schauer E, Elbert T, Neuner F. Community-implemented trauma therapy for former child soldiers in Northern Uganda: A randomized controlled trial. *JAMA*. 2011; **306**(5): 503–12.
29. Parnini SN. The crisis of the Rohingya as a Muslim minority in Myanmar and bilateral relations with Bangladesh. *Journal of Muslim Minority Affairs*. 2013; **33**(2): 281–97.
30. International Organisation of Migration. *Assessment of Suicide Risks and Factors in a Refugee Camp in Thailand*. Geneva: International Organisation of Migration; 2017. https://progressivevoicemyanmar.org/wp-content/uploads/2017/06/IOM-Mission-in-Thailand-Assessment-of-Suicide-Risks-and-Factors-in-a-Refugee-Camp-in-Thailand.pdf.
31. Ireland S. *The Impact of Displacement on Syrian Refugee and Iraqi Internally Displaced Youth in Iraq*. London: Save the Children; 2016. https://resourcecentre.savethechildren.net/pdf/save_the_children_uncertain_futures_iraq.pdf/.
32. McDonald A. *Invisible Wounds*. London: Save the Children UK; 2017. https://resourcecentre.savethechildren.net/document/invisible-wounds-impact-six-years-war-mental-health-syrias-children/.
33. Caroline A. *A Better Tomorrow: Syria's Children Have Their Say*. London: Save the Children International; 2019. https://resourcecentre.savethechildren.net/document/better-tomorrow-syrias-children-have-their-say/.
34. Salah TT, Abdelrahman A, Lien L, Eide AH, Martinez P, Hauff E. The mental health of internally displaced persons: an epidemiological study of adults in two settlements in Central Sudan. *International Journal of Social Psychiatry*. 2013; **59**(8): 782–8.
35. Colucci E, Jorm AF, Kelly CM, Minas H. Suicide first aid guidelines for assisting persons from immigrant or refugee background: A Delphi study. *Advances in Mental Health*. 2018; **16**(2): 105–16.
36. Ellis BH, Winer JP, Murray K, Barrett C. Understanding the mental health of refugees: Trauma, stress, and the cultural context. In Parekh R, Trinh NH, eds., *The Massachusetts General Hospital Textbook on Diversity and Cultural Sensitivity in Mental Health: Current Clinical Psychiatry*. Totowa, NJ: Humana Cham; 2019.
37. Chu J, Floyd R, Diep H, Pardo S, Goldblum P, Bongar B. A tool for the culturally competent assessment of suicide: The Cultural Assessment of Risk for Suicide (CARS) measure. *Psychological Assessment*. 2013; **25**(2): 424.

38. Bunney WE, Kleinman AM, Pellmar TC, Goldsmith SK, eds. *Reducing Suicide: A National Imperative*. Washington, DC: National Academies Press; 2002.

39. Vijayakumar L, Jotheeswaran AT. Suicide in refugees and asylum seekers. In Bhugra D, Craig T, Kamaldeep B, eds., *Mental Health of Refugees and Asylum Seekers*. Oxford: Oxford University Press; 2010.

40. Gopalkrishnan N. Cultural diversity and mental health: Considerations for policy and practice. *Frontiers in Public Health*. 2018; **6**: 308538.

41. World Health Organization. *Preventing Suicide: A Global Imperative*. Geneva: WHO Press; 2014. https://apps.who.int/iris/handle/10665/131056.

42. Patel V, Minas H, Cohen A, Prince M, eds. *Global Mental Health: Principles and Practice*. Oxford: Oxford University Press; 2013.

43. Akhtar A, Engels MH, Bawaneh A, Bird M, Bryant R, Cuijpers P, Hansen P, Al-Hayek H, Ilkkursun Z, Kurt G, Sijbrandij M. Cultural adaptation of a low-intensity group psychological intervention for Syrian refugees. *Intervention Journal of Mental Health and Psychosocial Support in Conflict Affected Areas*. 2021; **19**(1): 48–57.

44. Chowdhary N, Jotheeswaran AT, Nadkarni A, Hollon SD, King M, Jordans MJ, Rahman A, Verdeli H, Araya R, Patel V. The methods and outcomes of cultural adaptations of psychological treatments for depressive disorders: A systematic review. *Psychological Medicine*. 2014; **44**(6): 1131–46.

45. Shehadeh MH, Heim E, Chowdhary N, Maercker A, Albanese E. Cultural adaptation of minimally guided interventions for common mental disorders: A systematic review and meta-analysis. *Journal of Medical Internet Research: Mental Health*. 2016; **3**(3): e5776.

46. Ratkowska KA, De Leo D. Suicide in immigrants: An overview. *Open Journal of Medical Psychology*. 2013; **2**(3): 124–33.

47. World Health Organization. *Suicide Worldwide in 2019*. Geneva: WHO Press; 2021. www.who.int/publications/i/item/9789240026643.

48. Vijayakumar L. Suicide in women. *Indian Journal of Psychiatry*. 2015; **57**(Suppl 2): S233–8.

49. Tay AK, Riley A, Islam R, Welton-Mitchell C, Duchesne B, Waters V, Varner A, Moussa B, Alam AM, Elshazly MA, Silove D. The culture, mental health and psychosocial wellbeing of Rohingya refugees: A systematic review. *Epidemiology and Psychiatric Sciences*. 2019; **28**(5): 489–94.

50. Al-Haidary A, Al-Badri S. Deliberate self harm cases presented to the emergency unit of Al-Hussein General Teaching Hospital in Karbala/Iraq. *Al-Qadisiyah Medical Journal*. 2015; **11**(20): 92–7.

51. Yüzbaşıoğlu Y, Işık GÇ. Retrospective analysis of forensic cases in refugees admitted to emergency department. *American Journal of Emergency Medicine*. 2019; **37**(9): 1691–3.

52. El Halabi S, El Hayek R, Kahil K, Nofal M, El Hayek S. Characteristics of attempted suicide in the Middle East and North Africa Region: The mediating role of Arab culture and religion. *Mediterranean Journal of Emergency Medicine and Acute Care*. 2020; **1**(3).

53. Mekaoui N, Karboubi L, Ouadghiri FZ, Dakhama BS. Epidemiological aspects of suicide attempts among Moroccan children. *Pan African Medical Journal*. 2016; **24**(1): 2–5.

54. World Health Organization. *LIVE LIFE: An Implementation Guide for Suicide Prevention in Countries*. Geneva: WHO Press; 2021. www.who.int/publications/i/item/9789240026629.

55. UN Inter Agency Standing Committee. *IASC Guidance, Addressing Suicide in Humanitarian Settings*. Geneva: United Nations Office for the Coordination of Humanitarian Affairs; 2022. https://interagencystandingcommittee.org/iasc-reference-group-mental-health-and-psychosocial-support-emergency-settings/iasc-guidance-addressing-suicide-humanitarian-settings.

56. World Health Organization. *mhGAP Humanitarian Intervention Guide (mhGAP-HIG) Training of Health-Care Providers*. Geneva: WHO and UNHSCR; 2023. www.who.int/publications/i/item/9789240045361.

57. Colucci E, Jaroudy S, Rossmann M. Piloting of a suicide first aid gatekeeper training (online) for children and young people in conflict affected areas in Syria. *International Review of Psychiatry*. 2022; **34**(6): 640–8.

58. Persaud S, Rosenthal L, Arora PG. Culturally informed gatekeeper training for youth suicide prevention in Guyana: A pilot examination. *School Psychology International*. 2019; **40**(6): 624–40.

59. Perera C, Salamanca-Sanabria A, Caballero-Bernal J, Feldman L, Hansen M, Bird M, Hansen P, Dinesen C, Wiedemann N, Vallières F. No implementation without cultural adaptation: A process for culturally adapting low-intensity psychological interventions in humanitarian settings. *Conflict and Health*. 2020; **14**: 1–12.

60. Colucci, E, Lester, D. Suicide and Culture 2.0. *Hogrefe Publishing*. 2025

Chapter 10

Suicide and Occupation

Ananta Dave and Ellen Wilkinson

10.1 Introduction

Internationally, suicide continues to be a leading cause of death. The devastating impact of suicide on loved ones, communities and colleagues cannot be underestimated. Suicide is strongly associated with socio-economic disadvantage [1]. Poverty, inequality, deprivation and unemployment are linked with increased suicide rates at both an individual and a community level, with a predictable increase in suicide rates during and after periods of economic recession. In most societies, suicide is much more common in men. However, beyond these demographic factors, within the employed population, some occupations have been historically associated with higher rates of suicide deaths. There is a disproportionate impact of those deaths by suicide on other people within those occupations and their wider communities. It is important to understand the intersection of occupational factors with socio-economic disadvantage. Occupational groups are heterogeneous, so that different risk indicators within occupations may be amplified or masked [2].

Occupations which are commonly associated with an increased prevalence of deaths by suicide include those in the armed forces, farmers, health care workers (including doctors) and 'blue light' emergency workers, or 'first responders' (e.g., police, ambulance, rescue and fire personnel). These will be the focus of our discussion. These occupations may offer insights and opportunities for research into specific risk indicators and preventive factors. Understanding occupational risk factors over the span of a career from recruitment, self-selection and selection, through work environments and cultures, occupational trauma and stresses, offers the tantalising prospect of more generalisable suicide prevention. If we can develop effective interventions to prevent suicide in these professions, the overall number of suicides could be reduced.

Suicide prevention is a public health issue. Suicide affects a society's productivity and sustainability, including health care and community-critical service delivery. Each death of a doctor, health care worker, farmer, armed forces worker and emergency worker brings an economic cost to society in terms of replacing that lost working life. There is a moral, ethical and financial case to be made to understand and effectively implement suicide prevention measures in these occupational groups.

Over the course of this chapter, we discuss the evidence on the relative numbers of suicides in specific occupational groups; the risk indicators and protective factors for suicide at the individual, organisational and systemic level; and potential interventions over the course of a worker's career. Where possible, we have drawn upon systematic reviews and meta-analyses, which report comprehensive literature searches and aggregated statistical summaries, respectively. By modifying or eliminating the factors which put a worker at risk of suicide, and by strengthening or amplifying protective factors, it might be possible to reduce the number of people experiencing suicidal thoughts. In addition, other interventions might help prevent suicidal thoughts progressing to fatal acts.

While most work referenced is from developed countries, we hope that the insights gained and the interventions discussed will be applicable and adaptable across all societies and nations.

10.2 What Does the Evidence Tell Us about Occupational Risk?

Information about occupational risks for suicide is rarely based on consistently applied statistical methods. A comprehensive review of the literature concerning suicides by occupation reported on the 34 highest-quality studies [3]. Appropriate control populations for comparison are either the general population or another occupational group. This review used an international coding for occupations (ICSO) and found that out of nine occupational groupings, only two had a lower-than-average suicide mortality: group 1, managers and legislators, and group 4, clerical workers. Elevated suicide mortality rates were described in many occupations with mainly manual skills, including labourers, cleaners, machine operators, ships' deck crew, farmers, agricultural workers, builders and electricians. Different statistical terms give varying and sometimes confusing perspectives on occupational risk (see Table 10.1 for definitions of statistical terms). Also, the 'healthy worker effect' refers to the concept that the working population is, by definition, healthier than people who have been screened out of the workforce due to current or historic ill health.

The fourth progress report of the UK National Suicide Prevention Strategy [4] noted a 44% higher risk of suicide in males working in the lowest-skilled occupations and a 35% higher risk among males in skilled trades than the male national average. The risk of suicide was elevated for those in culture, media and sport occupations; for males the risk was 20% higher than the male national average, and for females the risk was 69% higher than the female

Table 10.1 Statistical terms used in reporting occupational risks of suicide

Acronym	Statistic	Formula	Comment
OR	Odds ratio	Compares odds of occurrence between two groups	Quantifies the strength of an association. Correlation does not imply causation.
RR	Rate ratio	Compares rate of occurrence between two groups	
	Suicide rate per 100,000	Suicide or open verdict / population at risk (e.g., census population in occupation)	Used to report crude suicide rates
	Age standardised suicide rate	Number of deaths in age group / mid-year population in same age group	Allows populations with different age structures to be compared

Table 10.1 (cont.)

Acronym	Statistic	Formula	Comment
PMR	Proportionate mortality ratio	Deaths by suicide / all deaths in same occupation	>100 indicates increased mortality. Widely used to measure occupational suicide rates in the absence of age-specific occupational population counts. Affected by mortality due to other causes (i.e., occupations with low mortality rates from other causes will have a higher PMR). Can be calculated in the absence of census data. Not useful in tracking change over time.
SMR	Standardised mortality ratio	Number of deaths (observed) for specified occupation / age matched rates in the general population (expected) × 100	>100 indicates increased mortality. Suicide rate can be compared with the age matched general population. SMR is not useful in tracking change over time. A SMR where the 95% confidence interval does not encompass 100 implies there is a statistically significant difference in rates when comparing the occupational population with the general population.

national average. Internationally, more recent data are less reliable due to variable delays in death investigation and registration. This makes it difficult to comment at the present time on the impact of the COVID-19 pandemic on occupational mortality by suicide.

The following paragraphs summarise what is known about the prevalence, risk and protective factors and potential interventions in the selected occupations.

For agricultural workers, variations in the definition of farmers, fishers and forestry workers create challenges in making temporal, international and national data comparisons. However, a systematic review of 65 international population studies, which led to a meta-analysis of 32 studies, confirmed a statistically significant increased suicide rate in this occupational group across the world and over time [5]. 'Farmers' comprise people with diverse socioeconomic status, from owners of large agricultural businesses, through skilled people who are directly employed, to unskilled, casual and migrant labourers. In India, farmer suicides have been in the spotlight for several years, and in 2020 a total of 10,677 persons involved in farming (farmers/cultivators and agricultural labourers) died by suicide, accounting for 7% of total suicide deaths [6]. In a country where suicide numbers are listed in crime statistics, it is probable that there is systematic under-estimation. Suicide was not fully decriminalised in India until 2017.

UK Armed Forces statistics are released annually by the UK Defence Statistics Authority [7]. For regular UK armed forces, since 2017, the British Army has experienced similar suicide rates to the age-matched general population, and the Royal Navy and Royal Air Force have experienced significantly lower rates. Suicide rates (age standardised) among males for UK combined armed forces were 8 per 100,000 over 20 years. However, in the last five years, the rate of suicide increased among army males from 6 per 100,000 in 2014 to 17 per 100,000 in 2019, but this remains lower than that of the age-matched UK male population. International comparisons are fraught with difficulties of definition and methodology, but the North Atlantic Treaty Organisation (NATO) Science and Technology Organisation surveys rates worldwide [8]. In the US, active service members reported a suicide mortality rate of 28.7 per 100,000 in 2020. The most recent comparison with data from the age-matched general population in 2019 showed similar rates. Evidence of elevated rates of suicide in people after leaving military service is also mixed, with stronger evidence for a rise in those leaving involuntarily, after a shorter period of service or serving at lower ranks [9]. In the US in 2017, the suicide rate for veterans was 1.5 times the rate for non-veteran adults, after adjusting for population differences in age and sex [10].

For health care workers, studies in Europe and North America over the last few decades using the standardised mortality ratio (SMR) have looked at suicide rates in health care professionals in general as well as in doctors (or physicians) in particular, with varying results. The studies consistently point to a higher rate of suicide among female health care workers.

An early analysis by Lindeman and colleagues using SMR found that all doctors were at higher risk and had higher rates of suicide compared to the general population, with female rates being the highest [11]. In England, Hawton concluded that between 1979 and 1995 the suicide rate using SMR in female doctors was significantly higher than in the general population [12].

Using SMR, the Office for National Statistics in England suggests that health professionals as a whole are not at increased risk of suicide compared to the general population, with a 16% reduced risk of suicide relative to the national average between 2011 and 2015 [13]. Low risk of suicide was particularly reported among medical practitioners (37% lower). However, over the same period (2011–15), the risk of suicide among female health professionals was 24% higher than the national average. This finding is largely explained by the higher risk of suicide among nurses, which was 23% above the national average in this analysis. Overall, in males and females, there were more than 40 suicides by nurses per year in 2011–20.

A more recent meta-analysis from the US and Europe showed that doctors (referred to as 'physicians' in this article) were at higher risk of suicide compared to the general population across America and Europe, with an overall SMR of 1.44 and SMR for female doctors of 1.9, and with some specialties, such as anaesthesiologists, psychiatrists, general practitioners and general surgeons, at higher risk within this group [14]. These discrepant numbers may be explained by geographical and temporal differences. There may also be variation across subgroups (e.g., gender, speciality and age).

Emergency services workers, otherwise known as 'blue light' workers or first responders, include fire, ambulance, police and search and rescue workers. International evidence for suicide rates in emergency personnel is mixed. However, it has been frequently noted that police are more likely to die from suicide than in the line of duty. In a meta-analysis of police suicides there were regional differences, with rates in the Americas and Europe higher than in the Caribbean and Asian regions [15]. There were also differences in rates among federal, regional and municipal police forces. In a detailed systematic review in which 63 studies were included, the majority examined police officers, with firefighters, emergency medical technicians and paramedics included [16]. An elevated risk of suicide, suicidal thoughts and behaviours relative to the general population in first responders was reported in some. However, in studies where risk relative to general population samples did not appear higher (or, indeed, were lower), it was suggested that this could be an artefact of the healthy worker effect.

10.3 Understanding Risk Indicators and Protective Factors

Suicide is multifactorial. Risk indicators for suicide in these specific occupations may be related to underlying characteristics of those employed, the quality of working conditions and common occupational stressors, access to means or many other associated factors. Vulnerabilities across the lifespan may interact, and it is widely recognised that the progression from predisposition to action is unlikely to follow a linear causal chain.

10.4 Agriculture

Suicide rates in farmers appear elevated in the absence of higher rates of diagnosed mental illness [17]. Rurality is a recognised risk factor, and isolation may reduce access to support services. Poor mental health and suicide risk in farming have been attributed to complex interconnected cultural, environmental, geographical, social and psychological risk factors. Qualitative research in Australia proposes two distinct pathways to suicide in farmers: (1) an acute situational pathway (reflecting risk factors associated with interpersonal relationships, financial stressors and retirement) and (2) a more protracted pathway linked with mental illness [18]. Unsustainable long working hours, time pressures and physical demands of the role of farming may drive an inability to prioritise well-being. Also, cultural attitudes of vulnerability may discourage health-seeking behaviour, especially in relation to mental ill health or psychological distress.

Access to lethal firearms and pesticides has been linked internationally with farmer suicides, but this explanation does not tell the whole story. Woollacott [19] explored the term 'rural stress', suggesting that the masculine social construction of esteem as a 'provider' to the community triggers significant loss of status in the face of suicidal feelings. Modern farming requires adaptability to change as farming practices evolve due to new economic models and environmental challenges. Farming as a family business within a close-knit community can be supportive. However, the interdigitation of family stresses with business complicates expectations and compounds the impact of agricultural crises. Unpredictable weather, climate change, disease, rapidly changing commodity prices and catastrophic situations beyond the control of the farmer can threaten the livelihoods of individuals, families and communities. Especially in low- and middle-income countries (LMICs), the politics and economics of farming may lead to debt, bankruptcy and subsequent shame and loss of honour.

10.5 Armed Forces

For serving armed forces personnel, predisposing factors to suicide may lie in early childhood adversity, including a family or close history of suicide. A link exists between childhood adversity, moral injury and a range of mental health disorders, though not specifically suicide [20]. Suicide may be precipitated by personal stress, including loss events, impairment associated with physical illness or professional challenges (e.g., an investigation, disciplinary or legal process). Military personnel experience extreme stress in their normal duties – the intense, traumatic environment of conflict. Mental illness may increase risk in isolation or by compounding antecedents. Substance misuse can be a cause and/or consequence of other risk factors. A culture of stigma and self-stigma about what is perceived as weakness or fragility may impede help-seeking for acute distress or mental illness. Fear and anxiety about threats to job security or career progression can prevent disclosure of a psychological problem. This could block information sharing – for example, self-harm, a sign of escalating risk, could be managed in a civilian setting with information withheld from military health services due to patient confidentiality. Sometimes, access to and familiarisation with weapons becomes a final enabler to acting on suicidal thoughts. In the US Armed Forces, most suicide deaths involve firearms, although the weapons are predominantly privately owned [21]. There are recognised protective factors, including 'the healthy worker effect'. The armed forces have an acculturation, a strong culture of camaraderie with support from colleagues and managers which can promote resilience, with strong group loyalty, bonding and mutual dependence encouraged at all levels in the services, particularly in small combat units.

10.6 Health Care

Gerada noted that personality traits which make good doctors are also linked to self-criticism, guilt, self-blame and difficulty seeking help [22]. Doctors may lack a safe outlet to process the emotional impact of their work, increasing their risk of depression, substance misuse and suicide.

Meltzer and Teoh both summarise risk indicators in health professionals related to individual factors: personal characteristics, socio-demographic background and personality [23,24]. Mental illness is common in health care workers, interacting with other vulnerabilities. Health care workers report higher rates of work-related stress, depression and anxiety than any other sector. Common causes are perceived high workload, intensity and complexity of work, rapid organisational change, low control and support, and personal experiences of bullying and harassment. Rates of burnout in doctors are high, possibly increasing, even early in their careers.

Conflict between work and personal life is a risk factor for mental health problems in doctors, especially among general practitioners (GPs). Stigma and self-stigma may mean the problem is under-estimated and creates barriers to treatment in health care workers. Occupational factors may include the nature of work, such as speciality, seniority, the emotional demands of the job and dealing with death. Organisational factors concern how work is designed and organised, such as workload, working hours, staffing levels, autonomy, support and resourcing. Additional professional stressors include complaints or regulatory referrals. Though rewarding work can be a protective factor, it can engender time-based conflict (time spent working reduces that available to relax or participate in family life) and strain-based conflict (strain relating to the job, such as anxiety or irritability, or ruminating excessively about work).

Easy access to lethal drugs and relevant knowledge on methods of suicide has been proposed as an explanation for the increased risk in health care workers. In a detailed UK review of 281 nurses who died by suicide between 2011 and 2016, a total of 204 (73%) were women [25]. The commonest suicide method for female nurses was self-poisoning (42%) using psychotropics, opiates and/or paracetamol.

10.7 Emergency Services

For emergency services workers, a baseline survey was published in 2015 by MIND, a leading UK mental health charity. Self-reported mental health service usage among ambulance (24.56%), fire (29.17%) and police personnel (30.82%) was above the general population level [26]. A total of 87.6% of personnel reported stress and poor mental health. This could reflect greater need among emergency service personnel or the self-selecting sample of this survey. Emergency personnel were less likely to take sickness leave, reflecting a culture of 'presenteeism'. They were twice as likely as the general workforce to identify problems at work as the main cause of mental health problems. Workload and management pressure were perceived to be greater stressors than exposure to trauma, notably including excessive workload (56%), pressure from management (55%), organisational upheaval (52%) and long hours (45%). One MIND press release stated that 'one in four emergency services workers has thought about ending their lives'.

A small US study of 200 first responders highlighted similar trends: 14% reported moderate-severe and severe depressive symptoms, 28% reported moderate-severe and severe anxiety symptoms, 26% reported significant symptoms of post-traumatic stress disorder (PTSD) and 31% reported harmful/hazardous alcohol use and dependence [27].

A large UK study of 40,299 police staff [28], which did not focus on mental health, showed probable depression was most frequently reported (9.8%), followed by anxiety (8.5%) and post-traumatic stress disorder (3.9%). Rates of anxiety or depression in police employees were doubled in those exposed to recent traumatic incidents compared to those without trauma exposure, with a sixfold increase in post-traumatic stress disorder. These rates are lower than the general population, perhaps reflecting the healthy worker effect.

10.8 Interventions

Prospective research with a defined primary outcome of suicide is rare due to the power required to signal statistically significant change for a rare event [29]. Many interventions are deemed effective based on proxy outcomes of non-fatal self-harm or suicidal ideation. Given the multifactorial aetiology of suicide, interventions may be made at three levels: the whole population (or universal level), an intermediate selected group with some indicators of increased risk or an individual known or predicted to be at risk. In the context of occupational prevention, there are individual, workplace-based, occupational and population-based interventions.

Employing organisations, trade unions, professional bodies and welfare organisations, especially those familiar and trusted by the occupational group, have an important role in shaping a help-seeking culture, making support acceptable and accessible to individuals in distress or becoming unwell. They can also set standards for employers in managing common occupational stresses and play a part in postvention – ensuring that those bereaved by the suicide of a colleague, friend or family member receive timely, effective support, thus reducing their own risk [30].

10.9 Farmers

Individual farmers can be helped by improved access to treatment for mental illness and support with distress. Farmers need encouragement to override their instinct to manage alone and to recognise the benefits of support from family and friends – or even the vital companionship of their farm dog. Welfare and insurance services that are already acceptable to farmers can provide targeted psychological support in places where farmers routinely visit, such as agricultural markets. They can also offer peer support from people who understand the industry, reducing cultural stigma in seeking help [31]. Organisations such as the Farming Community Network, which is specifically mentioned in the fourth progress report on the UK National Suicide Prevention Strategy [32], can provide advice and support via help-lines and direct access. Suspect, Connect, Ask, Refer, Follow-Up (SCARF), a well-being and suicide prevention education workshop in New South Wales, significantly and immediately increased suicide literacy and confidence to assist others, with significantly improved mental well-being at three-month follow-up [33]. The primary care team and any specialist mental health providers need to understand the industry, recognise emotional and practical difficulties in accessing appointments, address stresses holistically and treat illness.

Focussing on the safe management of firearms by using gun locks and gun safes within the therapeutic process can prevent suicides at an individual level. At a governmental level, guidance, along with firearm and pesticide legislation, have restricted access to means and suicide levels have fallen. Effective gun licensing can reduce the risk of impulsive fatal firearm use. Hawton studied 719 suicides involving firearms in farmers of both genders in England and Wales between 1981 and 1993 [34]. There was a reduction in firearm death rates and in farming suicides, particularly after 1989 when there was national legislation on firearm ownership, registration and storage. Bonvoisin has summarised the impact of pesticide bans on reducing suicides in India, Sri Lanka, Bangladesh and South Korea and has called for further reductions in pesticide availability [35].

Wherever possible, developing a fair business model through legislation and regulation, financial and emotional support during unexpected crises, and action on climate change could cushion the precarious nature of farming. Whole industry data collection is more challenging where there is no single employer or employment structure, and the only source of data is national statistics.

10.10 Military Personnel

For armed forces personnel, surveillance data, preferably available in real time, can clarify risk indicators and inform responses to emerging challenges. Leadership and accountability, with the belief that suicides are preventable, has driven detailed strategies to reduce military and veteran suicides worldwide. In 2003 Knox published on a US Air Force programme demonstrating a sustained 33% decline of relative risk in the suicide rate between 1990–6 and 1997–2002 after its implementation [36]. Leadership features strongly, promoting resilience, adaptive behaviours and cultures, fostering the 'wingman culture', encouraging responsible help-seeking and intolerance of belittling or humiliation which might deter airmen from seeking professional help. Leaders are expected to be aware of suicide risk factors and signs. They are expected to provide guidance and support, and to disseminate their knowledge so that colleagues have tools to identify distress signals and seek care.

Whole military systems aim to reduce stigma, using male-friendly terms like 'mental fitness'. Peer support includes awareness and advice for family and friends to support colleagues in crisis. Timely and accessible treatment for mental disorders, including substance misuse, psychological distress and moral injury, can reduce risk. Appropriate information sharing, with safe management of confidentiality, is a vital component of treatment. Recognition that self-harm is a risk factor facilitates the provision of effective and non-judgmental support. Media portrayal of suicide in military personnel can be particularly critical or celebratory, increasing risk within the local military and civilian community. Managerial support when dealing with career-threatening situations such as disciplinary processes, managing transitions such as leaving military service, can reduce risk. Reducing access to weapons can reduce the harm associated with impulsive suicidal ideation. A change in UK policy in the mid-1990s that restricted access to weapons in the army resulted in a decrease in suicides by 'firearms and explosives'.

10.11 Health Care Workers

For health care workers, the most modifiable factor is to improve access to treatment for mental illness and substance misuse, with reduced stigma, secrecy and fair management of confidentiality. The Practitioner Health Programme in the UK is a good example of this approach [37]. Education and support are needed to help workers recognise and prioritise their health and well-being needs early, and to normalise help-seeking. Services should be specific for various levels of need and should reduce isolation. For example, the fifth progress report on the UK suicide strategy, building on a study of suicides by female nurses, describes a comprehensive package of emotional, psychological and practical support for NHS staff [38]. A toolkit for suicide prevention has been produced by NHS Employers in the UK [39].

Effective treatment and rehabilitation for mental illness sends a strong message that doctors with mental illness can not only survive but thrive. In turn, they can bring unique empathy and understanding, further reducing stigma. Action is needed to address discrimination in referrals to the regulator. Employer referrals to the General Medical Council (GMC) are twice as likely for Black, Asian and minority ethnic doctors and International Medical Graduates [40]. Health care workers need autonomy, a sense of control, fairness and a compassionate culture. Actions to reduce discrimination, improve inclusion and effective remediation could reduce distress associated with referrals [41]. In view of the potential impact of suicide on the health care community, active postvention needs to be optimal [42].

For emergency workers, initiatives from Canada and the UK have followed a systematic preventative approach. A multifaceted intervention for police in Montreal reported on a 12- and 22-year follow-up [43]. The programme trained all officers, supervisors, and union representatives as volunteers, and established a help-line and publicity campaign. It showed a significant reduction in police suicide after 12 years, which was sustained at 22 years. There were positive differences between Montreal and Quebec, which did not receive the intervention, although demographic changes over time could have created bias.

In the UK a mental health charity implemented interventions to improve mental health (not specifically aiming to preventing suicide) as part of the Blue Light Programme involving ambulance staff. This involved a combination of addressing stigma, training and empowering staff, and building networks [44]. Between 2015 and 2019, compared to staff and volunteers who were not involved in the programme, participants felt more encouraged by their organisation to talk about mental health (64% compared with 29%), support people with mental health problems (53% versus 34%) and became more aware of support available to manage their mental health.

The Houston Fire Service developed psychologist-led interventions over three phases which focussed on raising awareness and augmenting education, targeting managers and leaders to empower them [45]. An online presentation taught various skills around identification of a problem and crisis, communication techniques, how to deal with a suicidal member, the Firefighter Support Network (FSN) and other helpful resources. Although numbers were small, there was some reduction in suicides in active service firefighters, with a five-year gap of no suicides between 2007 and 2012 after 8 in the preceding 24 years.

10.12 Discussion

The workers discussed throughout this chapter share a strong and distinct identity, a quasi-heroic status within the wider community and a reputation for invulnerability. All experience highly stressful working conditions, long hours and routine exposure to trauma or disaster. They may have to cope with unpredictability at work, a lack of control over external factors and a significant, potentially catastrophic impact of their actions. Some characteristics like being obsessional, hard-working and self-critical may be desirable; they may also worsen the impact of a deviation from 'normal function' with overzealous self-blame and demoralisation. Factors which make a good doctor, farmer, soldier or emergency worker may therefore present their own risks. This makes it important to instil a sense of the inherently stressful but rewarding nature of the occupation at the beginning of a career.

A primacy of work over personal life may contribute to problems in relationships and friendships or a default to dysfunctional coping mechanisms such as alcohol and substance misuse. The possible consequences of seeking help, such as regulatory sanctions or ostracism, may make access to services challenging, with understandable fear of confidentiality breaches. The high status of the work, and stigma associated with perceived weakness, may make it difficult to prioritise self-care. In society, people in these careers are either deified or vilified with a corresponding adverse impact on workers:

> The days of the doctor being the superhuman, all-giving, sacrificing individual are over. It is now time to have a more realistic contract with our patients and with the health systems in which we work, a contract where the doctor is cared for and can expect the same compassion as the patients they treat. [46]

Historically, accountability and leadership at the organisational or occupational level in relation to workforce well-being have been weak and avoidant, but there are examples where strong leadership and vision have demonstrated benefits, including the US Air Force (USAF), Montreal Police, Houston Fire Service and the NHS in the UK.

National surveillance using robust standardised statistical methods and definitions, ideally providing real-time data, could offer early warning signs of occupational health trends. Many armed forces now systematically collect data at the national level to inform their prevention strategies. It is important to consider the risks related to the demographics of the profession, like the higher risk to female health professionals in a workforce where females increasingly predominate. Farmers are more dispersed, but a Union or welfare organisation could track deaths and share learning. Societal or cultural incentives to under-report suicide deaths should be considered.

Within organisations, embedding protective practices like induction, education and specific models of support can make a difference. Senior and respected people willing to show vulnerability can act as positive role models.

Employers, regulators, trade unions or welfare organisations could embed targeted strategies for key occupations to reduce stigma around mental ill health. This could include stories of hope and recovery from those who have survived a crisis and returned to their careers or successfully moved on with their lives. Facilitating networks of peer support can strengthen prevention and augment other interventions. 'Mental fitness' has been successfully introduced as a targeted occupational intervention in military settings. Insight and help-seeking are reframed as strengths rather than weaknesses.

Stress at work can be perceived as being due to stressful working conditions rather than simply the traumatic nature of the work. It can lead to suicidality directly or indirectly via mental illness. The UK Health and Safety Executive (HSE) describe six main areas that can prevent work-related stress if well managed. These are demands, control, support, relationships, role and change [47].

Suicide awareness work by the voluntary sector can overcome some of the barriers to seeking help while instilling some useful skills around supportive conversations with, for example, people expressing suicidal ideas or behaviours. This may be through learning specific intervention skills such as Mental Health First Aid (MHFA) or Applied Suicide Intervention Skills Training (ASIST).

Whole population or community approaches are important interventions. These may include legislation and regulation to reduce access to means at population, occupational or individual levels, raising awareness and inspiring culture change. Successful examples of using legislation to reduce suicides include reduction of access to firearms through legislation, restriction of sales of analgesic medication in the UK, and tightening of requirements for the sale and storage of pesticides in South Asia.

Media coverage of deaths by suicide, including in those in high-status occupations, should be especially cautious and accompanied by positive stories of hope and recovery, with an awareness of the *Papageno* v. *Werther* effects [48]. Guidelines should inform and govern media coverage [49,50]. The media portrayal of suicides may be judgmental, speculative or prurient, which risks creating a ripple effect within the close-knit 'work family' and community, heightening the adverse impact of a colleague's suicide. Postvention (specialist bereavement support following death by suicide) within the workplace is recommended to reduce contagion.

The recently completed GMC commissioned review of doctors' deaths undertaken by Professor Louis Appleby made very useful recommendations for high-risk groups comprising real-time surveillance, targeted postvention and media management [50].

For each of these occupations, at an individual level, the focus needs to be firmly on keeping people well from the time they enter the profession or occupation and throughout their career. People within an occupation may move into an at-risk group because of changes and transitions which can create significant stresses. Improved rapid and normalised access to individual support is needed for stressful life events (whether occupational or personal), preferably close to the workplace, ideally intervening before someone becomes mentally unwell or suicidal.

Opportunities to remediate, rehabilitate and successfully return to practice should be accessible wherever possible. If this is not accepted by the worker, then clear, well-supported pathways out of an occupation are needed. Resignation, redeployment or early retirement when it is not of the individual's choice need addressing. If there is a career threatening disciplinary, regulatory, criminal or legal process, appropriate agencies must be accessible to offer advocacy and non-judgmental support.

Access to care and effective treatment for mental illness and substance misuse must be improved, keeping in mind common barriers to help-seeking and assuring confidentiality and privacy. A good example of this is the Practitioner Health Programme for UK doctors [51].

When a person becomes suicidal, whether through mental illness or situational distress, early intervention can prevent suicidal ideation progressing to suicidal behaviour. Essentially, suicide prevention should start well before a person becomes suicidal.

10.13 Conclusions

We have considered the suicide rates in specific occupational groups: doctors, health professionals, emergency 'blue light' workers, farmers and armed forces personnel.

The rates of suicide in these professional groups have fluctuated above the rates for the general population. Just as significantly, suicide in these professions can impact on colleagues, students, trainees, patients, families and whole communities, adversely affecting services, and the economy and health of nations.

Intervention should be multifaceted across the whole community and shared across organisations and agencies, driven by clear and compassionate belief and leadership. The pact with society needs to change so that everyone can do something to prevent the tragic loss of life of a suicide death.

The contribution to suicide prevention of those who have been bereaved by suicide is immense. We owe a debt of gratitude to them. Their losses have led to learning for many, and we offer hope that they find some solace and healing by inspiring future change for the better.

References

1. Samaritans. *Dying from Inequality: Socioeconomic Disadvantage and Suicidal Behaviour*. 2017. www.samaritans.org/wales/about-samaritans/research-policy/inequality-suicide/socioeconomic-disadvantage-and-suicidal-behaviour.
2. Roberts SE, Jaremin B, Lloyd K. High-risk occupations for suicide. *Psychological Medicine*. 2013; **43**(6): 1231–40.
3. Milner A, Spittal M, Pirkis J, et al. Suicide risk by occupation: Systematic review and meta-analysis. *British Journal of Psychiatry*. 2013; **203**: 409–16.
4. HM Government. *Preventing Suicide in England: Fourth Progress Report of the Cross-government Outcomes Strategy to Save Lives*. 2019. https://assets.publishing.service.gov.uk/media/5c459a9de5274a6e40f38fc1/national-suicide-prevention-strategy-4th-progress-report.pdf.
5. Klingelschmidt J, Milner A, Khireddine-Medouni I, et al. Suicide among agricultural, forestry, and fishery workers: A systematic literature review and meta-analysis. *Scand J Work Environ Health*. 2018; **44**(1): 3–15.
6. National Crime Records Bureau. *Accidental Deaths and Suicides in India*. New Delhi: Ministry of Home Affairs; 2020.
7. UK Ministry of Defence. *Suicides in the UK Regular Armed Forces: Annual Summary and Trends over Time 1 January 1984 to 31 December 2021*. London: UK Ministry of Defence; 2022.
8. North Atlantic Treaty Organisation, Science and Technology. *Military Suicide Prevention: Report Prepared for NATO Leadership*. Salisbury: STO NATO; 2018.
9. Kapur N, While D, Blatchley N, et al. Suicide after leaving the UK Armed Forces: A cohort study. *PLoS Medicine*. 2009; **6**(3): e1000026.
10. Schernhammer ES, Colditz GA. Suicide rates among physicians: A quantitative and gender assessment (meta-analysis). *American Journal of Psychiatry*. 2004; **161**: 2295–302.
11. Lindeman S, Laara E, Hakko H, et al. A systematic review on gender-specific

suicide mortality in medical doctors. *British Journal of Psychiatry*. 1996; **168**(3): 274–9.

12. Hawton K. Suicide in doctors: A study of risk according to gender, seniority and speciality in medical practitioners in England and Wales 1979–1995. *Journal of Epidemiology and Community Health* 2001; **55**(5): 296–300.
13. Office for National Statistics. *Suicide by Occupation, England: 2011 to 2015*. ONS; 2017.
14. Dutheil F, Aubert C, Pereira B, et al. Suicide among physicians and health-care workers: A systematic review and meta-analysis. *PLoS One*. 2019 December; **14**(12): e0226361.
15. Loo R. A meta-analysis of police suicide rates: Findings and issues. *Suicide and Life Threatening Behavior*. 2003; **33**(3): 313–25.
16. Stanley IH, Hom MA, Joiner TE, et al. A systematic review of suicidal thoughts and behaviors among police officers, firefighters, EMTs and paramedics. *Clinical Psychology Review*. 2016; **44**(3): 25–44.
17. Malmberg A, Hawton K, Simkin S. A study of suicide in farmers in England and Wales. *Journal of Psychosomatic Research*. 1997; **43**(1): 107–11.
18. Kennedy A, Brumby S, Versace VL, et al. Online assessment of suicide stigma, literacy and effect in Australia's rural farming community. *BMC Public Health*. 2018; **18**(1): 846.
19. Woollacott R. *Walking with Farmers and Talking about Suicidal Feelings: An Interpretative Phenomenological Analysis*. Bristol: University of the West of England; 2020.
20. Williamson V, Greenberg N, Murphy D. Predictors of moral injury in UK treatment seeking veterans. *Child Abuse and Neglect*. 2021 February; **112**: 104889.
21. US Government. *Reducing Military and Veteran Suicide: Advancing a Comprehensive, Cross-Sector, Evidence-Informed Public Health Strategy*. Washington, DC: Government Printing Office; 2021.
22. Gerada C. Doctors, suicide and mental illness. *BJPsych Bulletin*. 2018; **42**(4): 165–8.
23. Meltzer H, Griffiths C, Brock A, et al. Patterns of suicide by occupation in England and Wales: 2001–2005. *British Journal of Psychiatry* 2008; **193**(1): 73–6.
24. Kinman G, Teoh K. *What Could Make a Difference to the Mental Health of UK Doctors? A Review of the Research Evidence*. Society of Occupational Medicine; 2018. www.som.org.uk/sites/som.org.uk/files/What_could_make_a_difference_to_the_mental_health_of_UK_doctors_LTF_SOM.pdf.
25. National Confidential Inquiry into Suicide and Safety in Mental Health (NCISH). *Suicide by Female Nurses: A Brief Report*. Manchester: University of Manchester; 2020.
26. MIND. Wellbeing and Mental Health Support in the Emergency Services. London: MIND UK; 2020.
27. Jones S, Nagela C, McSweeney J, et al. Prevalence and correlates of psychiatric symptoms among first responders in a Southern State. *Archives of Psychiatric Nursing*. 2018; **32**(6): 828–35.
28. Stevelink S, Opie E, Pernet D, et al. Probable PTSD, depression and anxiety in 40,299 UK police officers and staff: Prevalence, risk factors and associations with blood pressure. *PLoS One* 2020; **15**(11): e0240902.
29. Riblet V, Shiner B, Young-Xu Y, et al. Strategies to prevent death by suicide: Meta-analysis of randomised controlled trials. *Br J Psych*. 2017; **210**: 396–402.
30. McDonnell S, Nelson PA, Leonard S, et al. Evaluation of the impact of the PABBS suicide bereavement training on clinicians' knowledge and skills: A pilot study. *Journal of Crisis Intervention and Suicide Prevention*. 2020; **10**: 1–8.
31. Bowersox NW, Jagusch J, Garlick J, et al. Peer based interventions targeting suicide prevention: A scoping review. *American Journal of Community Psychology*. 2021; **689**(1–2): 232–48.
32. HM Government. *Preventing Suicide in England: Fifth Progress Report of the Cross-government Outcomes Strategy to Save Lives*. London: HMSO; 2021. https://assets.publishing.service.gov.uk/media/605e4e

f48fa8f53927b08b2e/fifth-suicide-prevention-strategy-progress-report.pdf.

33. Perceval M, Reddy P, Ross V, et al. Evaluation of the SCARF wellbeing and suicide prevention programme for rural Australian communities. *Journal of Rural Health* 2020; **36**(2): 247–54.

34. Hawton K, et al. Methods used for suicide by farmers in England and Wales: The contribution of availability and its relevance to prevention. *British Journal of Psychiatry*. 1998; **173**(10): 320–4.

35. Bonvoisin T, Utyasheva L, Knipe D, et al. Suicide by pesticide poisoning in India: A review of pesticide regulations and their impact on suicide trends. *BMC Public Health*. 2020; **20**(1): 251.

36. Knox KL, Pflanz S, Talcott GW, et al. The US Air Force suicide prevention program: Implications for public health policy. *American Journal of Public Health*. 2010; **100**(12): 2457–63.

37. Brooks S, Gerada C, Chalder T. The specific needs of doctors with mental health problems: Qualitative analysis of doctor-patients' experiences with the Practitioner Health Programme. *J Ment Health*. 2017; **26**(2): 161–6.

38. HM Government. *Preventing Suicide in England: Fifth Progress Report of the Cross-government Outcomes Strategy to Save Lives*. 2021. London: HMSO; 2021. https://assets.publishing.service.gov.uk/media/605e4ef48fa8f53927b08b2e/fifth-suicide-prevention-strategy-progress-report.pdf.

39. www.nhsemployers.org/articles/suicide-prevention-and-postvention.

40. General Medical Council. *Fair to Refer: Reducing Disproportionality in Fitness to Practice Concerns Reported to the GMC*. 2019. www.gmc-uk.org/-/media/documents/fair-to-refer-report_pdf-79011677.pdf.

41. Dave A, Bhatti N, Geddes R. Does a narrow definition of medical professionalism lead to systemic bias and differential outcomes? *Journal of Health Policy & Opinion*. 2021; **14**: 1–12.

42. Torry R, Kinman G. *Responding to the Death by Suicide of a Colleague in Primary Care*. Louise Tebboth Foundation. www.som.org.uk/sites/som.org.uk/files/LTF_SOM_Responding_to_the_death_by_suicide_of_a_colleague_in_Primary_Care.pdf.

43. Mishara B, Fortin L. Long term effects of a police suicide prevention programme. *Crisis: Journal of Crisis Intervention and Suicide Prevention*. 2022; **43**: 234–43.

44. MIND. *Wellbeing and Mental Health Support in the Emergency Services*. 2023. www.mind.org.uk/media-a/4572/20046_mind-blue-light-programme-legacy-report-v12_online.pdf.

45. Finney E, Buser S, Schwartz J, et al. Suicide prevention in fire service: The Houston Fire Department (HFD) model. *Aggression and Violent Behaviour*. 2015; **21**: 1–4.

46. Gerada C. *The Wounded Healer: Report on the First 10 Years of Practitioner Health Service*. Practitioner Health Programme; 2018. www.practitionerhealth.nhs.uk/media/content/files/PHP-report-web%20version%20final%20copy.pdf.

47. Health and Safety Executive. *Tackling Work-Related Stress Using the Management Standards Approach: A Step-by-Step Approach*. 2019. www.hse.gov.uk/pubns/wbk01.htm.

48. Niederkrotenthaler T, Voracek M, Herberth A, et al. Role of media reports in completed and prevented suicide: *Werther v. Papageno* effects. *British Journal of Psychiatry*. 2010; **197**: 234–43.

49. Samaritans. *Media Guidelines for Reporting Suicide*. 2017. https://media.samaritans.org/documents/Samaritans_Media_Guidelines_UK_Apr17_Final_web.pdf.

50. World Health Organization. *Preventing Suicide: A Resource for Media Professionals*. September 2017. www.who.int/publications/i/item/WHO-MSD-MER-17.5.

51. General Medical Council. *Doctors Who Commit Suicide while under GMC Fitness to Practise Investigation*. 2014. www.gmc-uk.org/-/media/documents/Internal_review_into_suicide_in_FTP_processes.pdf_59088696.pdf.

Chapter 11

Substance Use Disorders and Suicide

Mohammed T. Abou-Saleh

11.1 Introduction

Suicide is a global public health issue. The World Health Organization (WHO) report on suicide estimated that globally 804,000 people died by suicide in 2012. The majority of suicides occur in low- and middle-income countries (75.5%), with a higher prevalence among men compared to women, peaking between the age of 15 and 24 years among women and between the age of 25 and 45 years among men [1].

The 2016 Global Burden of Disease Study reported that suicide was one of the top-ten leading causes of death in Western European countries. Globally age-standardised mortality rates for suicide have greatly reduced since 1990, but suicide remains an important contributor to mortality worldwide. Suicide mortality was variable across locations, between sexes and between age groups [2].

The WHO comprehensive action plan 2013–20 has adopted a multisectoral approach, through coordinated services from the health and social sectors, with an emphasis on promotion, prevention, treatment, rehabilitation, care and recovery. The plan mandates all countries to take actions and proposes key indicators and targets that can be used to evaluate levels of implementation, progress and impact. The action plan has, at its core, the globally accepted principle that there is 'no health without mental health' [3].

Importantly, the plan has essential conceptual and strategic links to the global strategy to reduce the harmful use of alcohol, draws on WHO's regional action plans and strategies for mental health and substance abuse, and builds upon the work of WHO's Mental Health Gap Action Programme (mhGAP).

The plan considered suicide prevention an important priority, with the global target that the rate of suicide in countries will be reduced by 10% by the year 2020. Importantly, the plan was followed by the *WHO Report on Preventing Suicide: A Global Imperative* that provides guidance on the way forward to suicide prevention.

The scope of this chapter is to provide an overview of the relationship between substance use disorders (SUDs) and suicidal behaviour, its epidemiology, determinants and common clinical presentations, and critically discusses the research findings to inform policy and best practice in prevention strategies of suicidal behaviour in persons with SUDs.

11.2 Substance Use Disorders

The ICD-10 Classification of Mental and Behavioural Disorders contains a wide variety of disorders that differ in severity (from uncomplicated intoxication and harmful use to dependence) that are all attributable to the use of one or more psychoactive substances (which may or may not have been medically prescribed).

In the *Diagnostic and Statistical Manual of Mental Disorders, 5th edition* [4], also known as *DSM-5*, the DSM-4 diagnoses of substance abuse and substance dependency were merged into the category of SUDs. The severity of SUDs is qualified as mild, moderate or severe on the basis of how many of the 11 diagnostic criteria are met. *The International Classification of Diseases, 11th revision* (ICD-11) divides SUDs into two categories: (1) harmful pattern of substance use and (2) substance dependence [5].

The Global Burden of Disease study showed that mental and substance use disorders were the leading cause of years of healthy life lost to disability (YLDs) worldwide, with illicit drug use disorders accounting for 10.9% (8.9–13.2%) and alcohol use disorders for 9.6% (7.7–11.8%) of disability adjusted life years (DALYs) caused by mental disorders and SUDs [6]. Moreover, SUDs are associated with high mortality, including deaths by accidental overdoses and suicide (diseases of despair). SUDs are more common in communities with high deprivation and psychosocial disadvantage and are associated with serious social hams and criminality. Their aetiology is complex, with contributing genetic and psychosocial factors, and occurs against a background of childhood adversity, family breakdown and high rates of familial abuse and other traumatic experiences.

SUDs are treatable and preventable: there is extensive evidence for the effectiveness and cost-effectiveness of treatment, whether pharmacological and psychosocial interventions. Moreover, SUDs are the most preventable psychiatric disorders: international evidence on the prevention of drug and alcohol use has been critically reviewed for their effectiveness at universal (primary), selective (secondary) and indicated (tertiary) levels [7].

In the US, the primary prevention of SUDs has been a challenging strategy, given misconceptions about SUDs, shortages in behavioural health professionals and the population-based focus on specific substances. These findings prompted a developmental approach to the identification and primary prevention of SUDs that does not fully rely upon behavioural health workers [8]. The proposed approach is based on risk factors for developing the disease according to different age groups that emphasises screening, education and empowerment, wherein individuals are screened for risk factors according to their age group and screening results are used to customise interventions in the form of education and empowerment. While this individualised approach is plausible, its effectiveness has not been demonstrated.

Abou-Saleh and colleagues [9] have advocated a person-centred approach as uniquely befitting for the optimal comprehensive assessment, integrated treatment and preventions of addictions: addictions, particularly addiction to illegal drugs, have long been considered criminal, immoral, self-inflicted conditions and importantly the most stigmatising health conditions in all communities and cultures. In recent decades, addictions have been dignified by their recognitions as serious health conditions included under mental disorders in international classification systems and accumulating evidence for effective treatment and preventative interventions that now shape policy, including issues of decriminalisation and legalisation.

A US study showed that addiction counsellors' education and experience do not improve suicide knowledge, beliefs or confidence in treating suicidal clients advocating the need for more specialist and effective training in this area [10].

The United Nations Office on Drugs and Crime (UNDOC) introduced international standards for preventative interventions and policies that are set out across the life course, that have been found to be effective by the scientific evidence in preventing substance use and that could serve as the foundation of an effective health-centred national substance use prevention system [11].

11.3 Epidemiology of SUDs and Suicide

The Global Burden of Disease Study 2010 reported that mental and SUDs were responsible for 22.5 million (14.8–29.8 million) of the 36.2 million (26.5–44.3 million) DALYs allocated to suicide in 2010. Capturing the suicide burden attributable to mental and SUDs allows for more accurate estimates of burden [12]. The study showed that the pooled relative risk of suicide was 19.9 for depression, 9.8 for alcohol dependence, 6.9 for opioid dependence, 8.2 for psychostimulant dependence, 4.5 for amphetamine dependence and 16.9 for cocaine dependence.

A cross-national analysis of the associations among mental disorders and suicidal behaviour in findings from the WHO World Mental Health Surveys in 21 countries provided informative results: each lifetime disorder including SUDs examined significantly predicts the subsequent first onset of suicide attempt, and after controlling for comorbidity, these associations decreased substantially but remained significant in most cases [13]. Overall, mental disorders were equally predictive in developed and developing countries, with a key difference being that the strongest predictors of suicide attempts in developed countries were mood disorders, whereas in developing countries impulse control, substance use and post-traumatic stress disorders were most predictive. Disaggregation of the associations between mental disorders and non-fatal suicide attempts showed that these associations are largely due to disorders predicting the onset of suicidal thoughts rather than predicting progression from thoughts to attempts. In the few instances where mental disorders predicted the transition from suicidal thoughts to attempts, the significant disorders are characterised by anxiety, SUDs and poor impulse control. The limitations of this study include the use of retrospective self-reports of lifetime occurrence and age-of-onset of mental disorders and suicidal behaviours, as well as the narrow focus on mental disorders as predictors of non-fatal suicidal behaviours.

A systematic review of substance use and suicidal ideation and behaviour (SIB) in low- and middle-income countries that included 108 studies showed a consistent positive association between substance use and SIB across all substances (alcohol, tobacco, cannabis, illicit drugs, non-medical use of prescription drugs); all substance use dimensions (intoxication, use and pathological use) and all SIB dimensions [14]. The authors noted that most of the studies focussed on alcohol and tobacco while neglecting substances such as cannabis, opioids, sedatives, stimulants, misuse of prescription medication, inhalants and hallucinogens. Most of the studies employed a cross-sectional design, were conducted within a risk-factor paradigm and provided little information about the potential interaction between variables.

In adolescents aged 12–15 years from 21 low- and middle-income countries, cannabis use in the past 30 days was significantly associated with suicide attempts (OR = 2.03; 95% CI: 1.42–2.91) and lifetime cannabis use was also independently associated with suicide attempts (OR = 2.30; 95% CI: 1.74–3.04) [15].

A meta-analysis of 35 case-control psychological autopsy studies published worldwide over a 30-year period reported that the presence of major depression and drug use disorder are associated with ninefold and sevenfold increase in suicide, respectively [16].

In the US, a case control study of SUDs and risk of suicide of a general population reported that all categories of SUDs were associated with an increased risk of suicide mortality. Adjusted odds ratios (adjusted for age, gender, poverty level, education and psychiatric diagnoses) ranged from 2.0 (CI 1.7, 2.3) for patients with tobacco use disorder only to 11.2 (CI 8.0, 15.6) for patients with multiple alcohol, drug and tobacco use disorders. SUDs were associated with increased relative risk of suicide for both women and men across all categories, but the relative risk was more pronounced in women [17].

11.4 Mediating Mechanisms

Suicidal behaviour ranges from suicidal ideation to suicidal attempts to completed suicide. It is conceived as a complex process which develops over time and is influenced by interacting biological, psychological, environmental and current situational factors indicating a stress-vulnerability model of aetiology [18]. While suicidal behaviour is strongly associated with any mental disorder, including SUD, it also occurs in the absence of mental disorders in crisis situations and in settings of socio-economic deprivation.

Explaining the association of mental disorders with suicidal behaviour, Mishara and Chagnon [19] proposed a model in which different mechanisms are combined with several critical factors: the presence of a crisis situation, the availability of an acceptable means, a lack of help or social support and poor coping skills. A first mechanism suggests that suicide and psychiatric disorders may share a common aetiology, such as the genetic predisposition to depression and impulsivity or the experience of early negative life events. A second mechanism suggests that some conditions, such as SUDs, are thought to develop as an attempt to avoid or diminish suicidal impulses. A third mechanism proposes that suicide can be the consequence of cognitive distortions that characterise mental disorders, such as depressive delusions, psychotic command hallucinations or extreme hopelessness. Furthermore, living with a mental disorder may generate negative experiences, such as social exclusion, unemployment, relational problems, stigma and discrimination, which in turn contribute to suicide. Finally, suicide can be considered as an iatrogenic result of inadequate, inappropriate or incomplete treatment of mental disorders [20].

The association of suicidal behaviour with SUDs may be mediated by increased impulsivity, behavioural disinhibition and aggression. Individual and social mechanisms may explain the increased risk for suicide related to alcohol consumption [21]. Alcohol intoxication impairs cognitive functions; increasing feelings of despair and sadness, impulsivity and aggression; and weakens or removes barriers to self-harm, reducing coping abilities [20]. Furthermore, alcohol use seriously reduces the level of social integration. A study by Khemiri and colleagues [22] showed that the experience of violence in childhood and the expression of violent behaviour, coupled with increased impulsivity, were found to be overrepresented in patients with alcohol dependence and associated with an elevated risk for suicidal thoughts and behaviour.

11.5 Alcohol Use Disorders and Suicide

Among SUDs, alcohol use disorders (AUDs) are the most harmful condition and are associated with high physical and mental comorbidity and high mortality, including suicide. Suicides, alcohol-related liver disease and accidental poisoning (opioid overdose) are considered 'diseases of despair'. A retrospective cohort study of diseases of despair in the

US, 2009–18, reported the prevalence of alcohol-related, substance-related and suicide-related diagnoses respectively increased by 37%, 94% and 170% [23].

A recent study of alcohol consumption and suicide rates in 183 countries showed positive associations between per capita alcohol consumption and suicide rates among males and females in all income groups of countries [24]. People with heavy alcohol use are five times more likely to die by suicide than social drinkers [25]. A meta-analysis of the literature reported a significant association between AUDs and suicidal ideation, suicide attempts and completed suicide [26]. Young people with AUDs are more likely to exhibit suicidal ideas and exhibit attempts while the elderly with AUDs are more likely to commit suicide (particularly those with comorbid depressive disorders) [27].

Studies have shown a high prevalence of AUDs in psychiatric units [28]. In a series of 200 psychiatric admissions in London, 48.5% scored 8 or more on the Alcohol Use Disorders Identification Test (AUDIT), indicating hazardous or harmful alcohol use, and 22.5% scored 16 or more, indicating alcohol dependence [29]. Alcohol misuse was strangely associated with suicidality: 70% with an AUDIT score of 8 and above and 86.7% with a score of 16 and above reported suicidal behaviour. Suicidality was positively associated with illicit drug use and mood disorders and negatively associated with psychosis.

In the US, a study of patterns of treatment utilisation before suicide among male veterans with SUDs reported that more than half of the patients were seen during the month before suicide, and 25.4% were seen during the week before suicide [30]. Most of the last visits before suicide (56.6%) were in a general medical setting, 32.8% were in a specialty mental health setting and 10.5% were in SUD treatment.

A national cohort and nested case-control study of health care utilisation prior to suicide in persons with AUDs was conducted in Sweden [31]. Of the people with AUDs who died by suicide, 39.7% and 75.6% had a health care encounter less than two weeks or less than three months before the index date, respectively, compared with 6.3% and 25.4% of controls, and of last encounters, 48.1% were in primary care and 28.9% were in specialty outpatient clinics, mostly for non-psychiatric diagnoses.

A series of longitudinal population-wide Swedish medical, criminal and pharmacy registries were used to evaluate the risk of death by suicide as a function of AUD history [32]. AUDs remained robustly associated with suicide persisting after accounting for confounding factors, including the occurrence of other psychiatric disorders. A recent narrative review of research evidence showed a strong association between AUDs and suicidal behaviour, including acute alcohol use particularly at the time of suicidal attempts [20].

In summary, AUDs are a very potent risk factor for suicidal ideation, attempts and importantly completed suicide in general community and clinical studies. This robust finding provides a central and powerful element of suicide prevention action plans.

11.6 Impact of Alcohol Policies on Suicidal Behaviour

A systematic review of the impact of alcohol policies on suicidal behaviour identified 19 studies conducted in Western and Eastern Europe and the US [33]. The studies were 'natural experiments' examining the effects of changes in alcohol policies on suicide rates at the population level. The results showed associations of increased alcohol availability, lower pricing and less restrictive drunk-driving counter-measures with increased suicidal behaviour. The findings could not be generalised to countries outside Europe and North

America. Notwithstanding the notion that the studies were open to various biases, the findings were informative and robust, leading the authors to conclude, 'Policies targeting harmful alcohol consumption may contribute towards a reduction in suicidal behaviour at the population level' [33].

11.7 Opioid Use Disorders and Suicide

Globally excess mortality from SUDs has been found to be highest for AUDs followed by opioid use disorders (OUDs), particularly in Latin America and Central, Eastern Europe and Central Asia. However, in high-income countries excess mortality from SUDs is marginally greater for OUDs than AUDs [34]. A meta-analysis of 43 studies confirmed the existence of an association between SUDs and suicidal ideation, suicide attempt and suicide death, with opioid substances having a stronger effect than other substances [35].

The global prevalence and trends in unintentional drug overdoses have been critically reviewed [36]. An overall trend of increasing deaths from prescription opioid use and decreasing deaths from illicit drug use has been noted. Moreover, cocaine, prescription opioids and heroin are the drugs most commonly associated with non-intentional drug overdoses worldwide, and the demographic and psychiatric correlates associated with non-intentional drug overdoses are similar globally.

Deaths attributed to OUDs (illegal opiates, particularly injecting heroin use and/or medicinal opioids) include intentional (suicides) and non-intentional overdoses [37]. A meta-analysis by Wilcox and colleagues [38] showed that heroin use increased the risk of suicide by 13.5 times compared with the tenfold increase with AUD. Another study investigating the association between prescription opioid use and suicide among patients with chronic non-cancer-related pain revealed that an increased opioid dose was related to an increased risk of suicide, even after controlling for demographic and clinical factors [39]. The link between intentional (suicides) and non-intentional overdose is complex and has been critically reviewed for specific pathways towards vulnerability to overdose and suicide, including medical and social factors [40]. Chronic pain leading to prescription of opioids in high doses contributes to overdoses and suicides at the population and patient levels. The increase in opioid overdoses is driven by increased demand and supply but less so for suicides. Some overdoses may be masked suicides: suicide notes were found in less than a third of overdose deaths [41]. Patients receiving prescriptions for opioids are at greater risk of death from overdose or suicide after stopping opioid treatment, with an increase in risk, the longer patients had been treated before stopping [42].

Bohnert and Ilgen [40] identified shared risk factors as well as specific risk factors for overdoses and suicides: demographic (age, gender and ethnicity) and the occurrence of comorbid mental disorders, particularly depressive disorders. The authors concluded:

> Opioid use plays a critical role in fuelling both of these public health problems. Consequently, interventions that address the shared causes and risk factors, such as programs to improve the quality of pain care, expand access to psychotherapy, and increase access to medication-assisted treatment for opioid use disorders, have the potential to be high-value investments by addressing both problems simultaneously. [40]

A cross-sectional study of suicidal motivations described by opioid overdose survivors showed that over half reported some desire to die prior to their most recent overdose, with 36% reporting a strong (>7/10) desire to die and 21% reporting 10/10 'I definitely wanted to die' [43]. The role of suicide in the opioid overdose epidemic has been aptly titled as a 'hidden tragedy', and the two are considered twin epidemics [44].

It has been proposed that the opioid crisis, suicides and related conditions constitute multiple clustered syndemics and not singular epidemics: numerous other related conditions, including pain disorders, adverse childhood experiences, post-traumatic stress disorders, HIV/AIDS, polydrug use and toxicity and certain social determinants of health, may interact in a multiplicative and/or cumulative manner to adversely impact individuals and populations [45].

11.8 Comorbidity and Suicidal Behaviour

The co-occurrence of SUDs and other psychiatric disorders has been shown to be the norm, not the exception. The term 'dual diagnosis' has been introduced to describe this phenomenon, but 'comorbidity' might be a better term. Community-based surveys reported high rates of comorbidity, particularly substance misuse in people with severe mental disorders [46,47].

The pattern of this comorbidity varies between comorbid mood, anxiety and personality disorders in patients accessing addiction services and comorbid alcohol, cannabis and cocaine misuse in patients accessing general psychiatric services [48]. Comorbidity is associated with increased risk of violence, suicide and worse clinical and social outcomes. The National Confidential Inquiry into Suicide and Safety in Mental Health reported that 57% of patients who died by suicide had a history of drug or alcohol misuse, including people with serious mental illness [49].

The severity of this morbidity also varies between these specialist settings: severe psychiatric disorder is associated with non-dependent use of substances (problematic substance use), whereas severe addiction is associated with borderline and antisocial personality disorder with or without minor psychiatric disorder. The pattern and severity of this comorbidity are therefore related to the clinical setting in which it presents, which may not be representative of comorbidity occurring in the community [50]. The implications of these findings for the provision of effective interventions and competent services have been addressed [51], and the implications have also been considered for severe mental illness via the National Institute for Health and Care Excellence (NICE) guidelines on psychosis with coexisting substance misuse [52].

11.9 Suicide and SUDs in Clinical Populations

A Norwegian national registry study of suicide after contact with substance misuse services showed that more women (73.5%) than men (60.6%) had contact with mental health services in their last year, and poisoning was more common among women who were more likely to be diagnosed with a sedative, hypnotic or anxiolytic use disorder [53].

A Danish national record-linkage study of suicide among people treated for drug use disorders showed that increased risk for completed suicide was associated with younger age at enrollment, history of psychiatric care, opioid use and alcohol use. Lower risk for suicide was associated with cannabis use. Moreover, compared with age- and gender-matched controls without a history of treatment for SUDs or recent psychiatric care, the standardised mortality ratio due to suicide was 7.13 for people with drug use disorders without a history of psychiatric care, 13.48 for people with drug use disorders and psychiatric history, and 13.61 for people with psychiatric history only [54].

Motivations for suicide attempts among psychiatric inpatients were explored: interpersonal motivations were associated with lower age and higher problematic alcohol use while intrapersonal motivation was related to having previous suicide attempts, more past-year negative life events and higher depressive symptoms [55].

11.10 SUDs and Suicides in the Health Profession

Mental health issues, including substance misuse in health professionals, are associated with higher rates of suicide in the general population [56,57]. A systematic review and meta-analysis of suicide among physicians reported an overall standardised mortality rate (SMR) of 1.44 (95 CI 1.16, 1.72), with women particularly at risk. Some specialties might be at higher risk, such as anaesthesiologists, psychiatrists, general practitioners and general surgeons. Of the physicians surveyed, 1% had made a suicide attempt and 17% experienced suicidal ideation. The rate of suicide in physicians decreased over time, especially in Europe [58].

A study of physicians and nurses treated in a dedicated specialist mental health service in Catalonia reported high risk of suicide of 5% among physicians and 5.2% among nurses, particularly those with concurrent mental disorders and SUDs [59]. A National Confidential Inquiry into Suicide and Safety in Mental Health (NCISH) report on suicide by female nurses indicated that overall, 41% had a history of alcohol misuse and 20% reported a history of drug misuse [60].

Doctors suffer high rates of burn-out, particularly doctors working in conflict zones and psychiatric trainees [57]. A study of large groups of medical students in 12 countries shows that students in all 12 countries across 5 continents reported very high levels of 'caseness' on validated measures of psychiatric symptoms and burn-out. Rates of substance misuse, often a cause of or coping mechanism for this distress, and identified sources of stress also varied across cultures [61]. These epidemiological findings have led to the establishment of dedicated specialist health programmes in North America and Europe. In the UK, the Practitioner Health Programme (PHP) was established in 2008 and has regularly reported good outcomes for doctors who accessed its services. A report on doctors with addiction disorders under PHP over an eight-year period demonstrated successful treatment of these doctors, with a high proportion of abstinence (77.6%) and nearly twofold increase in the proportion in active employment [62].

11.11 Preventing Suicide: International Action

The WHO report *Preventing Suicide: A Global Imperative* provides guidance on the way forward to suicide prevention: a global knowledge base on suicide and suicide attempts to guide governments, policymakers and relevant stakeholders, along with actionable steps for countries based on their current resources and contexts [63]. In addition, this report is a significant resource for developing a comprehensive multisectoral strategy that can prevent suicide effectively. Substance abuse is considered a major risk factor for suicidal behaviour. All SUDs increase the risk of suicide. Alcohol and other SUDs are found in 25–50% of all suicides, and suicide risk is further increased if alcohol or substance use is comorbid with other psychiatric disorders. Of all deaths from suicide, 22% can be attributed to the use of alcohol, which means that every fifth suicide would not occur if alcohol were not consumed in the population. Dependence on other substances, including cannabis, heroin or nicotine, is also a risk factor for suicide [63].

SUDs are highlighted as risk factors for suicide with relevant interventions at the universal level (raising awareness), selective level (interventions for vulnerable groups) and indicated level (assessment and management of mental disorders and SUD). The evidence-based interventions discussed in this chapter are relevant for low- and middle-income countries, highlighting restricting access to means, responsible media reporting, introducing mental health and alcohol policies, early identification and treatment, training of health workers, and follow-up care and community support following a suicide attempt [64].

The UNODC and WHO have introduced international standards for the treatment of drug use disorders [11] to support member states in their efforts to develop and expand effective, evidence-based and ethical treatment for drug use disorders. The standards are intended for all those involved in policy development, which involves planning, funding, delivery, monitoring and evaluation of treatment services and interventions for drug use disorders. The document is based on currently available scientific evidence on treatment for drug use disorders and sets out a framework for their implementation in line with principles of public health care. The standards identify major components and features of effective systems for the treatment of drug use disorders. They describe treatment modalities and interventions to match the needs of people at different stages and severities of drug use disorders, in a manner consistent with the treatment of any chronic disease or health condition.

11.12 Preventing Suicide in the UK

The UK government's national strategy for England, *Preventing Suicide in England: A Cross-government Outcomes Strategy to Save Lives*, that is translated into local suicide prevention plans. The ambition of 'zero suicides' was advocated. Such an aspirational aim may be achieved by taking a quality improvement approach rather than one driven by a target [65].

This strategy identified the key action of a tailored approach to promote and improve the health in users of drug and alcohol services. Public Health England (PHE) introduced changes to the National Drug Treatment Monitoring System to enable local areas and PHE to better capture information about co-occurring mental health, drug and alcohol treatment needs, and to be able to better monitor the extent to which those needs are being met. PHE addressed the underlying causes of drug-related deaths, including suicides, providing practical advice on reducing these deaths. Moreover, PHE has produced updated UK-wide clinical guidelines for treating drug misuse and dependence. One of the most important advances in preventing drug-related deaths, including suicides, is the self-use of naloxone by drug users and carers that has been adopted worldwide.

NICE has produced a plethora of guidelines on preventing suicide, including guidelines on coexisting severe mental illness and substance misuse, community health and social care services. Health Education England produced the *Self-Harm and Suicide Prevention Competence Framework* in 2018 for professionals and volunteers who work in mental health, physical health and social care. Finally, the Royal College of Psychiatrists produced a practice-focussed guidance for psychiatrists and other mental health professionals on suicide and self-harm [66]. The guidance addressed the needs of high-risk groups, including patients presenting with SUDs. According to the NCISH [49], more than half of patients who died by suicide had a drug or alcohol use disorder. The report found that only a small number of those patients had been in contact with specialist substance misuse services. It noted lower suicide rates in patients in contact with 'dual diagnosis' services. The confidential inquiry recommended that specialist alcohol and drug services should be available, with the ability to manage clinical risk, working closely with mental health services, establishing agreed-upon arrangements for 'dual diagnosis' patients.

The second most common suicide method reported by the NCISH [48] was self-poisoning. The most common drugs in fatal overdoses are opiates, both prescription and non-prescription. Internationally, opiate misuse and dependence are rising. The confidential inquiry recommended that opiate prescriptions should be reviewed carefully. It suggested that they should be subject to 'safer prescribing', including reduced use overall and short-term supplies.

Patients with addictions present frequently to emergency departments, and this can cause frustration for staff. Public Health England [67] reported that in one year, more than a million patients were admitted to the hospital with alcohol-related problems. This figure has more than doubled over the last 15 years. Around 70% of emergency department admittances between midnight and 5:00 a.m. on weekend nights are alcohol related. The provision of specialist addiction liaison services not only benefits patients but also reduces the length of stay and the number of repeat admissions to general hospitals.

11.13 Prevention of Suicidal Behaviour

Suicidal behaviour is caused by a complex set of contributing factors that are in many circumstances interconnected psychosocial, cultural and clinical factors – importantly the occurrence of depression and other psychiatric disorders, particularly SUD. Hegerl and Heinz [68] advanced the clinical explanatory model of the pivotal cause of depression and other psychiatric disorders, including SUDs combined with life adversities, that is evidenced-based, in preference of the model that assumes the social determinants of suicidal behaviour. The clinical model accords with clinical experience and practice and has been translated into the European Alliance Against Depression (EAAD), a complex intervention that has been shown to be highly effective in the prevention of suicidal behaviour in many regions in Germany and other European countries [69]. However, it has been argued that 'the dramatic decline of global suicide mortality observed in the last few decades' [70] can only be explained if we consider big social changes affecting urbanisation, social stability, social freedom and policies that have an impact on the consumption of alcohol, the improvement on the lives of the elderly and/or access to the means to kill oneself, among others. It is clear that no single approach can solve the complex challenge that is the reduction of suicide mortality, and there is still room for simultaneously testing and implementing measures that may have an impact on different modifiable factors [71].

A 10-year systematic review of suicide prevention strategies concluded that evidence is limited for interventions other than means restriction, schools-based awareness programmes and treatment of psychiatric conditions [72]. Moreover, two systematic reviews of psychosocial and pharmacological interventions for self-harm (irrespective of intent), in adults specifically, were also limited in their findings [73,74]. A review of psychosocial interventions found low- to moderate-quality evidence indicating a reduction in repetition of self-harm following cognitive behavioural therapy (CBT)–based interventions, along with low-quality evidence regarding the repetition of self-harm following dialectical behaviour therapy (DBT)–based interventions. Evidence for a range of other approaches was inconclusive. The review of pharmacological interventions included only seven trials of 546 patients in total, and the quality of the evidence was low or very low, prohibiting conclusions from being drawn. Many of the studies included in these reviews excluded people with a history of substance misuse.

A narrative synthesis of the evidence relating to the effectiveness of 13 different approaches (interventions) that have been incorporated into national suicide prevention programmes reported strongly supportive evidence concerning the effectiveness of structural interventions (restrictions on access to bridges, tall buildings and railways) and restriction on access to pharmacological agents. Weakly supportive evidence of effectiveness is available for community-based multilevel programs, education and training targeted at primary care physicians, lithium, cognitive behavioural therapy and dialectical behavioural therapy, and brief contact [75]. The authors concluded:

> There is insufficient or conflicting evidence concerning the effectiveness of the remaining approaches. We conclude that the evidence base for effective suicide prevention is far from convincing. Major improvement in the extent and quality of collaboration between researchers, policymakers, and practitioners and a considerable increase in funding for evaluation studies in suicide prevention are required if the current knowledge gap about effective interventions is to be bridged. [75]

A recent systematic review and meta-analysis of the effectiveness of suicide prevention in 15 controlled studies of various psychosocial interventions reported a significant effect for suicide prevention interventions on completed suicides and on suicide attempts [76]. Importantly the studies were conducted on clinical populations in Europe, North America and a few low- and middle-income countries. Moreover, multilevel interventions were more effective than single-level interventions.

11.14 Preventing Suicide in People with SUDs

While the evidence for a strong association of SUDs and suicidal behaviour is compelling, there has been little research on preventing suicide in people with SUDs. In two Cochrane reviews of psychosocial and pharmacological interventions for self-harm, more than a quarter of studies specified a type of substance misuse in their exclusion criteria [73,74]. A recent systematic review and meta-analysis of randomised controlled trials evaluated the effects of interventions to prevent suicide or reduce self-harm among people with SUDs [77]. The review identified six RCTs from four countries (Australia, Iran, the United States of America and the United Kingdom), with 468 participants in total. All but one study investigated psychosocial interventions. On average, across studies there was weak evidence of a small positive effect of interventions on suicide or self-harm outcomes. The studies were heterogeneous in terms of population, intervention, controls and outcome. There were some concerns regarding bias for all trials that were also liable to type II error, concluding that evidence is currently lacking regarding the effectiveness of interventions to prevent suicide and reduce self-harm among people with SUD.

Systematic reviews on dual diagnosis of treatment of depression in patients with alcohol or other drug dependence [78] and of psychosocial interventions for people with both severe mental illness and substance misuse [79] have not explored suicide- or self-harm-related outcomes [77]. A review by Padmanathan and colleagues referred to other trials measuring suicide- or self-harm-related outcomes as secondary or supplementary outcomes, or reported the suicide component of other scales separately, such as scales for depression or aggression, and concluding that 'in keeping with the studies reviewed here, these studies also found little evidence for treatment effects but again were frequently subject to similar limitations as the studies included in this review' [77].

An open pilot study of a suicide prevention intervention for patients attending group-based addiction treatment reported positive preliminary results [80]. A randomised, controlled trial of this intervention, with an estimated enrolment of 900 participants, is currently in progress [81].

11.15 Dynamic and Static Risk Factors Associated with Suicide and Protective Factors

In the absence of solid evidence for a tool or schema for effective assessment of risk of suicide in SUD, a credible schema to assist in evaluating individuals for potential suicide risks has been proposed by Esang and Ahmed [37], with reference to Simon and colleagues [81]. The schema categorises risk factors as either dynamic (acute) or static (long-term). As proposed, in patients who are suicidal and have a concurrent SUD, clinicians should pay attention to dynamic risk factors that affect the individual's life. These factors can change rapidly but are easy to target for treatment intervention. They also proposed protective factors: reasons for living; being clean and sober; attending 12-step support groups; religious attendance and/or internalised spiritual teachings against suicide; the presence of a child in the home and/or child-rearing responsibilities; intact marriage; trusting relationship with a counsellor, physician or other service provider; and employment.

In response to the findings of a study by Lynch and colleagues [17] on the association of suicide mortality and SUDs in the US, the Suicide Safer Care project was proposed as one model to address the need for training health professionals in suicide assessment and screening for patients with SUDs in health settings, such as primary care practices and emergency departments [82]. Data collected from pre- and post-training surveys of participants demonstrates the success of the training in increasing knowledge and confidence in identification and treatment of patients at risk of suicide.

11.16 Towards an Evidence-Based Suicide Prevention Strategy in SUDs

The findings of the present overview on the epidemiology of suicidal behaviour in people with SUDs in general and clinical populations strongly indicate that SUDs are a robust risk factor for suicidal behaviour, particularly in people with dual disorders of SUDs and comorbid other mental disorders, including mood, psychotic and personality disorders.

It is remarkable that the contribution of SUDs to suicidal behaviour is universal. However, there are important variations in the association of SUDs with suicidal behaviour between high-income countries and low- and middle-income countries in relation to gender, socio-economic deprivation, culture and comorbid physical and mental disorders. Two particular associations of SUDs with suicidal behaviour are highlighted, and AUDs and OUDs are presented as 'diseases of despair' that need particular strategies for the prevention of suicidal behaviour.

Importantly, and in the absence of solid evidence for a tool or schema for the effective assessment of risk of suicide in SUD, a credible and intelligible schema has been proposed to assist in evaluating individuals for potential suicide risks in clinical settings: assessment of dynamic and static risk factors associated with suicide and protective factors. Research indicates that thus far there is limited, low- to moderate-quality evidence for effective psychosocial or pharmacological interventions in the prevention of suicidal behaviour in people with mental disorders and SUD. However, there is evidence for multilevel and complex interventions in preventing suicide. Hence an evidence-based strategy for preventing suicidal behaviour in SUDs should be a key component of a general strategy.

SUDs are treatable and preventable: there is extensive evidence for the effectiveness and cost-effectiveness of treatment, whether pharmacological or psychosocial interventions. Moreover, SUDs are known as some of the most preventable psychiatric disorders: international evidence on preventative interventions for drug and alcohol use disorders has been critically reviewed for their effectiveness at universal (primary), selective (secondary) and indicated (tertiary) levels.

An evidence-based strategy includes the following key elements:

- It is of paramount importance that all health care professionals are trained and have the competencies to assess, detect and recognise SUDs and suicidal risk in primary care, specialist general hospital and community-based medical and mental health care and in criminal justice settings.
- Health care professionals in all settings should be empowered by knowledge, skills and attitudes that promote good engagement of people with SUDs and/or suicidal ideation or attempts, providing treatment that includes psychoeducation and brief psychosocial interventions.
- People with AUDs or OUDs, including those with non-intentional overdoses and those with comorbidity, need particular attention in view of their high mortality, high risk of suicide and the availability of effective interventions.
- Ongoing suicide risk assessment allows for an integrated treatment plan that enables health professionals to continuously address acute and modifiable suicide risk factors and the identification of protective factors that mitigate the risk of suicide.

References

1. World Health Organization. *Suicide in the World: Global Health Estimates*. Geneva: World Health Organization; 2019.
2. Naghavi M. Global burden of disease self-harm collaborators. *BMJ*. 2019 Feb 6; **364**: 194.
3. World Health Organization. *Mental Health Action Plan, 2013–2020*. Geneva: World Health Organization; 2013.
4. Hasin DS, O'Brien CP, Auriacombe M, Borges G, Bucholz K, Budney A, et al. DSM-5 criteria for substance use disorders: Recommendations and rationale. *American Journal of Psychiatry*. 2013 Aug; **170**(8): 834–51.
5. Poznyak V, Reed GM, Medina-Mora ME. Aligning the ICD-11 classification of disorders due to substance use with global service needs. *Epidemiology and Psychiatric Sciences*. 2018 Jun; **27**(3): 212–18.
6. Whiteford HA, Degenhardt L, Rehm J, Baxter AJ, Ferrari AJ, Erskine HE, et al. Global burden of disease attributable to mental and substance use disorders. *Lancet*. 2013 Nov 9; **382**(9904): 1575–86.
7. Griffin KW, Botvin GJ. Evidence-based interventions for preventing substance use disorders in adolescents. *Child Adolescent Psychiatry Clinics of North America*. 2010; **19**(3): 505–26.

8. Afuseh E, Pike CA, Oruche UM. Individualized approach to primary prevention of substance use disorder: Age-related risks. *Substance Abuse Treatment, Prevention and Policy*. 2020; **15**: 58.

9. Abou-Saleh MT, Tarter RE, Salloum IM. Substance use disorders. In Mezzich J, Botbol M, Christodoulou G, Cloninger C, Salloum I, eds., *Person Centered Psychiatry*. Springer: Cham; 2016.

10. Fruhbauerova M, Comtois KA. Addiction counselors and suicide: Education and experience do not improve suicide knowledge, beliefs, or confidence in treating suicidal clients. *Journal of Substance Abuse Treatment*. 2019 Nov; **106**: 29–34.

11. United Nations Office on Drugs and Crime/World Health Organization. *International Standards on Drug Use Prevention*, 2nd updated ed. Vienna: United Nations; 2020.

12. Ferrari AJ, Norman RE, Freedman G, Baxter AJ, Pirkis JE, Harris MG, et al. The burden attributable to mental and substance use disorders as risk factors for suicide: Findings from the Global Burden of Disease Study 2010. *PLoS One*. 2014 Apr 2; **9**(4): e91936.

13. Nock MK, Hwang I, Sampson N, Kessler RC, Angermeyer M, Beautrais A, et al. Cross-national analysis of the associations among mental disorders and suicidal behavior: Findings from the WHO World Mental Health Surveys. *PLoS Med*. 2009 Aug; **6**(8): e1000123.

14. Breet E, Goldstone D, Bantjes J. Substance use and suicidal ideation and behaviour in low- and middle-income countries: A systematic review. *BMC Public Health*. 2018 Apr 24; **18**(1): 549.

15. Carvalho AF, Stubbs B, Vancampfort D, Kloiber S, Maes M, Firth J, et al. Cannabis use and suicide attempts among 86,254 adolescents aged 12–15 years from 21 low- and middle-income countries. *European Psychiatry*. 2019 Feb; **56**: 8–13.

16. Conner KR, Bridge JA, Davidson DJ, Pilcher C, Brent DA. Meta-analysis of mood and substance use disorders in proximal risk for suicide deaths. *Suicide and Life Threatening Behavior*. 2019 Feb; **49**(1): 278–92.

17. Lynch FL, Peterson EL, Lu CY, Hu Y, Rossom RC, Waitzfelder BE, et al. Substance use disorders and risk of suicide in a general US population: A case control study. *Addiction Science and Clinical Practice*. 2020 Feb 21; **15**(1): 14.

18. Wasserman D, Rihmer Z, Rujescu D, Sarchiapone M, Sokolowski M, Titelman D, et al. The European Psychiatric Association (EPA) guidance on suicide treatment and prevention. *European Psychiatry*. 2012 Feb; **27**(2): 129–41.

19. Mishara BL, Chagnon F. Why mental illness is a risk factor for suicide: Implications for suicide prevention. In O'Connor RC, Pirkis J, eds., *The International Handbook of Suicide Prevention*, 2nd ed. Hoboken: Wiley; 2016: 594–608.

20. Wasserman D, Carli V, Iosue M, Javed A, Herrman H. Suicide prevention in psychiatric patients. *Asia Pacific Psychiatry*. 2021 Feb 18: e12450.

21. Norström T, Rossow I. Alcohol consumption as a risk factor for suicidal behavior: A systematic review of associations at the individual and at the population level. *Archives of Suicide Research*. 2016 Oct–Dec; **20**(4): 489–506.

22. Khemiri L, Jokinen J, Runeson B, Jayaram-Lindström N. Suicide risk associated with experience of violence and impulsivity in alcohol dependent patients. *Scientific Reports*. 2016 Jan 19; **6**: 19373.

23. Brignone E, George, DR, Sinoway, L, Katz, C, Sauder, C, Murray A, et al. Trends in the diagnosis of diseases of despair in the United States, 2009–2018. *BMJ Open*. 2020 Nov 9; **10**(10): e037679.

24. Kim, AM. Alcohol consumption and suicide rate. *Psychiatry Research*. 2021 Jan; **295**: 113553.

25. Harris EC, Barraclough B. Suicide as an outcome for mental disorders. *British*

Journal of Psychiatry. 1997 Mar; **170**: 205–28.

26. Darvishi N, Farhadi M, Haghtalab T, Poorolajal J. Alcohol-related risk of suicidal ideation, suicide attempt, and completed suicide. *PLoS One*. 2015 May 20; **10**(5).
27. Blow FC, Serras AM, Barry KL. Late-life depression and alcoholism. *Current Psychiatry Reports*. 2007 Feb; **9**(1): 14–19.
28. Hulse GK, Saunders JB, Roydhouse RM, Stockwell TR, Asso MR. Screening for hazardous alcohol use and dependence in psychiatric in-patients using the AUDIT questionnaire. *Drug and Alcohol Review*. 2000; **19**: 291–8.
29. McCloud A, Barnaby B, Omu N, Drummond C, Aboud A. Relationship between alcohol use disorders and suicidality in a psychiatric population. *British Journal of Psychiatry*. 2004 May; **184**: 439–45.
30. Ilgen MA, Conner KR, Roeder KM, Blow FC, Austin K, Valenstein M. Patterns of treatment utilization before suicide among male veterans with substance use disorders. *American Journal of Public Health*. 2012 Mar; **102**(suppl 1): S88–92.
31. Crump C, Edwards AC, Kendler KS, Sundquist J, Sundquist K. Healthcare utilisation prior to suicide in persons with alcohol use disorder. *British Journal of Psychiatry*. 2020 Dec; **217**(6): 710–16.
32. Edwards AC, Ohlsson H, Sundquist J, Sundquist K, Kendler KS. Alcohol use disorder and risk of suicide in a Swedish population-based cohort. *American Journal of Psychiatry*. 2020 Jul 1; **177**(7): 627–34.
33. Kõlves K, Chitty KM, Wardhani R, Värnik A, de Leo D, Witt K. Impact of alcohol policies on suicidal behavior: A systematic literature review. *International Journal of Environmental Research and Public Health*. 2020 Sep 25; **17**(19): 7030.
34. Charlson FJ, Baxter AJ, Dua T, Degenhardt L, Whiteford HA, Vos, T. Excess mortality from mental, neurological, and substance use disorders in the Global Burden of Disease Study 2010. *Epidemiology and Psychiatric Sciences*. 2015 Sep 25; **17**(19): 7030.
35. Poorolajal J, Haghtalab T, Farhadi M, Darvishi N. Substance use disorder and risk of suicidal ideation, suicide attempt and suicide death: a meta-analysis. *Journal of Public Health (Oxford)*. 2016 Sep; **38**(3): e282–91.
36. Martins SS, Sampson L, Cerdá M, Galea S. Worldwide prevalence and trends in unintentional drug overdose: A systematic review of the literature. *American Journal of Public Health*. 2015 Nov; **105**(11): e29–49.
37. Esang M, Ahmed SA. Closer look at substance use and suicide. *American Journal of Psychiatry Residents*. 2018; **13**(6): 6–8.
38. Wilcox HC, Conner KR, Caine ED. Association of alcohol and drug use disorders and completed suicide: An empirical review of cohort studies. *Drug and Alcohol Dependence*. 2004 December; **76**: S11–19.
39. Ilgen MA, Bohnert ASB, Ganoczy D, Bair MJ, McCarthy JF, Blow FC. Opioid dose and risk of suicide. *Pain*. 2016; **157**: 1079–84.
40. Bohnert ASB, Ilgen MA. Understanding links among opioid use, overdose, and suicide. *New England Journal of Medicine*. 2019 Jan 3; **380**(1): 71–9.
41. Rockett IRH, Caine ED, Connery HS, D'Onofrio G, Gunnellm DJ, Miller TR, et al. Discerning suicide in drug intoxication deaths: Paucity and primacy of suicide notes and psychiatric history. *PLoS One*. 2018 Jan 10; **13**(1): e01902.
42. Oliva EM, Bowe T, Manhapra A, Kertesz S, Hah JM, Henderson P, et al. Associations between stopping prescriptions for opioids, length of opioid treatment, and overdose or suicide deaths in US Veterans. *BMJ*. 2020 Mar 4; **368**: 283.
43. Connery HS, Taghian N, Kim J, Griffin M, Rockett IRH, Weiss RD, et al. Suicidal motivations reported by opioid overdose survivors: A cross-sectional study of adults with opioid use disorder. *Drug and Alcohol Dependence*. 2019 Dec 1; **205**: 107612.

44. Oquendo MA, Volkow ND. Suicide: A silent contributor to opioid-overdose deaths. *New England Journal of Medicine*. 2018 Apr 26; **378**(17): 1567–9.

45. Fornili K. The opioid crisis, suicides, and related conditions: Multiple clustered syndemics, not singular epidemics. *Journal of Addictions Nursing*. 2018 Jul/Sep; **29**(3): 214–20.

46. Harrison C, Abou-Saleh MT. Psychiatric disorders and substance misuse psychopathology. In Hussain RG, ed., *Dual Diagnosis: Substance Misuse and Psychiatric Disorders*. Oxford: Blackwell; 2002.

47. Abou-Saleh MT, Janca A. The epidemiology of substance misuse and comorbid psychiatric disorders. *Acta Neuropsychiatrica*. 2004 Feb; **16**(1): 3–8.

48. Abou-Saleh MT. Substance misuse and comorbid psychiatric disorders. *CPD Bulletin in Psychiatry*. 2000; **2**: 61–7.

49. Appleby L, Kapur N, Shaw J, Ibrahim S, Turnbull P et al. *The National Confidential Inquiry into Suicide and Safety in Mental Health. Annual Report: England, Northern Ireland, Scotland and Wales*. 2019. Manchester: University of Manchester.

50. Abou-Saleh, MT. Dual diagnosis: Management within a psychosocial context. *Advances in Psychiatric Treatment*. 2004; **10**(5): 352–60.

51. Lowe AL, Abou-Saleh MT. The British experience of dual diagnosis in the National Health Service. *Acta Neuropsychiatrica*. 2004 Feb; **16**(1): 41–6.

52. Abou Saleh MT, Crome I. National Institute for Health and Clinical Excellence (NICE) Guideline: Psychosis with coexisting substance misuse. *Addiction*. 2012 Jan; **107**(1): 1–3.

53. Myhre MØ, Kildahl AT, Walby FA. Suicide after contact with substance misuse services. *British Journal of Psychiatry Open*. 2020 May 7; **6**(3): e45.

54. Hesse M, Thylstrup B, Seid AK, Skogen JC. Suicide among people treated for drug use disorders. *BMC Public Health*. 2020; **20**(1): 146.

55. Suzuki T, Comtois KA, Dickens H, Bagge CL. Motivations for suicide attempts amongst psychiatric inpatients. *Psychiatry Research*. 2021 Jan; **295**: 113574.

56. Meltzer H, Griffiths C, Brock A, Rooney C, Jenkins R. Patterns of suicide by occupation in England and Wales: 2001–2005. *British Journal of Psychiatry*. 2008; **193**: 73–6.

57. Abou-Saleh MT. Doctors' impaired fitness to practise for health issues: The pivotal role of psychiatrists. *Arab Journal of Psychiatry*. 2020; **23**(1): 17–24.

58. Dutheil F, Aubert C, Pereira B, Dambrun M, Moustafa F, Mermillod M, et al. Suicide among physicians and health-care workers: A systematic review and meta-analysis. *PLoS One*. 2019 Dec 12; **14**(12): e0226361.

59. Braquehais MD, González-Irizar O, Nieva G, Mozo X, Llavayol E, Pujol T, et al. Assessing high risk of suicide amongst physicians and nurses in treatment. *Psychiatry Research*. 2020 Sep; **291**: 113237.

60. The National Confidential Inquiry into Suicide and Safety in Mental Health (NCISH). *Suicide by Female Nurses: A Brief Report*. Manchester: University of Manchester; 2020.

61. Molodynski A, Lewis T, Kadhum M, Farrell SM, Lemtiri Chelieh M, Falcão De Almeida T, et al. Cultural variations in wellbeing, burnout and substance use amongst medical students in twelve countries. *International Review of Psychiatry*. 2021 Feb–Mar; **33**(1–2): 37–42.

62. Sathanandan S, Abrol E, Aref-Adib G, Keen J, Gerada K. The UK Practitioner Health Programme: 8-year outcomes in doctors with addiction disorders. *Research and Advances in Psychiatry*. 2019; **6**(2): 43–9.

63. World Health Organization. *Preventing Suicide: A Global Imperative*. Geneva: World Health Organization; 2014.

64. Fleischmann A, Arensman E, Berman A, Carli V, De Leo D, Hadlackzy G, et al. *Overview Evidence on Interventions for Population Suicide with an Eye to*

Identifying Best-Supported Strategies for LMICs. Cambridge: Global Mental Health (Cambridge); 2016.

65. UK Department of Health. *Preventing Suicide in England: A Cross-government Outcomes Strategy to Save Lives*. London: Department of Health; 2012.
66. Royal College of Psychiatrists. *Self-Harm and Suicide in Adults, Final Report of the Patient Safety Group CR229*. London: Royal College of Psychiatrists; 2020.
67. Public Health England. *Alcohol Treatment in England 2013–2014*. London: Public Health England; 2014.
68. Hegerl U, Heinz I. Reflections on causes of suicidal behaviour. *Epidemiology and Psychiatric Sciences*. 2019 Oct; **28**(5): 469–72.
69. Hegerl U, Wittenburg L, Arensman E, Van Audenhove C, Coyne JC, McDaid D, et al. An optimizing suicide prevention programs and their implementation in Europe (OSPI Europe). *BMC Public Health*. 2009 Nov 23; **9**: 428.
70. Ayuso-Mateos JL. Suicide prevention: Towards an evidence-based policy. *Epidemiology and Psychiatric Sciences*. 2019 Oct; **28**(5): 468–8.
71. Zalsman G, Hawton K, Wasserman D, van Heeringen K, Arensman E, Sarchiapone M, et al. Suicide prevention strategies revisited: 10-year systematic review. *Lancet Psychiatry*. 2016; **3**: 646–59.
72. Hawton K, Witt KG, Taylor Salisbury TL, Arensman E, Gunnell D, Hazell P, et al. Pharmacological interventions for self-harm in adults. *Cochrane Database of Systematic Reviews*. 2015; **6**(7): CD011777.
73. Hawton K, Witt KG, Taylor Salisbury TL, Arensman E, Gunnell D, Hazell P. Psychosocial interventions for self-harm in adults. *Cochrane Database Systematic Reviews*. 2016; **12**(5): CD012189.
74. Platt S, Niederkrotenthaler T. Suicide prevention programs. *Crisis*. 2020 Mar; **41** (suppl 1): S99–124.
75. Hofstra E, van Nieuwenhuizen C, Bakker M, Özgül D, Elfeddali I, de Jong SJ, et al. Effectiveness of suicide prevention interventions: A systematic review and meta-analysis. *General Hospital Psychiatry*. 2020 Mar–Apr; **63**: 127–40.
76. Padmanathan P, Hall K, Moran P, Jones HE, Gunnell D, Carlisle V, et al. Prevention of suicide and reduction of self-harm among people with substance use disorder. *Comprehensive Psychiatry*. 2020 Jan; **96**: 152135.
77. Nunes EV, Levin FR. Treatment of depression in patients with alcohol or other drug dependence: A meta-analysis. *JAMA*. 2004; **291**: 1887–96.
78. Hunt GE, Siegfried N, Morley K, Sitharthan T, Cleary M. Psychosocial interventions for people with both severe mental illness and substance misuse. *Cochrane Database of Systematic Reviews*. 2013; **10**: CD001088.
79. Voss WD, Kaufman E, O'Connor SS, Comtois KA, Conner KR, Rie RK. Preventing addiction related suicide. *Journal of Substance Abuse Treatment*. 2013; **44**: 565–9.
80. Comtois K. *Preventing Addiction Related Suicide (PARS)*. 2018. https://clinicaltrials.gov/study/NCT03166709?cond=Suicide&term=Comtois%20&viewType=Card&rank=1.
81. Simon RI. Suicide risk: Assessing the unpredictable. In Simon RJ, Hales RE, eds., *The American Psychiatric Publishing Textbook of Suicide Assessment and Management*, 1st ed. Washington, DC: American Psychiatric Publishing; 2006.
82. Little V, James MC. Commentary on substance use disorders and risk of suicide in a general us population. *Addiction Science and Clinical Practice*. 2020 Jun 29; **15**(1): 21.

Chapter 12

Decriminalising Suicide Attempts in Ghana

The Journey Thus Far

Joseph Osafo and Johnny Andoh-Arthur

12.1 Introduction

Suicide and suicide attempts ravage societies and are now considered a top priority on the Global Health Agenda. In Ghana, lack of systematic reporting and recording hamper genuine efforts to prevent the problem. Among the many factors militating against progress in this direction is the strong taboo associated with suicidal behaviours in general and the criminalisation of suicide attempts in particular [1].

12.2 Prevalence of Suicidal Behaviour in Ghana

Prevalence estimates reveal frightening and staggering levels of suicidal behaviours in Ghana. A three-year suicide attempts trend in Ghana showed that 797 persons attempted suicide in Ghana in the year 2018. The number went up to 880 in 2019. A slight decline was recorded in the year 2020, with 777 suicide attempts. By June 2021, 417 persons had attempted suicide (figures from Ghanaian Ministry of Health in 2021). Evidence from other studies also shows that one in five adolescents engage in self-harm annually in Ghana [2]. Three in 10 junior high school students in Ghana report attempting suicide in the previous 12 months [3], and 2 out of 10 senior high school students report attempting suicide during the previous 12 months [4]. Studies conducted among school-going deaf adolescents reveal that 1 in 10 students report attempting suicide in the previous 12 months. Studies conducted among the LGBT population in Ghana show that 2 out of 5 adolescents who identify as LGBT engage in self-poisoning or self-injurious behaviours [2], whereas another study among the police showed nearly 3 in 10 police officers in urban Ghana report having had thoughts about taking their own lives during the previous 12 months [5].

Given the evidence that a single most important risk factor for suicide is a previous suicidal attempt [6], the high prevalence of suicide attempts among the various population in Ghana, as the evidence shows, calls for urgent steps towards addressing the problem. Unfortunately, the cultural context of Ghana, with its proscriptive attitudes towards suicidal behaviour and attempts, make such an effort a daunting task. Notwithstanding, some progress have and continue to be made in this respect. The next section will throw some light on the cultural context of suicidal behaviour and steps that have been taken so far to address the problem of suicidal behaviours, particularly decriminalisation of suicide attempt.

12.3 Suicide in the Cultural Context of Ghana

Suicide is perceived by the various ethnic groups in Ghana as an extraordinary moral evil with grave consequences for the entire community [7,8]. For this reason, incidents of suicide and suicide attempts are strongly met with reparative and retributive reactions from the people [1]. Suicide is construed as a social injury [9] that leaves an indelible scar on the bereaved family and is disruptive of societal harmony. Reparative reactions such as pouring of libation and ritual cleansing serve to appease the Gods and prevent them from visiting their wrath on the living. They also restore harmony between the seen and the unseen forces.

Retributive reactions, including perfunctory burials, insults and canning of the corpse of the deceased, as practiced in some traditional societies of Ghana, are meant to humiliate and exact vengeance against the deceased and to deter the living from pursuing such a course of action [10]. The pervasive stigma of suicide, according to Osafo and colleagues [11], is thus institutionalised at three levels – namely community, religion and law. As a perceived extraordinary moral evil that brings shame and dishonour to both family and community, there exist strong social norms against suicide and suicidal behaviours. The suicidal person is seen as an aggressor or an antisocial/communal person. He or she thus usually is on the receiving end of public opprobrium and social taunts, whether dead or alive. Cultural injunctions prohibit family members from engaging in the act and speaking about it [12]. It has been found that such harsh reactions to suicidal behaviours actually heighten the risk for subsequent suicides [13]. In one such case in a community in Ghana, social taunts by community members following suicidal attempts pushed someone to eventually take his life after three previous unsuccessful attempts. Studies have shown how some bereaved family members express shock and anger at the persons who take their lives or attempt to take their lives [13,14].

At the religious level, suicide constitutes a violation of a sacred injunction against the taking lives of others and, by extension, oneself. The act is construed as a 'sin' among all religious groups in Ghana [15], and evidence shows how some persons who attempted suicide construed the act as a sin against God [16]. Perceived as sin, suicides are usually not given church burials among most Christian communities.

The strong societal abhorrence to suicide is institutionalised legally under Ghana's criminal code (1960, Act 29), which states, 'Whoever attempts to commit suicide shall be guilty of a misdemeanor'. Persons who attempt suicide are swiftly apprehended and prosecuted, and upon conviction, they receive criminal penalties ranging from hefty fines to prison terms between one and three years [17].

12.4 Action for Decriminalisation Thus Far

Research and advocacy have been the main mechanisms for shifting public perception away from harsh public attitudes and reactions that view suicidal behaviour as an antisocial act, a sin and a crime, in favour of views that suicide is a life crisis that requires help rather than punishments. These advocacies have been in the form of media engagements; stakeholder consultative meetings with specific groups such as psychology students, nurses, doctors and queen mothers (in the traditional chieftaincy system where some ethnic groups' male leaders are supported by queen mothers); media personnel; and news editors. Some modest progress is being made in this respect, including, for example, evidence from a study showing that some nurses are transitioning from seeing suicide as a moral infraction to seeing it as a life crisis and thus showing more empathy to people in suicidal crisis [18].

12.5 Action against the Criminalisation of Suicide Attempt

Suicide attempts continue to be a criminal offence in Ghana despite evidence from across the world suggesting underlying psychological, psychiatric and socio-cultural factors. A global effort to decriminalise suicides in member countries of the World Health Organization (WHO) is a response to the mutual awareness among practitioners that criminalisation of the act is anachronistic, backward and counterproductive to effective prevention.

In Ghana, although studies have shown a heightened awareness among some groups about the need to change the status quo, others remain committed to the law and want to have it retained. For instance, in a recent study that explored the views of 11 members of parliament (MPs) in Ghana on the call to decriminalise attempted suicide, findings showed 9 MPs in support of the call for decriminalisation while 2 MPs were opposed to it [19]. Another study that explored views of 12 lawyers and judges in Ghana on the law criminalising suicide revealed 3 participants who were in defence of the law, 5 participants who were against the law and called for its repeal, and 4 other participants who wanted the law reformed to meet the needs of offenders [20]. A similar study conducted among clinical psychologists, emergency ward nurses and police officers in Ghana showed the majority of participants disagreeing with the law criminalising attempted suicide in Ghana, while a few participants agreed with the law [21].

It can be gleaned from the provided studies that perhaps a groundswell of support for advocacy towards decriminalisation of suicide attempts may exist among some important groups in Ghana, which only needed to be identified and harnessed for meaningful progress. It is from this belief that a number of significant steps have been taken to galvanise stakeholder support of decriminalisation of suicide attempts in Ghana. The next section will highlight a few of these significant steps and how they have shaped the decriminalisation agenda thus far in Ghana.

12.6 The Path to Decriminalisation of Attempted Suicides in Ghana

The very first practical steps towards advocacy for decriminalisation occurred in 2008, when a group of health professionals presented a petition to Parliament requesting the house to expunge the code that condemns attempted suicide. This initial effort was accentuated when the first author and a group of health professionals organised another petition (this time backed by some data) in 2012 and led a group of colleagues and students to present a petition to the Parliament of Ghana as part of the celebration of World Suicide Prevention Day. Since the petition, a series of gatekeeper training programmes have been organised to sensitise specific target populations and also to mobilise their support for a stronger advocacy towards discrimination. One such gatekeeper training was organised for media personnel on 9 September 2015 on the University of Ghana campus. Fifteen journalists drawn from eight public and private electronic and print media participated in the training. The training programme was to deepen their awareness about the dangers of irresponsible media reportage of suicide and expose them to the WHO guidelines for responsible media reporting of suicides. After the training, we monitored the media landscape on suicide reporting and found some modest gains, as far as adherence to WHO guidelines were concerned [22]. Some media personnel who attended the training recounted the difficulties they encountered in applying the WHO guidelines due to editorial policies.

Another gatekeeper training event held on 8 September 2016 involved 21 police personnel drawn from three main units: Homicide, Domestic Violence and Victim Support (DOVVSU) and Crime Scene. These units play key roles in the investigation, handling and recording of suicidal cases, and thus constituted potential partners for addressing and preventing suicides. The personnel were taken through various topics, including understanding attitudes towards suicide in Ghana, along with protocols regarding whether it is appropriate to arrest an individual or to provide them with help. The attendees also discussed police views of suicidal persons and the law in Ghana, with a plenary discussion on the topic 'Should Attempted Suicide Be Decriminalised in Ghana?'. The gatekeeping role of the police in suicide prevention was also discussed, along with a series of vignettes on attempted suicide and police diversion. A key upshot of the training has been the establishment of a collaboration between the police and our centre (the Centre for Suicide and Violence Research, CSVR) for managing suicidal cases. When suicide attempts are reported to the police, some personnel will now refer cases to us to help or refer family members bereaved by suicides to our team for psychosocial support. The mutual collaboration developed with the police after the training programme paved the way for the second author to conduct a first-ever qualitative psychological autopsy study into suicides in Ghana. The police assisted in accessing suicide cases and bereaved families for the study [23]. Again, the synergy with the police also led to another study that sought to gauge the views of 18 police personnel on the law criminalising suicides. In that study, 14 police officers strongly opposed the law and wanted it repealed, while only 4 of the personnel agreed with the law [24].

12.7 The Zeitgeist: An Era of Stronger and Broader Advocacy towards Decriminalisation

In February 2017 a child of a member of Parliament who was a student in one of Ghana's prominent tertiary educational institutions took her life. This suicide shocked the entire nation and dominated the headlines of major news outlet. It led to a spirited public debate about the need to push the prevention of suicide to the front burner of national priorities. Unfortunately, what followed within six months after this incident was something akin to a suicide contagion in which seven well-publicised suicides occurred, including that of another student who took her life from another prominent public university in Ghana where the authors of this chapter work. Advocacy for national suicide prevention policies and decriminalisation soared.

A consultative stakeholder forum was held on 30 March 2017 to chart the way forward towards suicide prevention. The forum was organised by the Centre for Suicide and Violent Research (CSVR) and was attended by a total of 105 stakeholders, including mental health professionals, physicians, religious leaders, student leaders, lawyers, non-governmental organisations, researchers, educationists, community-based organisations, media personnel, nursing and midwifery professionals, community leaders, police officers and lay persons. The forum discussed various issues under two key themes aimed at strategising the development of the National Policy for Suicide Prevention and Public Education and Training. It presented an opportunity to show evidence of underlying factors for suicides recorded in Ghana and helped fashion a road map for stronger advocacy for national suicide prevention plans. The forum was unanimous on the issue of the hindering effect of the existing criminal code against suicide attempt. Soon after the forum, together with a group of mental health professionals called Mental Health Advocacy, a new petition was drafted and submitted to the Law Reform Commission. While the commission engaged us, copies of the petition were shared with parliamentarians and some members at our centre. Mental Health Advocacy and Mental Health Authority were invited to meet with various Parliamentary Select Committees on Gender and Children and also Health for interaction and discussion. The petition was in three parts. The first part sought a repeal of section 57(2) of the Criminal Offences Act 1960 ((Act) 29) on the criminalisation of attempted suicide. The second part of the petition was to push for the amendment of section 58(2) and section (102) of Act (29), to remove derogatory words. The final part of the petition was an appendix that contained supporting empirical evidence of the petition for the repeal of section 57(2) of (Act) 29 on the criminalisation of attempted suicide. The consultative stakeholder forum finally led to the formation of the Association of Suicide Prevention in Ghana (GASP), which championed advocacy programmes. Together with our centre, various gatekeeper trainings have been held, detailed as follows.

From 24 July through to 8 August 2017, our centre, CSVR, was approached by the Ghana Pentecostal and Charismatic Council (GPCC) to train various women's groups and their leaders in the Greater Accra Region on *Depression and Suicide in Ghana*. More than 2,000 individuals participated in these meetings. After the training, several referrals were made to the centre, and various churches engaged the centre on similar programs.

The training was extended to queen mothers (on 5 September 2017), a key stakeholder group in Ghanaian local political leadership in our communities. The theme for the training was 'The Role of the Traditional Leader (Queen Mothers) in Suicide Prevention'. The purpose of the training was to equip queen mothers to serve as gatekeepers in their respective communities as far as suicide prevention is concerned. The issues addressed included suicide and attitudes towards suicide in Ghana, what protects/what puts people at risk of suicide, domestic abuse, culture and suicide, decriminalising suicide in Ghana and the role of the traditional leader (queen mother) in suicide prevention. A total of 24 influential queen mothers were in attendance. The impact of the programme reverberated through various communities, as the centre kept receiving referrals for help and interventions. School counsellors in pre-tertiary schools were also considered key stakeholders, given the amount of self-injurious behaviours and suicidality being reported by the media. The training was to sharpen their awareness of the reality of suicides and their respective roles towards prevention. It was also to galvanise their efforts in support of the advocacy for decriminalisation. On 5 October 2018 the centre organised a training workshop for Second Cycle School Teachers and Counsellors in the Greater Accra Region. A total of 53 participants from 18 schools were in attendance. The theme was 'Self-Harm and Suicide among Adolescents in Accra'. Topics included an introduction to adolescent mental health, adolescent self-harm and suicide in Ghana, building competencies to support adolescents in crisis and creating a pro–mental health school environment. Participants have since related with the centre and have been seeking knowledge on how to manage students in mental health and suicidal crisis.

12.8 Ghana's Mental Health Act 846, Diversion and Engagement of the Judiciary

It is important at this stage to emphasise that Ghana's Mental Health Act [25] makes provision for diversion. The act thus identifies the court as a key actor that can facilitate the transfer of persons with mental health challenges from the criminal justice system to the mental health systems for urgent and appropriate care. Clear provision is made in article 76 of Mental Health Act 846 for diversion of offenders with potential mental health problems from (1) the point of arrest (police), (2) during trial (in court) and even (3) after trial (in prison). To ensure progress on this, the need to also engage officers of the courts (judges and magistrates) and sensitise them became even more paramount in the wake of the rising number of suicides that were recorded in the year 2017.

Throughout July 2017 a group of suicide researchers, members of the newly formed GASP working in closer collaboration with Ghana's Mental Health Authority and the Judicial Services of Ghana, organised a sensitisation workshop and training for judges and magistrates across the length and breadth of the country. In all, a total of 247 judges and magistrates participated in the one-month nationwide programme. We began the outreach first with about 25 judges from the Supreme and Appeal Courts at Ghana's Supreme Court premises, after which we went around various parts of the country to meet high court judges, judges from district courts and magistrates. During the encounters, the judges recounted their experiences handling persons put before them with suicidal problems. It was apparent that most of these judges empathised with stories of the accused, yet they had the unpleasant duty of showing fidelity to the law. Some admitted that they only advised the accused and discharged them. The programme provided an opportunity for the judges and the magistrates to share some of the distress that comes with their work. The team of trainers took the eminent judges through some relaxation therapies and equipped them with other practical ways of managing the stress of work. In the end, we received, in practical ways, sound advice and direction from the judges on the best strategies to be adopted to expedite the decriminalisation process. The programme was thus a win-win for the judges and the team of mental health professionals who trained them.

12.9 Decriminalisation Advocacy: A Watershed Moment[1]

In 2021 there were series of suicides among police officers from the Ghana Police Service. The police administration took steps to consult with the Centre and Ghana Psychological Association to provide them with mental health services. A team made up of clinical and industrial psychologists organised workshops in three key police administrative areas where suicide occurred. The key issues addressed included stress and stress management, organisational leadership, police suicide and its prevention, and optimising one's mental health. Large numbers of police officers attended this program, and eventually the police administration commissioned a counselling department to address all mental health issues and training in the police service. The centre is manned by clinical psychologists and psychiatrists. The police administration has also included mental health and relevant organisational topics in police recruit training. The collaboration between the Ghana Police Service and mental health workers in Ghana has been tighter in recent times, which has created a strong awareness that persons experiencing suicidal crisis are not criminals but persons in need of mental health services.

A watershed moment in our quest to decriminalise suicide in Ghana occurred on 1 June 2022. On this date, the chairperson of the Parliamentary Select Committee on Constitutional, Legal and Parliamentary Affairs and other members met the lead author (the executive director for CSVR), Ghana Psychological Association, Psychiatry

[1] The Bill repealing the suicide attempt law in Ghana has received a Presidential assent.

Association of Ghana, Mental Health Advocacy, Mental Health Society of Ghana and Mental Health Authority to discuss a Private Member's Bill they are sponsoring to expunge the code that criminalises attempted suicide in Ghana. At the sitting, expert views were sought from us and, finally, resolution on decriminalisation was reached. Subsequently, the Committee contacted the centre for data on suicide and related issues in Ghana to strengthen the bill, presented to the floor of Parliament for consideration. What is interesting in this new move is that the sponsor of the bill had lost a daughter through suicide five years earlier but had, however, mustered courage to confront the antiquated criminal code that punishes the vulnerable instead of providing adequate and timely support.

12.10 Challenges Encountered Thus Far

The fight against criminalisation of suicide attempts encountered several challenges, including financial resources, inertia on the part of government, the delay in implementing the legal framework for the Mental Health Bill and absence of a national suicide prevention plan. These are discussed in the following sections.

12.11 Lack of Financial Resources

Efforts towards decriminalisation have been mainly driven by individual pockets of key persons, including the authors and team of mental health experts and suicide researchers. This hindered progress to the extent that we could not engage the members of Parliament, especially those on the Select Committee on Health, en bloc at private workshops. Fortunately, we identified a few of the MPs whom we considered to be very disposed to the decriminalisation agenda, furnished them with the trove of evidence garnered from Ghana and, at some points, personally engaged them for a thorough discussion on the petition.

12.12 Inertia on the Part of Government

Despite several engagements we had with some government officials in the media and at workshops, it was apparent that suicide and suicide prevention still was not considered a priority on the part of the government. Inertia on the part of the government was a serious drawback in the process until a member of Parliament belonging to the ruling party decided to sponsor the Private Member's Bill. The aftermath of this incident saw open mention and discussion of the matter among some government officials in the media.

12.13 The Lack of Implementation of the Legal Framework of Ghana's Mental Health Act, 2012 (Act 846)

Since the Mental Health Act was passed in the year 2012, Ghana still does not have the legal framework that should guide the implementation of the specific clauses of the act, including diversion of mentally ill persons from the criminal justice system to the mental health system. So even though there has been evidence of flagrant violation of specific clauses of the act, the present lacuna orchestrated by the lack of implementation of the legal framework to operationalise the act hinders any genuine efforts to redress the situation.

12.14 Lack of National Suicide Prevention Plan

The WHO recommendation for national governments to fashion out contextually relevant national suicide prevention sought to encourage national government to have a framework to harmonise all the efforts towards suicide prevention. Unfortunately, Ghana still does not have a national suicide prevention plan. The situation led to disjointed advocacy, which hampered progress. For instance, despite several trainings conducted for the media on responsible suicide reporting in line with WHO guidelines, there continues to be gross violation of the WHO guidelines on responsible reporting by some media organisations.

Furthermore, there remains no registry for recording suicides and suicidal behaviours. Only suicides that catch the attention of the media come to the attention of the media, even though suicides continue to happen in communities. The absence of reliable statistics leads to a crude underestimation of the problem and, perhaps, heightens the inertia on the part of the government, as far as prioritising suicide is concerned.

12.15 The Way Forward

Although the journey has been long, there is a light at the end of the tunnel, and we envisage that the outcome of the recent meeting with the select committee in Parliament will lead to an expedited action on decriminalisation. At the time of the last review of this chapter, Ghana's Parliament has voted to decriminalise suicide attempt. The amended bill is awaiting presidential assent to become a law. It is important to underscore that decriminalisation is just one side of the coin. What is left now is setting up a National Suicide Prevention Centre and developing a national suicide prevention policy. We also need to engage in serious public education to change attitudes, as well as a strong advocacy towards improvement of the mental health sector generally. This is important because decriminalisation is likely to lose its intent in Ghana when people attempt suicide, and instead of being helped within the mental health system, they are left to the harsh treatment of the public. In the several years of our work on suicide and suicide prevention, we have encountered several persons who after attempting suicide are subjected to negative treatment, which heightens their distress, leading some to take the route of finally killing themselves. It is important that an eagle eye is kept on renewed efforts towards decriminalisation, while at the same time a strong push for needed reforms in mental health is sustained. We suggest interprofessional collaboration in mental health care and suicide prevention [26]. Particularly, the need for orthodox mental health practitioners to work closely with faith healers cannot be underestimated as we seek to scale up resources for helping persons who may be going through mental health challenges and suicidal crisis in the aftermath of the decriminalisation. Such synergies are urgently needed to help close the yawning treatment gap in Ghana.

References

1. Andoh-Arthur J, Quarshie ENB. Suicide attempt and 'social suffering': Disrupting dangerous binary discourse and fostering kinship between the mental health and legal systems in Ghana. In Chan HCO, Adjorlolo S, eds., *Mental Health & Criminal Justice System in Africa*. London: Palgrave Macmillan; 2021.
2. Quarshie ENB, Waterman MG, House AO. Prevalence of self-harm among lesbian, gay, bisexual, and transgender adolescents: A comparison of personal and social adversity with a heterosexual sample in

Ghana. *BMC Research Notes*. 2020; **13**(1): 1–6.

3. Quarshie ENB, Andoh-Arthur J. Suicide attempt among 1437 adolescents aged 12–17 years attending junior high schools in Ghana: Prevalence and psychosocial correlates. *Crisis: The Journal of Crisis Intervention and Suicide Prevention*. 2021; **43**(1): 8–17.
4. Asante KO, Kugbey N, Osafo J, Quarshie ENB, Sarfo JO. The prevalence and correlates of suicidal behaviours (ideation, plan and attempt) among adolescents in senior high schools in Ghana. *SSM – Population Health*. 2017; **3**: 427–34.
5. Quarshie ENB, Odame SK, Annor F. Suicidal behaviors in the Ghana Police Service: Prevalence and correlates in the Greater Accra Region. *Crisis: The Journal of Crisis Intervention and Suicide Prevention*. 2021; **42**(3): 194.
6. World Health Organization. *Preventing Suicide: A Global Imperative*. Geneva: World Health Organization; 2014.
7. Gyekye K. *African Philosophical Scheme: The Akan Conceptual Scheme*. Cambridge: Cambridge University Press; 2005.
8. Adinkrah M. Better dead than dishonored: Masculinity and male suicidal behavior in contemporary Ghana. *Social Science and Medicine*. 2012; **74**(4): 474–81.
9. Osafo J, Hjelmeland H, Akotia CS, Knizek BL. The meanings of suicidal behaviour to psychology students in Ghana: A qualitative approach. *Transcultural Psychiatry*. 2011; **48**(5): 1–17.
10. Adinkrah M. Suicide and mortuary beliefs and practices of the Akan of Ghana. *OMEGA – Journal of Death and Dying*. 2016; **74**(2): 138–63.
11. Osafo J. *Attitudes towards Suicide: Exploring the Cultural Meaning(s) of Suicide in Ghana*. PhD dissertation submitted to Norwegian University of Science and Technology (NTNU), Trondheim, Norway, 2012.
12. Andoh-Arthur J, Knizek BL, Osafo J, Hjelmeland H. Societal reactions to suicides in Ghana: A qualitative study. *Crisis: The Journal of Crisis Intervention and Suicide Prevention*. 2019; **41(2)**: 128–34.
13. Osafo J, Akotia CS, Andoh-Arthur J, Quarshie ENB. Attempted suicide in Ghana: Motivation, stigma, and coping. *Death Studies*. 2015; **39**(5): 274–80.
14. Asare-Doku W, Osafo J, Akotia CS. The experiences of attempt survivor families and how they cope after a suicide attempt in Ghana: A qualitative study. *BMC Psychiatry*. 2017; **17**(1): 178.
15. Osafo J, Hjelmeland H, Akotia CS, Knizek BL. Social injury: An interpretative phenomenological analysis of the attitudes towards suicide of lay persons in Ghana. *International Journal of Qualitative Studies on Health and Well-Being*. 2011; **6**(4): 8708–18.
16. Akotia CS, Knizek BL, Kinyanda E, Hjelmeland, H. 'I have sinned': Understanding the role of religion in the experiences of suicide attempters in Ghana. *Mental Health, Religion & Culture*. 2013; **17**(5): 437–48.
17. Adinkrah M. Criminal prosecution of suicide attempt survivors in Ghana. *International Journal of Offender Therapy and Comparative Criminology*. 2013; **57**(12): 1477–97.
18. Osafo J, Akotia CS, Boakye KE, Dickson E. Between moral infraction and existential crisis: Exploring physicians and nurses' attitudes to suicide and the suicidal patient in Ghana. *International Journal of Nursing Studies*. 2018; **85**: 118–25.
19. Quarshie ENB, Oppong Asante K, Andoh-Arthur J, Akotia CS, Osafo J. To keep the law or to repeal it: Views of parliamentarians on the call to decriminalise attempted suicide in Ghana. *OMEGA – Journal of Death and Dying*. 2024; **89**: 39–56.
20. Osafo J, Akotia CS, Andoh-Arthur J, Boakye KE, Quarshie, ENB. 'We now have a patient and not a criminal': An exploratory study of judges and lawyers' views on suicide attempters and the law in Ghana. *International Journal of Offender Therapy and Comparative Criminology*. 2018; **62**(6): 1488–1508.

21. Hjelmeland H, Osafo J, Akotia CS, Knizek BL. The law criminalizing attempted suicide in Ghana. *Crisis: The Journal of Crisis Intervention and Suicide Prevention*. 2014; **35**(2): 132–6.

22. Quarshie ENB, Andoh-Arthur J, Asante KO, Asare-Doku W. Online media reporting of suicidal behaviour in Ghana: Analysis of adherence to the WHO guidelines. *International Journal of Social Psychiatry*. 2020; **67**(3): 251–9.

23. Andoh-Arthur J, Hjelmeland H, Osafo J, Knizek BL. 'Walking a tightrope': Reflections on police gatekeeping in suicide research in Ghana. *International Journal of Social Research Methodology*. 2018; **21**(3): 289–301.

24. Osafo J, Akotia CS, Quarshie ENB, Boakye KE, Andoh-Arthur J. Police views of suicidal persons and the law criminalizing attempted suicide in Ghana: A qualitative study with policy implications. *Sage Open*. 2017; **7**(3).

25. Parliament of Republic of Ghana. *The Mental Health Act 2012: Act 846*. 2012. www.refworld.org/pdfid/528f243e4.pdf.

26. Osafo J, Andoh-Arthur J. Inter-sectoral management of suicidal persons in Ghana: Tensions and Prospects. *Community Mental Health Journal*. 2021; **57**(6): 1010–16.

Chapter 13

Suicide Prevention in Clinical Practice

Linda Gask and Alex Thomson

13.1 What Does 'Good Clinical Practice' in Suicide Prevention Look Like?

Various guides have been developed in recent years to advise on how to provide safe and effective care to people at risk of suicide and self-harm and those presenting after self-harm in health care settings [1–5]. Management depends to some degree on the context in which a person is presenting (e.g., a general practitioner's (GP's) office, therapy room or emergency department), their prior relationships with the consulting professional, the boundaries of confidentiality pertaining to that relationship and the confidence of the professional to explore and discuss suicidal ideation. We will explore the common attitudes, skills and knowledge required by professionals working across different settings, then consider how these are modified by the different contexts in which they work – primary care, therapy settings and secondary mental health care teams and providers, and what else is required in those settings to ensure quality of care.

13.2 Interpersonal Aspects of Care

With its '10 Ways to Improve Safety' study, the National Confidential Inquiry for Suicide and Homicide (NCISH) [4] emphasises the importance of a personalised risk assessment: 'All patients' management plans should be based on the assessment of individual risk and not on the completion of a checklist'. This should be underpinned by respect, person-centredness and compassion, along with an ability to demonstrate appropriate flexibility and based on the best evidence.

13.3 Engagement Skills

Engaging a person in discussion about suicide and self-harm requires not only effective communication skills but being able to listen, demonstrate empathy, and pick up and sensitively explore verbal and nonverbal cues. Jobes [6] emphasises the importance of developing the therapeutic relationship: working in *collaboration* with the person to achieve a shared understanding of their problems, listening to their story non-judgmentally and, where suicide is expressed as an option, exploring what has led them to concluding that this is the only alternative. The consultation is not simply an assessment but a therapeutic intervention too, in terms of working together in a joint effort and conveying hope. This is *very* different from a routine checklist assessment interview (which many people who use services almost know by heart).

13.4 Talking about Suicide and Self-Harm

Specific questions about suicide and self-harm must be asked. The progress of the interview can be influenced by picking up on emotional cues to explore with key questions, such as '*When you say you feel low, can you tell me a little what that is like?*'; '*Does that ever reach a point that you feel unable to go on?*'; '*Have you ever felt that life isn't worth living?*'; '*Have you had thoughts of ending your life?*', possibly prefixed with a normalising phrase: '*This is a question that I ask everyone …*'. Further questions can then be signposted: '*There are a few more questions I'd like to ask about that …*', followed by questions about duration, frequency and severity of those thoughts; whether and exactly what plans have been considered; how close the person has come to enacting them; and what has stopped them from doing this. More than one method may have been considered. Similarly, when talking to someone who has self-harmed, signposting can be used to indicate the need to ask more detailed questions about duration, methods, frequency and severity of self-harm. Permission should be respectfully asked before looking at scars and wounds, and no assumptions should be made that a person must want to, or should, stop self-harming. Instead there should be careful exploration of situations in which it occurs, what it means to the person and what impact it has on their emotional state.

13.5 Assessing Risk of Suicide

Risk assessment includes the evaluation of a wide range of biological, social and psychological factors that are relevant to the individual and, in the judgment of the health care professional conducting the assessment, relevant to future risks, including not only thoughts of suicide, degree of planning and consideration of other methods (noted previously), but also context, underlying vulnerability and current mental state. Risk assessment is *one element* of a comprehensive clinical assessment, alongside diagnostic assessment, personalised formulation, assessment of social needs and identification of modifiable risk factors, all of which should inform treatment planning.

Context: What has been happening recently in this person's life? Are there any particular trigger events? Who else is around for them? Can they be involved? If the person has recently harmed themselves, what was their perception of what the outcome would be?

Vulnerability: What specific risk factors are there? These include past history of self-harm and mental illness; family history of suicide; health risk behaviours, including alcohol and drug use; impulsivity; physical health and psychosocial factors such as difficult relationships, bereavement, financial problems, looming deadlines and difficult anniversaries.

What are the specific risk factors and protective factors (social, psychological, pharmacological and motivational) that may increase or decrease the risks associated with self-harm? What are the coping strategies that the person has used in the past? Are there significant relationships that may either be supportive or represent a threat (such as abuse or neglect) and may lead to changes in the level of risk?

Current mental state: Evidence of depression or other mental illness, but also specific emotional states that indicate higher risk, including hopelessness, sense of entrapment or burdensomeness, shame, humiliation and self-hatred. If this is after an attempt at taking their life, how do they now feel about the outcome?

As an approach to predicting suicide, risk assessment is notoriously unreliable. Rather, the information collected in the assessment should be used to develop a *formulation of risk*, including the nature of current problems, predisposing, precipitating, perpetuating and protective factors derived from the assessment, which should then be clearly recorded. Risk formulation identifies 'why' someone engages in problematic behaviour, not just 'if' they will engage in it, and encourages a shift away from simply identifying risk factors to thinking about how key variables interact and connect in the expression of risk.

13.6 Clinical Environments and Primary Care

The vast majority of people with mental health problems are treated in primary care. Guidance from NCISH following a case-control study of suicide in primary care [7] advises that there is a mechanism in place:

- For safer prescribing of opiate analgesics and tricyclic antidepressants (i.e., reduced, short-term supplies). Opiates were found to be the most commonly used drug in fatal overdose.
- To ensure that patients who present with major physical illness are assessed and monitored for depression and risk of suicide (71% of people who died by suicide and presented to their GP had a diagnosis of depression).
- To ensure that patients with certain markers of risk (i.e., frequent consultations, multiple psychotropic drugs and specific drug combinations) are further assessed and considered for referral to specialist mental health services. (Only 8% of people who died by suicide had been referred to specialist mental health services in the previous 12 months.)

When a person consults following self-harm, a primary care professional should be able to carry out an assessment as noted previously and refer as necessary but will also likely have the benefit of prior knowledge of the person and their family. In the assessment and management of self-injury in primary care, health care professionals should refer service users for urgent treatment, if assessment suggests there is a significant risk. Effective liaison in the community, between primary and secondary care and other care providers, is essential to ensure that advice and consultation is available where required and that key information about patients is conveyed back to their GP.

13.7 Counselling and Therapy Settings

Many people with common mental health problems now receive care in these settings in the community. Some therapy training courses still do not adequately address suicide prevention [8,9], and counsellors should be able to carry out an assessment of risk and formulate a safety or crisis plan with a client (as discussed later). Confidentiality is a major concern for therapists, but careful contracting from the outset, in which the exceptions to confidentiality are clarified, together with an explanation of what will happen in these circumstances, may avoid potential problems with disclosure. Consultation with the supervisor will be key, along with clear record-keeping. If a therapist feels that despite talking things through, the client remains at immediate risk to themselves and is unwilling or unable to consent to the disclosure of information to a third party, it is important that they act on their concerns quickly and appropriately. This may include contacting the client's GP or crisis services.

13.8 Secondary Care

A well-functioning, integrated secondary care mental health system is vital in effective care delivery for suicide prevention. Elements include timely access to community treatment and support, specialist treatment services, ability to respond to emergencies and inpatient treatment, where needed. In secondary care, the mainstay of suicide prevention is access to diagnostic assessment, collaborative formulation and condition-specific, evidence-based mental health treatment in primary or secondary care. Preventative care planning must consider prescribing, psychotherapy, support to maintain social functioning and relationships, and addressing social risk factors. Secondary mental health services must therefore have good relationships with social services and local services working to address common suicide risk factors such as domestic violence, homelessness, asylum and immigration problems, sexual violence, financial problems and harmful use of alcohol or other drugs [10–15].

The focus of care delivery should be on a prompt response to referrals and responsive community mental health teams who can review treatment and provide additional support in response to deterioration. For mental health emergencies, which may include rapid deterioration or difficulties accessing help, a 24/7 service is needed. Emergency mental health services need to liaise with other emergency services where people might seek help, such as police, ambulance and hospital emergency departments. Specialist mental health help-lines can give advice in emergencies and, where necessary, dispatch mental health staff to attend. 'Street triage' services, involving joint working between police and mental health services, have been developed to ensure that there is clinical support when police are called to emergencies [16]. Mental health ambulance response teams have been developed to minimise police involvement, though there are currently few formal evaluations of this model [17]. In hospital emergency departments, on-site specialist liaison psychiatry services can provide immediate response to mental health emergencies and make arrangements for ongoing care and treatment [18].

Where patients need high-intensity, short-term treatment for a severe episode of illness, the crisis team model can provide an alternative to hospital admission [19].

13.9 Inpatient Care

Although the issue of when to admit has long been the topic of research and discussion, it remains a matter of professional judgment [20]. Factors affecting decisions have been identified, including suicidality, absence of support, lack of self-care, severity of psychiatric symptoms, existing diagnosis, discontinuation of medication and previous involuntary admissions, though these describe rather than guide decision-making [21]. Decision support tools have been developed, though it is likely that these are context-dependent, and the availability of local services is as important as individual patient factors in admissions [22]. Patient preference to avoid hospitalisation and managing health care costs are both considerations in service configuration. Specialist assessment by clinicians experienced in emergency psychiatry or intensive home treatment, third-party information from carers or treating clinicians, and the development of psychiatric emergency assessment units have been identified as factors associated with lower likelihood of hospitalisation [23,24]. However, suicide rates in patients under the care of home treatment teams are higher than in inpatients, indicating that careful assessment and regular review of treatment setting is essential, particularly for people who live alone [25].

While inpatient care can assure close supervision and treatment of the most unwell patients at greatest risk of suicide, risk factors for suicide still exist. Suicide associated with inpatient treatment is most common during the first few days of admission, during time off the ward and the first few days after discharge [26]. Preventing suicide in the inpatient setting requires prompt access to both pharmacological and psychotherapeutic treatment, support to address psychosocial stressors while in hospital, and attention to staffing levels, compassionate culture and the physical environment. Access to means can be limited by medicines management and minimising ligature points, including low-lying ligatures. The need for supervision and restriction of access to means must be balanced against the risk of creating an overly restrictive and sparse, unstimulating environment. Alongside physical and environmental safety, it is important to consider psychological safety, which includes freedom from fear, trust in staff and freedom from disempowerment. Important factors in maintaining psychological safety include minimising the use of restrictive practices or physical restraint, ensuring access to compassionate staff with time to listen and support, and measures to address the risk of physical or sexual assault by other patients and staff [27,28,29]. Patients with experience of inpatient treatment report the importance of empathic connection, being acknowledged as a human being, being protected from death, receiving support and re-establishing control over their lives [30]. Although inpatients may express a preference for single-sex wards as a means of managing both past traumatic experiences and immediate safety, the need for such arrangements is not universally accepted by service providers [31,32].

13.10 Treatment and Interventions

Given the varied causes of suicide, intervention must include bio-psychosocial needs assessment and care planning, including diagnostic assessment of mental illness and treatment planning, identification of interpersonal and social stressors with support to address these, and long-term care and support for both physical and mental health-related disabilities. While there is no generic treatment for suicidality, some specific approaches have been evaluated for their contribution to overall care in people who have self-harmed or attempted suicide.

13.11 Safety Planning

Formal safety planning involves the collaborative production of a plan of actions [33] to consider in terms of (a) ensuring personal safety (e.g., someone else taking care of medication), (b) coping strategies for emotional distress (e.g., distraction, breathing exercises, listening to music), and (c) sources of support – both personal (e.g., friends) and from professional or volunteer agencies (GP, secondary care, help-lines such as Samaritans). Future safety planning for longer-term planning involves, as in relapse prevention work, identifying the early warning signs of increasing distress (in terms of thoughts, feelings, physical symptoms and behaviour changes) and then putting plans into action – both first line to avert worsening of symptoms and then in a developing crisis. Safety planning is now widely recommended – particularly in the Royal College of Psychiatrists' guidance on self-harm, and online safety plans are available [34]. However, the evidence for it is based on a relatively small number of studies [35,36,37], none of which were carried out in primary care. There are risks that if not *truly* carried out collaboratively, and used as the basis for follow-up contact and further therapeutic discussion between patient and professional, it can become a box-ticking exercise and even unhelpful [37].

13.12 Specific Psychological Interventions

The evidence for specific psychological interventions for people who self-harm remains patchy and not easy to interpret. In 2011 the National Institute for Health and Care

Excellence (NICE) reviewed the field's extensively considered therapies with cognitive-behavioural, psychodynamic and problem-solving approaches. They recommended 3–12 sessions *tailored for individual need* from the provided approaches and specifically structured for people who self-harm. These should be provided by fully trained and supervised therapists experienced in working with people who self-harm, working collaboratively with service users to identify problems causing distress or factors maintaining their self-harm. They also noted that dialectical behavioural therapy (DBT) showed some benefit in reducing rates of self-harm for people with a diagnosis of borderline personality disorder (BPD).

Hawton and his colleagues [38], in a more recent systematic review, concluded that CBT (comprising cognitive-behavioural and problem-solving elements) seemed to be effective after self-harm, with few trials of any other promising interventions. They also concluded that DBT did not reduce the *proportion* of patients repeating self-harm but did reduce the *frequency* of self-harm. The challenge with evaluating generic psychological interventions for self-harm and suicidality is that the underlying factors, circumstances and mental illnesses are highly heterogeneous. In our opinion, as with other therapies, the attitude and behaviour of the practitioner, the relationship with a patient, and the integration with condition- and social circumstance-specific treatments or interventions are more important than the structure of a generic intervention.

13.13 Maintaining Patient Safety and Avoiding Iatrogenic Harm: Excessive Focus on Risk

While considering suicide risk is a necessary and vital component of clinical practice, there are some ways in which, when misapplied, this focus may become counterproductive. The *low-risk paradox* refers to the observation that the majority of people who died by suicide following contact with mental health services were judged to be 'low risk' at last service contact [7]. This observation leads to several interpretations and implications. People judged to be moderate or high risk are likely to receive a higher level of support and treatment to prevent suicide. People judged as low risk outnumber those judged moderate or high risk, so the absolute number of suicide deaths may be higher even if the rate is lower [39]. Checklists and scoring tools based on identified risk factors for self-harm or suicide perform poorly when compared to professional judgment [40]. A formulaic focus on risk may paradoxically worsen outcomes by inhibiting authentic connection and validation of distress, leaving patients feeling judged and needing to prove they are worthy of help, thus impairing trust in services [41].

This leads to the conclusion that the approach of determining eligibility for secondary care by identifying who is at risk of dying by suicide is based on the fallacy that we can do this with any accuracy or confidence [43]. While risk assessment tools may act as an aide memoire in order to structure professional judgment, they are no substitute for the approach of risk formulation and management. To be effective at preventing suicide, health care services must ensure that people with suicidal ideation or mental illnesses have access to effective treatment regardless of perceived suicide risk. Where services are at full capacity, this may put staff in a difficult position where some eligibility criteria are necessary to manage demand. In such circumstances it is important that mental health assessments remain therapeutic, with feedback and an opportunity to reflect, and focussed on need rather than eligibility. Where a service is unable to take a patient on for treatment, they should provide an assessment with feedback and advice for support and treatment, and information about alternative sources of support, communicating this with both the patient and their primary care practitioner [3].

13.14 Falling through the Gaps

Vital to the effective operation of clinical services is the integration and management of interfaces or transfers of care. Where different services are commissioned or operated in isolation, it may be possible for a person to be considered too high risk by a primary care service but not high risk enough by secondary care [42]. It is similarly possible for a person to be considered too high risk for every available service, leaving them in a position where all professionals agree that they are highly likely to die by suicide in the foreseeable future, but no service believes that they have the expertise or the responsibility to provide treatment. In both examples, the person is left in a liminal space where the only access to treatment or support is dependent on their primary care practitioner [43]. It is similarly vital that primary care and secondary care mental health services have good working arrangements with the necessary agencies to address common risk factors for suicide, such as harmful use of alcohol or other drugs, domestic violence advocacy, homelessness services and financial or benefits advice. A person with mental health needs exacerbated by their environment or social circumstances may require support to engage with other agencies.

13.15 Behavioural Management Approaches to Self-Harm and Suicidality

'Behavioural management' approaches to self-harm and suicidality were an accepted part of clinical practice in the late twentieth century. These were based on the theory that suicidality, self-harm and suicide attempts were behaviours which could be reinforced or rewarded by responding with care and compassion, and extinguished by the use of punishment [44]. The use of explicit punishments such as electric shocks, ice showers, painful restraint and seclusion has quite rightly fallen from favour on the grounds that they are neither ethical nor helpful. However, the belief that it is justified to withhold attention, or even respond aversively, to self-harm and expressions of distress lingers in contemporary clinical practice and in the use of derogatory terms such as 'manipulative' or 'attention-seeking' [45]. In some cases patients continue to experience derogatory responses or even refusals to assist from health care staff [46,47,48]. The observation that health care staff without specialist mental health training may view people who have self-harmed more sympathetically suggests that there may be elements of training and culture which need to be addressed [49,50].

There is no evidence to suggest that empathic, caring responses to self-harm or suicidality worsens outcomes or increases suicide rates. Rather, the opposite is the case: aversive responses may worsen outcomes or increase the likelihood of suicide by deterring future help-seeking or engagement, while leaving mental health conditions untreated and suicide risk factors unaddressed [51]. In cases of chronic self-harm and suicidality, attempts have been made to modify the behaviour of people identified as 'high intensity users of services' by the use of criminal behaviour orders or community protection notices. These measures aim to deter people from calling emergency services or attempting suicide in public places by threatening fines or imprisonment for the breach of an order. While these raise ethical questions about the roles and responsibilities of health care professionals, similar clinical considerations about lack of effectiveness and risk of harm apply as to other punishment-based responses to suicidality [52]. The evidence in this area suggests that the most effective response to frequent use of emergency services is a combination of key working and multi-agency care planning to meet need rather than exclusion [53].

There may be a further incorrect assumption that self-harm or suicidality indicates personality disorder. Suicidality and self-harm are features of a wide range of mental illnesses, including depression, obsessive-compulsive disorder, schizophrenia, post-traumatic stress disorder and bipolar affective disorder. Although the care of people with personality disorders may be challenging in clinical systems where there needs are not well served, effective treatments and service configurations are available, and this diagnosis should not be used to exclude a person from either emergency treatment or longer-term treatment [54].

13.16 Groupthink and Closed Cultures

Multidisciplinary working and shared decision-making are an important part of holistic care. It is important to recognise that teams may be at risk of developing a closed culture or groupthink, where a lack of external oversight and a focus on consensus and social conformity with colleagues leads staff to stray from good practice. While the risk is greatest in locked inpatient facilities, closed cultures may develop in community services, particularly in conditions of service pressure or where problems exist with governance and leadership [55]. 'Malignant alienation' describes the phenomenon whereby relations with a patient progressively deteriorate, resulting in a withdrawal of sympathy, support and treatment from staff, along with a tendency to construe needs and behaviour as provocative, unreasonable or overdependent. Such alienation can gather momentum and lead to fatal outcomes [56,57].

Where service culture is closed to feedback from incidents and complaints, attempts by patients to raise concerns may lead to defensive and hostile responses, with complaints ignored and dismissed, or even patients being deliberately and vexatiously excluded from treatment as reprisal [58,59,60]. Clinical practice safeguards include support for staff training, attendance at external conferences and networking events, opportunities for reflective practice, and regular monitoring of clinical outcomes, patient experience measures and complaints. Regulatory safeguards against the development of closed cultures include internal governance, peer review visits from other services and external inspection [15].

13.17 What Needs to Be Done to Maintain Positive Standards and Values?

13.17.1 Lived Experience and Co-production

There is increasing support for including people with open, lived experience of mental illnesses, self-harm or suicide attempts in research and in the design and delivery of clinical services. While peer support workers in mental health services can improve patients' sense of hope, support and connection, evidence of clinical benefit is mixed [61,62]. People with lived experience of mental illnesses and mental health services have insights into service delivery which may not be apparent to staff, and can mitigate against prejudice and assumptions. There is guidance on lived experience inclusion in research and service delivery [63,64]. However, the work can involve considerable psychological demand and emotional labour, and it is important for this to be appropriately remunerated and supported.

13.17.2 Staff Support and Networking

Support for staff, continuing professional education and networking has a role in the maintenance of professional identity, values and behavioural standards. Within teams, informal support and relationship-building should be supplemented by formal arrangements for supervision and reflective practice and clear arrangements for support with clinical challenges, work-related issues and more personal problems. A qualitative study of externally facilitated reflective practice for psychiatric liaison nurses, who have frequent contact with people who have self-harmed or attempted suicide, found that participants valued the practice. Themes identified included sharing and emotional expression, offering a perspective to see the value of their work, a safe space and development of supportive relationships [65].

External networking and benchmarking may mitigate the risk of closed cultures or groupthink by maintaining normative standards, for example membership of an external peer group or network and attending external conferences and continuing professional development events. A national UK audit of the quality of care of patients with significant mental health conditions who were admitted to a general hospital found a higher standard of care in hospitals which were members of a peer accreditation network [66]. Retrospective evaluations and randomised trials of peer networks have found increases in compliance with quality standards and positive qualitative evaluations, though it is unclear to what extent these translate into changes in clinical outcomes [67]. As a complex intervention, it is likely that potential benefits require careful definition, several years to realise, and are dependent on the development and maintenance of positive working cultures.

13.17.3 Patient Experience and Outcomes Monitoring

While it is generally agreed that mental health services should monitor clinical outcomes in the interests of patient safety and quality of care, there is limited consensus on approaches to implementation. Consequently, practice is inconsistent and there is greater focus on process measures. Although issues such as waiting times, admission rates and access to treatments are important, there may not be a direct association with clinical outcomes and there is a risk of unintended consequences though inappropriate incentivisation of unhelpful service behaviour. Patient experience and satisfaction is an important outcome in its own right and has been found to be positively associated with quality of care and patient safety [68]. Selection and implementation of service outcome monitoring should therefore be done in collaboration with people with lived and carer experience with mental health conditions, to identify and agree upon outcomes which are meaningful and relevant to patients' lives.

13.17.4 Training

Staff training is one of the planks of suicide prevention – despite the absence of good quality evidence from randomised controlled trials for its effectiveness [69]. It is difficult to see how clinicians can provide care without being trained in the necessary interventions to provide personalised risk assessment and effective management, and experience would suggest that training needs to be revisited regularly – with periodic review of the content and methods. Training that involves active role rehearsal and video feedback demonstrably leads to the acquisition of skills and changes in attitude and confidence [70], but on its own, this does not lead to a reduction in suicide [71]. Experience from a national rollout of training in Scotland suggests that a training strategy for suicide prevention should consider how to not only disseminate and implement training within organisations but what is required to establish a flourishing culture of high-quality skills acquisition and development [72] with both managerial and practical, organisational support for training.

13.18 Conclusions

- Assessment of risk does not begin with simply asking questions about suicide but with first engaging the patient. The consultation is not simply an assessment but a therapeutic intervention, in terms of working together in a joint effort and instilling hope.
- Risk assessment is one element of a comprehensive clinical assessment, alongside diagnostic assessment, personalised formulation, assessment of social needs and identification of modifiable risk – all of which should inform treatment planning.
- Effective working relationships and liaison in the community between primary and secondary care and other agencies is essential.
- Safety planning is good clinical practice, although the research evidence for it remains limited. It should be carried out collaboratively to avoid becoming a checklist exercise.
- The evidence for specific psychological interventions is patchy and not easy to interpret, but both cognitive behaviour therapy and dialectical behavioural therapy have been demonstrated to be effective. The attitude and behaviour of the practitioner may be the most important factor.
- To be effective at preventing suicide, health care services must ensure that people with suicidal ideation or mental illnesses have access to effective condition-specific treatment, regardless of perceived suicide risk.
- Behavioural management practices for self-harm and suicidality have no place in modern clinical services.
- It is incorrect to assume that self-harm and suicidality indicates personality disorder. In fact, they are features of a wide range of different mental illnesses.
- Clinical practice safeguards include support for staff training, opportunities for reflective practice, regular monitoring of clinical outcomes, and patient experience measures and complaints.
- Excellence in suicide prevention in clinical practice requires attention not only to the interpersonal and organisational aspects of delivering care, but also to the maintenance of patient safety, avoidance of iatrogenic harm, and ensuring the continued application of positive standards and values.

References

1. National Collaborating Centre for Mental Health. *Self-Harm: The Short-Term Physical and Psychological Management and Secondary Prevention of Self-Harm in Primary and Secondary Care*. Leicester: British Psychological Society; 2004.
2. National Institute for Health and Clinical Excellence. *Self-Harm: Longer-Term Management: CG 133*. London: NICE; 2011.

3. Stone H, Barrett K, Beales D, Cole-King A, Das S, Deshpande M, et al. *Self-Harm and Suicide in Adults: Final Report of the Patient Safety Group*. London: Royal College of Psychiatrists; 2020. www.rcpsych.ac.uk/improving-care/campaigning-for-better-mental-health-policy/college-reports/2020-college-reports/cr229.
4. National Confidential Inquiry into Suicide and Homicide (NCISH). *Safer Services: A Toolkit for Specialist Mental Health Services and Primary Care*. Manchester: NCISH; 2013.
5. Reeves, A. *Working with Suicidal Clients in the Counselling Professions: Good Practice in Action 042*. Lutterworth: British Association for Counselling and Psychotherapy; 2020.
6. Jobes DA. *Managing Suicidal Risk: A Collaborative Approach*. New York: Guilford; 2016.
7. National Confidential Inquiry into Suicide and Homicide (NCISH). *Suicide in Primary Care in England, 2002–2011*. Manchester: NCISH; 2014.
8. Wheeler S, Bowl R, Reeves A. Assessing risk: Confrontation or avoidance – what is taught on counsellor training courses. *British Journal of Guidance and Counselling*. 2004 May 1; **32**(2): 235–47.
10. Amiri S. Prevalence of suicide in immigrants/refugees: A systematic review and meta-analysis. *Archives of Suicide Research*. 2022; **26**(2): 370–405.
11. Ayano G, Tsegay L, Abraha M, Yohannes K. Suicidal ideation and attempt among homeless people: A systematic review and meta-analysis. *Psychiatry Quarterly*. 2019 Dec; **90**(4): 829–42.
12. Correia R, Jackson D. Risk to self: Identifying and managing risk of suicide and self-harm. *BJPsych Advances*. 2021 Mar; **27**(2): 126–36.
13. MacIsaac MB, Bugeja LC, Jelinek GA. The association between exposure to interpersonal violence and suicide among women: A systematic review. *Australia and New Zealand Journal of Public Health*. 2017 Feb; **41**(1): 61–9.
14. National Confidential Inquiry into Suicide and Safety in Mental Health. *Annual Report: England, Northern Ireland, Scotland and Wales*. Manchester: University of Manchester; 2019.
15. Thomson AB, Nyein C, Clarke M. Protection and safeguarding of vulnerable adults and children from violence. In Khwaja M, Tyrer P, eds., *Prevention and Management of Violence: Guidance for Mental Healthcare Professionals*, 2nd ed. Cambridge: Cambridge University Press; 2023.
16. Kirubarajan A, Puntis S, Perfect D, Tarbit M, Buckman M, Molodynski A. Street triage services in England: Service models, national provision and the opinions of police. *BJPsych Bulletin*. 2018 Dec; **42**(6): 253–7.
17. Trainer M. *Mental Health Joint Response Car Pilot – Evaluation Report*. London: NHS England and NHS Improvement; 2020 Aug. https://aace.org.uk/initiatives/mental-health-joint-response-car/.
18. Butler J, Hicks A, Brodie D, Bruce-Jones W, Cole-King A, Dahabra S, et al. *Liaison Psychiatry for Every Acute Hospital: Integrated Mental and Physical Healthcare*. London: Royal College of Psychiatrists; 2013. www.rcpsych.ac.uk/members/your-faculties/liaison-psychiatry/news-and-resources.
19. Johnson S. Crisis resolution and home treatment teams: An evolving model. *Advances in Psychiatric Treatment*. 2013 Mar; **19**(2): 115–23.
20. Apsler R, Bassuk E. Differences among clinicians in the decision to admit. *Archives of General Psychiatry*. 1983 Oct; **40**(10): 1133–7.
21. Marty S, Jaeger M, Moetteli S, Theodoridou A, Seifritz E, Hotzy F. Characteristics of psychiatric emergency situations and the decision-making process leading to involuntary admission. *Frontiers of Psychiatry*. 2018; **9**: 760.
22. McGarvey EL, Leon-Verdin M, Wanchek TN, Bonnie RJ. Decisions to initiate involuntary commitment: The role of intensive community services and other

factors. *Psychiatric Services*. 2013 Feb 1; **64**(2): 120–6.

23. Moss J, Nauranga D, Kim D, Rosen M, Wang K, Lanctot K. Variation in admission rates between psychiatrists on call in a university teaching hospital. *Annals of General Psychiatry*. 2018 Jul 10; **17**: 30.

24. Way BB. Relationships between patient, family, and significant other disposition preferences in psychiatric emergency services and the clinical symptom ratings and disposition decisions of psychiatrists. *Psychiatric Rehabilitation Journal*. 2005; **29**(2): 132–7.

25. Hunt IM, Appleby L, Kapur N. Suicide under crisis resolution home treatment – a key setting for patient safety. *BJPsych Bulletin*. 2016 Aug; **40**(4): 172–4.

26. National Confidential Inquiry into Suicide and Safety in Mental Health. *Annual Report: England, Northern Ireland, Scotland and Wales*. Manchester: University of Manchester; 2021. https://sites.manchester.ac.uk/ncish/reports/annual-report-2021-england-northern-ireland-scotland-and-wales/.

27. Care Quality Commission. *Sexual Safety on Mental Health Wards*. London: Care Quality Commission; 2018. www.cqc.org.uk/publications/major-report/sexual-safety-mental-health-wards.

28. National Collaborating Centre for Mental Health. *Sexual Safety Collaborative: Standards and Guidance to Improve Sexual Safety on Mental Health and Learning Disabilities Inpatient Pathways*. London: National Collaborating Centre for Mental Health; 2020.

29. Thibaut B, Dewa LH, Ramtale SC, D'Lima D, Adam S, Ashrafian H, et al. Patient safety in inpatient mental health settings: A systematic review. *BMJ Open*. 2019 Dec 23; **9**(12). www.ncbi.nlm.nih.gov/pmc/articles/PMC7008434/.

30. Berg SH, Rørtveit K, Aase K. Suicidal patients' experiences regarding their safety during psychiatric in-patient care: A systematic review of qualitative studies. *BMC Health Services Research*. 2017; **17**(1): 73. www.ncbi.nlm.nih.gov/pmc/articles/PMC5259991/.

31. Archer M, Lau Y, Sethi F. Women in acute psychiatric units, their characteristics and needs: A review. *BJPsych Bulletin*. 2016 Oct; **40**(5): 266–72.

32. Mezey G, Hassell Y, Bartlett A. Safety of women in mixed-sex and single-sex medium secure units: Staff and patient perceptions. *British Journal of Psychiatry*. 2005 Dec; **187**(6): 579–82.

33. Stanley B, Brown GK. Safety planning intervention: A brief intervention to mitigate suicide risk. *Cognitive and Behavioral Practice*. 2012 May 1; **19**(2): 256–64.

34. 'Staying Safe' website, www.stayingsafe.net.

35. Stanley B, Brown GK, Brenner LA, Galfalvy HC, Currier GW, Knox KL, et al. Comparison of the safety planning intervention with follow-up versus usual care of suicidal patients treated in the emergency department. *JAMA Psychiatry*. 2018 Sep 1; **75**(9): 894–900.

36. Miller IW, Camargo CA, Arias SA, Sullivan AF, Allen MH, Goldstein AB, et al. Suicide prevention in an emergency department population: The ED-SAFE study. *JAMA Psychiatry*. 2017 Jun 1; **74**(6): 563–70.

37. House A. Self-harm and suicide in adults: Will safety plans keep people safe after self-harm? *BJPsych Bulletin*. 2022 Feb; **46**(1): 1–3.

38. Hawton K, Witt KG, Salisbury TL, Arensman E, Gunnell D, Hazell P, et al. Psychosocial interventions following self-harm in adults: A systematic review and meta-analysis. *Lancet Psychiatry*. 2016 Aug 1; **3**(8): 740–50.

39. National Confidential Inquiry into Suicide and Safety in Mental Health. *The Assessment of Clinical Risk in Mental Health Services*. University of Manchester, 2018. www.research.manchester.ac.uk/portal/files/77517990/REPORT_The_assessment_of_clinical_risk_in_mental_health_services.pdf.

40. Quinlivan L, Cooper J, Meehan D, Longson D, Potokar J, Hulme T, et al. Predictive accuracy of risk scales following self-harm: Multicentre, prospective cohort study. *British Journal of Psychiatry*. 2017 Jun; **210**(6): 429–36.

41. Xanthopoulou P, Ryan M, Lomas M, McCabe R. Psychosocial assessment in the emergency department. *Crisis*. 2022 Jun; **43**(4): 299–306.

42. Coffey M, Cohen R, Faulkner A, Hannigan B, Simpson A, Barlow S. Ordinary risks and accepted fictions: How contrasting and competing priorities work in risk assessment and mental health care planning. *Health Expectations*. 2017; **20**(3): 471–83.

42. Lamph G, Baker J, Dickinson T, Lovell K. Personality disorder co-morbidity in primary care 'Improving Access to Psychological Therapy' services: A qualitative study exploring professionals' perspectives of working with this patient group. *Personality and Mental Health*. 2019; **13**(3): 168–79.

43. Appleton R, Elahi F, Tuomainen H, Canaway A, Singh SP. 'I'm just a long history of people rejecting referrals' experiences of young people who fell through the gap between child and adult mental health services. *European Child and Adolescent Psychiatry*. 2021 Mar; **30**(3): 401–13.

44. Kahng S, Iwata BA, Lewin AB. Behavioral treatment of self-injury, 1964 to 2000. *American Journal of Mental Retardation* 2002 May; **107**(3): 212–21.

45. Palombini E, Richardson J, McAllister E, Veale D, Thomson AB. When self-harm is about preventing harm: Emergency management of obsessive–compulsive disorder and associated self-harm. *BJPsych Bulletin*. 2021 Apr; **45**(2): 109–14.

46. DrEm_79. Self harm and the emergency department. *BMJ*. 2016 Apr 13; **353**: i1150.

47. Anonymous. I am more than a body to stitch up and label. *BMJ*. 2021 May 12; n1003.

48. Beale C. Magical thinking and moral injury: Exclusion culture in psychiatry. *BJPsych Bulletin*. 2022; **46**(1): 16–19.

49. Karman P, Kool N, Poslawsky IE, van Meijel B. Nurses' attitudes towards self-harm: A literature review. *Journal of Psychiatric and Mental Health Nursing*. 2015 Feb; **22**(1): 65–75.

50. McCarthy L, Gijbels H. An examination of emergency department nurses' attitudes towards deliberate self-harm in an Irish teaching hospital. *International Emergency Nursing*. 2010 Jan; **18**(1): 29–35.

51. Quinlivan LM, Gorman L, Littlewood DL, Monaghan E, Barlow SJ, Campbell SM, et al. 'Relieved to be seen' – patient and carer experiences of psychosocial assessment in the emergency department following self-harm: Qualitative analysis of 102 free-text survey responses. *BMJ Open*. 2021 May 1; **11**(5): e044434.

52. Thomson AB, Eales S, McAllister E, Molodynski A. Criminal sanctions for suicidality in the 21st Century UK. *British Journal of Psychiatry*. 2022; **221**(5): 653–4.

53. Soril LJJ, Leggett LE, Lorenzetti DL, Noseworthy TW, Clement FM. Reducing frequent visits to the emergency department: A systematic review of interventions, ed. Gupta V. *PLoS ONE*. 2015 Apr 13; **10**(4): e0123660.

54. National Collaborating Centre for Mental Health. *Borderline Personality Disorder: The NICE Guideline on Treatment and Management*. London: The British Psychological Society and The Royal College of Psychiatrists; 2009.

55. Care Quality Commission. *How CQC Identifies and Responds to Closed Cultures*. 2022. www.cqc.org.uk/guidance-providers/all-services/how-cqc-identifies-responds-closed-cultures.

56. Morgan HG, Priest P. Suicide and other unexpected deaths among psychiatric in-patients: The Bristol confidential inquiry. *British Journal of Psychiatry*. 1991 Mar; **158**(3): 368–74.

57. Watts D, Morgan G. Malignant alienation: Dangers for patients who are hard to like.

British Journal of Psychiatry. 1994 Jan; **164**(1): 11–15.

58. Sullivan P. Epistemic injustice and self-injury: A concept with clinical implications. *Philosophy, Psychiatry and Psychology*. 2019 Dec; **26**(4): 349–62.
59. Thomson AB, McAllister E, Veale D. Frequent attendance with self-harm: What might you be missing? *Emergency Medical Journal*. 2020 Jun 1; **37**(6): 331–44.
60. Thomson AB. Testimonial and hermeneutical injustices in adult protection and patient safety: Practical lessons for psychiatrists. Proceedings of the Philosophy Special Interest Group Biennial Conference (Online). London: Royal College of Psychiatrists; 2021.
61. Jones S, Riste L, Barrowclough C, Bartlett P, Clements C, Davies L, et al. *Reducing Relapse and Suicide in Bipolar Disorder: Practical Clinical Approaches to Identifying Risk, Reducing Harm and Engaging Service Users in Planning and Delivery of Care – The PARADES (Psychoeducation, Anxiety, Relapse, Advance Directive Evaluation and Suicidality) Programme*. Southampton: NIHR Journals Library; 2018. www.ncbi.nlm.nih.gov/books/NBK525339/.
62. Simpson A, Flood C, Rowe J, Quigley J, Henry S, Hall C, et al. Results of a pilot randomised controlled trial to measure the clinical and cost effectiveness of peer support in increasing hope and quality of life in mental health patients discharged from hospital in the UK. *BMC Psychiatry*. 2014 Feb 5; **14**: 30.
63. Faulkner A, Yiannollou S, Kalathil J, Crepaz-Keay D, Singer F, James N, et al. *4Pi National Involvement Standards: Involvement for Influence*. London: National Survivor User Network; 2015. www.nsun.org.uk/projects/4pi-involvement-standards/.
64. Watling D, Preece M, Hawgood J, Bloomfield S, Kõlves K. Developing an intervention for suicide prevention: A rapid review of lived experience involvement. *Archives of Suicide Research*. 2020 Oct 18; 1–16.
65. O'Neill L, Johnson J, Mandela R. Reflective practice groups: Are they useful for liaison psychiatry nurses working within the Emergency Department? *Archives of Psychiatric Nursing*. 2019 Feb; **33**(1): 85–92.
66. The National Confidential Enquiry into Patient Outcome and Death. *Treat as One*. 2017. www.ncepod.org.uk/2017mhgh.html.
67. Aimola L, Jasim S, Tripathi N, Bassett P, Quirk A, Worrall A, et al. Impact of a peer-review network on the quality of inpatient low secure mental health services: Cluster randomised control trial. *BMC Health Services Research*. 2018 Dec; **18**(1): 994.
68. Doyle C, Lennox L, Bell D. A systematic review of evidence on the links between patient experience and clinical safety and effectiveness. *BMJ Open*. 2013 Jan 3; **3**(1): e001570.
69. Mann JJ, Apter A, Bertolote J, Beautrais A, Currier D, Haas A, et al. Suicide prevention strategies: A systematic review. *JAMA*. 2005 Oct 26; **294**(16): 2064–74.
70. Appleby L, Morriss R, Gask L, Roland M, Lewis B, Perry A, et al. An educational intervention for front-line health professionals in the assessment and management of suicidal patients (The STORM Project). *Psychological Medicine*. 2000 Jul; **30**(4): 805–12.
71. Morriss R, Gask L, Webb R, Dixon C, Appleby L. The effects on suicide rates of an educational intervention for front-line health professionals with suicidal patients (the STORM Project). *Psychological Medicine*. 2005 Jul 1; **35**(7): 957–60.
72. Gask L, Coupe N, Green G. An evaluation of the implementation of cascade training for suicide prevention during the 'Choose Life' initiative in Scotland – utilizing Normalization Process Theory. *BMC Health Services Research*. 2019 Dec; **19**(1): 1.

Chapter 14

Community Action

Melissa Pearson and Thilini Rajapakse

14.1 Introduction

Globally, more than 700,000 deaths per year occur due to suicide. Of these, a majority of suicides occur in lower- to middle-income countries (LMICs). According to World Health Organization data from 2019 [1], more than half (58%) of global suicides occurred in those below the age of 50 years. Most adolescents who died by suicide were from LMICs. Worldwide, suicide is the fourth leading cause of death among young people aged between 15 and 29 years.

Suicide is often the result of a complex interplay of factors operating at community and individual levels. Societal and community factors can be understood as proximal or distal dimensions. Proximal dimensions include factors in one's immediate community directly contributing to risk of suicide and self-harm, such as the experience of trauma, abuse or conflict, dislocation or migration, financial hardship, social fragmentation, crime, and near experience of self-harm and suicide. In addition, many individual risk factors have distal connections to community-level factors such as exam pressures, peer pressure, interpersonal conflict, social isolation, exposure to self-harm methods through social media and media reporting of suicide [2]. Certain population groups, such as refugees, those exposed to conflict or trauma, or prisoners, are more vulnerable to dying by suicide.

Suicide and self-harm include a diverse range of antecedents, behaviours and people, and attempting to identify a single causative factor, or a stand-alone effective intervention, is simplistic and unlikely to be effective [3,4]. Given the multifactorial aetiology of suicide, prevention remains a challenge worldwide. Multiple evidence-based strategies, adopting a broad multisectoral approach implemented through the life course, are indicated [2,4,5]. Community-level interventions are an important part of any national suicide prevention strategy [2,6].

Many different approaches have been explored at a community level for the prevention of suicide, with varying levels of success. In this chapter we aim to provide evidence on effective interventions that are delivered in a community setting. While there is no specific definition for a community intervention, we have selected interventions where participation and delivery were in a community (non-health) setting where the individuals live or work. We have provided some examples of specific interventions where there is a clear description of the intervention that may help readers consider its application in their setting.

14.2 Suicide Preventive Strategies at the Community Level

14.2.1 Universal Preventive Strategies

Universal preventive strategies are measures aimed at the entire population, without particular focus on any high-risk or vulnerable groups. The aims are to maximise health and minimise risks associated with suicide in general.

14.2.2 Increasing Awareness Regarding Mental Health Issues among Primary Health Care Providers

This has emerged as an important measure in the identification and support of those at risk in the community. In the year prior to death, only one-third of those who commit suicide have contact with mental health services, whereas 75% have had contact with primary care providers [7]. In the month prior to suicide, primary care doctors and other non-specialist health care workers are reported to see 45% of those who go on to commit suicide. When considering older people who commit suicide (aged 55 years and over), primary health care providers had seen 58% in the month prior to the death. These findings are based mostly on data from high-income countries (HICs), but this disparity is likely to be even greater in LMICs, where specialised mental health services are scarcer.

Against this background, training of primary care providers (including doctors and nurses) in the identification and treatment of depression, together with support of psychiatrists, has been demonstrated to be an effective method of reducing suicide, suicidal attempts and suicidal ideation [4,8,9]. Repeating the training was shown to sustain reduction of suicide rates for years, but single-day training had no impact at three years [4]. Here the training was conducted together with interventions to strengthen the treatment of depression and support from psychiatrists. Thus it is important that regular educational training of primary health care staff go hand in hand with service development [10]. A computer-assisted, semi-structured, interviewer-rated package known as the Global Mental health Assessment Tool (GMHAT/PC) has been developed to be implemented by primary care workers [11]. The package aims to screen for mental disorders in primary care and link to the initiation of appropriate treatments by up-skilling primary care workers. This tool has been adapted and validated in a number of LMIC settings [12,13].

Several task-shifting approaches have been recommended for the treatment of mental disorders in LMICs [14]. Various interventions have been effective in reducing anxiety, depression and alcohol use disorders. There is some evidence that increased access to community mental health services can reduce hospitalisation for self-harm and shorten the periods of suicidal ideation; however, they had no impact on overall suicide rates [15,16].

14.2.3 Increase of Community Awareness Regarding Mental Health Disorders – In Schools

Studies have reported that provision of mental health education to young people in schools is effective for reducing suicidal behaviour. A US-based school health-education intervention found that students showed more adaptive attitudes towards problems, and lesser number of suicide attempts, in the three months following the intervention [17]. A European school-based educational program found that the group that received the intervention had lower rates of suicidal ideation and attempts at a 12-month follow-up [18]. A 2018 review of school-based interventions found that 7 of 11 randomised controlled trials (64%) reported a significant drop in suicidal ideation or attempts during postintervention or follow-up [19]. These interventions were mostly psycho-education, social support and skill building, often delivered by school counsellors. In contrast, while mental health education aimed at targeting in young people in schools has been found to have an effect, education targeting teachers appears to be of limited benefit [4]. Most published school-based interventions are reported from HICs, and such interventions may need to be locally adapted for effective delivery in LMICs.

14.2.4 Use of Social Media Platforms for Suicide Prevention

In recent years there has been growing interest in the possible use of social media platforms for prevention of suicide and suicide attempts (Box 14.1). Evidence is currently limited, although preliminary findings suggest that such platforms could be a way to reach otherwise hard-to-engage individuals [20]. More research is needed on the effectiveness and safety of this modality of intervention, particularly regarding risks related to difficulty in gauging user emotional status and challenges in controlling user behaviour.

Box 14.1 Overview of Chatsafe: A Young Person's Guide to Communicating Safely Online about Self-Harm

Description

The Chatsafe intervention was delivered to participants once a week for 12 weeks via a direct message sent by one of the research team to a social media account of the participants' choice. Each message included a link to one piece of social media content (a short video, animation or static image) that was hosted on the #chatsafe Instagram page (www.instagram.com/chatsafe_au). Each social media post directly mapped onto one of the themes from the guidelines (e.g., safe language to use when talking about suicide). In order to avoid overexposure to content relating specifically to suicide, every alternate week the content had a self-care theme. Self-care content included information about digital literacy and online and offline well-being.

Evidence

While the Chatsafe intervention has not been fully tested at the time of this writing, there are promising results from a pilot study. A sample of 189 young people aged 16–25 years completed three questionnaires across a 20-week period (4 weeks preintervention, immediately postintervention and at 4-week follow-up). The intervention took the form of a 12-week social media campaign delivered to participants via direct message. Participants reported finding the intervention acceptable, and they also reported improvements in their willingness to intervene against suicide and their perceived self-efficacy, confidence and safety when communicating on social media about suicide.

Applicability

This intervention is indicated for young people where they are accessing social media content. The team worked with young people to co-design content, and this may be an important element in its feasibility. The Chatsafe app is now being tested in multiple countries and has a useful list of resources.

Links

www.orygen.org.au/chatsafe/Resources/International-guidelines/UK-%E2%80%93-English.

https://journals.plos.org/plosone/article?id=10.1371/journal.pone.0253278.

14.3 Community Screening

A few studies in the past have suggested that screening for otherwise undetected individuals at risk of suicide, if coupled with effective referral and treatment, may be helpful in reducing suicide rates, but overall findings are inconclusive. Given the current evidence, screening of otherwise undetected individuals for risk of suicide is not recommended as a preventive strategy [4,9].

14.4 Restriction of Access to Means

Restriction of access to lethal and commonly available means of suicide has been shown to be an effective method of reducing rates of suicide in many different parts of the world. In Asia, where suicide by pesticide poisoning is common, restriction of access to pesticides through regulatory actions were associated with a significant drop in rates of suicides, with rates of method substitution being relatively low [4,21]. Safer storage of pesticides has been a promising area of research, but evidence is limited, and one study from Sri Lanka found no evidence that provision of safe storage methods of pesticides to local farmers reduced suicide attempts [22]. In areas where firearm suicides are prevalent, restriction of access to firearms has been associated with reduced suicide rates [4].

Zalsman and colleagues, in their review of suicide prevention strategies, found that studies from the UK report that reduced availability of toxic analgesics and restriction of pack sizes of analgesics are useful in reducing suicide-related deaths [9]. However, to date there is no evidence regarding analgesic restriction from LMICs, and generalisation of these findings to lower-income settings is not recommended, given the possibility of method substitution to other more lethal means, such as pesticides or more toxic medications, which are often freely available over the counter in LMIC settings.

Other methods of restriction of access to means include reduction of carbon monoxide emission through compulsory inclusion of catalytic converters in automobile exhaust systems, switching from coal gas (which has a high concentration of carbon monoxide) to natural gas and establishment of barriers at 'suicide spots' such as bridges and train stations [4,9].

14.5 Engaging the Media in Appropriate Reporting

Detailed depiction of suicide in mass media has been shown to be associated with increased suicidal behaviour [9,23]. The way the media portray suicide, the details given and the manner in which the event is portrayed can influence 'copy-cat' behaviours. Media are more likely to highlight 'dramatic' and highly lethal methods of suicide, drawing more attention to such methods [23]. The portrayal of suicide in entertainment media is reported to be associated with a 9–27% increase of suicides among the target audience [24]. Conversely, it has been argued that media blackouts or better-quality reporting will be associated with a protective effect (i.e., reduced suicidal behaviour), and there is some evidence to support this [23].

In response to this problem, many countries recommend and have established media reporting guidelines. However, the challenge lies in the fact that the effectiveness of these guidelines in reducing suicide rates is not established [9,25]. Exploration of innovative, effective methods of collaborating with the media on this important issue requires further exploration. The impact of suicide reporting in social media and the effect of fictional depictions of suicide (e.g., in movies) needs further evaluation.

14.6 Suicide Prevention through the Minimisation of Community Risk Factors

Several risk factors for suicide are linked to community and societal factors, and therefore harm reduction interventions in these areas have the potential to impact on suicide and suicidal behaviour. Such interventions could include support for people in financial hardship, livelihoods interventions, gender-based violence programs and substance misuse interventions. A recently reported pilot study of a community-based intervention aimed at supporting people through targeted support for financial distress in the UK [26]. The intervention recruited people following an admission for self-harm but utilised a community support model, with community workers engaging with young people to improve their independence, decision-making and confidence when dealing with problems. The intervention was found to be acceptable, but a further study is required to determine if it is effective in reducing suicide or suicidal behaviour, and whether it could be applied to the general population.

Some interventions targeted at adult women who have experienced gender-based violence have shown some effectiveness in reducing psychological distress. A study from Kenya employed community screening for psychological distress and impaired functioning, and provided women with a five-session behavioural treatment called Problem Management Plus (PM+), delivered by lay community workers [27]. They found that there was a significant medium-term reduction in psychological distress. However, there was no measurement of suicide or suicidal behaviour.

Alcohol and substance misuse is a well-known risk factor for suicide and suicidal behaviour. A recent systematic review of the impact of alcohol control policies found that where alcohol availability or use was restricted, there was a decrease in suicide [28]. This suggests that interventions targeted to reduce the harmful use of alcohol could have a positive impact on suicide. Brief interventions for alcohol have been found to be effective in a range of primary care settings, but there is little evidence for their effectiveness in community settings [29]. In addition, there are no studies of the impact on suicide and suicidal behaviour of interventions to reduce alcohol use in community settings.

A recent study from South Africa combined an economic empowerment intervention with an HIV and violence prevention program for out-of-school youth [30]. The intervention was delivered by community facilitators employed by local non-governmental organisations (NGOs). The combined intervention showed positive impacts on men's earnings, controlling behaviour in relationships, reduced depression symptomology and reduced suicidal thoughts. It also showed a reduction in women's experience of physical and sexual abuse. Thus community interventions that address the complex relationship between risk factors can have a positive impact on a range of health and social outcomes, including suicide.

14.7 Interventions for Accessible Support to Prevent Suicide

The provision of talking and listening support to people in crisis is a commonly provided service available to the public. These services are often referred to as 'crisis lines' and are primarily telephone based, but in recent years there has been an expansion into online chat and app-based support [31]. The effectiveness of such services is limited, and the lack of robust studies limits in-depth understanding of the overall impact.

A recent systematic review highlighted the positive impact of crisis lines to reduce distress at the time of the call and the important role they play in providing a safety net [32]. The review included 33 studies, only 2 of which were from LMICs (India [33] and China [34]). There has been an expansion of web-based support applications modelled on crisis line support. A recent review of Indian apps identified 43 mobile applications that provided educative elements, suicide risk assessment and strategies to manage suicidal thoughts [35]. A review of mobile app content in the UK revealed only 5 of 69 apps offered all six of the recommended suicide prevention strategies [36]. The diversity of content and suicide prevention strategies and the potential for harmful messages highlight the challenge in this rapidly evolving environment.

There have been recent elaborations of the talking and listening support in HICs, including a crisis cafes and safe havens that use a model of peer support, with or without clinical support, to provide alternative community spaces for people experiencing distress. Similar work from LMICs are more limited, but the recently reported 'Friendship Bench Intervention', which delivered a brief psychological intervention and peer support for rural Zimbabwean women, found significant reductions in rates of depression and suicidal ideation, although the impact on suicidal behaviour was not explored [37]. Such innovations are worth exploring further in LMIC settings where the availability of mental health services is limited.

14.8 Gatekeeper Training as a Specific Preventive Strategy

Gatekeepers could be described as those who frequently come into contact with community members, usually (but not always) through their occupation [10]. The idea is that gatekeepers come into contact with community members in non-medical local environments and may be well placed for early identification of risk factors for suicide, if they are trained to do so [10]. Gatekeepers from the general public can include a range of people, such as community leaders, spiritual leaders, social welfare workers, teachers and school staff, or police and other first responders. This has generated considerable interest, but gatekeeper training of the general public has not been shown to have a positive effect on the skills and attitudes of trainees, and it has not been demonstrated to be effective in reducing suicide rates [4,9].

Mental Health First Aid (MHFA) training courses have been developed in several countries [38] and has shown to have a small to moderate impact on knowledge, attitudes and confidence in providing first aid strategies to people suffering from mental illness [39].

There have been modules developed to specifically target suicide, and these have been adapted for a few LMIC settings [40–42]. There is no evidence yet of the effectiveness of this strategy, and a recent review found that MHFA training had no effect on adolescent mental health difficulties [43].

A different suggested approach is training of pesticide vendors with regard to the sale of pesticides and the risk of self-harm and suicide [44]. The intervention currently being trialled in Sri Lanka combined means restriction with pesticide vendors as gatekeepers. While the focus of the gatekeeper is to provide direct support or signpost to services, the pesticide vendor is trained to identify potential customers who may be purchasing pesticides with the intention of self-harm. The pesticide vendors are trained to ask specific questions about farming to identify non-farmers who attempt to buy pesticides and use observation skills to identify customers who may be intoxicated. These high-risk groups were identified through pilot studies. The pesticide vendors then attempt to delay the purchase, contact family members with permission or refuse sales [45]. This has the potential to be an important intervention in countries which have a high level of pesticide-suicides, but this requires further evaluation.

14.9 Peer Support Programmes

Peer-led community interventions for prevention of suicide and suicide attempts have become widely used. These interventions have drawn elements from other interventions and provide a wide variety of functions, including education, safety planning, crisis support, gatekeeper functions and social support. In community settings these interventions have often developed as outreach for hard-to-reach groups such as veterans' communities, schools, and men's and LGBTQ+ groups [46–51]. Evidence is currently limited on their effectiveness, and the heterogeneity in the interventions makes it difficult to draw firm conclusions [52,53]. Some of the divergence in interventions revolves around the definition of peer. In many programs a peer is someone with lived experience of suicidal thoughts and behaviours (lived experience), and in other programs the peer is considered a person from that community – men's groups, veterans, LGBTQ+ and rural communities (Box 14.2).

Box 14.2 Buddy Up: A Men's Suicide Prevention Campaign

Description

Buddy Up was a program that developed a range of educational materials through a co-production process and disseminated targeted advertising, promotional materials and educational resources. The campaign featured nine characters that depict men experiencing various mental illness symptoms. Individuals were encouraged to sign up as 'Buddy Up Champions' and promote men's mental health. The materials were made available to the champions and were placed around the home, workplace or community, to raise awareness and promote conversations about suicide prevention. During the month of June (Buddy Up Month), individuals and groups were invited to complete challenges (e.g., exercise with a buddy) for the chance to win prizes.

Evidence

The program was evaluated and found to be feasible and acceptable to the participants. The champions reported increased confidence in talking to other men about suicide and would recommend the program to others. There was qualitative evidence of diffusion and sustainability beyond the initial participant group signalling some potential of the intervention to raise awareness, address stigma, build social bonds and strengthen help-seeking.

Applicability

This intervention is a helpful model for using peer support to build connections in community settings for suicide prevention. The co-design of materials helped build the acceptability of the messages. Application in other settings would require the same approach to the development of community-specific resources. Additionally, the development of such initiatives needs to be carefully designed to ensure the safety of participants and the wider community.

Links

https://journals.sagepub.com/doi/full/10.1177/15579883231209189.
www.buddyup.ca.

14.10 Contact and/or Active Outreach Following a Suicide Attempt

After a suicide attempt, the risk of repetition is increased in the period after discharge from the hospital. Studies from HIC have reported a 15% repetition rate of non-fatal self-harm in the first year after a self-harm attempt [54,55]. The risk of completed suicide after hospital admission for attempted suicide has been reported as 2.46% at 3 years and 4.55% at 10 years, in varying studies [55,56].

Several trials have demonstrated that brief (follow-up) contact interventions (BCIs), such as sending postcards, text messages or follow-up phone calls, are effective for reducing suicidal ideation and repetition of suicide attempts [4,57,58]. The mechanism of action of BCIs appears to be related to a sense of increased social support, suicide prevention literacy and learning of alternative coping skills [59]. BCIs show promise as relatively inexpensive and scalable interventions for prevention of suicide in those who have attempted suicide and who have been recently discharged to the community. The low cost and ease of implementation suggest that such interventions could translate easily to low-income settings [60].

14.11 Multifaceted, Multilevel Community Interventions

Hergerl and colleagues conducted a two-year follow-up study that evaluated the effectiveness of several interventions applied at different levels, including primary care physician education, awareness campaign with the media and the community, training of community facilitators and self-help groups for those with depression or past self-harm [61]. They found that rates of suicide and suicide attempts were reduced at two-year follow-up, and the different intervention strategies tended to have a synergistic rather than a simple additive effect [61]. It was not clear which facet of the intervention was most effective.

A multimodal intervention developed by the White Mountain Apache Suicide Surveillance and Prevention System showed a 38.3% decrease in the suicide rate among those aged 15 to 24 years. This comprehensive program included universal awareness-raising activities, selected activities to better identify at-risk youths, increased coping skills and resiliency, and interventions targeted at young people who were exhibiting suicidal ideation or suicidal behaviour (see Box 14.3). This indicated that a community-driven, comprehensive program of activities targeting proximal and distal community risk factors through integrated support can reduce suicide and suicidal behaviour. Limitations of this study included a relatively small sample size and that this was not data from a randomised controlled trial (Box 14.3).

Box 14.3 A Multimodal Intervention: White Mountain Apache Suicide Surveillance and Prevention System

Description

Universal Programmes

The focus of the universal activities associated with the White Mountain Apache Suicide Surveillance and Prevention System was to coordinate planning among local agencies and raise community awareness. This included inter-agency meetings and a public education campaign, including print materials and radio broadcasted messages, a Substance Abuse and Mental Health Administration (SAMHSA) Native American Lifelines poster in a local newspaper every two weeks, eight public service announcements with a National Suicide Prevention Lifeline phone number that aired daily, talk shows about program events with audience-member call-in (monthly) and a series of four posters displayed in schools and tribal departments. This also included biannual suicide prevention walks; six suicide prevention conferences; a door-to-door campaign providing information and materials about the surveillance system mandate, services and lifeline; a series of empowerment educational workshops reaching about 391 tribal members; and information booths at local health and tribal fairs.

Selected Programmes

The goals of selected programming were to better identify at-risk youths and increase coping skills and resiliency. Activities included the Applied Suicide Intervention Skills Training for the community, the Sources of Strength suicide prevention program in two middle schools, community organisations and individuals (e.g., substance use and mental health centres, Head Start and casino employees). A coping skills curriculum was provided to seventh to eighth graders once a week for one year. Funding also supported strengths-based and culturally based activities led by Apache elders.

Indicated Programmes

Indicated interventions targeted youths who were exhibiting suicidal ideation and attempts. Activities included a brief intervention (two to four hours) with a powerful, locally adapted video and curriculum for youths to teach them risk reduction and motivate them to engage in services. A multisession life skills curriculum that included a family member taught communication, coping skills, problem-solving, goal-setting and how to connect to community resources. A curriculum was adapted for binge drinking. A community mental health specialist provided case management and monitoring.

Evidence

The overall Apache suicide death rates dropped from 40.0 to 24.7 per 100,000 (38.3% decrease), and the rate among those aged 15 to 24 years dropped from 128.5 to 99.0 per 100,000 (23.0% decrease). The annual number of attempts also dropped from 75 (in 2007) to 35 individuals (in 2012). National rates remained relatively stable during this time, at 10 to 13 per 100,000.

Limitations

Relatively small sample size and not a randomised controlled trial.

Applicability

This intervention is a comprehensive suicide prevention program that was culturally adapted for a high-suicide-risk indigenous community in the US. Other vulnerable populations or areas where there are high rates of suicide could also benefit from a multi-agency public health approach to suicide prevention, with adaptation to local socio-cultural environments.

Links

https://pubmed.ncbi.nlm.nih.gov/27736202/.
https://onlinelibrary.wiley.com/doi/10.1002/ajcp.12351.

14.12 Conclusions

Community-level interventions are a key part of suicide prevention, and many different preventive strategies have been explored. The effectiveness of these strategies varies. Given the nature of some of the community-level interventions, objective measurement of efficacy can be challenging. Prevention of access to means of suicide in the community has emerged as an important method of suicide prevention in many countries. Increased education and awareness among primary care health care professionals about mental illness and suicide have emerged as another important strategy. It is noteworthy that 'one-off' education sessions seem of limited efficacy, and effective psychoeducation strategies include several sessions, combined with enhanced availability or access to mental health services. Increasing awareness and mental health literacy among young people in schools shows promise, based on studies from HICs. Brief follow-up contact after an attempted suicide, in the form of postcards, text messages or phone calls, is emerging as a potentially scalable, cost-effective, targeted intervention to reduce repetition in those who have recently attempted suicide.

Other strategies, such as increased community awareness about mental illness and gatekeeper training of the general public, though popular, still lack evidence of efficacy. Improving the quality of media reporting on suicide has been identified as a key need to reduce suicide rates, but effective methods to do this remain challenging. Further research in these areas is recommended, to explore more effective and innovative ways to address these challenges.

It is also clear that multifaceted interventions, implemented at different levels on an ongoing basis, are more effective and often show a synergistic effect. Many complex factors underpin suicide and attempted suicide, and overall, evidence suggests that prevention would be most effective if a multimodal, multilevel, long-term approach is adopted [4,61,62].

References

1. World Health Organization. *Suicide Worldwide in 2019*. Geneva: World Health Organization; 2021.
2. World Health Organization. *Preventing Suicide: A Global Imperative*. Geneva: World Health Organization; 2014.
3. Jacob KS. The prevention of suicide in India and the developing world: The need for population-based strategies. *Crisis*. 2008; **29**(2): 102–6.
4. Mann JJ, Michel CA, Auerbach RP. Improving suicide prevention through evidence-based strategies: A systematic review. *American Journal of Psychiatry*. 2021; **178**(7): 611–24.
5. Mann JJ, Apter A, Bertolote J, Beautrais A, Currier D, Haas A, et al. Suicide prevention strategies: A systematic review. *JAMA*. 2005; **294**(16): 2064–74.
6. Hofstra E, van Nieuwenhuizen C, Bakker M, Ozgul D, Elfeddali I, de Jong SJ, et al. Effectiveness of suicide prevention interventions: A systematic review and meta-analysis. *General Hospital Psychiatry*. 2020; **63**: 127–40.
7. Luoma JB, Martin CE, Pearson JL. Contact with mental health and primary care providers before suicide: A review of the evidence. *American Journal of Psychiatry*. 2002; **159**: 909–16.
8. van der Feltz-Cornelis CM, Sarchiapone M, Postuvan V, Volker D, Roskar S, Grum AT, et al. Best practice elements of multilevel suicide prevention strategies: A review of systematic reviews. *Crisis*. 2011; **32**(6): 319–33.
9. Zalsman G, Hawton K, Wasserman D, van Heeringen K, Arensman E, Sarchiapone M, et al. Suicide prevention strategies revisited: 10-year systematic review. *Lancet Psychiatry*. 2016; **3**(7): 646–59.
10. World Health Organization. *Public Health Action for Prevention of Suicide: A Framework*. Geneva: World Health Organization; 2016.
11. Sharma VK, Lepping P, Krishna M, Durrani S, Copeland JR, Mottram P, et al. Mental health diagnosis by nurses using the Global Mental Health Assessment Tool: A validity and feasibility study. *British Journal of General Practice: Journal of the Royal College of General Practitioners*. 2008; **58**(551): 411–16.
12. Sharma VK, Durrani S, Sawa M, Copeland JR, Abou-Saleh MT, Lane S, et al. Arabic version of the Global Mental Health Assessment Tool-Primary Care version (GMHAT/PC): A validity and feasibility study. *Eastern Mediterranean Health Journal*. 2013; **19**(11): 905–8.
13. Sharma VK, Jagawat S, Midha A, Jain A, Tambi A, Mangwani LK, et al. The Global Mental Health Assessment Tool: Validation in Hindi – A validity and feasibility study. *Indian Journal of Psychiatry*. 2010; **52**(4): 316–19.
14. Purgato M, Uphoff E, Singh R, Thapa Pachya A, Abdulmalik J, van Ginneken N. Promotion, prevention and treatment interventions for mental health in low- and middle-income countries through a task-shifting approach. *Epidemiology and Psychiatric Sciences*. 2020 Aug 3; **29**: e150.
15. Aldridge LR, Garman EC, Luitel NP, Jordans MJD. Impact of a district mental health care plan on suicidality among patients with depression and alcohol use disorder in Nepal. *PloS One*. 2020; **15**(4): e0231158.
16. Machado DB, Alves FJ, Rasella D, Rodrigues L, Araya R. Impact of the new mental health services on rates of suicide and hospitalisations by attempted suicide, psychiatric problems, and alcohol problems in Brazil. *Administration and Policy in Mental Health*. 2018; **45**(3): 381–91.

17. Aseltine RH, James A, Schilling EA, Glanovsky J. Evaluating the SOS suicide prevention program: A replication and extension. *BMC Public Health*. 2007 Jul 18; 7: 161.

18. Wasserman D, Hoven CW, Wasserman C, Wall M, Eisenberg R, Hadlaczky G, et al. School-based suicide prevention programmes: The SEYLE cluster-randomised, controlled trial. *Lancet*. 2015; **385**(9977): 1536–44.

19. Robinson JCA, Bailey E. Suicide prevention in educational settings: A review. *Australasian Psychiatry*. 2018; **26**(2): 132–40.

20. Robinson J, Cox G, Bailey E, Hetrick S, Rodrigues M, Fisher S, et al. Social media and suicide prevention: A systematic review. *Early Intervention in Psychiatry*. 2016; **10**(2): 103–21.

21. Gunnell D, Fernando R, Hewagama M, Priyangika WD, Konradsen F, Eddleston M. The impact of pesticide regulations on suicide in Sri Lanka. *International Journal of Epidemiology*. 2007; **36**(6): 1235–42.

22. Pearson M, Metcalfe C, Jayamanne S, Gunnell D, Weerasinghe M, Pieris R, et al. Effectiveness of household lockable pesticide storage to reduce pesticide self-poisoning in rural Asia: A community-based, cluster-randomised controlled trial. *Lancet*. 2017; **390**(10105): 1863–72.

23. Sisask M, Varnik A. Media roles in suicide prevention: A systematic review. *International Journal of Environmental Research and Public Health*. 2012; **9**(1): 123–38.

24. Niederkrotenthaler T, Kirchner S, Till B, Sinyor M, Tran US, Pirkis J, et al. Systematic review and meta-analyses of suicidal outcomes following fictional portrayals of suicide and suicide attempt in entertainment media. *eClinicalMedicine*. 2021; **36**: 100922.

25. Pirkis J, Blood RW, Beautrais A, Burgess P, Skehans J. Media guidelines on the reporting of suicide. *Crisis*. 2006; **27**(2): 82–7.

26. Barnes MC, Haase AM, Scott LJ, Linton MJ, Bard AM, Donovan JL, et al. The help for people with money, employment or housing problems (HOPE) intervention: Pilot randomised trial with mixed methods feasibility research. *Pilot and Feasibility Studies*. 2018; **4**: 172.

27. Bryant RA, Schafer A, Dawson KS, Anjuri D, Mulili C, Ndogoni L, et al. Effectiveness of a brief behavioural intervention on psychological distress among women with a history of gender-based violence in urban Kenya: A randomised clinical trial. *PLoS Medicine*. 2017; **14**(8): e1002371.

28. Kõlves K, Chitty KM, Wardhani R, Värnik A, de Leo D, Witt K. Impact of alcohol policies on suicidal behavior: A systematic literature review. *International Journal of Environmental Research and Public Health*. 2020; **17**(19): 7030.

29. Platt L, Melendez-Torres GJ, O'Donnell A, Bradley J, Newbury-Birch D, Kaner E, et al. How effective are brief interventions in reducing alcohol consumption: Do the setting, practitioner group and content matter? Findings from a systematic review and metaregression analysis. *BMJ Open*. 2016; **6**(8): e011473.

30. Jewkes R, Gibbs A, Jama-Shai N, Willan S, Misselhorn A, Mushinga M, et al. Stepping Stones and Creating Futures intervention: Shortened interrupted time series evaluation of a behavioural and structural health promotion and violence prevention intervention for young people in informal settlements in Durban, South Africa. *BMC Public Health*. 2014; **14**(1): 1325.

31. Predmore Z, Ramchand R, Ayer L, Kotzias V, Engel C, Ebener P, et al. Expanding suicide crisis services to text and chat. *Crisis*. 2017; **38**(4): 255–60.

32. Hoffberg AS, Stearns-Yoder KA, Brenner LA. The effectiveness of crisis line services: A systematic review. *Frontiers in Public Health*. 2020 Jan 17; **7**: 399.

33. Chavan BS, Garg R, Bhargava R. Role of 24 hour telephonic helpline in delivery of mental health services. *Indian Journal of Medical Sciences*. 2012; **66**(5–6): 116–25.

34. Jianlin J. Hotline for mental health in Shanghai, China. *Crisis*. 1995; **16**(3): 116–20.

35. Sudarshan S, Mehrotra S. Suicide prevention mobile apps for Indian users: An overview. *Cureus*. 2021; **13**(7): e16770.

36. Martinengo L, Van Galen L, Lum E, Kowalski M, Subramaniam M, Car J. Suicide prevention and depression apps' suicide risk assessment and management: A systematic assessment of adherence to clinical guidelines. *BMC Medicine*. 2019; **17**(1): 231.

37. Fernando S, Brown T, Datta K, Chidhanguro D, Tavengwa NV, Chandna J, et al. The Friendship Bench as a brief psychological intervention with peer support in rural Zimbabwean women: A mixed methods pilot evaluation. *Global Mental Health*. 2021 Aug 26; **8**: e31.

38. Jorm AF, Kitchener BA, Reavley NJ. Mental Health First Aid training: Lessons learned from the global spread of a community education program. *World Psychiatry: Official Journal of the World Psychiatric Association (WPA)*. 2019; **18**(2): 142–3.

39. Morgan AJ, Ross A, Reavley NJ. Systematic review and meta-analysis of Mental Health First Aid training: Effects on knowledge, stigma, and helping behaviour. *PloS One*. 2018; **13**(5): e0197102.

40. Chandrasiri A, Fernando M, Dayabandara M, Reavley NJ. Cultural adaptation of the mental health first aid guidelines for assisting a person at risk of suicide for Sri Lanka: A Delphi expert consensus study. *BMC Psychiatry*. 2021; **21**(1): 466.

41. De Silva SA, Colucci E, Mendis J, Kelly CM, Jorm AF, Minas H. Suicide first aid guidelines for Sri Lanka: A Delphi consensus study. *International Journal of Mental Health Systems*. 2016; **10**(1): 53.

42. Requena SS, Cerqueira AV, Assumpção TA, Peres CHM, Loch AA, Reavley NJ. Cultural adaptation of the mental health first aid guidelines for assisting a person at risk of suicide in Brazil: A Delphi expert consensus study. *BMC Psychiatry*. 2022; **22**(1): 397.

43. Forthal S, Sadowska K, Pike KM, Balachander M, Jacobsson K, Hermosilla S. Mental health first aid: A systematic review of trainee behavior and recipient mental health outcomes. *Psychiatric Services*. 2022; 73(4): 439–46.

44. Weerasinghe M, Konradsen F, Eddleston M, Pearson M, Jayamanne S, Gunnell D, et al. Potential interventions for preventing pesticide self-poisoning by restricting access through vendors in Sri Lanka. *Crisis*. 2018; **39**(6): 479–88.

45. Weerasinghe M, Pearson M, Turner N, Metcalfe C, Gunnell DJ, Agampodi S, et al. Protocol: Gatekeeper training for vendors to reduce pesticide self-poisoning in rural South Asia – A study protocol for a stepped-wedge cluster randomised controlled trial. *BMJ Open*. 2022; **12**(4): e054061.

46. Brown LA, Webster JL, Tran JT, Wolfe JR, Golinkoff J, Patel E, et al. A suicide prevention intervention for emerging adult sexual and gender minority groups: Protocol for a pilot hybrid effectiveness randomized controlled trial. *JMIR Research Protocols*. 2023 Sep 29; **12**: e48177-e.

47. Ehret BC, Chalker SA, Pozun CT, Martinez-Ceren CS. A peer approach to suicide prevention and recovery: Study protocol for a feasibility and acceptability trial of Caring Cards for veterans. *Contemporary Clinical Trials Communications*. 2022; **29**: 100974.

48. Greden JF, Valenstein M, Spinner J, Blow A, Gorman LA, Dalack GW, et al. Buddy-to-Buddy, a citizen soldier peer support program to counteract stigma, PTSD, depression, and suicide. *Annals of the New York Academy of Sciences*. 2010; **1208**(1): 90–7.

49. Pickering TA, Wyman PA, Schmeelk-Cone K, Hartley C, Valente TW, Pisani AR, et al. Diffusion of a peer-led suicide preventive intervention through school-based student peer and adult networks. *Frontiers in Psychiatry*. 2018 Nov 15; **9**: 598.

50. Zachariah B, de Wit EE, Bahirat JD, Bunders-Aelen JFG, Regeer BJ. What is in it for them? Understanding the impact of a 'Support, Appreciate, Listen Team' (SALT)–based suicide prevention peer education program on peer educators. *School Mental Health*. 2018; **10**(4): 462–76.

51. Gorman JA, Chamberlin ES, Stevenson BJ, Calixte R, Crossman DM, Ahern ME, et al. Using veterans' socials to build a community: Feasibility of the VOICES intervention. *Community Mental Health Journal*. 2022; **58**(8): 1544–53.

52. Schlichthorst M, Ozols I, Reifels L, Morgan A. Lived experience peer support programs for suicide prevention: A systematic scoping review. *International Journal of Mental Health Systems*. 2020; **14**(1): 65.

53. Bowersox NW, Jagusch J, Garlick J, Chen JI, Pfeiffer PN. Peer-based interventions targeting suicide prevention: A scoping review. *American Journal of Community Psychology*. 2021; **68**(1–2): 232–48.

54. Owens D, Horrocks J, House A. Fatal and non-fatal repetition of self-harm: Systematic review. *British Journal of Psychiatry*. 2002 Sep; **181**: 193–9.

55. Liu BP, Lunde KB, Jia CX, Qin P. The short-term rate of non-fatal and fatal repetition of deliberate self-harm: A systematic review and meta-analysis of longitudinal studies. *Journal of Affective Disorders*. 2020 Aug 1; **273**: 597–603.

56. Gibb SJ BA, Fergusson DM. Mortality and further suicidal behaviour after an index suicide attempt: A 10-year study. *Australian and New Zealand Journal of Psychiatry*. 2005 Jan–Feb; **39**(1–2): 95–100.

57. Stanley B, Brown GK, Brenner LA, Galfalvy HC, Currier GW, Knox KL, et al. Comparison of the safety planning intervention with follow-up versus usual care of suicidal patients treated in the emergency department. *JAMA Psychiatry*. 2018; **75**(9): 894–900.

58. Hassanian-Moghaddam H, Sarjami S, Kolahi AA, Carter GL. Postcards in Persia: Randomised controlled trial to reduce suicidal behaviours 12 months after hospital-treated self-poisoning. *British Journal of Psychiatry*. 2011; **198**(4): 309–16.

59. Milner A, Spittal MJ, Kapur N, Witt K, Pirkis J, Carter G. Mechanisms of brief contact interventions in clinical populations: A systematic review. *BMC Psychiatry*. 2016; **16**: 194.

60. Chen H, Mishara BL, Liu XX. A pilot study of mobile telephone message interventions with suicide attempters in China. *Crisis*. 2010; **31**(2): 109–12.

61. Hegerl U, Althaus D, Schmidtke A, Niklewski G. The alliance against depression: 2-year evaluation of a community-based intervention to reduce suicidality. *Psychological Medicine*. 2006; **36**(9): 1225–33.

62. Fountoulakis KN, Gonda X, Rihmer Z. Suicide prevention programs through community intervention. *Journal of Affective Disorders*. 2011; **130**(1–2): 10–16.

Chapter 15

Surveillance

Catherine A. Robinson and Rob Poole

15.1 Does Surveillance Matter?

Disease surveillance, particularly of infectious diseases, has a long history. There are many book chapters and articles providing detailed accounts of systematically collated health information [1]. Conventionally, modern health surveillance commences with John Snow's observations of the epidemic of cholera in London's Soho district in 1854 [2], culminating in the iconic (but probably ineffective) removal of the handle from Broad Street pump. It is significant that although Snow did not know that the *Vibrio cholerae* bacterium was the causative organism, surveillance played a part in resolving the epidemic. Disease surveillance has a crucial role in evaluating and shaping responses to major public health problems, as was clearly demonstrated during the COVID-19 pandemic of 2020. Not all causes of untimely death or ill health are due to the disease of interest, but surveillance provides a firm foundation for public health interventions of all types [1].

In public health, surveillance is the systematic and continuous collection, analysis and interpretation of health-related information. The collation of data allows the identification of factors that increase or decrease risk, and the detection of changes and patterns of morbidity and mortality at a population level. The intention is to acquire data that can inform actions to achieve health benefits for the population. Hence the point of surveillance is practical. Someone must understand the data collected and do something to change morbidity or mortality frequency.

Surveillance has always been concerned with temporal and geographical parameters. However, the ability and interest in testing routinely collected surveillance data for clusters has developed over time [3]. Surveillance of self-harm is gradually increasing and improving globally. The detection of temporal and special clusters can enable service and clinical practice improvement and support the evaluation of interventions. According to McGill and Haddock [4], the establishment of a clinical quality registry for self-harm presenting in hospital has the potential to link data to improved care.

15.2 Surveillance Always Involves Compromises

Surveillance is rarely straightforward and often requires several separate elements to create a meaningful picture, building a total dataset that is adequately reliable and detailed. In the UK there are multiple sources of surveillance data. The following examples are by no means an exhaustive list. Information can be derived from routinely collected UK National Health Service (NHS) activity data or bespoke systems. There is a system of compulsory notification of certain diagnoses under the UK Health Protection (Notification) Regulations, 2010. There are 29 notifiable diseases at the time of writing [5]. A similar but voluntary system exists for the notification of possible adverse reactions to prescribed drugs run by the Medicines and Healthcare Products Regulatory Agency (MHRA). Death certification and non-clinical statutory processes such as coroners' verdicts result in centrally processed statistics. There is a National Confidential Inquiry into Suicide and Safety in Health (NCISH) that examines all suicides that occur whilst the patient is receiving, or recently received, mental health care [6]. Purpose-designed surveillance systems exist that are embedded in clinical settings and monitor a range of conditions. Some have an international platform (e.g., burns) [7].

Even within high-income countries (HICs) like the UK, health service information systems in different locations are not necessarily consistent or compatible This can militate against the collation of high-quality and comprehensive surveillance data. Health and data systems vary even more widely between countries, which can make international surveillance information difficult to collate or compare. In low-resource health systems, such as exist in many low- and middle-income countries (LMICs), health records are often paper-based or are non-existent. This creates major challenges to surveillance in those countries with the highest rates of many serious health problems.

Implementing a surveillance system involves the monitoring of the incidence of health events within a population, and this can be used to improve the efficiency and effectiveness of health systems. Surveillance information can be used to inform health and social policy development locally, regionally and nationally, including resource allocation. Over time, it can be used to evaluate the impact of health policy and initiatives in the form of trends in prevalence.

Disease surveillance usually involves compromises to 'ideal' research methods. For example, in most countries, rates of death from cirrhosis of the liver are taken as an indicator of deaths due to liver disease related to alcohol consumption [8]. There are many non-alcohol-related causes of cirrhosis, including fatty liver disease related to obesity or hepatitis C. Where rates of death due to non-alcoholic cirrhosis are stable, and where alcoholic liver disease is the commonest cause of cirrhosis, changes in overall rates of cirrhosis deaths can be taken to indicate the impact of alcohol consumption. Unfortunately, life is not so simple. The UK has seen a substantial increase in deaths due to cirrhosis over the past 50 years, and a substantial element of this is due to increased per capita alcohol consumption, itself related to decreases in the relative cost of alcohol and increased availability. However, hepatitis C infection has also substantially increased and, in a further complication, there is an interaction between high alcohol consumption and hepatitis C infection [9]. These factors have to be taken into account when interpreting the surveillance data, but they do not invalidate it.

This illustrates the difficulty in case definitions that is intrinsic to surveillance. Self-harm is not easy to define, and the same is true of suicide. In the UK the coronial system is used to differentiate suicide from other types of untimely death. However, some other types of coronial verdict include cases that are clinically judged to be suicides (e.g., open verdicts), and research has to be based upon a variety of coronial outcomes and not just suicide [10]. Legal categories change in small and large ways over time. In the UK, for example, narrative coronial verdicts were introduced in 2004. This introduced verdicts that are more challenging to aggregate than older, categorical verdicts [11].

There was much adverse comment in British newspapers during the height of the COVID-19 epidemic that the daily surveillance figures recorded deaths of people infected with the virus, rather than just those who unequivocally died solely from the effects of viral infection. This criticism entirely misunderstands the nature of disease surveillance and the difficulty in attributing death to a single cause. It would be impossible to collate an unequivocal figure quickly enough to inform public health measures. Although the figures did not directly measure the events of greatest concern, the proxy figure did provide good-enough tracking of the UK epidemic in the context of a major public health emergency. Similar compromises have to be made in timely suicide and self-harm surveillance systems, which inevitably exclude some deaths where suicide was the intention and omits some deaths where the intention was unclear [12]. There have been moves to develop real-time suicide surveillance. Although a recent review of existing systems revealed differences across the five systems studies, there were common elements that the authors viewed as providing the potential for a common, replicable system that could be adapted to local circumstances [13].

15.3 Where There Is No Surveillance for Suicide Prevention Purposes

As many of the chapters in this book attest, suicide is a global public health problem that especially affects LMICs. Suicide is an indicator in the United Nations' Sustainable Development Goals (SDGs) [14]. Despite repeated statements from international bodies such as the World Health Organization (WHO) that reducing rates of suicide is a global imperative, the allocation of resources to suicide prevention is limited. Current estimates suggest that the global target set in the SDGs (to reduce suicide mortality by one-third by 2030) will not be met on time or reduced to anywhere near this target.

Understanding population rates in suicide and self-harm, and trends as they change over time, are key data in prevention strategies. In 2014 the WHO recommended that governments should develop comprehensive suicide surveillance systems as part of national suicide strategies [15]. The WHO campaign on suicide has continued with its 2022 'LIVE LIFE' campaign, which includes surveillance as one of its six pillars [16].

15.4 Self-Harm as a Proxy for Suicide

It is generally accepted that for every death by suicide there are likely to be 20 non-fatal events, which are referred to in a variety of terms: non-suicidal self-harm, suicide attempt, non-accidental injury, self-injury and so on. The 2019 Global Burden of Disease report suggested in excess of 14 million individuals affected globally each year [17]. In HICs, this behaviour is commoner amongst women than men, a reversal of gender patterns compared with suicide. The iceberg model of surveillance can be applied to suicide and self-harm, the larger number of events being non-fatal self-harm and the top level being deaths by suicide [18].

Comprehensive surveillance systems must monitor the commoner, less severe events as well as those of most concern. Self-harm carries its own morbidity, and it is worth monitoring in its own right. It is associated with later suicide and is often used as proxy for suicide in statistics, even though there are marked differences in the two behaviours. The difficult question is which deaths and self-inflicted injuries to include, given the unclear boundary with deaths due to domestic violence.

15.5 Death Registration

Ambitious goals to capture all deaths related to self-inflicted harm are a distant dream, as many countries lack systems to record instances of suicide and self-harm surveillance, and some collect no reliable statistics at all [19]. The obstructions to change are not just related to inadequate resource allocation to suicide and self-harm surveillance per se. For example, some countries have no death registration system, partly because a very large number of deaths occur without medical involvement. This can be compounded by religious or cultural requirements that the body of the deceased should be interred or destroyed very quickly after death. However, international interest in the lack of comprehensive death or consistent death registration processes has sharply increased as a consequence of the COVID-19 pandemic [20].

The existence of effective and accurate death registration is crucial to evaluating progress against a number of the SDGs. Consequently, the existence of reliable national death registration systems is itself an SDG indicator, with a target of 80% of deaths being registered (via SDG indicator 17.19.2) by 2030. A study by the Economic and Social Commission for Asia and the Pacific (ESCAP) [20] suggests that rates of death registration have increased in a number of areas in recent years. However, those most at risk of being excluded from death registration are those populations with the least access to health care (and most at risk of suicide), such as people living in rural areas, Indigenous groups, people with disabilities, migrants, people without documentation and domestic workers. Women and girls may be generally under-represented in death registrations [21].

Suicide is thus under-reported in many countries [22]. There are specific problems in collating national statistics on suicide amongst other causes of death. Basic death registration captures the medical cause of death but cannot reliably record how a person came to die. All legal systems derived from English law emphasise the importance of intention, which cannot be measured directly. Deciding on intention, and therefore whether a death is due to suicide or not, involves collating much circumstantial detail. Determining that a death was due to suicide following accepted legal and clinical opinion involves making an inference as to the person's intentions immediately prior to their death. Classification of a death as suicide follows different processes in different countries. There is no internationally agreed standardised recording and certification process in determining suicide deaths. There are significant factors that lead to resistance to reporting individual deaths as suicide in most countries, including the UK. Strong religious prohibition of suicide is a major reason for under-reporting [23]. Attempting to take one's own life is a crime in some countries with large populations, and this is known to increase the likelihood of misclassification [24]. Humanitarian considerations underpin calls to decriminalise attempted suicide, such as that by the International Association for Suicide Prevention (2019) [25]. The impact on surveillance, and therefore on suicide prevention, lends further support to the argument for decriminalisation.

15.6 Routinely Collected Data

Even where there is systematic collation of statistics on suicide deaths, there are problems in understanding the data. Legal processes to determine that a death is by suicide can take variable lengths of time. In some cases, there can be delays of years [12], as is the case in some UK coroners' inquests. In most systems, published figures reflect the date when a suicide was reported, not the date when the death occurred, which is potentially highly misleading when trying to relate death rates to events. Such delays are sufficiently common to demand some caution in interpreting raw national data. This has implications for both primary and secondary prevention efforts [26]. There have been changes to the reporting of coronial data in the UK as a consequence, as well as the development of real-time monitoring. Timeliness of analysis and regular reporting of surveillance data are important components of self-harm and suicide surveillance systems [27]. As Public Health England [28] has suggested, different organisations and suicide prevention projects need different data from surveillance systems to support their work, and this may involve aggregating or disaggregating data in a variety of ways.

It is widely recognised that establishing rigorous and sustainable self-harm surveillance systems is challenging, but there are calls to do so in different regions of the globe [29,30]. The WHO notes the need for sustained investment to support the development of systems to monitor presentations of self-harm and makes the assumption that resources for this should come from governments, regional or national [31]. However, the location of data is not uniform across the world. In HICs, episodes of self-harm are generally captured through presentations to secondary health care emergency departments (EDs). EDs are an excellent source of information in many cases [32], but this relies on good information systems. Furthermore, not all countries operate EDs for all areas. In some places, emergency responses are in casualty departments, which primarily offer triage and onward referral. It is noteworthy that, in some countries, incidents of suicide and self-harm are captured and collated through medicolegal processes that belong to the criminal justice system. Even in countries where attempted suicide has recently been decriminalised, such as India, medicolegal systems of notification are unchanged. National suicide statistics are based upon such notifications, rather than the public health system, with a resultant difference in the reliability of the data collected.

By international standards, the UK generates high-quality suicide and self-harm surveillance data. There are three main continuous processes. The first is the generation of national statistics, particularly rates of death by suicide. The latter is based on coronial verdicts. The second level is the detailed investigation of deaths by suicide amongst people who are, or who have recently been, under the care of specialist mental health services, the National Confidential Inquiry into Suicide and Safety in Health (NCISH). The third level is locally held self-harm registers. There are a number of these, which are selective and non-uniform, collate somewhat different data items and therefore provide different information. Each of these levels has been important in supporting and evaluating population-level suicide prevention measures. There is a paucity of systems in LMICs [33]. Even in HICs with well-developed systems, death misclassification or under-reporting is a problem. Overall, self-harm is recorded less well than suicide, especially at the national level.

There are some long-standing examples of third-level, local surveillance which use clinician completed paper-based proforma. Others, more recently designed, utilise routinely collected data at a minimum from emergency departments' electronic records, sometimes from a cluster of hospitals and, in some cases, utilising other records like liaison psychiatry [34]. Nonetheless some older local systems have informed national suicide prevention strategies [35], and some have been developed with the intention to feed directly into the refinement of local health and care services [36].

15.7 Establishing Self-Harm Registers

Despite calls for national self-harm registers [30,37], there are a only few examples of national schemes [38]. Our own experience of setting up self-harm registers in LMICs highlights some of the reasons why this is the case. Data *quality* needs to be balanced against data *quantity*, both in terms of the number of variables and the number of self-harm events that are recorded. The number of variables will be, in part, dependent upon the sources of data and the ability to influence either the scope of routinely produced datasets or the resources to create bespoke data collection frameworks; both depend on clinicians asking, and recording the answers to, all of the questions in a given dataset.

Where electronic records are pervasive and reliable, the issue of repeat self-harm and the risks associated with self-harm and suicide can be explored. For example, on the basis of the extant evidence in the public domain, repeat self-harm is a risk factor for suicide in the UK but rare in South Asia. However, it is hard to link data between hospitals in South Asia. It is possible that non-repetition in South Asia is an artefact of the mixed heath economy prevalent there. Where it is possible to link data together (e.g., because a national health service exists), there may be greater scope for analysis and interpretation.

15.8 Definitions

Whilst there is much agreement about the utility of self-harm surveillance, how to define it and what sort of data to collect are not universally agreed upon. Definitions are open to some international debate [39]. Some health systems base their routinely collected data around the US Centre for Disease Control and Prevention's ICD_10_CM codes for non-fatal suicide attempts and intentional self-harm [36]. However, ICD codes are difficult to apply in LMIC settings and are agreed upon through a political, rather than scientific, process. Use of ICD codes does not of itself guarantee rigour. The variation in the content of self-harm registries is in part due to the reliance of routinely collected information in health service systems, which may not always include important information about individuals or communities. For example, the health system in Canada at one point did not include Indigenous identifiers and excluded some regions completely [40].

The Bristol Self-Harm Register [41] is 'a composite of self-reported and abstracted data from NHS records'. Emergency department records are searched electronically for potential self-harm cases. 'Intentional self-injury or self-poisoning regardless of motivation or suicidal intent' extraction uses a bespoke framework. This is a local data set which provides information about employment, relationships, precipitating factors, treatments and referrals, and thus provides more detail than the hospital episode documentation. However, the Bristol register concerns relatively smaller numbers of people.

15.9 New Sources of Data

At the other end of the spectrum of data extraction and processing, there have been digital developments. The techniques of natural language processing and machine learning have been used to detect mention of keywords like *depression* and *suicide ideation*. One such system is being developed in Australia, where a natural language processing classifier is using machine learning to identify episodes of self-harm via both free text triage notes and some categorical data [30].

Another example is big data research of social media platforms (or so-called *infoveillance* or *digital epidemiology*). The hypothesis is that one can model population-level trends by using social media data [42]. This process is based on the assumption that suicide interventions involve recognising warning signs, with an ability to identify groups based on basic demographics. These new techniques have major challenges and limitations. For example, they depend on the accuracy of labelling and involve data that can be skewed in a number of ways. For example, social media users are overrepresented in the demographic of 18–34 year olds, who are more likely to be female; geographical information and other important demographics are not universally included in profiles.

Data mining social media, including blogs, creates a number of ethical challenges to this sort of research, none more so than protecting the privacy of social media data and not revealing the identity of individual users. On the one hand, the data is put by the user in the public domain. On the other hand, personal data should not be used without the permission of the individual. Although the data is in the public domain, guidance recommends obtaining an ethical review and considering consent [43]. Where quotes from social media postings are used in presentations or papers, this runs the risk of being identifiable. Careful consideration needs to be given to anonymisation processes which are complex and involve much more than simply removing names. There are limitations to going too far to anonymise information, in that there is a risk it will lose context and meaning and strays too far away from the producer's views and perceptions.

15.10 The South Asia Self-Harm Initiative (SASHI)

The South Asia Self-Harm Initiative (SASHI) is a major project on surveillance that has several arms but started in south India, with later involvement in Pakistan and Sri Lanka. It was funded by the UK Research and Innovation–Global Challenges Research Fund (UKRI-GCRF), but there was alternative funding before and after that, several spin-offs having secured separate funding.

SASHI's programme of work started with a request from colleagues in India to provide some advice about how to explore the characteristics and care and treatment pathways of people presenting at the hospital with self-harm. We led the team to meet a very local need in Mysuru, Karnataka, India. From the outset of the SASHI programme, it was clear that the challenge is much greater in LMICs, particularly where self-harm and suicide are stigmatised or subject to legal sanction [44].

We progressed to establish a small international team and a common aim to test the feasibility, acceptability and utility of identification and mental health assessment of individuals presenting to a large state government hospital following an episode of self-harm [45]. We achieved a series of small collaborative grants which enabled us to synthesise relevant literature, meet with international experts in the field and pilot a data collection framework [46]. Based on what we learned from the pilot work, we refined our aims to shift the focus away from mental health assessment to a much broader project which included socio-economic antecedents of self-harm, in addition to mental health problems.

Having completed this essential early work, we were successful in achieving research funding from UKRI/GCRF for a large-scale study to design, establish and evaluate self-harm registers in South Asia. The WHO guidance [31] presumes that most self-harm surveillance takes place in emergency departments, but as previously noted, emergency medicine is not universally available in LMIC settings. The large state government hospital we worked in included a casualty triage with the potential for outpatient care from a relevant department, admission or transfer for further treatment elsewhere. Another large not-for-profit hospital we worked in operated an emergency department with the potential for emergency care, admission or transfer. Both sites had in-patient burn units.

During our work with SASHI, it was necessary to decide which data to collect at what nodal points on the patient journey. Both decisions were tempered by what information is routinely collected and maintained and by the feasibility of collecting some information directly from people presenting after an episode of self-harm or their families; this in turn relied on the willingness of people to be interviewed, space and privacy in the different hospital settings, timely access to the clinical and administrative information and permissions and approvals. Medical records were for the most part paper-based, with some non-clinical transactions in digital form. We used process mapping to fully understand the patient pathways, administrative and legal frameworks and the clinical and physical environment [47]. This was critical to setting up a workable self-harm register in each setting and to avoid omissions evident in our pilot project.

Routinely collected information in the Indian state government hospital was entirely paper based, with handwritten medical records held in large card-bound files. Bound ledgers documented all presentations to the casualty and bound registers of all presentations that fell into certain legal categories. Ultimately, of course, information is provided by the person presenting with self-harm and the assessing or treating clinician.

In India the Medicolegal Register (MLR; all cases admitted that have a legal implication) proved to be the most consistent source of data, as it was a high priority for the hospital to complete it and it contained details about incidents of interest. Our process mapping enabled us to identify the MLR as a key data source and to understand that timely access to the register could be problematic in a busy environment. Each country's health system and setting have different optimal points of data collection and process mapping, with input from register planners outside the immediate clinical environment. Our experience suggests that few clinicians in any setting, HIC or LMIC, will have sufficient knowledge of how all of the relevant systems in their own hospitals work. The additional input external to the immediate clinical team reduced the risk of loss of relevant cases in the surveillance system and helped highlight the range and utility of existing routine data to populate a register.

This process has been brought into sharp focus by deep-dive work on the routinely collected data on burns in the large state government hospital. In large parts of the world outside of Europe, self-immolation is a common method of suicide and self-harm. Our work with the routinely collected data in medical records showed that it was difficult to discern those cases that were due to either assault or self-harm from accidents. This was reflected in some overwriting of categories during the course of a hospital stay. The relationship between self-harm and domestic violence is complicated in HIC and LMIC settings. Perpetrators as well as victims of domestic violence have an elevated risk of self-harm, and misclassification is of increasing interest to service providers and researchers.

During our time with the SASHI project, we came to move away from the difficult task of determining *intention* (which may not clearly exist in any case, being a legal rather than a clinical phenomenon) and towards the alterative of determining *likely agency*. The latter is less vulnerable to alteration, though such a risk still exists, as patients are frequently interviewed by clinicians with family members present in LMICs. This can include perpetrators of domestic violence. The determination of agency focusses on *Who did what?*, not *Why?* No inferences are made about anyone's state of mind at the time. This is not an idiosyncrasy of ours. This difficulty led to a change in how ICD codes such incidents between ICD-9 and ICD-10. Measurement of self-harm is difficult at a population level, but we do not believe it to be impossible.

The SASHI data is still under analysis, and there will be an open-access manual available to replicate the work in other countries. Needless to say, the processes are important; the precise solution found in South Asia may not apply to other settings. Our work does create a question as to whether self-harm registers should include instances of suspected domestic violence, at least in those settings where immolation or self-immolation are common.

15.11 Clinical Challenges in Data Collection

The major challenge in maintaining self-harm registers over time is to get clinicians who are very busy to record information for surveillance purposes. In our experience, they respond well to explanation, but the challenge is to get their attention. It is important that the gap between data collection and implementation of findings is not too short, so that the burden of data collection is seen to solve a problem for clinicians and for individual patients. The critical step is between the clinician and the record. Psychiatrists have a perverse incentive to avoid saying that someone is suicidal, because if they die, it is then your fault. This is true in HICs and may influence what is recorded unconsciously. This is a further good reason to record *what* has happened rather than *why* it has happened. More neutral information is recorded more reliably.

15.12 Other Sources of Surveillance Data

It is only in recent years that non–health care sources of routine data have been explored (e.g., see Lubman and collegues' work on ambulance data) [48]. Wales and England have each developed a scheme to record police attendances at suspected suicide incidents [49]. These rely on the judgment of individual police officers that a given episode is a likely suicide or self-harm. Whilst this judgement may cause false positives and false negatives, the speed that data can be collated gives real-time information, with marked advantages over the coronial data, which can be delayed for a considerable time. Other potential new data sources include ambulance services, schools and third-sector facilities. So far these data sources are under-explored, but there are good grounds to suppose that they capture self-harm incidents that do not present to EDs. It is more a question of the data being different rather than less reliable.

15.13 Who Is Data For?

There is no point in collecting data if you do not do something with it. Statistics, on their own, achieve little. The WHO recommends at least annual reporting, which is important, but statistical findings must be acted upon by someone with agency in the situation at social, clinical or public health levels. Amongst those of us who have worked hard to establish self-harm registers in places that have historically produced no statistics, there is a tension between the need to publish peer-reviewed papers/reports for funders and the extra effort necessary to do something different. There is a need for 'Memoranda of Understanding' with clinical services (and the temptation of informal arrangements is to be avoided). Western researchers should seek to facilitate local ownership of both the problem and the solution. Local surveillance can help identify subgroups of people, whether in terms of geographical location [50], health condition [51] or in terms of different methods [52]; this can also help identify who self-harms and therefore support better targeting of interventions [53]. In low-resource settings, statistics can assist with the deployment of limited resources. There are constant problems with staff retention and continuing funding, which can be withdrawn very suddenly.

In trying to ensure that data is used, the research is drawn into a type of suicide prevention activism. This is difficult for scientists but inevitable. The alternative is that surveillance effort is not used as a political fig leaf to hide inactivity, whereby something is done (the establishment of a register) but nothing is done (no action is taken based on the findings of a register).

15.14 Conclusion

The establishment of self-harm registers is a major part of suicide prevention. There is no need to await action by governments. Indeed, locally owned and implemented registers carry major advantages over larger-scale schemes. Although details of the registers differ according to local needs, and definitions vary so that data cannot be easily compared, all registers depend on rigour, especially at the clinical/data collection interface. Although there is a principle that randomised controlled trials depend on the size of the dataset, it is important to recognise that large datasets can amplify, rather than reduce, error where it is systematic. In particular, it is important to recognise that findings may challenge preconceptions. Surprises of this sort are the most important findings that justify the existence of registers. It is particularly important to avoid inadvertently confirming preconceived ideas to the exclusion of new, potentially useful ones.

References

1. Choi BC. The past, present, and future of public health surveillance. *Scientifica*. 2012; **1**: 875253.
2. Cameron D, Jones IG. John Snow, the Broad Street pump and modern epidemiology. *International Journal of Epidemiology*. 1983; **12**(4): 393–6.
3. Thacker SB, Berkelman RL. Public health surveillance in the United States. *Epidemiologic Reviews*. 1988; **10**(1): 164–90.
4. McGill K, Haddock R. Hospital treated self-harm: Improved care through improved data. *Issues Brief No. 47. Deeble Institute for Health Policy Research*. 2022; https://ahha.asn.au/wp-content/uploads/2023/11/deeble_issues_brief_no_47_hospital_treated_self_harm_improving_care_through_improved_data.pdf.
5. HM Government. *Health Protection (Notification) Regulations, 2010*. 2010. www.legislation.gov.uk/uksi/2010/659/schedule/1.
6. Appleby L. Safer services: Conclusions from the report of the National Confidential Inquiry. *Advances in Psychiatric Treatment*. 2000; **6**(1): 5–15.
7. Bebbington E, Miles J, Young A, van Baar ME, Bernal N, Brekke RL, et al. 2024. Exploring the similarities and differences of burn registers globally: Results from a data dictionary comparison study. *Burns*. **50**(4): 850–65.
8. Younossi ZM, Wong G, Anstee, QM, Henry L. The global burden of liver disease. *Clinical Gastroenterology and Hepatology*. 2023; **21**(8): 1978–91.
9. Shukurullayevna BS, Kamolidinovna IL, Nabijonovna, KZ. Differential diagnosis of alcoholic and viral hepatitis. *World Bulletin of Public Health*. 2023; **21**: 8–11.
10. Linsley KR, Schapira K, Kelly TP. Open verdict v. suicide – importance to

research. *British Journal of Psychiatry*. 2001; **178**(5): 465–8.

11. Carroll R, Hawton K, Kapur N, Bennewith O, Gunnell D. Impact of the growing use of narrative verdicts by coroners on geographic variations in suicide: Analysis of coroners' inquest data. *Journal of Public Health*. 2012; **34**(3): 447–53.
12. Ikeda R, Hedegaard H, Bossarte R, Crosby AE, Hanzlick R, Roesler J, et al. Improving national data systems for surveillance of suicide-related events. *American Journal of Preventive Medicine*. 2014; **47**(3 suppl 2): S122.
13. Benson R, Rigby J, Brunsdon C, Corcoran P, Dodd P, Ryan M, et al. Real-time suicide surveillance: Comparison of international surveillance systems and recommended best practice. *Archives of Suicide Research*. 2023; **27**(4): 1312–38.
14. da Costa BFC, Ramalho A, Gonçalves-Pinho M, Freitas A. Suicide mortality rate as a sustainable development goal (SDG): A bibliometric analysis. *Psychiatric Quarterly*. 2022; **93**(1): 15–26.
15. World Health Organization. *Preventing Suicide: A Global Imperative*. Geneva: WHO; 2014. www.who.int/publications/i/item/9789241564779#:~: text=The%20report%20provides%20a%20global%20knowledge%20base%20on, and%20context%20to%20move%20forward%20in%20suicide%20prevention.
16. World Health Organization. *LIVE LIFE: An Implementation Guide for Suicide Prevention in Countries*. Geneva: WHO; 2014. www.who.int/publications/i/item/9789240026629.
17. Institute for Health Metrics and Evaluation Seattle. *Evaluation, Global Burden of Disease Collaborative Network: Global Burden of Disease Study 2016 (GBD 2016) Results 2017*. Seattle: Institute for Health Metrics and Evaluation Seattle; 2019.
18. Geulayov G, Casey D, McDonald KC, Foster P, Pritchard K, Wells C, et al. Incidence of suicide, hospital-presenting non-fatal self-harm, and community-occurring non-fatal self-harm in adolescents in England (the Iceberg Model of Self-Harm): A retrospective study. *Lancet Psychiatry*. 2018; **5**(2): 167–74.
19. World Health Organization. *Suicide in the World: Global Health Estimates*. Geneva: World Health Organization; 2019.
20. Economic and Social Commission for Asia and the Pacific (ESCAP). *Reaching a Regional Estimate of Death Registration Completeness*. 2023.
21. Adair T, Gamage USH, Mikkelsen L, Joshi R. Are there sex differences in completeness of death registration and quality of cause of death statistics? Results from a global analysis. *BMJ Global Health*. 2021; **6**(10): e006660.
22. Sari E, Er ST, Demir E. Suicide as globalisation's black swan: Global evidence. *Public Health*. 2023; **217**, 74–80.
23. Gearing RE, Alonzo D. Religion and suicide: New findings. *Journal of Religion and Health* 2018; **57**: 2478–99.
24. Wu KCC, Cai Z, Chang Q, Chang SS, Yip PSF, Chen YY. Criminalisation of suicide and suicide rates: An ecological study of 171 countries in the world. *BMJ Open*. 2022 **12**(2): e049425.
25. International Association of Suicide Prevention. *Decriminalisation Position Paper*. 2024. www.iasp.info/wp-content/uploads/IASP-Decriminalisation-Position-Paper.pdf.
26. Nsubuga P, White ME, Thacker SB, Anderson MA, Blount SB, Broome CV, et al. Public health surveillance: A tool for targeting and monitoring interventions. In Jamison DT, Breman JG, Measham AR, Alleyne G, Claeson M, Evans DB, et al., eds., *Disease Control Priorities in Developing Countries*, 2nd ed. Washington, DC: The International Bank for Reconstruction and Development and The World Bank; 2006.
27. Witt K, Robinson J. Sentinel surveillance for self-harm. *Crisis*. 2019; **40**(1): 1–6.
28. Public Health England. *Public Health England: Approach to Surveillance*. London: Public Health England; 2017.

29. Chauhan N, Sharma M. National Self-Harm Registry: Is it time for India to have one? *Indian Journal of Preventive & Social Medicine*. 2020; **51**(4): 228–30.

30. Kolves K, Mathieu S, Fleischmann A. Suicide and self-harm surveillance across the Western Pacific: A call for action. *Lancet Regional Health: Western Pacific*. 2022; **19**: 100367.

31. World Health Organization. *Practice Manual for Establishing and Maintaining Surveillance Systems for Suicide Attempts and Self-Harm*. Geneva: World Health Organisation; 2016.

32. Sperandei S, Page A, Spittal MJ, Witt K, Robinson J, Pirkis J, et al. Using the 'presenting problem' field in emergency department data improves the enumeration of intentional self-harm in NSW hospital settings. *Australian and New Zealand Journal of Psychiatry*. 2021; **55**(10): 1019–20.

33. Vijayakumar L, Armstrong G. Surveillance for self-harm: An urgent need in low-income and middle-income countries. *Lancet Psychiatry*. 2019; **6**(8): 633–4.

34. Dalton TR, Knipe D, Feder G, Williams S, Gunnell D, Moran P. Prevalence and correlates of domestic violence among people seeking treatment for self-harm: Data from a regional self-harm register. *Emergency Medicine Journal*. 2019; **36**(7): 407–9.

35. Hawton K, Bergen H, Casey D, Simkin S, Palmer B, Cooper J, et al. Self-harm in England: A tale of three cities – Multicentre study of self-harm. *Social Psychiatry and Psychiatric Epidemiology*. 2007; **42**: 513–21.

36. Williams S. Establishing a self-harm surveillance register to improve care in a general hospital. *British Journal of Mental Health Nursing*. 2015; **4**(1): 20–5.

37. Witt K, Robinson J. Sentinel surveillance for self-harm. *Crisis*. 2019; **40**(1): 1–6.

38. Troya MI, Griffin E, Arensman E, Cassidy E, Mughal F, Lonergan CN, et al. Hospital-presenting self-harm among older adults living in Ireland: A 13-year trend analysis from the National Self-Harm Registry Ireland. *International Psychogeriatrics*. 2024; **36**(5): 396–404.

39. Hedegaard H, Schoenbaum M, Claassen C, Crosby A, Holland K, Proescholdbell S. Issues in developing a surveillance case definition for nonfatal suicide attempt and intentional self-harm using *International Classification of Diseases, Tenth Revision, Clinical Modification* (ICD-10-CM) coded data. *National Health Statistics Reports*. 2018; **108**: 1–19.

40. Pollock NJ, Healey GK, Jong M, Valcour JE, Mulay S. Tracking progress in suicide prevention in Indigenous communities: A challenge for public health surveillance in Canada. *BMC Public Health*. 2018; **18**(1): 1320.

41. Mummé M, Redaniel T, Boyd A, Jackson J, Mars B, Macleod J. The Bristol Self Harm Register (BSHR) dataset: Linked self-harm register records of the children in the Avon Longitudinal Study of Parents and Children (ALSPAC). *Wellcome Open Research*. 2023; **7**: 195.

42. Keyes KM, Kandula S, Olfson M, Gould MS, Martínez-Alés G, Rutherford C, Shaman J. Suicide and the agent–host–environment triad: Leveraging surveillance sources to inform prevention. *Psychological Medicine*. 2021; **51**(4): 529–37.

43. Benton A, Coppersmith G, Dredze M. Ethical research protocols for social media health research. In *Proceedings of the First ACL Workshop on Ethics in Natural Language Processing*. Valencia, Spain: Association for Computational Linguistics; April 2017. www.cs.jhu.edu/~mdredze/publications/ethicsnlp_2017.pdf.

44. Vichianchai V, Kasemvilas S, Kaewhao S, Youdkang O. Prediction of revisit of repeated attempted-suicide patients. *Information Technology Journal*. 2018; **14**(1): 23–31.

45. Krishna M, Rajendra R, Majgi SM, Heggere N, Parimoo S, Robinson C, Poole R. Severity of suicidal intent, method and behaviour antecedent to an act of self-harm: A cross sectional study of survivors of self-harm referred to a tertiary hospital in Mysore, south India. *Asian Journal of Psychiatry*. 2014; **12**: 134–9.

46. Rajendra R, Krishna M, Majgi S, Heggere N, Robinson C, Poole R.

A feasibility study to establish a Deliberate Self-Harm Register in a state hospital in southern India. *British Journal of Medical Practitioners*. 2015; **8**(1): a807.

47. Bebbington E, Poole R, Kumar SP, Krayer A, Krishna M, Taylor P, et al. Establishing self-harm registers: The role of process mapping to improve quality of surveillance data globally. *International Journal of Environmental Research and Public Health*. 2023; **20**(3): 2647.

48. Lubman DI, Heilbronn C, Ogeil RP, Killian JJ, Matthews S, Smith K, et al. National Ambulance Surveillance System: A novel method using coded Australian ambulance clinical records to monitor self-harm and mental health-related morbidity. *PloS One*. 2020; **15**(7): e0236344.

49. Meurk C, Wittenhagen L, Steele ML, Ferris L, Edwards B, Bosley E, Heffernan E. Examining the use of police and ambulance data in suicide research. *Crisis*. 2020; **42**(5): 386–95.

50. Cox GR, Owens C, Robinson J, Nicholas A, Lockley A, Williamson M, et al. Interventions to reduce suicides at suicide hotspots: A systematic review. *BMC Public Health*. 2013 Mar 9; **13**: 1–12.

51. Jones S, Somashekar R, Bharath DU, Maiji SM, Taylor L, Nagaraj S, Krishna M. Physical health impairment, disability and suicidal intent among self-harm survivors in South India. *International Journal of Community Medicine and Public Health*. 2021; **8**(5): 2370–7.

52. Daly C, Griffin E, Ashcroft DM, Webb RT, Perry IJ, Arensman E. Intentional drug overdose involving pregabalin and gabapentin: Findings from the National Self-Harm Registry Ireland, 2007–2015. *Clinical Drug Investigation*. 2018; **38**(4): 373–80.

53. Barrett P, Griffin E, Corcoran P, O'Mahony MT, Arensman E. Self-harm among the homeless population in Ireland: A national registry-based study of incidence and associated factors. *Journal of Affective Disorders*. 2018; **229**: 523–31.

Chapter 16

Postvention Following Bereavement by Suicide

Alexandra Pitman and Keith Hawton

16.1 Introduction

Suicide bereavement describes the period of grief, mourning and adjustment after a suicide death that is experienced by family members, friends and close contacts of the deceased [1]. This group is sometimes termed *suicide survivors* or the *suicide bereaved*, and are considered the group most directly affected by a suicide. Suicide bereavement is distinct from *exposure* to (or awareness of) the suicide of someone in one's wider social networks. Although both are associated with suicidality [1,2], probably through differing mechanisms, closeness to the deceased is a key influence on the severity of psychiatric morbidity and suicidal ideation [3]. Irresponsible *media reporting of suicide* represents a more distal exposure to suicide, with demonstrated impacts on population suicide rates, particularly in the case of a celebrity's suicide [4]. *Suicide clusters* are thought to be a manifestation of exposure to suicide, although in spatial clusters the links between the deceased may not always be clear [5]. The psychological mechanisms implicated in the phenomenon of suicide clusters intersect with the risk factors that apply where there is an established kinship and include (a) social transmission, where there is exposure to suicidal behaviour (including method) on social networks or the media; (b) distorted perception of the frequency of suicidal behaviour, again perhaps influenced by media reporting, together with online social networking; (c) assortative relating, whereby people with similar problems or backgrounds establish social groups or networks; and (d) sharing of information within social groups representing isolated tight-knit communities [6]. This chapter focusses on suicide bereavement (the most proximal exposure) and responses to this, as distinct from broader interventions mitigating the effects of exposure to suicide, although there is some overlap.

Suicide bereavement is associated with a range of adverse health and social outcomes, including suicide and psychiatric illness [1] and also disruptive effects on family cohesion [7]. These adverse sequelae highlight the importance of providing support to people bereaved by suicide to mitigate the risk of new onset or deteriorating mental illness and further family disruption. Understanding the basis for the elevated risk of suicide and other adverse outcomes after suicide loss is critical in tackling modifiable risk factors through preventive initiatives. This is the focus of current research efforts. However, until we understand these mechanisms better, it is difficult to be clear about the most effective means of reducing suicide risk after suicide loss.

The term *postvention* is used broadly to describe any support provided to the bereaved after a suicide, with the intention of reducing distress and Preventing adverse outcomes, including suicidal behaviour [8]. More narrowly, it can be defined as a specific suicide prevention intervention provided after suicide loss [8]. Supporting people bereaved by suicide is one of five key messages in the World Health Organization's (WHO's) suicide prevention strategy [9]. It is one of the overarching aims of the suicide prevention strategy for England [10] and a key component of numerous international suicide prevention strategies [11]. These include some low- and middle-income countries, despite the lack of observational evidence describing the impact of suicide loss in those settings. Despite the prominence given to provision of support after suicide, no interventions have been shown to reduce suicide risk in people bereaved by suicide, and only a few have demonstrated effectiveness in improving mental health or social functioning [12].

16.2 How Common Is Suicide Bereavement?

Early estimates of the number of people severely affected by each suicide loss were between five and ten individuals [13], but these results were not empirically based. Empirical work since then has derived differing estimates depending on definitions used (i.e., bereaved versus exposed). A survey of suicide survivors estimated that between 60 people (20 relatives, 20 friends and 20 colleagues) were directly affected (i.e., bereaved) by each loss [14]. Surveys yield estimates of between 135 [15] and 425 people [16] exposed to each suicide. Estimates of the prevalence of suicide bereavement also vary due to differing definitions. A meta-analysis of population-based studies estimated that 4% of the population reported past-year exposure to suicide; 22% reported lifetime exposure [17]. Estimates of lifetime exposure in some studies represent more than half the general population: 51% in a US sample [18] and 58% in an Australian sample [19]. The proportion of the bereaved who experience serious psychological sequelae is related to the bereaved's perception of closeness to the deceased [3].

These figures allow for a crude estimate of the burden of suicide bereavement. The WHO estimates 700,000 suicides per year globally [20]. A conservative estimate indicates that 60 people are directly affected by each suicide death [14]. There is also a survey finding that 9% of people bereaved by suicide subsequently make a suicide attempt [21]. An estimated 42 million people are bereaved by suicide annually, and 3.78 million of them might go on to make a suicide attempt. With a greater awareness of the adverse psychiatric outcomes of suicide bereavement and support sources available, clinicians who encounter this risk factor in patients may recognise their greater vulnerability and help address modifiable suicide risk factors (such as psychiatric illness, financial hardship and loneliness).

16.3 Risk of Suicide after Suicide Bereavement

There is now strong evidence from population registry studies that suicide risk is elevated after the suicide of a child [22,23], parent [24], sibling [25,26], cousin [25] or partner [22,27]. Studies investigating the impact of peer suicide demonstrate an elevated risk of suicide attempt but have not measured risk of suicide [2]. Generally, suicide risk is greater in those exposed to suicide more than once when compared to those reporting one suicide exposure [2]. Most research on this topic has been conducted on the suicide of a parent, with consistent evidence that exposure to parental suicide in childhood carries an increased risk of suicide in adulthood [28,29].

The mechanisms of the link between suicide bereavement and suicide remain unclear, but other adverse outcomes (described later) are likely contributors. The genetic heritability of suicide risk is well established [30,31] and forms the basis for the routine practice of eliciting a family history of suicide within a mental health assessment. However, a narrow focus on genetics to inform suicide risk assessment ignores the emotional trauma associated with suicide loss. Clinicians reading this chapter might think back to patients they have assessed in the past who reported a family history of suicide and realise they neglected to pause the assessment, acknowledge the traumatic nature of this event, and inquire about its impact on life course and social, emotional, and occupational functioning. The environmental component of suicide risk after suicide loss is now better acknowledged and is evident in the increased risk of suicide attempt [2,21] and suicide [2,27] among non-relatives of people who die by suicide. While spouses and friends do share genetic similarities, termed *assortative mating* with respect to partners [32] and *assortative relating* with respect to friends [33], studies that account for shared traits for psychiatric illness when estimating suicide risk after the suicide of a spouse conclude that assortative mating is less likely an explanation than environmental factors [22,34]. The gender differences observed when assessing the magnitude of the risk of suicide after a partner's suicide also suggest that genetic susceptibility may be a less important factor for suicidal behaviour than environmental factors such as help-seeking [22]. Thus environmental factors also include the social and emotional dimensions of suicide loss, such as stigma, lack of support, psychiatric illness and the burden of grief, as well as shared social and economic adversity.

Differing impacts of suicide bereavement by age at loss also provide clues as to mechanisms, although this has only been explored with respect to parental suicide loss. Generally the younger the age of a parent at the time of their suicide, the greater the suicide risk in their children [24,35]. This is likely to relate to the age at which a child experienced a traumatic life event and an abrupt change in parenting. After the death of one parent, children may also experience a sense of a (temporary) loss of the other grieving parent. Parental suicide loss in early development is particularly predictive of later suicide [36], with the most sensitive period being up to 6 years of age [37]. Risk of suicide remains elevated 25 years after parental suicide in childhood [38], long after societal expectations of having 'moved on' with their grief [39]. There are also gender differences, with suicide risk being greatest in older female offspring and lowest in older male offspring [40].

Qualitative research among adolescents demonstrates that the suicide of a sibling or friend can affect the way a young person relates to others and maintains progress in education [41,42]. The suicide of a sibling, as for that of a parent, may erode the capacity of a surviving parent to contain the grief of others in the family unit [41]. Qualitative accounts from young adults describe complex family dynamics after suicide loss, in which bereaved parents are perceived to be those in greatest need but young children are seen as much lower down this hierarchy [43], potentially leaving children feeling neglected. Clearly, clinical practice needs to change. Instead of just asking about a family history of suicide, clinicians should inquire about suicide among friends and (current/former) partners as well as relatives, and explore the emotional impact in relation to the stage of life at which these occurred. This is also a good opportunity for the clinician to screen for known adverse health and social outcomes. It is also important for clinicians to highlight to reassure the bereaved about the low absolute risk of suicide after parental suicide loss [44] and to be aware that for many people, witnessing the devastation wreaked by a peer or relative's suicide may serve to inhibit suicidal behaviour [45].

16.4 Other Adverse Health Outcomes of Suicide Bereavement

16.4.1 Mortality

The adverse mortality outcomes of suicide bereavement include not only suicide but also an increased risk of all-cause mortality [27].

16.4.2 Psychiatric Illness

The risk of psychiatric illness following bereavement by suicide is apparent in a number of studies. These include an elevated risk of depression in spouses [27,46] and children [35,47,48] bereaved by suicide, including psychiatric admission specifically for unipolar depression [49], bipolar disorder [49] or first onset mania [50]. There is also evidence of increased risk of post-traumatic stress disorder in spouses [27] and, for children and adolescents, psychotic disorders [35] and personality disorders [35]. Studies also describe an elevated probability among children and young adults of being initiated on antidepressants [51] and, among parents, psychiatric admission [52,53].

16.4.3 Suicide Attempt

Risk of suicide attempt is elevated in people bereaved by the suicide of a relative or a friend [2,21]. Among relatives, this risk has been investigated most commonly in relation to parental suicide, where suicide attempt risk is increased in children and adolescents [28,35,37,54]. Findings from a Swedish sample show that trajectories of suicide attempt risk differ markedly for children who lose a parent to suicide, depending on the age at which they experience the loss. For those who experience parental suicide loss during childhood, suicide attempt risk increases steadily throughout childhood and into midlife; for those who experience suicide loss in adolescence, suicide attempt risk peaks sharply after the loss and then declines over ensuing decades [36].

The impact of peer suicide bereavement on suicide attempt has been investigated most commonly in relation to adolescents [2,55]. These studies show conflicting findings, which is likely to relate to statistical power and/or differing definitions of closeness to the deceased. US and Canadian cohort data show a clear association of a schoolmate's suicide with suicide attempt within a year of the loss [56], as well as one year [57,58] and two years [59] later. However, survey data from US adolescents show no increased risk of suicide attempt when assessed at six months [45], seven months [60] and three years [61] after a peer's suicide. In a Hong Kong school-based study, the peers of suicide attempters carried a higher risk of suicide attempt than peers of suicide completers [62]. It is not clear whether those close to the deceased received the most support or whether their greater awareness of the impacts on family and other friends inhibited suicidal behaviour [45].

16.4.4 Substance Use

Although substance use is a common coping response to bereavement more generally [63], an increased risk of substance use may not be specific to suicide loss. Such work tends to describe a greater probability of having an alcohol or drug use disorder when compared with non-bereaved adults, but not when compared to adults bereaved by other causes [27,52]. For example, suicide-bereaved parents are three times more likely to have alcohol use disorders than non-bereaved control parents, both before and after the suicide [52].

However, individuals bereaved by suicide are no more likely to have a drug or alcohol use disorder than controls bereaved by motor vehicle collision, both before and after the loss [52].

Studies describing the risk of substance misuse among children bereaved by suicide tend to use self-report measures and are therefore less reliant on a formal diagnosis made on physician contact. There is evidence from US cohort studies that adolescents have an increased probability of smoking, marijuana use and binge-drinking after the suicide of a relative [54] or peer [56] when compared to non-bereaved adolescents. Cohort study data also show that adolescents bereaved by parental suicide are at higher risk of developing an alcohol or drug use disorder than bereaved controls two years after the loss [64] but not at five years [65]. Age at bereavement is likely to be an influence. In a Swedish registry-based study, offspring bereaved by parental suicide did not differ from bereaved controls in their risk of alcohol or drug use disorders [35]. However, subgroup analysis found that those who lost a parent to suicide in childhood were more likely to be admitted for drug use disorders than non-bereaved controls and that this association was stronger than for those who lost a parent to suicide later in young adulthood [35].

A British study of young adults bereaved by the sudden death of a friend or relative found that a greater proportion of those bereaved by suicide and other unnatural deaths increased their use of drugs or alcohol after the loss than people bereaved by sudden natural causes [66]. However, there is also some evidence that suicide loss has a deterrent effect on others, who in contrast reduce or stop their drug use [67]. Qualitative data suggest that increasing one's use of drugs and alcohol after suicide bereavement may form part of a bereaved person's coping strategies, used as part of the grieving process to help deal with overwhelming thoughts and emotions [68]. This works suggests a need for monitoring of substance use after suicide loss, using sensitive approaches when judging whether and when to intervene [66–68]. Men may be more prone to using substances to cope with grief after suicide, and in a British sample illicit drug use and alcohol use were slightly more commonly reported by men [69].

16.4.5 Physical Health Problems

Evidence from a relevant systematic review of studies comparing suicide bereavement to other bereavements describes an elevated risk in those bereaved by suicide of pain and physical illness, such as cardiovascular disease, hypertension, diabetes and chronic obstructive pulmonary disease, as well as poorer general health [70]. However, studies that measure physical health prior to the loss show that some of these differences apply even before bereavement [52]. A Canadian registry-based study described a significant increase in physician visits by parents for physical illness after a child's suicide death and significantly worse physical health after the loss than for parents bereaved by a child's motor vehicle death [52]. In a Danish registry-based study, suicide-bereaved spouses were more likely to report physical health problems than non-bereaved spouses but less likely than spouses bereaved by all other causes [27]. The same study provided striking gender differences in help-seeking. Women bereaved by spousal suicide were significantly less likely than the general population to be hospitalised for physical health disorders or to visit their general practitioner [27]. Men bereaved by spousal suicide were significantly less likely than spouses bereaved by other causes to visit their general practitioner [27]. It may be that some of these inconsistencies in physical health disparities are explained, at least in part, by gender differences in help-seeking in the context of the culture around grief. It seems important for clinicians to inquire about physical health after suicide loss, particularly if there are concerns about self-neglect, poor motivation in the context of depression, substance use or a sense of being unworthy of help.

16.4.6 Grief

People bereaved by violent deaths are more likely than those bereaved by natural causes to develop complicated grief, but this is not specific to suicide loss [71]. However, where people bereaved by suicide do develop complicated grief, as measured using the 'Inventory of Complicated Grief', this is associated with an increased probability of reporting suicidal ideation [72]. Of the various dimensions of grief, surveys describe an increased probability of reporting perceived stigma, shame, guilt, blame, responsibility, avoidance and rejection after suicide loss [21,73,74]. Where compared directly to people bereaved by non-suicide violent causes, also highly stigmatised, suicide-bereaved people are more likely to report greater rejection and shame but not stigma, guilt or responsibility [1].

16.4.7 Social Functioning

People bereaved by the suicide of a friend or relative are more likely than those bereaved by other causes to report problems in social functioning [21] and are more likely to drop out of a course or leave their job [21], thereby disrupting social and occupational trajectories. Suicide-bereaved spouses are more likely to claim benefits than spouses bereaved by other causes [27]. They are also more likely to experience marital break-up [52]. In a British survey of people bereaved by suicide, 13% had experienced financial problems after the loss, 8% experienced unemployment or job loss and 6% experienced divorce or separation [69].

16.5 Support Provided after Suicide Loss

16.5.1 Timing of Support

Postvention can operate at various levels and at different time points. The long-term risk of suicide risk after bereavement [38] suggests that support should be available for decades after the loss. The elevated risk of suicide immediately after suicide loss [75] suggests that support should be provided in the immediate aftermath of the loss, as proactive outreach. Appropriate timing of support is a key issue for the suicide-bereaved, many of whom report feeling abandoned for the first few weeks after the loss and express a need for longer-term support from informal and formal sources [76]. The need for early and proactive intervention from professionals (and from informal networks) has been identified, not requiring the bereaved to take the first initiative in contacting services immediately after the loss [76]. Reluctance to seek help in the early stages of loss is related partly to stigma and a sense of being unworthy of support, and partly to a lack of motivation during the acute phase of grief, along with a lack of clarity over what support might be available [76].

16.5.2 Formal Support

Formal interventions developed to support people after a suicide include bereavement counselling, family-based interventions, cognitive-behavioural group or individual therapy, writing therapy, online support and group or one-to-one peer support. These interventions tend to take supportive, psychotherapeutic and psychoeducational approaches, involving bereaved peers and/or professionals (known as peer support), but they are not always available through health services. The evidence to support their effectiveness in reducing suicide risk is also weak [12].

National or local suicide bereavement support organisations provide the majority of suicide bereavement support resources across many countries (see Box 16.1). Such services tend to be based in the voluntary sector, with funding reliant on charitable donations or grants. Support organisations are listed in directories of suicide bereavement support, such as 'Help Is at Hand' [77] and these directories are considered helpful for the bereaved [78]. Although some services are available online, addressing inconsistent geographical provision, people in remote areas and the digitally excluded remain underserved. Several organizations offer the following resources: online psychoeducation about the impacts of suicide loss, online practical information (e.g., on inquests), a telephone help-line, counselling and group therapy. Many of these organisations provide peer support from people who have themselves experienced suicide loss. International studies describing the perceived needs of people bereaved by suicide highlight the importance placed on peer support (whether individual, group or online) for gaining a shared understanding of the unique experience of suicide loss [76].

Suicide bereavement support organisations can offer their services throughout the grief trajectory, but some require a minimum period (for example three months) to have elapsed before commencing counselling. Coordination at the local level with police, paramedics and other first responders provides a link with local suicide bereavement support organisations, allowing systems of proactive outreach immediately after the loss. Where evaluated, these are perceived to be effective and acceptable by providers and the suicide-bereaved [79].

For those who experience the most severe psychological sequelae of suicide bereavement, formal support might also include psychiatric treatment where mental illness arises following the loss. Voluntary sector bereavement support organisations and primary care serve a role in identifying those who may be struggling and referring them on so that they receive appropriate treatment.

16.5.3 Informal Support

International studies of people bereaved by suicide identify that they strongly value social support from family and friends (including, for example, practical support such as help with childcare), professional support from health care services or bereavement services, clear information and, more broadly, being able to access a wide range of sources of support [76]. Such informal support from family and friends is particularly important in the immediate aftermath of the loss, when a bereaved person may not be ready to accept formal psychological support or may not be aware of available voluntary sector support. Indeed, informal support may sometimes be preferred to support from health care services, from the voluntary sector or provided in an online forum [69].

16.6 Population-Level Interventions

16.6.1 Interventions at the Organisational Level

Some countries offer postvention response programs tailored for schools or universities, provided after the suicide of a student. They include advice on how to communicate the news to students, staff and parents; how to handle media interest; and how to identify and support the students who might be most impacted. These appear to increase the confidence of staff in coping with the aftermath of a student's suicide [80]. Other guidance exists to support health service staff after the suicide of a patient and after the suicide of a colleague (see Box 16.1).

16.6.2 Public Awareness of Suicide Bereavement Support

It is important that friends, relatives, general practitioners and other professionals involved are aware of suicide support resources and proactive in signposting to them. This is particularly important given qualitative work showing that suicide-bereaved people often perceive their general practitioners as uncertain of how to respond in providing support [81], with general practitioners also expressing a lack of confidence in communicating with families after suicide loss [82]. Coalitions of suicide support organisations help raise awareness of the services available to people affected by suicide loss, and this also has an important role in addressing the stigma of suicide loss at the population level.

16.6.3 Disparities in Access to Support

A British survey of the experiences of 7,158 people bereaved by suicide found that only 40% accessed any support beyond their informal networks after their loss [69]. Overall, 16% had accessed GP services, 14% had used private counselling or bereavement support and 13% had sought information on suicide loss via the internet [69]. Less than 10% of the sample had used UK National Health Service (NHS) counselling/bereavement support, suicide bereavement support services, online forums or blogs, group support via self-help groups, information leaflets (such as those left by first responders), general bereavement services or group support via the NHS [69]. Within the first week of the bereavement, the organisations most commonly accessed were police officers (85%), emergency services (80%), faith leaders (66%) and funeral directors (64%). For the 60% of respondents who reported not having accessed the sources of support listed here, the commonest explanations were having supportive families and friends, feeling able to cope alone or not knowing what services were available [69]. There is clearly a problem of geographical access to suicide support services; 12% of respondents in a UK sample reported there were no local support services available to them [69]. In a younger British sample, 60% of young adults bereaved by suicide had accessed formal support, and 62% had accessed informal support, but 23% reported receiving no support at all [83].

When compared with people bereaved by other losses, people bereaved by the suicide of a friend or relative are more likely to perceive delays in receiving support than people bereaved by other causes. They are also less likely to receive informal support [83], which is thought to be partly explained by stigma [83,84]. Stigma is implicated as a major contributor to the preparedness of others to offer help, as well as bereaved people's willingness to seek help [43,85,86]. This is also an issue in psychiatric settings, where stigma may explain the lack of contact made with some families after a patient's suicide [87]. Addressing this stigma is a key factor in facilitating access to support and reducing distress. Clinicians have a key role in addressing the stigma of suicide loss and can do this by informing the bereaved about sources of support (Box 16.1).

16.6.4 The Effectiveness of Postvention in Preventing Suicide

There are very few trials of interventions delivered to people bereaved by suicide, and the evidence for their effectiveness in reducing psychiatric morbidity is weak [12]. There is a suggestion that complicated grief therapy (CGT) may reduce suicidal ideation among suicide-bereaved people with complicated grief, defined as scoring above a threshold on the 'Inventory of Complicated Grief' [88], but this study lacked the power to test this formally. No postvention interventions evaluated to date have been found to reduce suicide risk, although there is evidence that some reduce the intensity of grief, sense of blame and risk of low mood and anxiety [12].

In the absence of clear evidence of effectiveness in reducing suicide risk, public health authorities in England have produced guidance to address the postvention needs of the local population by suggesting how local services might be provided [89,90] and evaluated [91]. It is important that the clinical and research community continue to develop and evaluate interventions tailored to the needs of people bereaved by suicide. Comparisons of the effects of suicide bereavement to those of bereavement related to other sudden violent deaths demonstrate that there are many similarities between these two groups on outcomes, such as grief intensity, stress reactions and psychopathology [1]. Future service planning might consider how to offer support to both groups, recognising shared vulnerabilities and simplifying referral pathways while creating economies of scale and reducing stigma.

16.6.5 What Health Services Can Do to Address Gaps in Support

Every healthcare provider and local health and social care commissioner should review their 'Serious and Untoward Incident' (SUI) policy to ensure that it addresses the needs of relatives, other patients and staff after a patient's suicide. This should include sources of local and national suicide bereavement support (Box 16.1) and encourage managers to communicate this information to bereaved relatives, patients and staff after a suicide. Senior suicide lead clinicians are valued by staff for managing systemic learning [92]. Training of those undertaking SUI investigations following suicide would help identify who might need support and direct this appropriately. SUI policies should be clear that relatives should be involved in the process of post-suicide multidisciplinary reviews, explaining to relatives clearly what to expect from this process and what is likely to change as a result of the outcome. Partnerships with local universities also offer an opportunity to form collaborations between clinicians, researchers and people with lived experience, who can develop interventions based on available evidence for acceptability and design rigorous evaluations.

16.7 Conclusions

This chapter has outlined the range of adverse outcomes associated with the suicide of a friend or relative, and the limited evidence available for the effectiveness of interventions to reduce suicide risk in this group. The difficulties faced by this group include psychiatric illness, physical health problems, stigma, shame, poor social functioning and problems accessing support. Informal support from family and friends is particularly valued, as is peer support. Clinicians can potentially mitigate the risk of suicide in this group by screening and treating mental illness and addressing modifiable risk factors for suicide. They can also counter stigma by showing a willingness to acknowledge distress, offer early on and signpost to available resources.

Box 16.1 Suicide Bereavement Support Sources

This box provides a list of directories of support and resources for suicide bereavement.

Public Health England

See the following resource for more information:

- Public Health England, *Help Is at Hand: Support after Someone May Have Died by Suicide* (2021), https://supportaftersuicide.org.uk/wp-content/uploads/2020/04/HIAH_Booklet_2021_V5.pdf.

This is a co-produced resource for people bereaved by suicide and other sudden, traumatic death. It provides advice and the contact details of other organisations offering support, including advice for friends, family and colleagues of the bereaved.

Scottish Association of Mental Health

The Scottish Association of Mental Health (SAMH), in conjunction with NHS Health Scotland and Choose Life (a 10-year national strategy and action plan to prevent suicide in Scotland), has produced a booklet that describes practical issues that need to be faced after a suicide, some of the emotions that people bereaved by suicide might experience and sources of support:

- Scottish Association of Mental Health, *After a Suicide*, www.samh.org.uk/documents/After_a_suicide.pdf.

Support after Suicide Partnership (SASP)

This is a UK-wide network of national and local organisations involved in delivering suicide bereavement support. The site also includes links to downloadable support guides, including *Help Is at Hand, After a Suicide, You Are Not Alone* and *Finding the Words*.

- https://supportaftersuicide.org.uk/support-guides/
- https://supportaftersuicide.org.uk/

Resources for Teachers Supporting Individual Students

MindEd provides free e-learning modules such as 'Overview of Children and Young People's Mental Health (Introductory Level)', which includes a module entitled 'Post Suicide-Bereavement and Postvention'. These modules are designed to provide those who work with young people with the skills and resources to open up conversations around suicide loss. The lessons include videos modelling how teachers and professionals working in child and adolescent mental health services (CAMHS) might approach the issue with a young bereaved person and how to explain this to their friends.

- www.minded.org.uk/Catalogue/Index?HierarchyId=0_36571_43882_43883&programmeId=36571.

Guidance to Support Health Service Staff after the Suicide of a Patient

The Royal College of Psychiatrists provides the following resources for health service staff who experience the suicide of a patient:

- *If a Patient Dies by Suicide: A Resource for Psychiatrists*. www.rcpsych.ac.uk/members/workforce-wellbeing-hub/if-a-patient-dies-by-suicide. This guide is aimed at psychiatrists of all levels, from trainees to experienced consultants.
- *If a Patient Dies by Suicide: A Resource for Mental Health Professionals*. www.rcpsych.ac.uk/docs/default-source/members/supporting-you/if-a-patient-dies-by-suicide/if-a-patient-dies-by-suicide—for-mental-health-professionals.pdf?sfvrsn=d9a8230b_2. This guide is aimed at all mental health professionals, including trainees and unqualified staff.

Guidance to Support Health Service Staff after the Suicide of a Colleague

The following resources are designed for health service staff after the suicide of a colleague:

- Samaritans, *NHS Employee Suicide Postvention Kit* (2023), https://www.nhsconfed.org/system/files/2023-03/NHS-employee-suicide-postvention-toolkit.pdf.
- R Riley, H Causer, J Spiers, et al., *Postvention Guidance: Supporting NHS Staff after the Death by Suicide of a Colleague* (2023), www.surrey.ac.uk/sites/default/files/2024-09/postvention-guidance.pdf.

Guidance to Support University Staff and Students after the Suicide of a Student

See the following resources for bereaved university staff and students:

- Universities UK, 'How to respond to a student suicide Main Guidance' (2022), www.universitiesuk.ac.uk/sites/default/files/uploads/Reports/postvention-main-guidance.pdf.

Resources for the Friends or Relatives of Someone Bereaved by Suicide

Finding the Words is a co-produced guide that gives advice on how to provide practical and emotional support to someone who has lost a friend or relative to suicide. See the following website for more information:

- www.thecalmzone.net/wp-content/uploads/2018/03/Finding_the_Words.pdf.

Support Organisations

Cruse Bereavement Care

Cruse Bereavement Care is a UK charity promoting the well-being of bereaved people and enabling anyone bereaved by death to understand their grief and cope with their loss. The charity provides free support, including a help-line (open Monday–Friday, with varying hours; 0808 808 1677), and offers information, advice, education and training services.

Samaritans

Samaritans provides confidential, non-judgmental emotional support, 24 hours a day, for people who are experiencing feelings of distress or despair, including those which could lead to suicide. Their services are offered by telephone, e-mail, letter and in-person in most of their branches.

The Compassionate Friends

The Compassionate Friends (TCF) is a UK organisation of bereaved parents and their families offering peer support to others after the death of a child or children, as well as to other relatives, friends and professionals who are helping the family. They provide a help-line (0345 123 2304), local befrienders and online support.

Child Bereavement UK

Child Bereavement UK (formerly the Child Bereavement and merged, since 2025, with Winston's Wish, another UK childhood bereavement charity) provides specialised support, information and training to all those affected when a baby or child dies, or when a child is bereaved. They offer an online forum for bereaved a helpline, training for professionals," (this compensates for the content taken out above for Winston;s Wish and a database of organisations that offer support to bereaved families and the professionals who care for them.

Suicide&Co

Suicide&Co is a British charitable organisation that supports people bereaved by suicide. It offers free one-to-one counselling, support information on their website and social media channels, and a national suicide bereavement helpline run by bereavement counsellors (open Monday–Friday, 9:00 a.m.–5:00 p.m; 0800 054 8400).

Grief Encounter

Grief Encounter is a UK organisation which helps families address difficult issues such as the death of a child's parent or significant loved one. They offer a help-line (open Monday–Friday, 9:30 a.m.–3:00 p.m.; 0808 802 0111) and support such as one-to-one counselling and residential camps.

Survivors of Bereavement by Suicide

Survivors of Bereavement by Suicide is a UK charitable organisation offering peer-led emotional and practical support to people bereaved by the suicide of a close relative or friend. The organisation provides a confidential telephone helpline (0300 111 5065), support information on their website, an email support service and monthly group meetings in specific locations.

The WAY Foundation

The Widowed and Young (WAY) Foundation is a UK organisation for people who have become widows or widowers at a young age (before their 51st birthday). It offers members a help-line and support group.

INQUEST

INQUEST is a charity that provides a free advice service to bereaved people on contentious deaths and their investigation, with a particular focus on deaths in custody. They offer an 'Information Pack' containing advice to bereaved families or friends facing an inquest in England and Wales, and a casework service for those bereaved after a death in custody. For more information, see www.inquest.org.uk.

References

1. Pitman A, Osborn D, King M, Erlangsen A. Effects of suicide bereavement on mental health and suicide risk. *Lancet Psychiatry*. 2014; **1**(1): 86–94.
2. Hill NTM, Robinson J, Pirkis J, Andriessen K, Krysinska K, Payne A, et al. Association of suicidal behavior with exposure to suicide and suicide attempt: A systematic review and multilevel meta-analysis. *PLoS Med*. 2020; **17**(3): e1003074.
3. Cerel J, Maple M, van de Venne J, Brown M, Moore M, Flaherty C. Suicide exposure in the population: Perceptions of impact and closeness. *Suicide and Life Threatening Behaviour*. 2017; **47**(6): 696–708
4. Niederkrotenthaler T, Braun M, Pirkis J, Till B, Stack S, Sinyor M, et al. Association between suicide reporting in the media and suicide: Systematic review and meta-analysis. *BMJ*. 2020; Mar 18; 368: m575.
5. Haw C, Hawton K, Niedzwiedz C, Platt S. Suicide clusters: A review of risk factors and mechanisms. *Suicide and Life Threatening Behaviour*. 2013 Feb; **43**(1): 97–108.
6. Hawton K, Hill NTM, Gould M, John A, Lascelles K, Robinson J. Clustering of suicides in children and adolescents. *Lancet Child and Adolescent Health*. 2020 Jan 1; **4**(1): 58–67.
7. Cerel J, Jordan JR, Duberstein PR. The impact of suicide on the family. *Crisis*. 2008; **29**(1): 38–4.

8. Andriessen K. Can postvention be prevention? *Crisis.* 2009; **30**(1): 43–7.

9. World Health Organization. *Preventing Suicide: A Global Imperative.* Geneva: World Health Organization; 2014. www.who.int/publications/i/item/9789241564779.

10. Department of Health and Social Care. *Suicide Prevention in England: Fifth Progress Report of the Cross-government Outcomes Strategy to Save Lives.* London: HMSO; 2021. www.gov.uk/government/publications/suicide-prevention-in-england-fifth-progress-report.

11. Schlichthorst M, Reifels L, Spittal M, Clapperton A, Scurrah K, Kolves K, et al. Evaluating the effectiveness of components of national suicide prevention strategies: An interrupted time series analysis. *Crisis.* 2023 Jul; **44**(4): 318–328.

12. Andriessen K, Krysinska K, Hill NTM, Reifels L, Robinson J, Reavley N, et al. Effectiveness of interventions for people bereaved through suicide: A systematic review of controlled studies of grief, psychosocial and suicide-related outcomes. *BMC Psychiatry.* 2019 Jan 30; **19**(1): 49. https://bmcpsychiatry.biomedcentral.com/articles/10.1186/s12888-019-2020-z.

13. Fleischmann A, Bertolote JM, Mishara BL, Andriessen K, Farberow NL, Grad OT, et al. *Preventing Suicide: How to Start a Survivors Group.* Geneva: World Health Organization, Department of Mental Health and Substance Abuse; 2008.

14. Berman AL. Estimating the population of survivors of suicide: Seeking an evidence base. *Suicide and Life Threatening Behaviour.* 2011; **41**(1): 110–6.

15. Cerel J, Brown MM, Maple M, Singleton M, van de Venne J, Moore M, et al. How many people are exposed to suicide? Not six. *Suicide and Life Threatening Behaviour.* 2019; **49**(2): 529–534.

16. Crosby AE, Sacks JJ. Exposure to suicide: Incidence and association with suicidal ideation and behavior: United States, 1994. *Suicide and Life Threatening Behaviour.* 2002; **32**(3): 321–8.

17. Andriessen K, Rahman B, Draper B, Dudley M, Mitchell PB. Prevalence of exposure to suicide: A meta-analysis of population-based studies. *Journal of Psychiatric Research.* 2017 May; **88**: 113–120.

18. Feigelman W, Cerel J, McIntosh JL, Brent D, Gutin N. Suicide exposures and bereavement among American adults: Evidence from the 2016 General Social Survey. *Journal of Affective Disorders.* 2018 Feb; **227**: 1–6.

19. Maple M, Sanford R, Pirkis J, Reavley N, Nicholas A. Exposure to suicide in Australia: A representative random digit dial study. *Journal of Affective Disord.* 2019 Dec **1**; 259: 221–227.

20. World Health Organization. *Suicide Worldwide in 2019.* Geneva: World Health Organization; 2021. www.who.int/publications/i/item/9789240026643.

21. Pitman A, Osborn D, Rantell K, King M. Bereavement by suicide as a risk factor for suicide attempt: A cross-sectional national UK-wide study of 3432 young bereaved adults. *BMJ Open.* 2016; **6**(1): E009948.

22. Agerbo E. Midlife suicide risk, partner's psychiatric illness, spouse and child bereavement by suicide or other modes of death: A gender specific study. *Journal of Epidemiolology and Community Health.* 1978/2005; **59**(5): 407–12.

23. Qin P, Mortensen PB. The impact of parental status on the risk of completed suicide. *Archives of General Psychiatry.* 2003; **60**(8): 797–802.

24. Garssen J, Deerenberg I, MacKenbach JP, Kerkhof A, Kunst AE. Familial risk of early suicide: Variations by age and sex of children and parents. *Suicide and Life Threatening Behaviour.* 2011; **41**(6): 585–93.

25. Tidemalm D, Runeson B, Waern M, Frisell T, Carlström E, Lichtenstein P, et al. Familial clustering of suicide risk: A total population study of 11.4 million individuals. *Psychological Medicine.* 2011; **41**(12): 2527–34.

26. Rostila M, Saarela J, Kawachi I. Suicide following the death of a sibling: A nationwide follow-up study from

Sweden. *BMJ Open*. 2013 Apr 26; **3**(4): e002618.

27. Erlangsen A, Runeson B, Bolton JM, Wilcox HC, Forman JL, Krogh J, et al. Association between spousal suicide and mental, physical, and social health outcomes a longitudinal and nationwide register-based study. *JAMA Psychiatry*. 2017; **74**(5): 456–64.
28. Hua P, Bugeja L, Maple M. A systematic review on the relationship between childhood exposure to external cause parental death, including suicide, on subsequent suicidal behaviour. *Journal of Affective Disorders*. 2019; **257**(1): 723–34.
29. del Carpio L, Paul S, Paterson A, Rasmussen S. A systematic review of controlled studies of suicidal and self-harming behaviours in adolescents following bereavement by suicide. *PLoS ONE*. 2021 Jul 9; 16(7): e0254203.
30. Runeson B, Åsberg M. Family history of suicide among suicide victims. *American Journal of Psychiatry*. 2003 Aug; **160**(8): 1525–6.
31. Tsuang MT. Risk of suicide in the relatives of schizophrenics, manics, depressives, and controls. *Journal of Clinical Psychiatry*. 1983 Nov; **44**(11): 396–7, 398–400.
32. Eckland B. Assortative mating: Theories of mate selection. *Journal of Social Biology*. 1982; **29**(1–2): 7–21.
33. Joiner TE. Contagion of suicidal symptoms as a function of assortative relating and shared relationship stress in college roommates. *Journal of Adolescence* 2003; **26**(4): 495–504.
34. Agerbo E. Risk of suicide and spouse's psychiatric illness or suicide: Nested case-control study. *BMJ*. 2003; **327**(7422): 1025–6.
35. Wilcox HC, Kuramoto SJ, Lichtenstein P, Långström N, Brent DA, Runeson B. Psychiatric morbidity, violent crime, and suicide among children and adolescents exposed to parental death. *Journal of the American Academy of Child and Adolescent Psychiatry* 2010; **49**(5): 514–23.
36. Kuramoto SJ, Runeson B, Stuart EA, Lichtenstein P, Wilcox HC. Time to hospitalization for suicide attempt by the timing of parental suicide during offspring early development. *JAMA Psychiatry*. 2013; **70**(2): 149–57.
37. Rostila M, Berg L, Arat A, Vinnerljung B, Hjern A. Parental death in childhood and self-inflicted injuries in young adults: A national cohort study from Sweden. *European Child and Adolescent Psychiatry*. 2016 Oct; **25**(10): 1103–11.
38. Guldin MB, Li J, Pedersen S, Obel C, Agerbo E, et al. Incidence of suicide among persons who had a parent who died during their childhood: A population-based cohort study original investigation. *JAMA Psychiatry*. 2015; **72**(12): 1227–34.
39. Hybholt L, Higgins A, Buus N, Berring LL, Connolly T, Erlangsen A, et al. The spaces of peer-led support groups for suicide bereaved in Denmark and the Republic of Ireland: A focus group study. *International Journal of Environmental Research and Public Health*. 2022 Aug 11; **19**(16): 9898.
40. Lee KY, Li CY, Chang KC, Lu TH, Chen YY. Age at exposure to parental suicide and the subsequent risk of suicide in young people. *Crisis*. 2018; **39**(1): 27–36.
41. Andriessen K, Krysinska K, Rickwood D, Pirkis J. 'It changes your orbit': The impact of suicide and traumatic death on adolescents as experienced by adolescents and parents. *International Journal of Environmental Research and Public Health*. 2020 Dec 14; **17**(24): 9356.
42. Andriessen K, Draper B, Dudley M, Mitchell PB. Pre- and postloss features of adolescent suicide bereavement: A systematic review. *Death Studies*. 2016; **40**(4): 229–46.
43. Pitman A, De Souza T, Putri AK, Stevenson F, King M, Osborn D, et al. Support needs and experiences of people bereaved by suicide: Qualitative findings from a cross-sectional British study of bereaved young adults. *International Journal of Environmental Research and Public Health*. 2018 Apr 3; **15**(4): 666.

44. Calderaro M, Baethge C, Bermpohl F, Gutwinski S, Schouler-Ocak M, Henssler J. Offspring's risk for suicidal behaviour in relation to parental death by suicide: Systematic review and meta-analysis and a model for familial transmission of suicide. *British Journal of Psychiatry*. 2022 Mar; **220**(3): 121–129.
45. Brent DA, Perper J, Moritz G, Allman C, Friend A, Schweers J, et al. Psychiatric effects of exposure to suicide among the friends and acquaintances of adolescent suicide victims. *Journal of the American Academy of Child and Adolescent*. 1992; **31**(4): 629–39.
46. Spiwak R, Elias B, Sareen J, Chartier M, Katz LY, Bolton JM. Spouses bereaved by suicide: A population-based longitudinal cohort comparison of physician-diagnosed mental disorders and hospitalized suicide attempts. *Journal of Psychiatric Research*. 2020; Nov; **130**: 347–54.
47. Pfeffer CR, Karus D, Siegel K, Jiang H. Child survivors of parental death from cancer or suicide: Depressive and behavioral outcomes. *Psychooncology*. 2000; **9**(1): 1–10.
48. Kuramoto SJ, Stuart EA, Runeson B, Lichtenstein P, Långström N, Wilcox HC. Maternal versus paternal suicide and offspring risk of hospitalization for psychiatric disorders and suicide attempt. *Pediatrics*. 2010; **126**(5): e1026–32.
49. Appel CW, Johansen C, Deltour I, Frederiksen K, Hjalgrim H, Dalton SO, et al. Early parental death and risk of hospitalization for affective disorder in adulthood. *Epidemiology*. 2013; **24**(4): 608–15.
50. Kessing LV, Agerbo E, Mortenssen PB. Major stressful life events and other risk factors for first admission with mania. *Bipolar Disorder*. 2004; **6**(2): 122–9.
51. Appel CW, Johansen C, Christensen J, Frederiksen K, Hjalgrim H, Dalton SO, et al. Risk of use of antidepressants among children and young adults exposed to the death of a parent. *Epidemiology*. 2016; **27**(4): 578–85.
52. Bolton JM, Au W, Leslie WD, Martens PJ, Enns MW, Roos LL, et al. Parents bereaved by offspring suicide: A population-based longitudinal case-control study. *JAMA Psychiatry*. 2013; **70**(2): 158–67.
53. Ljung T, Sandin S, Långström N, Runeson B, Lichtenstein P, Larsson H. Offspring death and subsequent psychiatric morbidity in bereaved parents: Addressing mechanisms in a total population cohort. *Psychological Medicine*. 2014; **44**(9): 1879–87.
54. Cerel J, Roberts TA. Suicidal behavior in the family and adolescent risk behavior. *Journal of Adolescent Health*. 2005; **36**(4): 352.e9–16.
55. Quigley J, Rasmussen S, McAlaney J. The associations between children's and adolescents' suicidal and self-harming behaviors, and related behaviors within their social networks: A systematic review. *Archives of Suicide Research*. 2016; **21**(2): 185–236. www.tandfonline.com/action/journalInformation?journalCode=usui20.
56. Cerel J, Roberts TA, Nilsen WJ. Peer suicidal behavior and adolescent risk behavior. *Journal of Nervous and Mental Disease*. 2005; **193**(4): 237–243.
57. Thompson MP, Light LS. Examining gender differences in risk factors for suicide attempts made 1 and 7 years later in a nationally representative sample. *Journal of Adolescent Health*. 2011; **48**(4): 391–7.
58. Feigelman W, Gorman BS. Assessing the effects of peer suicide on youth suicide. *Suicide and Life Threatening Behaviour*. 2008; **38**(2): 181–94.
59. Swanson SA, Colman I. Association between exposure to suicide and suicidality outcomes in youth. *Canadian Medical Association Journal*. 2013; **185**(10): 870–7.
60. Brent DA, Perper JA, Moritz G, Allman C, Schweers J, Roth C, et al. Psychiatric sequelae to the loss of an adolescent peer to suicide. *Journal of the American Academy of Child and Adolescent Psychiatry*. 1993; **32**(3): 509–17.
61. Brent DA, Moritz G, Bridge J, Perper J, Canobbio R. Long-term impact of exposure to suicide: A three-year

controlled follow-up. *Journal of the American Academy of Child and Adolescent Psychiatry*. 1996; **35**(5): 646–53.

62. Ho TP, Leung PW, Hung SF, Lee CC, Tang CP. The mental health of the peers of suicide completers and attempters. *Journal of Child Psychology and Psychiatry*. 2000 Mar; 41(3): 301–8.

63. Stroebe M, Schut H, Stroebe W. Health outcomes of bereavement. *Lancet*. 2007 Dec 8; **370**(9603): 1960–73.

64. Brent D, Melhem N, Donohoe MB, Walker M. The incidence and course of depression in bereaved youth 21 months after the loss of a parent to suicide, accident, or sudden natural death. *American Journal of Psychiatry*. 2009. Jul; **166**(7): 786–94.

65. Hamdan S, Melhem NM, Porta G, Soon Song M, Brent DA. Alcohol and substance abuse in parentally bereaved youth. *Journal of Clinical Psychiatry*. 2013; **74**(8): 828–33.

66. Pitman A, Stevenson F, King M, Osborn D. Self-reported patterns of use of alcohol and drugs after suicide bereavement and other sudden losses: A mixed methods study of 1,854 young bereaved adults in the UK. *Frontiers in Psychology*. 2020; **11**: 1024. https://doi.org/10.3389/fpsyg.2020.01024

67. Pitman A, Stevenson F, Osborn D. Investigating whether bereavement by suicide and other unnatural causes has a deterrent effect on alcohol or drug use in young adults. *International Journal of Environmental Research and Public Health*. 2022 Oct 14; **19**(20): 13245.

68. Eng J, Drabwell L, Stevenson F, King M, Osborn D, Pitman A. Use of alcohol and unprescribed drugs after suicide bereavement: Qualitative study. *International Journal of Environmental Research and Public Health* 2019 Oct 24; **16**(21): 4093.

69. McDonnell S, Hunt I, Flynn S, Smith S, McGale B, Shaw J. *From Grief to Hope: The Collective Voice of Those Bereaved or Affected by Suicide in the UK*. Manchester: University of Manchester; 2020. http://research.bmh.manchester.ac.uk/cmhs/research/centreforsuicideprevention/fromgriefto hope/.

70. Spillane A, Matvienko-Sikar K, Larkin C, Corcoran P, Arensman E. What are the physical and psychological health effects of suicide bereavement on family members? An observational and interview mixed-methods study in Ireland. *BMJ Open*. 018 Jan 13; **8**(1): e019472.

71. Lobb EA, Kristjanson LJ, Aoun SM, Monterosso L, Halkett GKB, Davies A. Predictors of complicated grief: A systematic review of empirical studies. *Death Studies*. 2010 Sep; **34**(8): 673–98.

72. Mitchell AM, Kim Y, Prigerson HG, Mortimer MK. Complicated grief and suicidal ideation in adult survivors of suicide. *Suicide and Life Threatening Behaviour*. 2005 Oct; **35**(5): 498–506.

73. Hanschmidt F, Lehnig F, Riedel-Heller SG, Kersting A. The stigma of suicide survivorship and related consequences: A systematic review. *PLoS One*. 2016 Sep 22; **11**(9): e0162688.

74. Kõlves K, Zhao Q, Ross V, Hawgood J, Spence SH, de Leo D. Suicide and other sudden death bereavement of immediate family members: An analysis of grief reactions six-months after death. *Journal of Affective Disorders*. 2019 Jan **15**; 243: 96–102.

75. Pitman A, Logeswaran Y, McDonald K, Cerel J, Lewis G, Erlangsen A. Investigating risk of self-harm and suicide on anniversaries after bereavement by suicide and other causes: A Danish population-based self-controlled case series study. *Epidemiology and Psychiatric Sciences*. 2023 Aug **8**; 32: e53.

76. Dyregrov K. What do we know about needs for help after suicide in different parts of the world? A phenomenological perspective. *Crisis*. 2011; **32**(6): 310–18.

77. Support After Suicide Partnership. *Help Is at Hand: Support after Someone May Have Died by Suicide*. 2021. HM Government. https://supportaftersuicide.org.uk/wp-content/uploads/2020/04/HIAH_Booklet_2021_V7.pdf

78. Hawton K, Sutton L, Simkin S, Walker DM, Stacey G, Waters K, et al. Evaluation of a resource for people bereaved by suicide. *Crisis*. 2012; **33**(5): 254–64.

79. Hill NTM, Walker R, Andriessen K, Bouras H, Tan SR, Amaratia P, et al. Reach and perceived effectiveness of a community-led active outreach postvention intervention for people bereaved by suicide. *Frontiers in Public Health*. 2022 Dec **22**;10: 1040323.

80. Rickwood D, Telford N, Kennedy V, Bailey E, Robinson J. The Need For and Acceptance of a Suicide Postvention Support Service for Australian Secondary Schools. *Journal of Psychologists and Counsellors in Schools*. 2018;28(1):55–65.

81. Wainwright V, Cordingley L, Chew-Graham CA, Kapur N, Shaw J, Smith S, et al. Experiences of support from primary care and perceived needs of parents bereaved by suicide: A qualitative study. *British Journal of General Practice*. 2020 Jan 30; **70**(691): e102–e11.

82. Foggin E, McDonnell S, Cordingley L, Kapur N, Shaw J, Chew-Graham CA. GP's experiences of dealing with parents bereaved by suicide: A qualitative study. *British Journal of General Practice*. 2016 Oct; **66**(651): e737–46.

83. Pitman AL, Rantell K, Moran P, Sireling L, Marston L, King M, et al. Support received after bereavement by suicide and other sudden deaths: A cross-sectional UK study of 3432 young bereaved adults. *BMJ Open*. 2017 May 29; **7**(5): e014487.

84. Pitman A, Rantell K, Marston L, King M, Osborn D. Perceived stigma of sudden bereavement as a risk factor for suicidal thoughts and suicide attempt: Analysis of British cross-sectional survey data on 3387 young bereaved adults. *International Journal of Environmental Research and Public Health*. 2017 Mar 9; **14**(3): 286.

85. Pitman AL, Stevenson F, Osborn DPJ, King MB. The stigma associated with bereavement by suicide and other sudden deaths: A qualitative interview study. *Social Science and Medicine*. 2018 Feb; **198**: 121–129.

86. Evans A, Abrahamson K. The influence of stigma on suicide bereavement: A systematic review. *Journal of Psychosocial Nursing and Mental Health Services*. 2020 Apr 1; **58**(4): 21–27.

87. Pitman AL, Hunt IM, McDonnell SJ, Appleby L, Kapur N. Support for relatives bereaved by psychiatric patient suicide: National confidential inquiry into suicide and homicide findings. *Psychiatric Services*. 2017 Apr 1; **68**(4): 337–344.

88. Zisook S, Katherine Shear M, Reynolds CF, Simon NM, Mauro C, Skritskaya NA, et al. Treatment of complicated grief in survivors of suicide loss: A HEAL report. *Journal of Clinical Psychiatry*. 2018 Mar/Apr; **79**(2): 17m11592.

89. National Suicide Prevention Alliance, Support after Suicide Partnership *Support after a Suicide: Developing and Delivering Local Bereavement Support Services*. Public Health England; 2016. https://assets.publishing.service.gov.uk/media/5a7f3db6ed915d74e6229407/support_after_a_suicide.pdf

90. PHE. *Support after a Suicide: A Guide to Providing Local Services*. 2017.

91. NSPA, SASP. *Support after a Suicide: Evaluating Local Bereavement Support Services*. London; 2016.

92. Gibbons R, Brand F, Carbonnier A, Croft A, Lascelles K, Wolfart G, et al. Effects of patient suicide on psychiatrists: Survey of experiences and support required. *BJPsych Bulletin*. 2019; **43**(5): 236–241.

Index

For EU product safety concerns, contact us at Calle de José Abascal, 56–1°, 28003 Madrid, Spain or eugpsr@cambridge.org.

www.ingramcontent.com/pod-product-compliance
Lightning Source LLC
LaVergne TN
LVHW052311200926
848481LV00002B/531